OXFORD COMPARATIVE CONSTITUTIONALISM

Series Editors

RICHARD ALBERT

William Stamps Farish Professor of Law,
The University of Texas at Austin School of Law

ROBERT SCHÜTZE

Professor of European and Global Law,
Durham University and College of Europe

Gender Diversity in Public Law

OXFORD COMPARATIVE CONSTITUTIONALISM

Comparative constitutional law has a long and distinguished history in intellectual thought and in the construction of public law. As political actors and the people who create or modify their constitutional orders, they often wish to learn from the experience and learning of others. This cross-fertilization and mutual interaction has only accelerated with the onset of globalization, which has transformed the world into an interconnected web that facilitates dialogue and linkages across international and regional structures. Oxford Comparative Constitutionalism seeks to publish scholarship of the highest quality in constitutional law that deepens our knowledge of local, national, regional, and global phenomena through the lens of comparative public law.

ALSO PUBLISHED IN THIS SERIES

Politicized Religion and the Reframing of Fundamental Rights
Susanna Mancini and Michel Rosenfeld

Constitutional Change Under Autocracy
Anna Fruhstorfer

City, State
Constitutionalism and the Megacity
Ran Hirschl

The Politics of Constitutional Rigidity
Unveiling Pathways to Change in Mexico
Mariana Velasco-Rivera

Courts and LGBTQ+ Rights in an Age of Judicial Retrenchment
Rehan Abeyratne

Ex-Ministers as Constitutional Judges
Mathias Möschel

Redefining Comparative Constitutional Law
Essays for Mark Tushnet
Edited by Madhav Khosla and Vicki C. Jackson

Foreign Relations Federalism
The EU in Comparative Perspective
Thomas Verellen

Responsive Judicial Review
Democracy and Dysfunction in the Modern Age
Rosalind Dixon

Outsourcing Rulemaking Powers
Constitutional limits and national safeguards
Cedric Jenart

Abusive Constitutional Borrowing
Legal globalization and the subversion of liberal democracy
Rosalind Dixon and David Landau

A Theory of African Constitutionalism
Berihun Adugna Gebeye

Eternity Clauses In Democratic Constitutionalism
Silvia Suteu

Deliberative Peace Referendums
Ron Levy, Ian O'Flynn, Hoi L. Kong

Scales of Memory Constitutional Justice and Historical Evil
Justin Collings

The Global South and Comparative Constitutional Law
Edited by Philipp Dann, Michael Riegner, and Maxim Bönnemann

Gender Diversity in Public Law

Between Recognition and Control

STEFANO OSELLA
Assistant Professor, Faculty of Law,
The University of Hong Kong

OXFORD
UNIVERSITY PRESS

OXFORD
UNIVERSITY PRESS

Great Clarendon Street, Oxford, OX2 6DP,
United Kingdom

Oxford University Press is a department of the University of Oxford.
It furthers the University's objective of excellence in research, scholarship,
and education by publishing worldwide. Oxford is a registered trade mark of
Oxford University Press in the UK and in certain other countries.

Published in the United States of America by Oxford University Press
198 Madison Avenue, New York, NY 10016, United States of America.

British Library Cataloguing in Publication Data
Data available

Library of Congress Control Number: 2026934589

ISBN 9780198935049

DOI: 10.1093/9780198935070.001.0001

Printed and bound by
CPI Group (UK) Ltd., Croydon, CR0 4YY

The manufacturer's authorized representative in the EU for product safety is
Oxford University Press España S.A. of Parque Empresarial San Fernando de Henares,
Avenida de Castilla, 2 – 28830 Madrid (www.oup.es/en or product.safety@oup.com).
OUP España S.A. also acts as importer into Spain of products made by the manufacturer.

MIX
Paper | Supporting responsible forestry
FSC
www.fsc.org
FSC® C013604

Normality is a paved road: It's comfortable to walk, but no flowers grow on it
(Often attributed to Vincent Van Gogh, though probably apocryphal)

Acknowledgements

Research is a relational activity. No one is an island, and my work is the outcome of a web of relationships that have supported and inspired me, from the sprouting of my first idea to the completion of this manuscript.

I have been engaged with the topic of gender diversity in comparative public law since 2014, when I began my doctoral studies at the European University Institute. While this book differs in many significant ways from my doctoral thesis, it completes the research that I started during my PhD studies. It is only fitting that I begin by thanking my alma mater, the beautiful EUI, for offering me that invaluable opportunity. My research has continued at other institutions as well, notably the Max Planck Institute for Social Anthropology and Bocconi University, to which I am much indebted. I am also grateful for the enriching research residencies at the Collegio Carlo Alberto of the University of Turin and at the Käte Hamburger Kolleg—*Recht als Kultur* at the University of Bonn. My deep gratitude goes to the University of Hong Kong, my academic home. The material and intellectual support I have received here have surpassed my highest expectations. I am thankful for the funding provided by the University of Hong Kong through the Seed Fund for Basic Research for New Staff for my project 'Recognizing and Controlling Gender Diversity: Models and Developments in Comparative Public Law, and Avenues of Research'. This funding was crucial to the development and completion of this book.

The care, encouragement, and love I received from those around me have not simply helped—they have been indispensable to completing this book. I am very grateful to my *Doktormutter* and long-time co-author, Ruth Rubio-Marín. I am also indebted to: Rehan Abeyratne, Richard Albert, Shreya Atrey, Gustavo Buss, Manuel José Cepeda Espinosa, Gráinne de Búrca, Erin Delaney, Rosalind Dixon, Marie-Claire Foblets, Hualing Fu, Michaela Hailbronner, Jed Kroncke, Anna Katharina Mangold, Nick Markwald, Irene Parra Prieto, Elizabeth Perham, Robert Schuetze, Amal Sethi, Alec Stone Sweet, Silvia Suteu, Davide Tomaselli, Sergio Verdugo, Marco Wan, Joseph H. H. Weiler, Po Jen Yap, and Simon N. M. Young. A special mention is due to Cora Chan, from whose example I learn daily. My appreciation goes to Brian Stone and Mirza Rizwaan Ahmed for their invaluable support during the editorial process.

Ju Liu, Susanna Roßbach, and Jeremy Yu have given me the best research assistance I could ask for, and I am most thankful for their help.

To my friends, I have no words to convey the depth of my appreciation for you: Daniela Alaattinoglu, Chiara Carpignano, Federica Coppola, Skander Galand, Simone Gerbaudo, Daniela Gervasio, Massimo Lando, Andrea Marengo, Elisa

Michelazzo, Elisabetta Morlino, and Graziella Romeo. Thank you to my dearest Alice Margaria, who is there for me every day. If my friends billed me for the hours spent listening to me, they would be rich, and I would be left *in braghe di tela.*

Grazie to my therapist, Chiara Saimandi. She deserves a medal. Perhaps a few. Possibly, a parade. I would like to thank my family (*cagnolini inclusi*, Pino especially), my parents (*in composizione allargata*), grandparents, and in particular my mother, Tiziana. Finally, my deepest gratitude and love go to Carlo, to whom I dedicate this book. They all taught me the meaning of unconditional love. And without unconditional love, there is no room for diversity. Or for anything, really.

For the largest part, this book encompasses a substantial body of new research and advances original scholarship and theories. Nevertheless, this monograph is the culmination of the research that has occupied me for almost ten years. This research underpinned my PhD dissertation, *The Legal Regime of Gender Identity: A Comparative Enquiry* (European University Institute, 7 May 2019), whose theoretical framework informs the book as a whole. However, the intellectual debt is especially clear in Chapters 2, 4, and 5. To a lesser extent, other portions of this volume draw upon and expand previous publications of mine, both single- and co-authored.[1] Full references are included at relevant points in the text.

The book relies on sources in multiple languages. I have endeavoured to translate all sources myself, unless otherwise indicated. When a translation is very close to the original wording, I have placed the passage in quotation marks. I am most thankful to Susanna Roßbach for her invaluable help with understanding and verifying sources in German. This book has been edited for language by Brian Donahoe, whose help I gratefully acknowledge. The credit for the excellent index goes to Maria Sosnowski, whom I sincerely thank.

[1] In particular, portions of the book—especially Chapter 4—draw upon, at times reproduce, and expand: Stefano Osella, *When Comparative Law Walks the Path of Anthropology: The Case of Third Gender in Europe*, 23 German Law Journal 920 (2022); Stefano Osella, *Reinforcing the Binary and Disciplining the Subject: The Constitutional Right to Gender Recognition in the Italian Case-Law*, 20 International Journal of Constitutional Law 454 (2022). To a lesser degree, other sections of this volume draw upon and develop: Stefano Osella & Ruth Rubio-Marín, *Gender Recognition at the Crossroad: Four Models and the Compass of Comparative Law*, 21 International Journal of Constitutional Law 574 (2023); Stefano Osella, *Come Evolve il Diritto all'Identità di Genere? Fattori Strutturali, Culturali e Dogmatici nella Giurisprudenza Costituzionale Italiana e Colombiana. Un'Analisi Comparata*, Diritti Comparati 1 (2023); Marie-Xaviere Catto & Stefano Osella, *The Sexed Subject*, *in* The Cambridge Companion to Gender and the Law 25 (Stephanie Hennette-Vauchez & Ruth Rubio-Marín eds., 2023); Stefano Osella & Ruth Rubio-Marín, *The Right to Gender Recognition Before the Colombian Constitutional Court: A* Queer/Travesti *Theory Analysis*, 40 Bulletin of Latin American Research 650 (2022); Stefano Osella, *De-gendering the Civil Status? A Public Law Problem*, 20 International Journal of Constitutional Law 471 (2020); Ruth Rubio-Marín & Stefano Osella, *El Nuevo Derecho Constitucional a la Identidad de Género entre la Libertad de Elección, el Incremento de Categorías y la Subjetividad y Fluidez de sus Contenidos. Un Análisis desde el Derecho Comparado*, 40 Revista Española de Derecho Constitucional 45 (2020); Stefano Osella & Ruth Rubio-Marín, *Between Rights and Pragmatism: Intersex Rights Before the Colombian Constitutional Court*, *in* The Legal Status of Intersex Persons (Jens Scherpe, Anatol Dutta & Tobias Helms eds., 2018); Stefano Osella, *'Harmonic Bodies': Intersex Persons, Corrective Treatments, and Gender Violence in Italian Law. A Research Proposal*, LGBTI Persons and Access to Justice (Anna Lorenzetti & Maria Federica Moscati eds., 2015).

Contents

1
Introduction

1. Prologue

Try to think (or feel) that your gender identity diverges from the sex/gender assigned to you at birth.[1] Suppose that the sex under which you are legally registered, as indicated on your ID or passport, does not align with your gender identity. Imagine that this mismatch makes people and public officers question who you are every time you attempt to use a public service, board a plane, or in any way need to identify yourself. Finding employment is not easy, either. Being outed as trans by your mismatching documents is not going to help you secure a good job in precarious times and intolerant contexts. The mismatch may also cause legal troubles. For all intents and purposes, your legal sex is still the birth-assigned one. Your retirement age, the facilities you can use, possibly the person you can marry, and other aspects of daily life may depend on your legal registration. Without being able to change your legal sex to reflect your gender identity—without legal recognition—it may be difficult for you to feel confident in public and be perceived by others as the person you are.

Legal recognition of the sex/gender you identify with (hereinafter, 'gender identity recognition' or 'gender recognition') might improve things. Suppose that you are Italian. Italian law allows you to change your legal sex. Lucky for you, you identify in a binary sex/gender—no third option is available, but your identity is male or female. To amend your legal sex, you must file a case before a judge. You will have to change yourself (and the judge will check). Although Italian law no longer requires surgical sterilization, you will have to transform your physical characteristics, behaviour, and psychological traits. Details might be a bit hazy, but, as a rule of thumb, you need to take hormones for a while. Some surgeries on your secondary sex characteristics—breast removal or augmentation, to name one—might strengthen your case. You need the support of a mental health specialist and a diagnosis of gender dysphoria. You must also show that your behaviour is 'appropriate'

[1] Gender identity is 'each person's deeply felt internal and individual experience of gender, which may or may not correspond with the sex assigned at birth, including the personal sense of the body (which may involve, if freely chosen, modification of bodily appearance or function by medical, surgical or other means) and other expressions of gender, including dress, speech and mannerisms'. For this definition, *see*: Yogyakarta Principles: Principles on the Application of International Human Rights Law in Relation to Sexual Orientation and Gender Identity (Nov. 2006). For a theoretical overview, refer to Chapter 2. I thank Rehan Abeyratne for his suggestion to start with an (imaginary) anecdote.

Gender Diversity in Public Law. Stefano Osella, Oxford University Press. © Stefano Osella 2026.
DOI: 10.1093/9780198935070.003.0001

to the legal sex you are claiming. This might be how you present yourself, dress, cut your hair, talk, and gesticulate. It could happen that the sex/gender of the person you date will be scrutinized, too.

This examination might be an irksome, if not traumatizing, experience. Or perhaps you lean more towards the pragmatic. You say whatever you have to say and *buonanotte*.[2] Or perhaps you tick all the boxes and make no effort to comply with all the requirements. Regardless, a few questions remain. Why all the fuss? Why should someone legally classified as a man, for example, wear trousers, keep short hair, and have a flat chest? Why should a doctor endorse your application? Why should a man have to act 'manly' and a woman have to act 'womanly' (whatever that means)? Ultimately, why does the law care that much?

2. The questions and the argument of this book

Intersex, trans, and nonbinary people—collectively, 'gender-diverse people'[3]—struggle to obtain legal protection. Intersex persons—whose physical characteristics diverge from typical male and female standards—may be subjected during infancy to involuntary, unnecessary, and harmful medical interventions intended to align their anatomy with 'gendered social corporeal norms'.[4] Tellingly, activists refer to such treatments as 'intersex genital mutilation' (IGM).[5] However, legal authorities may overlook or even condone these practices. Trans and nonbinary people face legal hurdles, too. Modifying the sex marker in public documents and being legally treated in conformity with one's gender identity can be life-changing for trans people.[6] Yet, in many jurisdictions, parliaments and courts subject gender recognition to onerous preconditions. The Italian Constitutional Court, to name one, requires physical, behavioural, and psychological transformation.[7] Article 61-5 of the French Civil Code requires one to present oneself in public and to be known in a sex different from one's birth-assigned sex. A nonbinary legal option—a

[2] Literally, 'Good night'; Figuratively, 'Goodbye and good riddance!'

[3] Sally Hines explains: '[a] gender-diverse person does not conform to their society's norms or values when it comes to their gendered physicality, gender identity, gender expression or a combination of these factors' (SALLY HINES, IS GENDER FLUID? A PRIMER FOR THE 21ST CENTURY 16 (2018)). To be sure, intersex, trans, and nonbinary people have different characteristics, needs, and demands (see Chapter 2). Nevertheless, their anatomy and gender identity differ from the understanding that is legally presupposed.

[4] Daniela Alaattinoglu & Kari Ragnarsson, *A Castle in the Sky? The Icelandic Ban on Non-Therapeutic, Non-Consensual Interventions on Intersex Children in Context*, 4 EUROPEAN HUMAN RIGHTS LAW REVIEW 408, 408 (2025).

[5] Markus Bauer, Daniela Truffer & Daniela Crocetti, *Intersex Human Rights*, 24 THE INTERNATIONAL JOURNAL OF HUMAN RIGHTS 724, 726 (2020).

[6] 'Trans' refers to all people whose gender identity and birth-assigned sex/gender do not match. As I explain in the following chapter, when I refer to the legal classification, I use the term 'sex', and sex/gender to refer to the individual's social identification.

[7] Constitutional Court [Corte Cost.], 21 ottobre 2015, n. 221 (see Chapter 4).

third sex—is absent from most jurisdictions to the detriment of nonbinary people. When granted, the nonbinary option may be limited to specific beneficiaries. For example, it may be granted to people who exhibit 'variations of sex/gender development' and who permanently identify as nonbinary.[8]

The past decades have been momentous for the human rights of gender-diverse persons. Trans and nonbinary people have managed to have the most burdensome preconditions for gender recognition eliminated in several national and supranational jurisdictions.[9] In a handful of cases, they have obtained a right to gender self-determination. All they have to do is declare the legal sex in which they want to be classified.[10] Involuntary medical treatments administered to intersex people have, in some jurisdictions, been limited, if not banned. Sometimes, gender diversity has been projected in a more positive light, as a source of learning rather than as something shameful to be erased.[11]

Regardless, public authorities have perceived the demands of gender-diverse people as a challenge. This book explains why this has been the case and why gender identity and sex characteristics matter for the 'relationship between individuals and the state'—or, in other words, for public law.[12] The focus of the book is largely (though not exclusively) on constitutional law. Indeed, sex-based public interests and fundamental rights are often grounded in constitutions. More significantly, gender diversity matters to central aspects of constitutionalism, as it 'engages with the institutions of government, the rights of individuals and groups, and the formulation of limitations on institutional power'.[13]

Taking a public law perspective, this book thus examines *how* and *why* gender diversity has been denied, limited, or recognized in several jurisdictions in Europe, Asia, and South America,[14] and, to do so, it identifies and examines some models of gender diversity recognition.[15] To be clear, this book does not propose an entirely

[8] Gesetz zur Änderung der in das Geburtenregister einzutragenden Angaben, 18 Dec. 2018. As discussed in Chapter 7, nonbinary recognition is now regulated in Germany by the Law on self-determination: Gesetz über die Selbstbestimmung in Bezug auf den Geschlechtseintrag [SBGG], 19 June 2024.

[9] Refer for example to Chapters 4 and 5, discussing Italy and France.

[10] This is the case, for example, in Colombia, as discussed in Chapter 6.

[11] Refer to Chapter 3, discussing the public law questions presented by intersexuality.

[12] Katherine G. Young, *Introduction: A Public Law of Gender*, *in* THE PUBLIC LAW OF GENDER: FROM THE LOCAL TO THE GLOBAL 1, 9 (Kim Rubenstein & Katherine G. Young eds., 2016).

[13] Beverley Baines, Daphne Barak-Perez & Tsvi Kahana, *The Idea and Practice of Feminist Constitutionalism*, *in* FEMINIST CONSTITUTIONALISM: GLOBAL PERSPECTIVES 1, 1–2 (Beverley Baines, Daphne Barak-Perez & Tsvi Kahana eds., 2012).

[14] Australia, Belgium, Colombia, France, Germany, India, Italy, Nepal, Pakistan, and the United Kingdom. On comparative methodology: Section 4 of this Introduction.

[15] For a brief overview of these models, please refer to Section 4 of this Introduction. Models are here understood as having a 'heuristic' function; they help us understand the key features of different manifestations of the right to gender recognition: Alison Young, *Constitutional Methodology and Brexit: Adopting a Model-Theoretic Approach*, *in* THE METHODOLOGY OF CONSTITUTIONAL THEORY (Dimitrios Kyritsis & Stuart Lakin eds., 2022).

comprehensive taxonomy of gender diversity (mis)recognition.[16] Rather, it analyses models where the public law implications of gender diversity are evident and observable.

Drawing on legal comparison, this book builds a theory of *gender diversity in public law*. First, I argue that *gender identity* and *sex anatomy* are central to public law, even though constitutions have been mostly silent about them.[17] This centrality has manifested following the legal demands of gender-diverse people. When gender-diverse people have advanced their claims and framed them as human or constitutional rights, public officials—such as courts, parliaments, and administrative authorities—have often placed limits on them. When this has been the case, or when such limits have been contested before courts, authorities have also had to provide reasons, thus making explicit how legal systems rely on cis identities and endosex anatomies.[18] The balancing of various legal and constitutional principles at play, in other words, has served as a platform for making it explicit that the legal system not only builds on men and women (and the clear distinction between them) but also on men and women with specific identities, roles, and sex/gender anatomies. To borrow from Mattias Kumm, proportionality favours 'Socratic contestation'.[19] Proportionality has forced public authorities to explain why recognizing gender diversity is a problem, or, in other words, why gender identity and sex characteristics matter in public law.

Intersex characteristics and trans and nonbinary identities can indeed complicate the legal assignment of a permanent and binary sex. This assignment determines the personal legal status that is, the '*relation* between the individual and the state ... [which] *qualifies the individual* [and] is to be seen as a state of affairs, rather than a right'.[20] Hence, gender diversity has been perceived as a source of

[16] Ruth Rubio-Marín and I have tried to offer the criteria for such a taxonomy in: Stefano Osella & Ruth Rubio-Marín, *Gender Recognition at the Crossroads: Four Models and the Compass of Comparative Law*, 21 International Journal of Constitutional Law 574 (2023).

[17] Some notable and recent exceptions are Article 42 of the 2019 Constitution of Cuba; Article 12 of the 2015 Constitution of Nepal; Articles 14 and 58 of the 2009 Plurinational Constitution of Bolivia; Articles 11(2) and 83(14) of the 2008 Constitution of Ecuador; Article 26(3) of the 2013 Constitution of Fiji. All constitutions were consulted on: https://www.constituteproject.org.

[18] 'Endosex' refers to people who do not display intersex characteristics (Morgan Carpenter, Katharine B. Dalke & Brian D. Earp, *Endosex*, 49 Journal of Medical Ethics 225, 225–26 (2023)). People whose gender identity corresponds to their birth-assigned sex/gender are usually referred to as 'cis' or 'cisgender'. For a discussion of the term 'cisgender': B. Aultman, *Cisgender*, 1 TSQ: Transgender Studies Quarterly 61 (2014).

[19] Mattias Kumm, *The Idea of Socratic Contestation and the Right to Justification: The Point of Rights-Based Proportionality Review*, 4 Law and Ethics of Human Rights 141, 152–57 (2010).

[20] Robert Alexy, A Theory of Constitutional Rights 164 (Julian Rivers trans., 2002) (emphasis in the original). On the notion of status, *see also*: Aldo Corasaniti, *Stato delle Persone*, *in* Enciclopedia del Diritto vol 43, 948, 954–55 (1990); Maryline Bruggeman, *Le Rôle de l'État Civil*, *in* L'Etat Civil Dans Tous ses états (Claire Neinrick ed., 2008); Guido Alpa, Status e Capacità. La Costruzione Giuridica delle Differenze Individuali (1993). I acknowledge that the definition of the notion of status is very much debated among scholars. For an overview: Geoffrey MacCormack, Status: *Problems of Definition and Use*, 43 Cambridge Law Journal 361 (1984). This debate clearly falls out of the scope of this analysis. Nevertheless, sex as status seems to be accepted in the scholarship: Davina Cooper & Robyn Emerton, *Pulling the Thread of Decertification: What Challenges Are Raised by the Proposal to*

uncertainty in defining the legal status of a person. This is consequential in legal systems that are gendered. Certainty as to the individual legal status matters, for example, for the welfare system, military conscription, gender equality, and the heterosexuality of marriage. That said, gender diversity is now being recognized in multiple legal systems. When this is the case, gender diversity remains important for public law. Recognition becomes a manifestation of a constitutional order that pays attention to the demands of minorities and that represents them.

Second, legal authorities have often attempted to restrict gender diversity. When faced with the choice of either changing the law to acknowledge the world's complexity or attempting to simplify the world to conform to the (over)simplicity of the law, courts, parliaments, and administrative authorities have often chosen the latter option. They have decided to make gender-diverse people 'legible' and have resorted to an array of legal instruments to do so. Legibility is indeed central to the creation of state authority. States, it is argued, are often less interested in representing the world's complexity and more interested in simplifications that are helpful for governance purposes.[21] In the cases discussed in this book, the presence of constitutional and human rights has not allowed the complete denial of gender diversity, but has determined various forms of balancing between individual rights and the needs of the legal order. On the other hand, in a few instances, public authorities have accepted human differences and transformed the role of the state in this regard from enforcing uniformity to protecting diversity. When this has happened, the rights of the individual have been deemed to outweigh the state's interest in the legibility of the person.

This dynamic reveals that the legal notion of sex—with its constitutional ramifications—is not ultimately intended to represent a factual, pre-legal reality. Instead, the legal definition of sex—of what it takes to be defined as a man or a woman—is the outcome of a balancing exercise, which, in the jurisdictions discussed in this book, usually takes the form of proportionality. In each instance discussed in this book, even when gender diversity has been denied by making reference to the 'biology' of sex, the legal category of sex is always defined to achieve specific purposes. Legal sex, even when purportedly grounded in 'biology', is the outcome of value judgments.

Reform Legal Gender Status?, 10 feminists@law (12 Nov. 2020), also available as King's College London Law School Research Paper, https://www.ssrn.com/abstract=3729490; Davina Cooper & Flora Renz, *If the State Decertified Gender, What Might Happen to Its Meaning and Value?*, 43 JOURNAL OF LAW AND SOCIETY 483 (2016).

[21] JAMES C. SCOTT, SEEING LIKE A STATE: HOW CERTAIN SCHEMES TO IMPROVE THE HUMAN CONDITION HAVE FAILED 1–8, 22–24 (1998) (presenting the notion of 'legibility' and the necessity of simplification for purposes of governance); Dean Spade, *Documenting Gender*, 59 HASTINGS LAW JOURNAL 731, 739–50 (2008); Jane Caplan & John Torpey, *Introduction*, *in* DOCUMENTING INDIVIDUAL IDENTITY: THE DEVELOPMENT OF STATE PRACTICES IN THE MODERN WORLD (Jane Caplan & John Torpey eds., 2001).

Third, legal or constitutional rights have been employed to both challenge and uphold this control system and to 'shape' the subject of the legal order. The rights of gender-diverse people function in a 'pragmatic' or 'ambivalent' manner.[22] On the one hand, rights have facilitated the recognition of diversity and have called into question the system of sex categories in law. On the other hand, restrictions on and controls over individual identities and bodies have been exercised through the invocation and application of rights. Rights have been the instrument that has both shaped individuals and allowed them to question this shaping.

Now, two warnings. In this book, I aim to be analytical. The arguments presented are intended as a diagnosis of the relations between gender diversity and public law. I do not aim to advance a normative argument in favour of gender diversity recognition. I know that doing so would require a robust and context-dependent line of reasoning that I cannot provide here. I leave this endeavour to future research. Rather, I try to offer insights to define a common language around these questions and contribute to producing 'another imaginary' on gender diversity in the law.[23] This new imaginary might perhaps be the starting point for future arguments that may protect gender-diverse people. This is my hope. That said, I should clarify my normative standpoint. I look upon the demands of gender-diverse people with great favour and sympathy. Intersex, trans, and nonbinary rights are human rights. Despite my best efforts to be objective, my normative standpoint might affect how I interpret legal developments.

Second, I acknowledge that the demands of gender-diverse people extend beyond the right to physical integrity and gender recognition. Feasibility considerations prompted me to narrow my focus to these two demands. Nevertheless, I am convinced that discussing these particular demands already serves to illustrate the relations between gender diversity and public law.

3. Advances in the field

3.1. Gender (diversity) constitutionalism

For the past two decades at least, constitutional law scholars have asked the 'woman question'[24] to fill a 'huge gap—a gender gap—in contemporary constitutional law analysis'.[25] The gender gap, however, becomes a gender chasm if we ask

[22] On the ambivalence of rights, *see*: Ben Golder, Foucault and the Politics of Rights 89–113 (2015); Wendy Brown, *Suffering Rights as Paradoxes*, 7 Constellations 208 (2000). With specific reference to gender identity: Osella & Rubio-Marín, *supra* note 16, at 581.

[23] I try to heed the advice of Judith Butler, Who's Afraid of Gender 10–11 (2024).

[24] Vicki C. Jackson, *Conclusion: Gender Equality and the Idea of a Constitution: Entrenchment, Jurisdiction, Interpretation*, *in* Constituting Equality: Gender Equality and Comparative Constitutional Law 312, 312 (Susan H. Williams ed., 2009).

[25] Beverly Baines & Ruth Rubio-Marín, *Introduction: Toward a Feminist Constitutional Agenda*, *in* The Gender of Constitutional Jurisprudence 1, 2 (Beverly Baines & Ruth Rubio-Marín

the gender diversity question. To be sure, gender diversity has not been entirely absent from the literature on gender constitutionalism. In part, the intersectional approach has led scholars to consider the position of 'women who are lesbian, bisexual, or transgendered', among others.[26] In part, gender-diverse people have received attention in their own right.[27] Just to mention a few names, Shreya Atrey has discussed the position of trans and nonbinary people in the case law of India's Supreme Court and has demonstrated that gender constitutionalism should be understood as an instance of 'boundaries in contestation', and always open to possible expansions.[28] Angioletta Sperti has examined the development of a global constitutional jurisprudence granting rights to LGB people;[29] Rehan Abeyratne has discussed the connection between LGBQTI+ rights and the crisis of liberal democracy;[30] Jessica Clarke has examined the different forms of legal identity and the challenges that gender-diverse people present to binary legal systems;[31] Julie Greenberg has discussed the tensions triggered by intersexuality in the US legal system, built as it is around the binary, and has demonstrated 'why sex matters'.[32] And Ruth Rubio-Marín has argued that the demands of trans people are contributing to transforming the constitutional gender order.[33] The study of gender diversity, in other words, belongs in public law.

Moreover, theoretical concerns suggest exploring the role of gender identity and sex characteristics from a public law perspective. As Ruth Rubio-Marín explains,

eds., 2004). Some fundamental works in the field are: CONSTITUTING EQUALITY: GENDER EQUALITY AND COMPARATIVE CONSTITUTIONAL LAW (Susan H. Williams ed., 2009); Baines, Barak-Perez & Kahana, *supra* note 13; HELEN IRVING, GENDER AND THE CONSTITUTION: EQUITY AND AGENCY IN COMPARATIVE CONSTITUTIONAL DESIGN (2008).

[26] Baines & Rubio-Marín, *supra* note 25, at 4. A reference to Kimberlé W. Crenshaw is here de rigueur: Kimberlé W. Crenshaw, *Demarginalizing the Intersection of Race and Sex: A Black Feminist Critique of Antidiscrimination Doctrine, Feminist Theory and Antiracist Politics*, UNIVERSITY OF CHICAGO LEGAL FORUM 139 (1989); Kimberlé W. Crenshaw, *Mapping the Margins: Intersectionality, Identity Politics, and Violence Against Women of Color*, 43 STANFORD LAW REVIEW 1241 (1991).

[27] Young, *supra* note 12, at 7–8 and 35–36. *See also*: Rohan Kapur & Kellin Kristofferson, *A Gender Critique of Accountability in Global Administrative Governance*, *in* THE PUBLIC LAW OF GENDER: FROM THE LOCAL TO THE GLOBAL 514 (Kim Rubenstein & Katherine G. Young eds., 2016).

[28] Shreya Atrey, *Feminist Constitutionalism: Mapping a Discourse in Contestation*, 20 INTERNATIONAL JOURNAL OF CONSTITUTIONAL LAW 611 (2022).

[29] ANGIOLETTA SPERTI, CONSTITUTIONAL COURTS, GAY RIGHTS, AND SEXUAL ORIENTATION EQUALITY (2017).

[30] REHAN ABEYRATNE, COURTS AND LGBTQ+ RIGHTS IN AN AGE OF JUDICIAL RETRENCHMENT (2025).

[31] Jessica A. Clarke, *They, Them, Theirs*, 132 HARVARD LAW REVIEW 894 (2019) (concerning the recognition of nonbinary identity); Jessica A. Clarke, *Identity and Form*, 103 CALIFORNIA LAW REVIEW 747 (2015) (discussing different forms of legal identity). I will rely on the categories introduced by Clarke in *Identity and Form*—and especially her distinction between 'ascriptive' and 'elective' identity—throughout the book. As Clarke acknowledges, these terms have been widely used (with different nuances) among legal scholars. *See Id.*, at 757 and at 763, and authors therein cited.

[32] JULIE A. GREENBERG, INTERSEXUALITY AND THE LAW: WHY SEX MATTERS (2012).

[33] RUTH RUBIO-MARÍN, GLOBAL GENDER CONSTITUTIONALISM AND WOMEN'S CITIZENSHIP: A STRUGGLE FOR TRANSFORMATIVE INCLUSION 295–309 (2022).

the 'separate sphere' tradition is central to liberal constitutionalism.[34] Indeed, as Ruth Rubio-Marín, Wen-Chen Chang, Kelley Loper, and Mara Malagodi argue, '[t]he modern constitutional project is defined … by a specific gender order: one premised on patriarchal and heteronormative gender roles as intrinsic to the political system it configures'.[35] In liberal thought, state and society are organized around the so-called separate sphere doctrine:[36] men are assigned to the public sphere of politics and paid employment, women to the private sphere of domesticity. In the age of contractualist theories, the legitimacy of the separate spheres rested on heterosexual marriage and on the—considering the social pressure to marry, arguably fictionalized—liberty to enter it. The separate sphere doctrine was also believed to reflect the ostensibly natural predispositions of men and women—in other words, binary conceptions of sex/gender and gender roles. It is not by chance that, as historian Thomas Laqueur argues, the cultural understanding of sex/gender changed during the eighteenth century, from a 'single sex' model—whereby the bodies of men and women were not understood as oppositional and complementary, but rather as a hierarchical and patriarchal continuum—to the idea that sex/gender anatomy was binary and incommensurable.[37]

In this political-constitutional context, binary and stable sex categories become a legal necessity. As Judith Butler explains in *Gender Trouble*, '[t]he internal coherence or unity of either gender, man or woman, … requires both a stable and oppositional heterosexuality…. [I]nstitutional heterosexuality both requires and produces the univocity of each of the gendered terms that constitute the limit of gendered possibilities within an oppositional, binary gender system'.[38] If the constitutional system builds on the separate spheres doctrine, it also needs a legal system where sex is an 'oppositional' binary. Gender-diverse people, however, are an ill fit for the 'univocity of each of the gendered terms' and ultimately upset the assumptions concerning 'men, women, and the rest of us',[39] thus causing some constitutional 'gender trouble'—on which this book will shed some light.

[34] This paragraph largely draws on the work of RUBIO-MARÍN (*Id.*).

[35] Ruth Rubio-Marín, Wen-Chen Chang, Kelley Loper & Mara Malagodi, *Gender Constitutionalism in Asia: A Comparative Framework*, *in* GENDER, SEXUALITY AND CONSTITUTIONALISM IN ASIA 1, 1 (Wen-Chen Chang, Kelley Loper, Mara Malagodi & Ruth Rubio-Marín eds., 2023).

[36] CAROLE PATEMAN, THE SEXUAL CONTRACT (1988). Some of the writings contained in this book reflect a controversial understanding of trans identity by today's standards (*Id.* at 223). Nevertheless, Pateman's theory remains valid for grounding an understanding of gender constitutionalism that can protect gender-diverse people.

[37] THOMAS LAQUEUR, MAKING SEX: BODY AND GENDER FROM THE GREEKS TO FREUD 193–207 (1992).

[38] JUDITH BUTLER, GENDER TROUBLE: FEMINISM AND THE SUBVERSION OF IDENTITY 30–31 (2d ed. 1999).

[39] KATE BORNSTEIN, GENDER OUTLAWS: ON MEN, WOMEN, AND THE REST OF US (2d ed. 2016).

3.2. Critical legal studies

This book is indebted to the work of those scholars who have argued that sex categories are an instrument of governance and a form of governmental rationality. Dean Spade has examined sex categorizations and the cis- and binary-normative assumptions that are ubiquitous in US administrative law and central to public governance.[40] Paisely Currah has suggested that the assignment of each person to a binary sex category serves governmental rationality.[41] Outside the United States, Alex Sharpe has explored the significance of gender identity in a number of common law jurisdictions and the importance thereof for legal theory. Sharpe's work on 'transgender jurisprudence' has, in fact, been a great source of inspiration for this book.[42] Chris Dietz has discussed the functioning of gender self-determination in Denmark, highlighting not only its advantages, but also how it connects to a specific form of governmentality. Dietz's contribution has been particularly helpful to understand that the right to gender recognition is no magical fix for the protection of gender diversity and that practical difficulties may remain.[43] Flora Renz has also demonstrated how sex categories—and the Gender Recognition Act 2004—have been used as a form of governmental rationality in the United Kingdom.[44]

This book offers comparative insights into multiple jurisdictions that have arguably been less central to the debate and yet are theoretically significant. It also offers a combination of doctrinal and critical investigation that is, to date, missing. Crucially, it connects these debates to public and constitutional law.

3.3. Human rights

The literature discussing the human rights of trans, nonbinary, and intersex people has blossomed in recent times. Scholars have criticized the shortcomings of the protections afforded to gender-diverse people, discussing both national and international law.[45] This book adds to this literature as it takes human rights as

[40] Dean Spade, Normal Life: Administrative Violence, Critical Trans Politics, and the Limits of Law (2d ed. 2015).

[41] Paisley Currah, Sex Is as Sex Does: Governing Transgender Identity (2022); Paisely Currah & Lisa Jean Moore, *'We Won't Know Who You Are': Contesting Sex Designations in New York City Birth Certificates*, 24 Hypatia 113 (2009).

[42] Alex Sharpe, Transgender Jurisprudence: Dysphoric Bodies of Law (2002).

[43] Chris Dietz, Self-Declaration in the Legal Recognition of Gender (2023).

[44] Flora Renz, Gender Recognition and the Law: Troubling Transgender People's Engagement with Legal Regulation (2024).

[45] *Ex multis*: Damien Gonzalez-Salzberg, Sexuality and Transsexuality Before the European Court of Human Rights (2019); The Legal Status of Transsexual and Transgender Persons (Jens Scherpe ed., 2015); The Legal Status of Intersex Persons (Jens Scherpe, Anatol Dutta & Tobias Helms eds., 2018); Peter Dunne, *Transgender Sterilisation Requirements in Europe*,

the starting point to question assumptions of gender identity and sex anatomy in public and constitutional law.

Finally, this research adds to the critical literature on rights. To mention but a few examples, critiques have addressed the limited concrete impact of legal rights, which at times fail to create real social change.[46] The effectiveness of rights to redress systemic discrimination against trans people and free them from the structures and strictures of gender has also been contested.[47] One critique that is especially relevant to the study of gender diversity in public law is the *ambivalence* and *ambiguity* of the rights approach. As Ben Golder explains, rights are inherently ambiguous because 'any attempt to definitively "ground" human rights upon a given conception of humanity or attribute of the human rights bearer ... can always be unmasked ... as a particular and unavoidably exclusionary interpretation of the human'.[48] Rights can 'produce subjects; they position, constrain, and conduct those who deploy them and subtly contour the subjectivity of self-understanding of the rights holder who is their supposed master'.[49]

In the context of gender diversity recognition, rights allow people to be different. When rights are demanded, courts and public authorities in general must explain *why* limits are placed on gender recognition or why intersex treatments are allowed. Demanding rights forces public authorities to face the 'Socratic contestation' that Kumm describes. On the other hand, rights may be used to curb diversity and trigger normalizing dynamics that take the form of disciplinary power. When rights are conferred on a particular rights-bearer, mechanisms that include hierarchical supervision, enforcement of detailed norms, and micro-penalties and rewards can take root. This research shows, through a combination of doctrinal analysis and critical theory, how this mechanism concretely works on gender-diverse—trans, nonbinary, and intersex—people.

4. Methodological notes

4.1. Why comparative law?

This book discusses gender diversity (mis)recognition in public law. Hence, it offers a micro-comparison, namely a discussion of 'individual legal rules (also

25 Medical Law Review 554 (2017); Peter Dunne, *(Trans)Forming Single-Gender Services and Communal Accommodations*, 26 Social & Legal Studies 537 (2017).

[46] Baines & Rubio-Marín, *supra* note 25, at 6.

[47] Spade, *supra* note 40; Heath Fogg Davis, Beyond Trans: Does Gender Matter (2017).

[48] Ben Golder, Foucault and the Politics of Rights 89 (2015); Brown, *supra* note 22, at 232; Wendy Brown, States of Injury: Power and Freedom in Late Modernity (1995).

[49] Golder, *supra* note 48, at 97.

individual legal concepts) which regulate broadly the same thing'.[50] To borrow a particularly fortunate expression from Ran Hirschl, the aim of this book is 'concept building through multiple description'.[51] More specifically, the purpose of this research is to 'generate concepts and analytical frameworks for thinking about constitutional norms and practices'.[52] Giuseppe de Vergottini has argued that 'legal comparison is an indispensable tool to facilitate knowledge',[53] and Ran Hirschl explains, '[b]y studying various manifestations of and solutions to roughly analogous constitutional challenges, our understanding of key concepts in constitutional law... becomes more sophisticated and analytically sharp'.[54] Comparison lends itself well to the study of gender diversity. Laws and decisions concerning gender diversity can be limited in any one jurisdiction. Despite being the source of essential insights on which this research draws, studies focusing on a single country might face constraints in advancing more general conclusions. Researching multiple jurisdictions instead favours the identification of a critical mass of comprehensive material.

More precisely, following Rosalind Dixon's taxonomy, the comparison contained in this book is 'reflective', 'moral cosmopolitan', and 'doctrinal'.[55] It is 'reflective' because it stimulates thought on the different models of gender diversity recognition, sharpening our critical understanding of what is distinctive about each of them. Comparison is 'moral-cosmopolitan' in that it identifies a few common elements in the relationship between gender diversity and public law. Furthermore, it grounds the argument that the role of gender identity and sex characteristics in public law is a transnational issue. Finally, the following chapters examine the doctrinal foundations of the recognition of gender diversity, as well as the discourses utilized to restrict or recognize it.

The legal developments presented in the book are also contextualized, at least to some extent. This helps us understand why gender diversity matters to public law in different jurisdictions and allows us to see its workings. That said, comparison is *not* used here to identify the 'independent variables' that determine the development of gender diversity across jurisdictions. It is not an 'inference-oriented small-N comparative study' as described by Hirschl.[56] Finally, as already mentioned,

[50] Jaakko Husa, Introduction to Comparative Law 105 (2023).

[51] Ran Hirschl, Comparative Matters: The Renaissance of Comparative Constitutional Law 117, 238–42 (2014). Although Hirschl explicitly encourages researchers to go beyond this 'concept building through multiple description' approach, he is also adamant about the importance of *this* kind of legal comparison. On this point: Rosalind Dixon, *Toward a Realistic Comparative Constitutional Studies. Review of Comparative Matters: The Renaissance of Comparative Constitutional Law (Oxford University Press, 2014)*, 64 The American Journal of Comparative Law 193 (2016).

[52] *Id.* at 238.

[53] Giuseppe de Vergottini, Diritto Costituzionale Comparato 52–53 (11th ed. 2022); Lucio Pegoraro, Diritto Costituzionale Comparato. La Scienza e il Metodo 27 (2014).

[54] Hirschl, *supra* note 51, at 238.

[55] Rosalind Dixon, *Comparative Constitutional Modalities: Towards a Rigorous but Realistic Comparative Constitutional Studies*, 2 Comparative Constitutional Studies 60 (2024).

[56] Hirschl, *supra* note 51, at 244–67.

comparative law in this book is *not* normative. Normative research is surely important to comparative law;[57] however, a *theory* of gender diversity in public law is needed before proposing normative solutions. The material presented here can contribute to the development of such a theory.

4.2. Selection of jurisdictions: Criteria

This study discusses legal developments in Australia, Belgium, Colombia, France, Germany, India, Italy, Nepal, Pakistan, and the United Kingdom, albeit not in equal measure. Throughout the book, references are also made to other jurisdictions, mostly to provide context and hints for future research.

In all these jurisdictions, courts, parliaments, and other government bodies have 'faced similar ... rights questions' but have arrived at different solutions, making them comparable for the purposes of this book.[58] To borrow from Dixon, the 'constitutional language' regarding gender diversity in these jurisdictions is similar, and, in this sense, public authorities 'have grappled with the same specific issues' conferring 'a strong degree of "general" and "topical" similarity'.[59] Indeed, this book examines a set of (broadly defined) rules that serve a similar function, namely, balancing the rights of gender-diverse individuals and competing public interests and fundamental rights in legal systems where sex classifications are heavily relied on for achieving a number of legal and constitutional goals.[60] These dynamics have led to constitutional developments in virtually all jurisdictions examined. In one jurisdiction under study, that is, France, this constitutional dimension (doctrinally speaking) is only marginally present; nevertheless, the interaction between public power and individual identity remains particularly evident.

As Konrad Zweigert and Hein Kötz advise, I have avoided 'all limitations and restraints' on the 'question of "sources of law", [as] the comparatist must treat as a source of law whatever moulds or affects the living law in his [*sic*] chosen system'.[61] To this purpose, this book examines multiple legal materials, including judicial decisions, statutes, administrative regulations, and soft law. These materials are not uniformly present in all jurisdictions. Nevertheless, they all serve a similar function.

[57] Vicki C. Jackson, *Comparative Constitutional Law: Methodologies*, *in* The Oxford Handbook of Comparative Constitutional Law 54, 60–62 (Michel Rosenfeld & Andras Sajo eds., 2012).

[58] Sandra Fredman, Comparative Human Rights 17 (2018).

[59] Dixon, *supra* note 55. As Pegoraro suggests, I approach the relations between the individual and public powers in a 'substantive' fashion (*supra* note 53, at 25–27).

[60] Konrad Zweigert & Hein Kötz, Introduction to Comparative Law 34–36 (Tony Weir trans, 3d ed. 1998). On 'functionalism': Roberto Scarciglia, Metodi e Comparazione Giuridica 80 (4th ed. 2025); Mathias Siems, Comparative Law 31–5 (3d ed. 2022).

[61] Zweigert & Kötz, *supra* note 60, at 35.

As Dixon recommends for this type of comparative study, the selection of these comparable cases is broad.[62] It includes jurisdictions of common[63] and civil law;[64] from the Global North[65] and from the Global South;[66] with decolonial[67] and postcolonial experience;[68] higher,[69] middle,[70] and lower income.[71] The presence of cases from the Global South deserves emphasis. Legal comparison may indeed be an 'antidote' to various forms of ethnocentrism,[72] especially when it comes to fundamental rights.[73] Further considerations for the selection included the accessibility of sources and languages, as well as the availability of legal materials. Finally, concerning contextualization, although I provide historical, anthropological, and legal background to understand the cases, I make no claims to providing an ethnography-like 'thick description'.[74] Another limitation of this study is that I could not conduct research 'in the field' in each jurisdiction discussed. Time and resources are, after all, limited.

Finally, as this book explores several issues related to gender diversity and public law, it is structured around themes. Depending on the topic under consideration, each chapter draws on one or more jurisdictions to illustrate a single theme. Some chapters explore multiple jurisdictions. Others, such as the discussions surrounding various standards of recognition—arguably one of the most debated areas in this field—require a more thorough analysis. In those cases, I have, therefore, chosen to focus on a single jurisdiction.

5. Overview of the chapters

Chapter 2 gives a brief account of the notions of sex and gender, and of the binary. It introduces the main protagonists of this study, explaining who intersex, trans, and nonbinary people are, what they ask, and what limits and objections their demands encounter. The chapter offers a brief overview of the social controversies associated with the demands of gender-diverse people and presents some counter objections.

62 Dixon, *supra* note 55.
63 Australia, India, Pakistan, United Kingdom.
64 Belgium, Colombia, France, Germany, Italy, Nepal.
65 Australia, Belgium, France, Germany, Italy.
66 Colombia, India, Nepal, Pakistan.
67 Colombia.
68 India and Pakistan.
69 Australia, Belgium, France, Germany, Italy, United Kingdom.
70 Colombia.
71 India, Nepal, Pakistan.
72 Husa, *supra* note 50, at 72–4.
73 As a positive exception: Holning Lau, *Decriminalizing Same-Sex Sexual Activity: Jurisprudence from the Global South*, 23 International Journal of Constitutional Law 61 (2025).
74 Ran Hirschl, *Methodology and Research Design*, *in* Constitutionalism in Context 41, 45–46 (David Law ed., 2022).

Intersexuality is a good starting point for understanding the relationship between gender diversity and public law. In Chapter 3, I argue that intersexuality may be perceived as a problem for legal authorities in systems where binary categories are presupposed and enforced. I concentrate first on Italy and France and explain that preserving the legal binary is *one* reason why public authorities might rely on medical knowledge to deny the existence of intersex people and favour a binary assignment at birth. Next, I refer to Belgian law where, despite nonbinary recognition being available, intersex rights are not yet satisfactorily protected, thus warning against any facile presumption of an automatic correlation between nonbinary recognition and the protection of intersex physical integrity. Finally, I examine German and Colombian law, showing how intersex constitutional rights have been acknowledged and the significance of transforming the binary legal order for this purpose.

I then focus on the right to gender recognition, identifying and discussing three forms thereof: the medico-behavioural, the socio-behavioural, and the self-determination models. Italy, discussed in Chapter 4, is an example of the medico-behavioural model. Italian law is characterized by an abundant constitutional jurisprudence in which the sex binary has been entrenched by requiring applicants for recognition to undergo a medically supervised transformation of their physical, behavioural, and psychological characteristics. These medico-behavioural requirements amount to a disciplinary mechanism that forces trans people into acceptable shapes. The Italian case shows how medicalization and standardized, normatively compelled sex/gender expression have been used to primarily preserve the heterosexuality of family law, which has constitutional status in Italy.

Medical requirements for being granted recognition are often criticized, and demands for de-medicalization have been successful in some cases. This may lead to what I call the 'socio-behavioural model', which is enshrined in French law and discussed in Chapter 5. Since 2016, medical transformations are no longer required, but applicants for gender recognition in France have to demonstrate the behaviour typically associated with, and be socially acknowledged in, their claimed legal sex. Although de-medicalized, the socio-behavioural model preserves external control over legal transitions. The chapter examines the rationales behind this approach, exploring the push for human rights and the resulting resistance based on the foundational principle of the 'inalienability of civil status', which courts, the legislature, and some scholars identify as conflicting with gender recognition.

More rarely, trans advocates achieve gender self-determination—that is, the right to simply declare one's legal sex without having to fulfil any requirements. Chapter 6 examines this model in Colombia, which boasts a body of constitutional case law on this subject that is qualitatively and quantitatively impressive. The chapter details the development of the self-determination doctrine and its application to specific circumstances and beneficiaries, arguing that gender self-determination transforms legal sex from an 'objective' characteristic to a 'subjective' declaration and is linked to broader structural changes enhancing LGBTQI+ rights, such as equal marriage and parental rights. The chapter also explains the Eurocentrism of binary-normative conceptions of sex/gender and the decolonizing potential of gender self-determination.

The legal sex binary is a crucial notion in this book. While the medico-behavioural and socio-behavioural models appear to reinforce it, gender self-determination questions it as it opens the door to previously non-legible gender identities. Several jurisdictions have examined nonbinary recognition directly and granted it, though in different models, which Chapter 7 explores. The chapter begins with *embodied recognition*, whereby nonbinary recognition is granted to individuals who show some form of physical diversity, be it congenital or the outcome of medical treatments. Examples of such a model can be found in the case law of the High Court of Australia and of the German Federal Constitutional Court and Federal Court of Justice.[75] This approach, I argue, reinforces mechanisms of control and supervision of individual identities, even though nonbinary identities are recognized. In contrast, the Colombian Constitutional Court represents a self-determination model, whereby nonbinary recognition is granted based on the person's self-declaration. Finally, the chapter examines the case law of the Supreme Courts of India, Nepal, and Pakistan, which have recognized nonbinary people based on the socio-historical experiences of identified vernacular identities, framing recognition as a form of redistributive justice and thus developing a type of nonbinary recognition of its own. Importantly, they further clarify the colonial dimension of the legal binary, illuminating the Eurocentric assumptions of the gender order in public and constitutional law.

The last chapter asks what is next and focuses on two opposite, ongoing developments: the erasure of sex categories and the 'biologistic' backlash. First, I investigate the challenges associated with removing sex categories from the law altogether. The first part of the chapter, hence, begins with examining the case law of the Italian Constitutional Court, the French Court of Cassation, and the Colombian Constitutional Court, which, each in its own way, found that sex categories are constitutionally necessary. In contrast, courts in Germany and Belgium have established the constitutional neutrality of civil status, thus in principle allowing the elimination of sex markers. Focusing on the United Kingdom's opposition to reforming the Gender Recognition Act 2004 and the rise of constitutional decisions denying gender recognition in central and eastern Europe, the chapter raises the issue of the comeback of biological narratives around sex in relation to gender registration. Finally, the conclusions summarize the findings, tie up the various threads contained in the book, and press for further research.

[75] In 2024, Germany passed legislation that moved German law towards self-determination (see Chapter 7). This development, however, is more uncertain when it comes to a *constitutional* right to nonbinary self-determination.

2

A Brief Theoretical Background

1. Definitions, clarifications, and a few introductory remarks

Much of this book relies on notions that are common currency in gender studies and which should be introduced before proceeding to the legal analysis. The present aim is not to offer a complete overview of a highly complex topic but, more modestly, to provide a concise explanation of some concepts to facilitate the reading of the volume.[1] I also aim to briefly introduce some of the social controversies that have accompanied the demands of gender-diverse people. I start with a definition of the notions of 'sex' and 'gender' and then move on to this book's main 'actors'—intersex, trans, and nonbinary people—and discuss their interactions with the law. I conclude with an examination of some objections to the rights of gender-diverse people and succinctly respond to them.

In this book, I employ 'sex' and 'gender' according to Judith Butler's theoretical framework. Butler has rejected the traditional differentiation between sex and gender, which posits the former as a biological core and the latter as a cultural construction. Butler argues that gender is a signifying mechanism that produces and assigns meaning to the sexed body:

> Gender ought not to be conceived merely as the cultural inscription of meaning on a pregiven sex (a juridical conception); gender must also designate the very apparatus of production whereby the sexes themselves are established. As a result, gender is not to culture as sex is to nature; gender is also the discursive/cultural means by which 'sexed nature' or 'a natural sex' is produced and established as 'prediscursive,' prior to culture, a politically neutral surface *on which* culture acts.[2]

[1] On queer legal theory: Brenda Cossman, *Queering Queer Legal Studies: An Unreconstructed Ode to Eve Sedgwick (and Others)*, 6 Critical Analysis of Law 23 (2019); Damien Gonzalez-Salzberg, Sexuality and Transsexuality under the European Convention on Human Rights: A Queer Reading of Human Rights Law (2019); Aeyal Gross, *Gender Outlaws Before the Law: The Courts of the Borderlands*, 32 Harvard Journal of Law & Gender 165 (2009); Janet Halley, Split Decisions: How and Why to Take a Break from Feminism (2007); Carl Stychin, Law's Desire: Sexuality and the Limits of Justice (1995).

[2] Judith Butler, Gender Trouble: Feminism and the Subversion of Identity 10 (2d ed. 1999) (emphasis in the original). *See also*: Judith Butler, Undoing Gender 42 (2004) (where Butler defines gender as a 'norm' and as 'the apparatus by which the production and normalization of masculine and feminine take place along with the interstitial forms of hormonal, chromosomal, psychic, and performative that gender assumes').

Gender Diversity in Public Law. Stefano Osella, Oxford University Press. © Stefano Osella 2026.
DOI: 10.1093/9780198935070.003.0002

Butler contends that our understanding of the body is mediated and situated. Myriad human bodies—with countless differences among them—are reinterpreted through gender (as a meaning-making apparatus) to fit a specific binary mould. The body and its materiality, it must be clear, are not in any way denied. Nevertheless, how we see the body cannot be abstracted from the cultural context. Butler's theory has been enormously influential across disciplines.[3] Interestingly, the rejection of the neat differentiation between sex and gender has been studied in science, too. As Agustín Fuentes explains, 'humans are biocultural', meaning that they are

> a product of dynamic relationships that interweave the biological and the cultural, as well as the historical, into a single result: us. Although we are biological organisms, the totality of the human experience cannot be reduced to either specific innate (biological) or external (environmental/cultural) influences. It is a synthesis of both.[4]

I will therefore use 'gender' to refer to the cultural mechanism that attributes meaning to the individual body and identity. I will employ 'sex/gender' to refer to the individual dimension, including social and self-identification. However, I will use 'sex' to refer to the *legal* sex in which each person is classified. This choice reflects the legal vocabulary.[5] To be clear, the difficulty of distinguishing the material from the cultural is evident in the law, too—and perhaps even more so than in other disciplines.[6] Sex is indeed rarely defined as purely biological—and even when courts or legislatures do so, they normally do it for legal purposes, which shows that defining sex is rarely (if ever) a fact-finding mission to determine a biological truth.

As noted above, Butler connected our 'binary' understanding of sex/gender—the mutually exclusive existence of two 'biological sexes' only, with everything else

[3] Just to mention a few non-exhaustive examples, Butler has stimulated research in history (THOMAS LAQUEUR, MAKING SEX: BODY AND GENDER FROM THE GREEKS TO FREUD (1992); ALICE DOMURAT-DREGER, HERMAPHRODITES AND THE MEDICAL INVENTION OF SEX (1998)), anthropology (KATRINA KARKAZIS, FIXING SEX: INTERSEX, MEDICAL AUTHORITY, AND LIVED EXPERIENCE (2008)), law (GONZALEZ-SALZBERG, *supra* note 1; Gross, *supra* note 1), and biology (ANNE FAUSTO-STERLING, SEXING THE BODY: GENDER POLITICS AND THE CONSTRUCTION OF SEXUALITY (2d ed. 2020)).

[4] AGUSTÍN FUENTES, SEX IS A SPECTRUM: THE BIOLOGICAL LIMITS OF THE BINARY 41 (2025). For an introduction to the scientific questioning of binary understandings of sex/gender, *see* section 4.2 of this chapter.

[5] For a similar choice, *see* PAISLEY CURRAH, SEX IS AS SEX DOES: GOVERNING TRANSGENDER IDENTITY 3 (2022).

[6] Anti-discrimination lawyers have argued that disaggregating the material from the cultural is a mistake for anti-discrimination law: Katherine M. Franke, *The Central Mistake of Sex Discrimination Law: The Disaggregation of Sex from Gender*, 144 UNIVERSITY OF PENNSYLVANIA LAW REVIEW 1 (1995); Mary Anne Case, *Disaggregating Gender from Sex and Sexual Orientation: The Effeminate Man in the Law and Feminist Jurisprudence*, 105 YALE LAW JOURNAL 1 (1995); JOANNE CONAGHAN, LAW AND GENDER 155–97 (2013).

being reduced to a minuscule and pathological exception—to the preservation of institutional heterosexuality.[7] To be sure, questioning the binary does not mean questioning the presence of men and women, but only their *exclusive* existence: it is not that men and women do not exist; simply, the argument goes, other people exist, too. As we shall see, the connection between the binary and institutional heterosexuality is extremely clear in public law, specifically in relation to the preservation of traditional marriage. That said, many public interests and rights may motivate limits on the recognition of gender diversity and the preservation of the binary, and, in general, legal sex. Hence, in the following, I will refer to the 'binary' not to indicate or question the existence of 'men' and 'women', but rather the insistence on their *exclusive* existence, mostly for legal purposes, at the expense of any other possibilities.

2. Intersex people

'Intersexuality' refers to people 'born with physical sex characteristics (such as sexual anatomy, reproductive organs, hormonal patterns and/or chromosomal patterns) that do not fit typical definitions for male or female bodies'.[8] Intersexuality represents a social challenge. Mauro Cabral defines it as all manifestations of the 'sexed body' that vary 'from the culturally prevailing standard of feminine or masculine corporeality'.[9] In the words of Michel Foucault, the 'hermaphrodite' was 'someone with two sexes [whom] one didn't know whether to treat as a boy or a girl, whether or not he/she should be allowed to marry and with whom, whether he/she could become the holder of an ecclesiastical living, whether he/she could take religious orders, and so on.'[10] Intersex people have been difficult to classify for legal purposes, too.[11] Considering the illegibility of intersexuality, it is unsurprising that the history of intersex people in Europe and North America is replete with discrimination.[12]

[7] Butler, Gender Trouble, *supra* note 2, at 24 and 30–31; Michel Foucault, History of Sexuality, Vol. 1: An Introduction 155 (Robert Hurley trans., 1990); Christine Delphy, *Rethinking Sex and Gender*, 16 Women's Studies International Forum 1 (1993); Monique Wittig, *The Category of Sex*, *in* Monique Wittig, The Straight Mind and Other Essays 2 (1992).

[8] United Nations Office of the High Commissioner for Human Rights, Free & Equal Campaign Fact Sheet: Intersex People (Sept. 2025), https://www.unfe.org/sites/default/files/download/Intersex%20factsheet%202025%20-%20EN_0.pdf.

[9] Mauro Cabral & Gabriel Benzur, *Cuando Digo Intersex: Un Diálogo Introductorio a la Intersexualidad*, 24 Cadernos Pagu 283, 284 (2005).

[10] Michel Foucault, Abnormal: Lessons at the College de France 1974–1975 65 (Graham Burchell trans., 2003).

[11] For a historical perspective, *see* Yan Thomas, *La Division des Sexes en Droit Romain*, *in* Histoire des Femmes en Occident. I. L'Antiquité 131 (Georges Duby & Michelle Perrot eds., 2002). For a general discussion, *see*: Julie A. Greenberg, Intersexuality and the Law: Why Sex Matters (2012).

[12] Geertje Mak, *Doubtful Sex in Civil Law: Nineteenth and Early Twentieth Century Proposals for Ruling Hermaphroditism*, 12 Cardozo Journal of Law and Gender 197 (2005); Geertje Mak,

Currently, the demands of intersex people—the ones that this book examines—primarily relate to the medical and surgical treatments motivated by the cultural imperative 'to make intersex children's bodies conform to gendered social corporeal norms':[13] that is, the treatments aimed to give a conventionally masculine or feminine appearance to children's genitals. Such treatments, it should be noted, might be unnecessary for preserving the life and health of intersex children.[14]

The origin of such treatments can be traced to the protocols designed by John Money and his team at Johns Hopkins University in the 1950s. As explained by Jemima Repo,[15] Money suggested that the 'gender role' (meaning, in effect, gender identity) of children is not biologically determined at birth, but develops according to perceptual stimuli, primarily the external genitalia. Money theorized that atypical external genitalia could lead to an undesirable 'ambiguous gender role'. It was feared that this presented the risk of 'psychological disturbances' and possible social ostracism.[16] As observed by Alice Domurat-Dreger, these protocols were also inspired by heteronormative values, as ambiguous genitalia could impair penile–vaginal sex.[17] Intersexuality was, therefore, seen as an undesirable abnormality.[18]

Protocols were devised to operate on genitals in early childhood. Doctors had to interpret biological markers to assign children a sex/gender of rearing, and administered surgical and medical treatments to shape genitals accordingly. Parents were advised to raise their child in the assigned sex/gender without informing them of their intersexuality. That said, sex/gender assignment did not depend only on biological characteristics. Other factors—such as practical feasibility—weighed in. For example, given the technical difficulties associated with the reconstruction of a penis, boys without a penis or with a micropenis could be assigned to the female sex/gender and operated on to create a conventional female anatomy.[19] In short, Repo has argued that such treatments were intended to 'normalise the child's sexuality and sex, and ultimately, the reproduction of life. . . . [T]he more "normal"

Conflicting Heterosexualities: Hermaphroditism and the Emergence of Surgery around 1900, 24 Journal of the History of Sexuality 402 (2015); Domurat-Dreger, *supra* note 3; Michel Foucault, Herculine Barbin (Richard McCougall trans., 1980).

[13] Daniela Alaattinoglu & Kari Ragnarsson, *A Castle in the Sky? The Icelandic Ban on Non-Therapeutic, Non-Consensual Interventions on Intersex Children in Context*, 4 European Human Rights Law Review 408, 408 (2025).

[14] *Id.* Bernard Dickens underlines that, when genitals are ambiguous at birth, medical attention should be advised because there might be an underlying condition that warrants medical treatment. This is the case, for example, of Congenital Adrenal Hyperplasia (Bernard Dickens, *Management of Intersex Newborns: Legal and Ethical Developments*, 143 International Journal of Gynecology & Obstetrics 255, 257–58 (2018)).

[15] The following account of the approach developed by John Money largely draws on Jemima Repo, The Biopolitics of Gender 24–49 (2015).

[16] Alice Domurat-Dreger, *Ambiguous Sex or Ambivalent Medicine? Ethical Issues in the Treatment of Intersexuality*, 28 Hastings Centre Report 24 (1998); Karkazis, *supra* note 3.

[17] Domurat-Dreger, *supra* note 3, at 197.

[18] Fausto-Sterling, *supra* note 3, at 49.

[19] Repo, *supra* note 15, at 35–36.

the genitalia looked, the more likely the subject was to successfully develop the corresponding gender role.'[20] Domurat-Dreger has contended that these treatments aimed 'to keep two clear sexes and to retain the notion that heterosexuality is normal and homosexuality is not'.[21]

Since the 1990s, activists have been vocal in opposing involuntary and culturally motivated medical and surgical interventions, particularly on children. They have highlighted the possible adverse effects of such treatments, which include psychological trauma, physical pain, sterility, and loss of sexual sensation.[22] As the European Parliament put it, such treatments may impact on intersex people's 'physical, psychological and sexual and reproductive health'.[23] Tellingly, some activists refer to such treatments as 'intersex genital mutilation' (IGM).[24] To be sure, changes have occurred in medical practice. A more attentive and respectful approach to the needs of intersex people has arguably developed.[25] Nevertheless, to this day, 'the rights to bodily autonomy and self-determination, and an end to stigmatisation' appear to be central demands of intersex activists,[26] as is evident in

[20] *Id.* at 38.

[21] DOMURAT-DREGER, *supra* note 3, at 197.

[22] Cheryl Chase, *Hermaphrodites with Attitude: Mapping the Emergence of Intersex Political Activism*, *in* THE TRANSGENDER STUDIES READER (Susan Stryker & Stephen Whittle eds., 2006). For a description of the adverse effects of such treatments on intersex people: Commissioner for Human Rights of the Council of Europe, Human Rights and Intersex People (2015); Morgan Carpenter, *The Human Rights of Intersex People: Addressing Harmful Practices and Rhetoric of Change*, 24 REPRODUCTIVE HEALTH MATTERS 74, 75 (2016); Markus Bauer, Daniela Truffer & Daniela Crocetti, *Intersex Human Rights*, 24 THE INTERNATIONAL JOURNAL OF HUMAN RIGHTS 724 (2020).

[23] Resolution 2016/2096(INI), of the European Parliament on Promoting Gender Equality in Mental Health and Clinical Research ¶ BC (14 Feb. 2017).

[24] Bauer, Truffer & Crocetti, *supra* note 22, at 726.

[25] This point deserves a deeper discussion that cannot be offered here. Nevertheless, a reference should be made to the 2006 Chicago Consensus Statement and its 2016 follow-up, which might be argued to be an example of a more respectful medical approach to intersexuality (Peter A. Lee, Christopher P. Houk, Faisal Ahmed & Ieuan A. Hughes, *Consensus Statement on Management of Intersex Disorders. International Consensus Conference on Intersex*, 118 PEDIATRICS 488 (2006); Peter A. Lee et al., *Global Disorders of Sex Development Update since 2006: Perceptions, Approach and Care*, 85 HORMONE RESEARCH IN PAEDIATRICS 158 (2016)). Karkazis explains that the 2006 Consensus Statement introduced new standards characterized by a joint effort of medical professionals and advocacy groups. The Consensus emphasizes the patient's perspective, acknowledges the heteronormative assumptions of the original protocols, stresses the necessity of using inclusive terminology, and advises a more cautious approach to medical treatments (KARKAZIS, *supra* note 3, at 237–38). Activists seem divided on the 2006 Chicago Consensus. Some have welcomed the Consensus lukewarmly (Bauer, Truffer & Crocetti, *supra* note 22, at 739), while others have criticized these protocols as ultimately 'validating' intersex genital mutilation (Carpenter, *supra* note 22, at 75–76). I should also acknowledge that some medical professionals have problematized the demands of intersex activists. In 2016, a group of healthcare professionals questioned whether intersex activists are genuinely representative of the intersex population. They argued that, even though some outdated approaches to intersex management unfortunately persist, the treatment of intersexuality is today more holistic, multidisciplinary, consent-driven, and technologically advanced than it used to be (Martine Cools, Margaret Simmonds, Sue Elford, Joke Gorter, S. Faisal Ahmed, Franco D'Alberton & Alex Springer, Olaf Hiort, *Response to the Council of Europe Human Rights Commissioner's Issue Paper on Human Rights and Intersex People*, 70 EUROPEAN UROLOGY 407, 407–09 (2016)).

[26] Carpenter, *supra* note 22, at 74 and 77; Bauer, Truffer & Crocetti, *supra* note 22, at 724, 726–27.

some of the main intersex rights declarations, such as the 2013 Malta Declaration,[27] the 2014 Statement of Riga,[28] and the 2017 Vienna Statement.[29] Principle 32 of the 2017 edition of the Yogyakarta Principles (Plus Ten) reads: 'No one shall be subjected to invasive or irreversible medical procedures that modify sex characteristics without their free, prior and informed consent, unless necessary to avoid serious, urgent and irreparable harm to the concerned person.'

Less unifying is the demand for recognition of an intersex identity.[30] To clarify, 'intersex' is not coterminous with a nonbinary gender identity. Intersex people may identify as binary or nonbinary, just like anyone else, and may not be interested in pursuing gender recognition. Katrina Karkazis has observed that: 'The goal of many people with an intersex condition is not to deconstruct or eliminate gender, or to advocate for a third sex or no sex, but rather to change treatment practices and improve the well-being of others with these conditions ... intersexuality, these activists argue, is primarily a problem of stigma and trauma, not of gender.'[31] As Julie Greenberg highlights, some intersex activists contend that 'altering the current medical protocol for the treatment of infants with an intersex condition can best be advanced by focusing on issues emphasized by disability rights advocates', thus distancing themselves from LGBTQ+ demands.[32] In the political arena, excessive emphasis on identity demands is perceived as extraneous by some intersex activists, who contend that a 'focus on honorifics, pronouns and toilets' is misplaced.[33] Some advocates have stressed that intersex treatments and identity recognition should be kept separate.[34] Another phalanx of intersex activists, however, appears to be more aligned with LGBTQ+ demands. These activists argue that 'the problems associated with intersex traits have to do with narrow views about gender' and criticize medical authorities, arguing that they constitute 'a powerful group that enforces gendered ideologies about bodies and identities'.[35] An intersex

[27] Third International Intersex Forum, Malta Declaration (1 Dec. 2013), https://www.oiieurope.org/malta-declaration/.

[28] Intersex Iceland, NNID of the Netherlands, OII Austria/VIMÖ, OII Belgium, Genres Pluriels, OII Bulgaria, OII Francophonie, OII Germany/IVIM, OII Scandinavia/Intersex Scandinavia, TransInterQueer e.V., Statement of Riga (8 Oct. 2014), https://www.oiieurope.org/statement-of-riga/.

[29] OII Europe, Statement of the 1st European Intersex Community Event (30–31 Mar. 2017), https://www.oiieurope.org/statement-1st-european-intersex-community-event-vienna-30st-31st-march-2017/.

[30] For a mapping of intersex activism: Maayan Sudai, *Revisiting the Limits of Professional Autonomy: The Intersex Rights Movement's Path to De-Medicalization*, 41 Harvard Journal of Law & Gender 1, 1–18 (2018). For a previous reflection of mine on these topics: Stefano Osella, *When Comparative Law Walks the Path of Anthropology: The Third Gender in Europe*, 23 German Law Journal 920 (2022). For a discussion of the socio-legal complexities entailed by nonbinary recognition of intersex people, *see* Fae Garland & Mitchell Travis, Intersex Embodiment. Legal Frameworks between Identity and Disorder 51–77 (2023).

[31] Karkazis, *supra* note 3, at 247.

[32] Greenberg, *supra* note 11, at 5.

[33] Carpenter, *supra* note 22, at 79.

[34] Bauer, Truffer & Crocetti, *supra* note 22, at 741.

[35] Georgiann Davis, Contesting Intersex: The Dubious Diagnosis 52 (2015).

legal identity, the argument goes, would have 'the potential to undermine medical assumptions and practices that surround intersex individuals'.[36]

Intersex demands for physical integrity are slowly gaining traction in human rights law.[37] For example, in 2025, the High Commissioner for Human Rights submitted a report to the UN General Assembly where 'medically unnecessary surgeries, hormonal treatments and other medical interventions intended to modify [intersex children's] physical appearance and traits to fit stereotypes of male or female bodies' were condemned.[38] In 2024, the Human Rights Council expressed 'grave concern' about the 'the violence and harmful practices that persons with innate variations in sex characteristics, including children, face in all regions of the world, including medically unnecessary or deferrable interventions, which may be irreversible, with respect to sex characteristics, performed without the full, free and informed consent of the person'.[39] Similar statements have been made by multiple human rights bodies, for example the Committee against Torture, the Committee on the Rights of Persons with Disabilities, the Committee of the Rights of the Child, as well as the Human Rights Committee.[40] The CEDAW Committee has condemned the violation of human rights suffered by intersex women.[41] At the regional level, the Council of Ministers and the Parliamentary Assembly of the Council of Europe,[42] the Commissioner for Human Rights of the Council of Europe,[43] the European Parliament,[44] and the Inter-American

[36] Sudai, *supra* note 30, at 33.

[37] For an overview: Alaattinoglu & Ragnarsson, *supra* note 13; Bauer, Truffer & Crocetti, *supra* note 22; GIOVANNA GILLERI, SEX, GENDER, AND INTERNATIONAL HUMAN RIGHTS LAW: CONTESTING BINARIES (2024); United Nations Human Rights Council, Discriminatory Laws and Policies, Acts of Violence and Harmful Practices Against Intersex Persons: Report of the Office of the United Nations High Commissioner for Human Rights, UN Doc. A/HRC/60/50, ¶ 4 (4 Sept. 2025).

[38] United Nations Human Rights Council, UN Doc. A/HRC/60/50, *supra* note 37, ¶¶ 10–14.

[39] United Nations Human Rights Council, Combating Discrimination, Violence and Harmful Practices Against Intersex Persons, UN Doc. A/HRC/55/L.9 (21 Mar. 2024).

[40] As discussed in Bauer, Truffer & Crocetti, *supra* note 22 and in GILLERI, *supra* note 37. *See*: Committee Against Torture, Concluding observations of the Committee against Torture: Germany, CAT/C/DEU/CO/5, ¶ 20 (12 Dec. 2011), https://www.ohchr.org/en/documents/concluding-observations/catcdeuco5-concluding-observations-committee-against-torture; Committee on the Rights of Persons with Disabilities, Concluding Observations on the Initial Report of France, CRPD/C/FRA/CO/1, ¶¶ 36–37 (14 Sept. 2021), https://intersexrights.org/un/crpd-c-fra-co-1/; Committee on the Rights of the Child, Concluding Observations on the Combined Second to Fourth Periodic Reports of Switzerland, CRC/C/CHE/CO/2-4, ¶¶ 42–43 (30 Jan. 2015), https://www.icj.org/sogiunjurisprudence/concluding-observations-crcccheco2-4-30-january-2015-switzerland.

[41] GILLERI, *supra* note 37, at 157. For a general overview of 'intersex mainstreaming' in international human rights law: *Id.*, at 154–64.

[42] Council of Europe, Committee of Ministers, Recommendation CM/Rec(2025)7 of the Committee of Ministers to Member States on Equal Rights for Intersex Persons (7 Oct. 2025); Parliamentary Assembly of the Council of Europe, Promoting the Human Rights of and Eliminating Discrimination Against Intersex People, Res. 2191 (12 Oct. 2017). *See also*: FRANCESCA ROMANA AMMATURO, EUROPEAN SEXUAL CITIZENSHIP: HUMAN RIGHTS, BODIES AND IDENTITIES 7–31 (2017).

[43] Commissioner for Human Rights of the Council of Europe, Human Rights and Intersex People (Issue Paper) (2015).

[44] Resolution 2018/2878(RSP), of the European Parliament on the Rights of Intersex People, 2019 O.J. (C 449) 142 (14 Feb. 2019).

Court[45] and Inter-American Commission on Human Rights have also expressed support for intersex rights.[46] In 2023, the European Court of Human Rights decided the *M v. France* case.[47] The applicant had been subjected to involuntary and unnecessary medical treatments as a child. They complained that the statute of limitations that French authorities had used to justify denying their request to start investigations into their medical history violated the right to be free from inhumane and degrading treatments (Article 3 ECHR). The Court found the claim to be procedurally inadmissible. Nevertheless, it referred to international human rights soft law, drew a parallel between involuntary intersex treatments and female genital mutilation and forced sterilization, and concluded that 'non-therapeutic, non-consensual interventions' on intersex children violate Article 3 ECHR.[48]

3. Trans and nonbinary people

'Transgender' emerged in the 1990s as a blanket term to indicate all people whose gender identity differs from their birth-assigned sex.[49] Over time, 'trans' has become the more popular, though largely overlapping, term, which will be used in this book.[50] 'Nonbinary' is used to designate individuals whose identity differs from male and female. The 2006 Yogyakarta Principles describe 'gender identity' as:

> [E]ach person's deeply felt internal and individual experience of gender, which may or may not correspond with the sex assigned at birth, including the personal sense of the body (which *may* involve, *if freely chosen*, modification of bodily appearance or function by medical, surgical or other means) and other expressions of gender, including dress, speech and mannerisms.[51]

[45] Identidad de Género e Igualdad y No Discriminación a Parejas del Mismo Sexo, Advisory Opinion OC-24/17, Inter-American Court of Human Rights (ser. A) No. 24 (24 Nov. 2017).

[46] Inter-American Commission on Human Rights, Press Release No. 250/23, IACHR Calls to Guarantee the Rights of Intersex Older Persons (23 Oct. 2023), https://www.oas.org/en/iachr/jsForm/?File=%2Fen%2Fiachr%2Fmedia_center%2Fpreleases%2F2023%2F250.asp; Inter-American Commission on Human Rights, Press Release No. 115/11, IACHR Creates Unit on the Rights of Lesbian, Gay, Bisexual, Trans, and Intersex Persons (3 Nov. 2011), https://www.oas.org/en/iachr/media_center/PReleases/2011/115.asp.

[47] M v. France, App. no. 42821/18 (26 Apr. 2022), https://hudoc.echr.coe.int/eng?i=001-217430.

[48] Daniela Alaattinoglu, *Intersex Interventions as Human Rights Violations: The European Court of Human Rights Sets Out Guiding Principles in M v France*, 86 THE MODERN LAW REVIEW 1265 (2023). I borrow the expression 'non-therapeutic, non-consensual interventions' from *Id.* at 1276.

[49] For definitions, *see also*: STEPHEN WHITTLE, RESPECT AND EQUALITY. TRANSSEXUAL AND TRANSGENDER RIGHTS xix–xxiii (2002).

[50] CURRAH, *supra* note 5, at 3.

[51] Yogyakarta Principles: Principles on the Application of International Human Rights Law in Relation to Sexual Orientation and Gender Identity, Preamble (Nov. 2006) (emphasis added).

A recurring and generalized term in the legal vocabulary of many jurisdictions is 'transsexual'. According to Stephen Whittle, this notion refers to trans individuals who 'intend to undergo, [are] undergoing, or [have] undergone' gender confirmation medical and surgical treatments. Transsexual people are sometimes described as 'trapped in the wrong body' and eager to change their anatomy.[52] The widespread use of 'transsexual' by courts and parliaments, it can be argued, reflects more than devotion to what has become outdated terminology; it can be understood as a strategic choice to correlate gender recognition with physical—hence, verifiable—transformations.[53]

The question of the pathological status of trans identity can only be briefly mentioned here. Suffice it to say that trans identity was considered a psychiatric disorder per se.[54] This is arguably no longer the case today, as the understanding of trans identity has evolved over time, but related conditions—for example, the distress associated with a trans identity or gender dysphoria—are still considered pathological.[55] The pathologization of trans identity has long been controversial. Some human rights activists and scholars have opposed it entirely,[56] arguing that

[52] Talia Mae Bettcher, *Trapped in the Wrong Theory: Rethinking Trans Oppression and Resistance*, 39 Signs 383 (2014). This definition of 'transsexual' relies on Whittle, *supra* note 49, at xxiii.

[53] On this point, refer to: Damian Gonzalez-Salzberg, *The Accepted Transsexual and the Absent Transgender: A Queer Reading of the Regulation of Sex/Gender by the European Court of Human Rights*, 29 American University International Law Review 797 (2014); Gonzalez-Salzberg, *supra* note 1.

[54] Titia F. Beek, Peggy Cohen-Kettenis & Baudewijntje P.C. Kreukels, *Gender Incongruence/Gender Dysphoria and Its Classification History*, 28 International Review of Psychiatry 5 (2016).

[55] The 5th edition of the *Diagnostic and Statistical Manual of Mental Disorders* of the American Psychiatric Association dropped the diagnosis of 'gender identity disorder' and adopted 'gender dysphoria' in 2013. As said, the focus shifted from the 'identity per se' to the distress experienced by trans people. At the same time, the terminology adopted reveals a spectrum-based, and no longer binary-normative, understanding of gender (American Psychiatric Association (APA), Diagnostic and Statistical Manual of Mental Disorders (5th ed. 2013). Despite the progress, criticisms have been addressed to this diagnosis (Zowie Davy, *The DSM-5 and the Politics of Diagnosing Transpeople*, 44 Archives of Sexual Behaviour 1165, 1166 (2015)). Both professionals and activists have called for a full depathologization (Jacob E. Perlson, Oakland C. Walters & Alex S. Keuroghlian, *Envisioning a Future for Transgender and Gender-diverse People beyond the DSM*, 219 The British Journal of Psychiatry 471 (2021); Zowie Davy, *The DSM-5 and the Politics of Diagnosing Transpeople*, 44 Archives of Sexual Behaviour 1165 (2015); Johann Drescher, Peggy Cohen-Kettenis & Sam Winter, *Minding the Body: Situating Gender Identity Diagnoses in the ICD-11*, 24 International Review of Psychiatry 568 (2012)). The WHO has dropped the previous diagnoses of 'gender identity disorders' from the 11th edition of the *International Classification of Diseases* (*ICD-11*, 2019). In lieu of that, a new 'gender incongruence' diagnosis has been added. This diagnosis has been moved from the chapter on 'Disorders of adult behaviour and personality' to the chapter on 'Conditions related to sexual health', signifying that it is no longer a psychiatric condition. A non-pathological understanding of trans identity has also been adopted by the World Professional Association for Transgender Health in the latest edition of the influential Standards of Care: Eli Coleman et al., *Standards of Care for the Health of Transgender and Gender Diverse People, Version 8*, 23 International Journal of Transgender Health S1 (2022), for example at S117. As for the diagnosis for children, the question remains controversial (Sam Winter et al., *ICD-11 and Gender Incongruence of Childhood: A Rethink is Needed*, 3 The Lancet Child and Adolescent Health 671 (2019); Jack Drescher, Peggy T. Cohen-Kettenis & Geoffrey M. Reed, *Gender Incongruence of Childhood in the ICD-11: Controversies, Proposal, and Rationale*, 3 Lancet Psychiatry 297 (2016)).

[56] Yogyakarta Principles, *supra* note 51, Principle 18.

the diagnostic criteria are stereotypical and outdated, and that pathologization causes stigma.[57] Others have advocated for a reform of diagnostic criteria, fearing that depathologization might be unrealistic and could jeopardize access to gender-affirming healthcare.[58] Regardless, the pathological status of trans identity is still presupposed in the law of several jurisdictions, and medical expertise may be used by public authorities to decide on applications for gender recognition. Public authorities have indeed capitalized on pathologization, seizing it as an opportunity to gatekeep changes in legal sex.[59]

As mentioned, gender recognition is of crucial importance for trans and nonbinary people. In this book, I understand gender recognition as *both* the possibility to change one's legal records and to obtain the legal status associated with one's gender identity. A trans or nonbinary person who is denied recognition becomes 'illegible' to the state. As a result, unrecognized trans and nonbinary people may become more vulnerable to poverty, deprivation, and violence.[60] Understandably, Sally Hines has argued that 'recognition lies at the heart of social justice'[61] and contributes to the full inclusion of trans people.[62]

Despite this importance, gender recognition is seldom granted without preconditions or requirements. Trans and nonbinary people have mobilized against restrictions on the recognition of their identities.[63] They are demanding 'a quick, transparent, and accessible mechanism that legally recognises and affirms each person's self-defined gender identity', and that 'no eligibility criteria, such as medical or psychological interventions, a psycho-medical diagnosis, minimum or maximum age, economic status, health, marital or parental status, or any other third party opinion, shall be a prerequisite to change one's name, legal sex or gender'.[64] Gender self-determination has become the central demand of trans and nonbinary advocates.

[57] Jens Theilen, *Depathologisation of Transgenderism and International Human Rights Law*, 14 Human Rights Law Review 327 (2014).

[58] Mary Burke, *Resisting Pathology: GID and the Contested Terrain of Diagnosis in the Transgender Rights Movement*, *in* Sociology of Diagnosis (P.J. McGann & David J. Hutson eds., 2011).

[59] The use of pathologizing discourses to contain non-normative sexualities is an old theme in gender and sexualities: Michel Foucault, History of Sexuality, Vol 1: An Introduction (Robert Hurley trans., 1990); Dagmar Herzog, Sexuality in Europe (2011).

[60] Dean Spade, *Documenting Gender*, 59 Hastings Law Journal 731, 739–59 (2008); Dean Spade, Normal Life: Administrative Violence, Critical Trans Politics, and the Limits of Law (2d ed. 2015); Council of Europe, Protecting Human Rights of Transgender Persons 5 (Nov. 2015).

[61] Sally Hines, Gender Diversity, Recognition, and Citizenship 10 (2013).

[62] *Id.* at 9–20.

[63] For an overview of the legal developments in the field in multiple jurisdictions: The Legal Status of Transgender and Transsexual Persons (Jens Scherpe ed., 2017).

[64] Principle 31, C(i) and C(iii), of Yogyakarta Principles plus10: Additional Principles and State Obligations on The Application of International Human Rights Law in Relation to Sexual Orientation, Gender Identity, Gender Expression and Sex Characteristics to Complement the Yogyakarta Principles (Sept. 2017).

It has been argued that gender recognition is a human right.[65] A few non-exhaustive examples seem to confirm this conclusion. The Human Rights Committee has called on states to repeal invasive preconditions for gender recognition, while the CEDAW Committee has expressed concern regarding such requirements.[66] The Special Rapporteur for Torture has called for the abrogation of laws allowing sterilization as a requirement for the recognition of gender identity.[67] At the regional level, the Organization of American States and the Inter-American Commission on Human Rights have called for the elimination of discriminatory laws against trans and nonbinary people and for gender self-determination.[68] In *Atala Riffo and Daughters v. Chile*, the Inter-American Court declared that sexual orientation and gender identity are protected grounds under the Convention. Such principles, Alec Stone Sweet and Wayne Sandholtz have argued, have become *jus cogens*.[69] The Inter-American Court of Human Rights has embraced the right to gender identity in its 2017 Advisory Opinion, where it specified that gender self-determination—within or beyond the binary—is integral to each person's dignity, privacy, personal autonomy, and self-determination.[70]

The ECtHR has not declared a right to gender self-determination or nonbinary recognition,[71] but it has repeatedly granted gender recognition within the binary,[72] banned coerced sterilizing treatments,[73] and guaranteed trans people the right

[65] Holning Lau, *Gender Recognition as a Human Right*, *in* THE CAMBRIDGE HANDBOOK OF NEW HUMAN RIGHTS 193 (Andreas von Arnauld, Kerstin von der Decken & Mart Susi eds., 2020); Michael O'Flaherty, *Sexual Orientation and Gender Identity*, *in* INTERNATIONAL HUMAN RIGHTS LAW 305 (4th ed., Daniel Moeckli, Sangeeta Shah & Sandesh Sivakumaran eds., 2022).

[66] For example: UN Human Rights Committee, Concluding Observations on Ukraine, UN Doc. CCPR/C/UKR/CO/7, ¶ 10 (22 Aug. 2013); UN Committee on the Elimination of Discrimination against Women, Concluding Observations on the Netherlands, UN Doc. CEDAW/C/NLD/CO/5, ¶ 46 (22 July 2014).

[67] UN Human Rights Council, Report of the Special Rapporteur on Torture and Other Cruel, Inhuman or Degrading Treatment or Punishment, UN Doc. A/HRC/22/53, ¶¶ 76–79 (2013).

[68] Advances and Challenges towards the Recognition of the Rights of LGBTI Persons in the Americas, Inter-American Commission on Human Rights, OEA/Ser.L/V/II.170, Doc. 184, ch. 3 (8 Dec. 2018), https://www.oas.org/en/iachr/reports/pdfs/lgbti-recognitionrights2019.pdf; Informe Sobre Personas Trans y de Género Diverso y Sus Derechos Económicos, Sociales, Culturales y Ambientales, Inter-American Commission on Human Rights, OEA/Ser.L/V/II. Doc. 239 (7 Aug. 2020); Violencia contra Personas Lesbianas, Gay, Bisexuales, Trans e Intersex en América, Inter-American Commission on Human Rights, OAS/Ser.L/V/II.rev.2 Doc. 36 (12 Nov. 2015).

[69] Atala Riffo and Daughters v. Chile, Merits, Reparations and Costs, Judgment, Inter-American Court of Human Rights (ser. C) No. 239 (Feb. 24, 2012). *See* ALEC STONE SWEET & WAYNE SANDHOLTZ, THE LAW AND POLITICS OF INTERNATIONAL AND HUMAN RIGHTS COURTS. THE DILEMMA OF EFFECTIVENESS 218 (2024).

[70] Identidad de Género e Igualdad y No Discriminación a Parejas del Mismo Sexo, Advisory Opinion OC-24/17, Inter-American Court of Human Rights (ser. A) No. 24, ¶ 160 (24 Nov. 2017).

[71] Y v. France, App. no. 76888/17 (31 Jan. 2023), https://hudoc.echr.coe.int/eng?i=001-223027 (concerning nonbinary recognition).

[72] Christine Goodwin v. the United Kingdom, App. no. 28957/95 (11 July 2002), https://hudoc.echr.coe.int/fre?i=001-60596; I v. the United Kingdom, App. no. 25680/94 (11 July 2002), https://hudoc.echr.coe.int/spa?i=001-60595.

[73] A.P., Garçon and Nicot v. France, App. nos. 79885/12, 52471/13, and 52596/13 (6 Apr. 2017), https://hudoc.echr.coe.int/eng?i=001-172913.

to preserve a legal relationship with their spouse—though not necessarily in the form of marriage.[74] The Parliamentary Assembly of the Council of Europe[75] and the European Parliament have invited states to introduce self-determination and nonbinary options.[76] Finally, the Court of Justice of the European Union has developed a body of law that is arguably capable of protecting the right to gender recognition.[77]

4. Trans rights and their critics: Some objections and counter objections

4.1. Gender-critical movements and the anti-gender advocates

Gender-critical claims

Adding to the legal complexities they generate in gendered legal systems, the demands of gender-diverse people have been opposed by actors across the social spectrum, from religion-inspired conservatives to certain branches of the women's rights movement usually known as 'gender-critical' feminists.[78] This section aims to provide a concise introduction to these debates. The aim is not to be exhaustive, but, more modestly, to acknowledge the intense social divisions that have accompanied the demands of gender-diverse people. Most of this section concerns the opposition to trans and nonbinary gender recognition, but this social opposition has implications for intersex people, too. Gender-critical activists' focus on the binary may conflict with the protection of intersex people,[79] as, for example, is manifested when intersex women are barred from sports competition.[80] Furthermore, '[moral

[74] Hämäläinen v. Finland, App. no. 37359/09 (16 July 2014), https://hudoc.echr.coe.int/eng?i=001-145768. GONZALEZ-SALZBERG, *supra* note 1, 28–57.

[75] Parliamentary Assembly of the Council of Europe, Discrimination against Transgender People in Europe, Res. 2048 (2015), ¶ 6.2 (22 Apr. 2015).

[76] Resolution 2018/2878(RSP), of the European Parliament on the Rights of Intersex People, 2020 O.J. (C 449) 142, ¶ 9 (14 Feb. 2019).

[77] Stefano Osella, *The Court of Justice and Gender Recognition: A Possibility for an Expansive Interpretation?* 87 WOMEN'S STUDIES INTERNATIONAL FORUM 102493 (2021); Alina Tryfonidou, *The Cross-Border Recognition of Changes in the Legal Sex of Transgender Persons: The Landmark ECJ ruling in the* Mirin case. ECJ, 4 Oct. 2024, Case C-4/23, M.-A. A. v. Direcția de Evidență a Persoanelor Cluj, Serviciul Stare Civilă and Others, EUROPEAN CONSTITUTIONAL LAW REVIEW (2025, forthcoming) (on file with author).

[78] Some theorists have questioned whether gender-critical feminists are feminists at all: Henry F. Fradella, *The Imperative of Rejecting 'Gender-Critical' Feminism in the Law*, 30 WILLIAM & MARY JOURNAL OF RACE, GENDER, AND SOCIAL JUSTICE 269 (2024).

[79] Surya Monro & Sean Saifa Wall, *Social Theories*, *in* INTERSEX, VARIATIONS OF SEX CHARACTERISTICS, DSD. CRITICAL APPROACHES 60, 79 (Surya Monro et al. eds., 2025).

[80] Ruth Pearce, Sonja Erikainen & Ben Vincent, *TERF Wars: An Introduction*, 68 THE SOCIOLOGICAL REVIEW MONOGRAPHS 677, 688 (2020). Although not immediately connected to the discussion presented in this volume, a reference to the saga of Caster Semenya is necessary, in particular considering the 2025 decision of the European Court of Human Rights. *See*: Semenya v. Switzerland, App. no. 10934/21 (10 July 2025), https://hudoc.echr.coe.int/eng?i=001-244348. For an overview: Matteo

conservatives such as those militating in] anti-gender movements ... make life difficult for intersex people because they enforce binaried, rigid notions of sex and gender.'[81]

Gender recognition has been targeted by gender-critical feminists, who claim a genealogical link to radical feminism—a connection that Butler, upon whose account this section substantially draws, contests.[82] Gender-critical feminists broadly oppose gender recognition and self-determination because they fear it would erase lesbianism, give undue advantages to 'biological men', exacerbate 'sex-based' discrimination against cis women, and jeopardize their safety.[83] Some gender-critical feminists insist that their focus is the discrimination that cis women suffer because of their biological characteristics, not trans identity per se.[84] Nevertheless, some have also acknowledged that their claims clash 'with gender identity ideology, which is at the heart of trans activism'.[85] Although some gender-critical feminists have admitted that many trans women do *not* represent a threat to cis women's safety and even express a degree of sympathy for them, they nonetheless remain very critical of gender recognition.[86] Others in the same camp have been more adversarial, claiming, for example, that 'men who transgender do not change sex, and have a lifetime's experience of being members of the male sex caste. ... [T]he behaviour of men who transgender is more likely to resemble that of other male persons rather than that of women, and men's behaviour [specifically, in public restrooms] can be very abusive.'[87]

Winkler & Giovanna Gilleri, *Of Athletes, Bodies, and Rules: Making Sense of Caster Semenya*, 49 Journal of Law, Medicine and Ethics 644 (2021).

[81] Surya Monro, *Introduction to Variations of Sex Characteristics, in* Intersex, Variations of Sex Characteristics, DSD. Critical Approaches 1, 4–5 (Surya Monro et al. eds., 2025).

[82] Judith Butler, Who Is Afraid of Gender 134–69 (2024). It should be noted that some LGB activists (intentionally excluding the 'T') have also questioned the rights of trans and nonbinary people, seeking to separate the advocacy for LGB rights from that of trans rights. The phenomenon appears understudied. *See, e.g.*: Helen Clarke, *(Re)producing Sex/gender Normativities: LGB Alliance, Political Whiteness and Heteroactivism*, Journal of Gender Studies (2024, online first) https://www.tandfonline.com/doi/full/10.1080/09589236.2024.2307602.

[83] Aleardo Zanghellini, *Philosophical Problems with the Gender-Critical Feminist Argument Against Trans Inclusion*, 12 SAGE Open 1–14 (2020). For a different perspective: Alessandra Asteriti & Rebecca Bull, *Gender Self-Declaration and Women's Rights: How Self Identification Undermines Women's Rights and Will Lead to an Increase in Harms: A Reply to Alex Sharpe, 'Will Gender Self-Declaration Undermine Women's Rights and Lead to an Increase in Harms?' (2020) 83(3) MLR 539*, ModernLawReview (22 July 2020) https://www.modernlawreview.co.uk/asteriti-bull-sharpe/; Christen Price, *Women's Spaces, Women's Rights: Feminists and the Transgender Rights Movement*, 103 Marquette Law Review 1509 (2020).

[84] Butler, *supra* note 82, at 138.

[85] Holly Lawford-Smith, 'Holly Lawford-Smith: What is Gender-Critical Feminism? (And why is everyone so mad about it?)' (*Holly Lawford-Smith, Political Philosopher*, 27 Aug. 2020), https://hollylawford-smith.org/what-is-gender-critical-feminism-and-why-is-everyone-so-mad-about-it/. *See*: Butler, *supra* note 82, at 138.

[86] Butler, *supra* note 82, at 155–69.

[87] Sheila Jeffreys, *The Politics of the Toilet: A Feminist Response to the Campaign to 'Degender' a Women's Space*, 45 Women's Studies International Forum 42, 47 (2014) (arguing against the desegregation of public toilets). For a critique: Butler, *supra* note 82, at 144.

Women's equality and safety are, needless to say, praiseworthy objectives. However, the necessity or suitability of denying or restricting gender identity rights in order to achieve them has been questioned. This book does not focus on disproving the claims of gender-critical advocates.[88] This said, it is fair to mention that such claims have been opposed, including among feminists. For example, Catharine MacKinnon has argued that trans equality 'does not, contrary to allegations of anti-trans self-identified feminists, endanger women or feminism, including what some in this group call "women's sex-based rights"'.[89] MacKinnon also stated:

> The key question here is not (the endlessly obsessed-over) what is a woman, but what accounts for the inequality of women to men. Women are not oppressed by our bodies—our hormones, chromosomes, vaginas, breasts, ovaries. We are placed on the bottom of the gender hierarchy by the misogynistic meanings male dominant societies create and project onto us.... *Trans women are, politically, women. They are our people too.*[90]

Furthermore, although more empirical research is always beneficial,[91] it has been contended that gender self-determination and the safety of cis women can coexist. For example, the Argentinian Parliament introduced self-determination in 2012. As of 2023, no cases of violence perpetrated by individuals taking advantage of self-determination appear to have been reported.[92] In 2024, the Commissioner for Human Rights of the Council of Europe stated that 'narratives presenting trans people as predatory and a threat to the physical safety of women or children *are not supported by evidence and are highly discriminatory*'.[93] Some empirical studies also suggest that there appears to be no evidence that 'gender identity inclusive'

[88] Ruth Rubio-Marín and I have expressed our support for trans and nonbinary rights in Ruth Rubio-Marín & Stefano Osella, *La Autodeterminación de Género: Gender Critical Radfems a la Prueba de la Proporcionalidad*, IberICONnect Blog (1 Feb. 2021), https://www.ibericonnect.blog/2021/02/la-autodeterminacion-de-genero-gender-critical-radfems-a-la-prueba-de-la-proporcionalidad/.

[89] Catharine A. MacKinnon, *A Feminist Defense of Transgender Sex Equality Rights*, 34 Yale Journal of Law and Feminism 88, 88 (2023). *See also*: Butler, *supra* note 82, at 139–40; Alex Sharpe, *Will Gender Self-Declaration Undermine Women's Rights and Lead to an Increase in Harms?*, 83 The Modern Law Review 539 (2020); Fradella, *supra* note 78.

[90] MacKinnon, *supra* note 89, at 91–92 (emphasis added).

[91] Fradella, *supra* note 78, at 272 (specifically discussing the ongoing research on sport competitions).

[92] Marian Cabarjal, *What the World Has to Learn from Argentina about Trans Rights*, Open Democracy (19 June 2023), https://www.opendemocracy.net/en/5050/argentina-trans-rights-luana-self-id-gabriela-mansilla-healthcare/. Gender self-determination was introduced in Argentina with: Ley 26.743, Identidad de Género, mayo 24, 2012.

[93] Commissioner for Human Rights of the Council of Europe, Human Rights and Gender Identity and Expression (Issue Paper) 100 (Mar. 2024), (emphasis added). *See also*: Transgender Europe (TGEU), Self-determination Models in Europe: Practical Experiences 15–24 (Nov. 2022).

accommodations put the safety or privacy of cis women at risk—while the lack of such accommodations does, in fact, jeopardize trans people's safety.[94]

Anti-gender advocacy

Political and legal conservativism and, most prominently, opposition to the so-called 'gender ideology', is another milieu where gender recognition and self-determination have been targeted. To be clear, there is no denying the differences between gender-critical feminists and anti-'gender ideology' advocates.[95] Nevertheless, their shared focus on opposing gender recognition creates an alignment that is difficult to dismiss.[96] Given the significant inconsistencies that animate anti-gender advocacy, Butler argues, it may be difficult to pin down the exact content of this very much feared 'phantasm' of gender ideology.[97] In short, the phantasmatic 'gender ideology' is a set of ideas attributed to proponents of women and LGBTQI+ rights and is presented by those who conjure it essentially as an assault on nature and tradition.[98] According to Mary Anne Case, the opposition to 'gender ideology' originates in the Vatican's reaction to the agenda for women's equality developed during the 1995 Fourth World Conference on Women in Beijing.[99] Anti-gender advocacy opposes transforming the gender order to include feminist and LGBTQI+ claims and the 'tight connection between and among all the components it incorporates under the "gender agenda," such as the dismantling of sex roles, the acceptance of homosexuality, the recognition of a diversity of family forms and of sexual and gender expression', among others.[100]

[94] Amira Hasenbush, Andrew R. Flores & Jody L. Herman, *Gender Identity Nondiscrimination Laws in Public Accommodations: a Review of Evidence Regarding Safety and Privacy in Public Restrooms, Locker Rooms, and Changing Rooms*, 16 Sexuality Research & Social Policy 70 (2018); Jody L. Herman, Andrew R. Flores & Elana Redfield, Williams Institute, Safety and Privacy in Public Restrooms and Other Gendered Facilities (Feb. 2025), https://williamsinstitute.law.ucla.edu/publications/safety-in-restrooms-and-facilites/.

[95] On this point: Butler, *supra* note 82, at 142. For an introduction to the political and constitutional complexities related to the opposition to the so-called gender ideology: Mara Malagodi, Stefano Osella & Elettra Stradella, *Introduction to the Special Section*, 21 European Constitutional Law Review 1 (2025); Mara Malagodi & Elettra Stradella, *Conceptualising the Link between Constitutional Degradation and Gender Populism*, 21 European Constitutional Law Review 8 (2025); Silvia Suteu, *The Rule of Law Crisis Was Always Gendered: The Anti-Gender Playbook in Europe*, 21 European Constitutional Law Review 58 (2025).

[96] Sally Hines, *Hands Towards the Right: UK Gender–Critical Feminism and Right-Wing Coalitions*, Journal of Gender Studies (online first) https://www.tandfonline.com/doi/full/10.1080/09589236.2025.2468805?src=recsys.

[97] The understanding of gender ideology as a 'phantasm' is borrowed from Butler, *supra* note 82, at 5.

[98] For a definition of 'gender ideology': Roman Kuhar & David Paternotte, *'Gender Ideology' in Movement: Introduction, in* Anti-Gender Campaigns in Europe: Mobilizing Against Equality 1, 4 (Roman Kuhar & David Paternotte eds., 2017).

[99] Mary Anne Case, *After Gender the Destruction of Man? The Vatican's Nightmare Vision of the 'Gender Agenda' for Law*, 31 Pace Law Review 802 (2011).

[100] *Id.* at 808.

Anti-gender activism now spreads well beyond its origins in Catholicism and has become truly global in its dimensions.[101] Although the adversaries of 'gender ideology' have received significant academic criticism,[102] the movement appears to be gaining strength at the constitutional level in multiple jurisdictions.[103] Clearly, anti-gender advocates are particularly worried by trans rights and gender recognition, which profoundly challenge discourses based on sex, biology, and the 'natural' division of roles between men and women,[104] and, it can be added, the separate spheres doctrine.

4.2. On (binary) sex/gender and the scientific discourse

Common among the various objections to trans and nonbinary gender recognition is the claim that advocates ostensibly disregard biology and the scientific reality of 'sex'.[105] I do not have the scientific expertise to take sides in this debate. I can, however, draw attention to some of the rebuttals that have been made against this claim.

First, we should acknowledge that science is not detached from social context.[106] The definition of 'sex' is no exception. Anne Fausto-Sterling has consistently argued that 'labeling someone a man or a woman is a social decision. We may use scientific knowledge to help us make the decision, but only our beliefs about gender—not science—can define our sex'.[107] Fausto-Sterling adds that no attempt is made to deny 'the material body':

> There *are* hormones, genes, prostates, uteri and other body parts and physiologies that we use to differentiate male from female .... But every time we try to return to the body as prior to socialization, prior to discourse about male and female ... Butler writes: 'we discover that matter is fully sedimented with discourses on sex and sexuality that prefigure and constrain the uses to which that term can be put'.[108]

[101] BUTLER, *supra* note 82, at 37–72.

[102] *Id.*; Kuhar & Paternotte, *supra* note 98.

[103] Ruth Rubio-Marín, *Anti-Gender Constitutionalism*, 21 EUROPEAN CONSTITUTIONAL LAW REVIEW 37 (2025).

[104] *See* Mary Anne Case, *Trans Formations in the Vatican's War on Gender Ideology*, 44 SIGNS 639, 640 (2019).

[105] Pearce, Erikainen & Vincent, *supra* note 80, at 687–89.

[106] THOMAS KUHN, THE STRUCTURES OF SCIENTIFIC REVOLUTIONS. 50TH ANNIVERSARY EDITION (4th ed. 2012).

[107] FAUSTO-STERLING, *supra* note 3, at 3.

[108] *Id.* at 24 (emphasis in the original), citing: JUDITH BUTLER, BODIES THAT MATTER: ON THE DISCURSIVE LIMITS OF 'SEX' 29 (1993)

We should also highlight that the notion of a binary 'biological sex'[109]—understood as two exclusive, 'uniform' and 'distinct … biological type[s]'[110]—has also been challenged. For example, Agustín Fuentes argues that:

> [E]verything about humans is a supercomplicated blend of biology and culture. … This is not to say that females and males are the same. They aren't. Nor is it that biological variation related to sex does not matter. It does. It's just that not all humans fit neatly into the categories of female or male, and biological measures of human bodies rarely segregate into two non-overlapping categories. Neither 'female' nor 'male' describes a uniform or distinct biological type.[111]

Not only are humans biocultural, Fuentes contends, but, even though 'there are patterned variations in sex biology in human bodies [and even though] they contribute to the shaping of people's lives … those patterns are not ubiquitous. They are seldom truly dimorphic, almost never binary, and do not always or usefully match to the categories of man or woman'.[112]

A great number of critical reflections on how the notion of 'biological sex' is scientifically and socially defined can now be found in other disciplines. Historian Sarah R. Richardson has highlighted 'cases in the history of human sex chromosome research in which different models or scientific theories vie for acceptance under conditions of incomplete empirical evidence' and has shown 'how gender conceptions may enter into and serve as a cognitive resource in the development of scientific theories'.[113] Philosopher Rebecca Jordan Young and anthropologist Katrina Karkazis have similarly discussed the interactions between social discourses and scientific research on testosterone (popularly known as the 'male hormone') and demonstrated the influence of the former on the latter.[114] Historians Thomas Laqueur,[115] Valerio Marchetti,[116] and

[109] This notion has been made official policy at times. *See, e.g.*, the 2025 executive order of the President of the United States on *Defending Women From Gender Ideology Extremism and Restoring Biological Truth to the Federal Government* (Exec. Order No. 14168 90 FR 8615 (2025)). The term 'biological sex' has been criticized. Jessica A. Clarke argues that it 'lend[s] a veneer of objectivity and scientism' to the restriction of trans rights (*Sex at Birth*, 122 COLUMBIA LAW REVIEW 1821, 1859 (2022)).

[110] FUENTES, *supra* note 4, at 4.

[111] *Id.* at 3–4.

[112] *Id.* at 124.

[113] SARAH S. RICHARDSON, SEX ITSELF: THE SEARCH FOR MALE AND FEMALE IN THE HUMAN GENOME 15–16 (2013).

[114] REBECCA JORDAN YOUNG & KATRINA KARKAZIS, TESTOSTERONE: AN UNAUTHORIZED BIOGRAPHY (2019); CORDELIA FINE, DELUSIONS OF GENDER: HOW OUR MINDS, SOCIETY, AND NEUROSEXISM CREATE DIFFERENCE (2010); REBECCA JORDAN-YOUNG, BRAIN STORM: THE STORMS IN THE SCIENCE OF SEX DIFFERENCES (2011). For a critical approach to this research: Diane Halpern, *How Neuromythologies Support Sex Role Stereotypes Reviewed Work(s): Brain Storm: The Flaws in the Science of Sex Differences by Rebecca M. Jordan-Young: Delusions of Gender: How Our Minds, Society, and Neurosexism Create Difference by Cordelia Fine*, 330 SCIENCE 1320 (2010).

[115] THOMAS LAQUEUR, MAKING SEX: BODY AND GENDER FROM THE GREEKS TO FREUD (1992).

[116] VALERIO MARCHETTI, L'INVENZIONE DELLA BISESSUALITÀ. DISCUSSIONI TRA TEOLOGI, MEDICI, E GIURISTI DEL XVII SECOLO SULL'AMBIGUITÀ DEI CORPI E DELLE ANIME (2008).

Alice Domurat-Dreger[117] have researched the history of sex and shown how its perception changes in connection to political and cultural movements.

In short, no one is denying science or the materiality of the body; rather, scholars and activists are trying to counter an oversimplified biological rhetoric that is being mobilized against gender-diverse people. As Karkazis has put it:

> Debates about sex are often framed falsely as scientific versus cultural arguments, whereby the former by virtue of being grounded in biology are seen as tied to nature and thus truth, whereas the latter are seen as hectoring from a postmodern gender La La Land.... This is not a case of science versus social constructionism, as some argue; it's about the calculated use of 'biological sex' to buttress obsolete thinking about sex.[118]

Second, the 'you-ignore-science' (or scientist) objection is based on a misapprehension of the meaning and functioning of sex assignment, both socially and legally. As Butler explains, 'sex assignment is not simply an announcement of the sex that an infant is perceived to be; it also communicates a set of adult desires and expectations. ... [S]ex assignment is not a simple description of anatomical facts, but a way of imagining what they will mean, or should mean.'[119] This is even more true when it comes to the law. When children are assigned a sex, they are assigned a set of legal positions, as this book shows. They see their relations with the state and fellow citizens determined. Arguably, they are assigned a legal status. And a legal status serves a legal or constitutional purpose, not a positivistic endeavour of representing reality. In all the legal decisions discussed in this book, including those that denied recognition and where judges invoked biologistic notions of sex, the aim is not a genuine effort to determine biological sex per se. Even when legal sex is defined with exclusive reference to biological markers, it is done to preserve some legal and social arrangement—whether justified or less so is a different matter.

4.3. What is diverse after all?

Anthropologists have debated gender diversity for decades[120] and observed that the presence of people who defy the binary is acknowledged and positively valued

[117] DOMURAT-DREGER, *supra* note 3.
[118] Katrina Karkazis, *The Misuses of 'Biological Sex'*, 394 THE LANCET 1898, 1899 (2019).
[119] BUTLER, *supra* note 82, at 30.
[120] A few sources are Tom Boellstorff, *Queer Studies in the House of Anthropology*, 36 ANNUAL REVIEW OF ANTHROPOLOGY 17 (2007); Kath Weston, *Lesbian/Gay Studies in the House of Anthropology*, 22 ANNUAL REVIEW OF ANTHROPOLOGY 339 (1993). Anthropologists have long been interested in gender diversity: William Schlesinger, *Sex, Gender, and Sexual Subjectivity: Feminist and Queer Anthropology*, *in* THE SAGE HANDBOOK OF CULTURAL ANTHROPOLOGY (Lene Pedersen & Lisa Cligget eds., 2021). For earlier examples: Willard W. Hill, *The Status of the Hermaphrodite and Transvestite in Navaho*

in many societies.[121] In fact, once one acknowledges the many manifestations of gender diversity that have been documented, binary views of sex become but *one* among the many ways of understanding gender identity and the human body. As Serena Nanda argues:

> Cross-cultural studies demonstrated such a wide variety of attributes of masculine and feminine roles and characteristics in different societies that the view of gender as a cultural construction, the content of which varies from society to society, is now widely accepted in the social sciences.[122]

Furthermore, many scholars regard the imposition of the sex/gender binary as a by-product of European colonialism. For instance, Maria Lugones has argued that the erasure of (what we may perceive as) gender-diverse pre-colonial identities alongside the imposition of compulsory heterosexuality was part of the violent European colonial governance in Latin America.[123] Similar impositions formed part of the British colonial project in India, where gender-diverse people were criminalized because they were deemed to be immoral and disorderly.[124] As Ruth Pearce, Sonja Erkainin, and Ben Vincent have pointed out, 'biological conceptualisations of sex are mediated by wider gendered as well as colonial and racialised norms that direct the social positions ascribed to different women and men'.[125] This colonial project intersects with a racial dimension. Scholars have pointed out

Culture, 37 AMERICAN ANTHROPOLOGIST 273 (1935); BRONISLAW MALINOWSKI, SEX AND REPRESSION IN SAVAGE SOCIETY (1927); MARGARET MEAD, COMING OF AGE IN SAMOA (1928); MARGARET MEAD, SEX AND TEMPERAMENT IN THREE PRIMITIVE SOCIETIES (1935). For a criticism of the globalization of the notion of transgender: Tom Boellstorff et al., *Decolonizing Transgender: A Roundtable Discussion*, 1 TSQ: TRANSGENDER STUDIES QUARTERLY 419 (2014); Aniruddha Dutta and Raina Roy, *Decolonizing Transgender in India: Some Reflections*, 1 TSQ: TRANSGENDER STUDIES QUARTERLY 320 (2014); Elijah Adiv Edelman, *The Subject of Trans Lives and Vitalities*, UNSETTLING QUEER ANTHROPOLOGY: FOUNDATIONS, REORIENTATIONS, AND DEPARTURES 209 (Margot Weiss ed., 2024).

[121] SERENA NANDA, NEITHER MAN NOR WOMAN: THE HIJRAS OF INDIA (1990); MARZIA MAURIELLO, AN ANTHROPOLOGY OF GENDER VARIANCE AND TRANS EXPERIENCE IN NAPLES: BEAUTY IN TRANSIT (2021); VANJA HAMZIĆ, SEXUAL AND GENDER DIVERSITY IN THE MUSLIM WORLD: HISTORY, LAW AND VERNACULAR KNOWLEDGE (2015); AFSANEH NAJMABADI, PROFESSING SELVES: TRANSSEXUALITY AND SAME-SEX DESIRE IN CONTEMPORARY IRAN (2013); DAVID VALENTINE, TRANSGENDER: ETHNOGRAPHY OF A CATEGORY (2007); BERNARD SALADIN D'ANGLURE, ÊTRE ET RENAÎTRE INUIT, HOMME, FEMME OU CHAMANE (2006); GAYATRI REDDY, WITH RESPECT TO SEX: NEGOTIATING HIJRA IDENTITY IN SOUTH INDIA (2005); DON KULICK, TRAVESTI: SEX, GENDER, AND CULTURE AMONG BRAZILIAN TRANSGENDERED PROSTITUTES (1998).

[122] NANDA, *supra* note 121, at 128.

[123] Maria Lugones, *Heterosexualism and the Colonial/Modern Gender System*, 22 HYPATIA 186 (2007); Maria Lugones, *Towards a Decolonial Feminism*, 25 HYPATIA 742 (2010). For more references to the literature, please refer to Chapter 5.

[124] GAYATRI REDDY, WITH RESPECT TO SEX: NEGOTIATING HIJRA IDENTITY IN SOUTH INDIA (2005); JESSICA HINCHY, GOVERNING GENDER AND SEXUALITY IN COLONIAL INDIA. THE HIJRA, C. 1850–1900 (2019); MUHAMMAD AZFAR NISAR, GOVERNING THIRDNESS. STATE, SOCIETY, AND NON-BINARY IDENTITIES IN PAKISTAN (2022).

[125] Pearce, Erikainen & Vincent, *supra* note 80, at 687–89.

the connection between whiteness and the sexual/gender binary. C. Riley Snorton and Hortense Spillers have exposed the troubling racialized history behind the definition of the binary, that is, the idea that, biologically speaking, there are only men and women.[126]

To be clear, as Ara Wilson has suggested, ethnographic accounts and anthropological elaborations, especially within queer and feminist anthropology, are not a 'chronicle' of gender diversity. In other words, these examples are not meant to be a cabinet of curiosities, preserved in amber or frozen in time. Quite the contrary, the contribution of anthropology lies in building an advanced theoretical framework to better understand the mutable and contingent nature of identity. These examples invite us to reflect on how assumptions regarding universal identity norms are overly simplistic, debatable, and not truly reflective of the diverse experiences as they actually exist in the real world.[127] The many ways sex/gender is perceived and treated should warn us about notions of naturalness. They point out that identity and corporeality vary according to many concrete factors.

5. Conclusion

In this chapter, I have synthesized various sources to construct a backdrop that contextualizes the legal discussions forming the core of this volume. I have offered definitions of sex/gender, and the gender binary, and given an account of the demands of gender-diverse people. I have tried to hew as closely as possible to the legal domain and prioritize those aspects that inhere in legal developments. The picture I have painted is surely simplified. The demands of gender-diverse people differ across geographical, social, and socio-economic contexts—just to name a few axes that might distinguish the characteristics of gender-diverse advocacy. Likewise, the opposition to these demands is surely more complex and nuanced than I have managed to convey. The main point of this chapter is not to contribute a much-needed reconstruction of the history of such concepts and movements or a normative argument; rather, my intention is to introduce the interactions of gender-diverse people with the law and the limits—both social and legal—that their demands encounter. How these interactions play out will become clearer in the coming chapters.

[126] C. Riley Snorton, Black on Both Sides: A Racial History of Trans Identity (2017); Hortense Spillers, *Mama's Baby, Papa's Maybe: An American Grammar Book*, 17 Diacritics 64 (1987).

[127] Ara Wilson, *Queer Anthropology*, Open Encyclopedia of Anthropology (2019, updated in 2023) http://doi.org/10.29164/19queer.

3

The Physical Foundation of the Legal Binary

The Question of Intersexuality

1. Introduction

Intersexuality—that is, the presence of *physical characteristics* 'that do not meet medical and social norms for female or male bodies'[1]—has long represented a social challenge, at least in the West. Individuals are usually sorted into sex/gender categories—male or female—at birth based on their external genitalia, which Suzanne Kessler and Wendy McKenna define as the 'essential insignia' of gender.[2] As outlined in Chapter 2, protocols including medical and surgical 'normalizing' treatments have been implemented to 'manage' intersexuality and the cultural questions raised by it. For the past three decades, however, activists and academics have contended that such treatments cause serious human rights concerns, and international and regional institutions have condemned medically unnecessary and culturally motivated involuntary interventions on intersex people.[3] As summarized by Daniela Alaattinoglu, the international human rights soft law signals that 'non-consensual interventions on people with variations of sex characteristics which are not medically necessary constitute a violation of physical integrity, bodily autonomy, the right to health, the right to respect for private and family life, the right to non-discrimination and other fundamental rights, especially pertaining to children'.[4] The 2023 decision of the European Court of Human Rights in *M v. France* is of particular significance in this regard.[5] Although the case was

[1] Morgan Carpenter, *The Human Rights of Intersex People: Addressing Harmful Practices and Rhetoric of Change*, 24 Reproductive Health Matters 74 (2016). *See* Chapter 2.

[2] Suzanne Kessler & Wendy McKenna, Gender: An Ethnomethodological Approach 154 (1985).

[3] Markus Bauer, Daniela Truffer & Daniela Crocetti, *Intersex Human Rights*, 24 The International Journal of Human Rights 724, 727–34 (2020) (offering an overview of human rights developments). *See* also Chapter 2, Section 2.2.

[4] Daniela Alaattinoglu, *Intersex Interventions as Human Rights Violations: The European Court of Human Rights Sets out Guiding Principles in* M v France, 86 Modern Law Review 1265, 1270 (2023).

[5] M v. France, App. No. 42821/18 (26 Apr. 2022), https://hudoc.echr.coe.int/eng?i=001-217430. For a commentary, *see* Alaattinoglu, *supra* note 4.

Gender Diversity in Public Law. Stefano Osella, Oxford University Press. © Stefano Osella 2026.
DOI: 10.1093/9780198935070.003.0003

inadmissible on procedural grounds, the Court of Strasbourg established some general principles detailing how, potentially, 'normalizing' treatments can be in violation of Articles 3 and 8 of the European Convention on Human Rights.

Intersexuality can complicate the *legal* assignment of sex, too.[6] Arguably, this complication can affect the certainty of the legal positions of the person. It may also challenge the public interests and fundamental rights grounded in the individual legal status, raising such questions as: What facilities is the intersex person going to use? Whom are they going to marry? and so forth. Starting from this consideration, I examine the extent to which intersexuality is perceived as a legal and constitutional problem in those systems where a binary identity must be legally assigned at birth and should, in principle, be permanent. In such cases, I argue that lawmakers may strategically rely on medical involvement, including 'normalizing' treatments, to erase the 'complications' posed by intersexuality.

At the same time, I also argue that the transformation of the binary legal order, for example, when nonbinary recognition is introduced, may ease the tensions caused by the legal necessity of assigning each person to a binary sex. In turn, this leads to decreasing the pressure to medically erase intersexuality. To be clear, I do not contend that the protection of intersexuality requires nonbinary recognition. Other factors may lead to the protection of intersex characteristics, even in binary systems. Nonetheless, when the law safeguards the physical integrity of intersex people, regardless of what led to this development, the understanding of intersexuality changes. Bodies that the law previously deemed pathological are perceived as healthy and acceptable. This change shakes the 'biological foundation' of the legal binary. As a result, the legal order may open up to gender diversity and shift away from traditional binary structures. When we look at all these developments together, it becomes clear that sex anatomy and sex categories in the law are deeply and inextricably connected.

To present my case, I track different approaches to the questions posed by intersexuality in comparative law. First, I identify the *erasure* model. In this model, legal authorities employ a medical discourse to erase any deviations from the binary. Italian law, for example, sees intersexuality as a problem for classification at birth. It also defines intersexuality as a cause of instability of legal sex later in life because of a debatable association between intersexuality and trans identity. As a result, Italian law encourages early medical and surgical interventions

[6] I have briefly discussed the transformative potential of recognizing intersexuality in Marie-Xavière Catto & Stefano Osella, *The Sexed Subject*, *in* THE CAMBRIDGE COMPANION TO GENDER AND THE LAW 25, 44–47 (Stephanie Hennette-Vauchez & Ruth Rubio-Marín eds., 2023). *See* also, in the same chapter, the insightful analysis of Marie-Xavière Catto on the production of two sexed bodies: *Id.* at 31–43. Please refer also to: JULIE A. GREENBERG, INTERSEXUALITY AND THE LAW: WHY SEX MATTERS (2012). Focusing on the United States, Greenberg's work has pioneered the analysis of how law can be mobilized to advance the claims of the intersex movement. Greenberg also highlighted the strictures posed by a binary system on intersexuality, especially in relation to marriage, the use of IDs, and separate facilities (*Id.* at 47–82).

on intersex children. French law offers yet another example of the erasure model. 'Standardizing' interventions on intersex children are discouraged. Nevertheless, medical expertise is employed to ensure the legal assignment of a binary sex to each person. By implication, the law relies on medical involvement to buttress the binary legal order.

Legal recognition of gender plurality does not necessarily lead to laws protecting intersex physical integrity. This chapter refers to Belgium, where nonbinary gender is recognized as a matter of constitutional law, but a ban on intersex treatments has not been introduced (at the time of this writing). The Belgian case does not detract from the argument that intersexuality may be perceived as a legal problem in binary systems. Yet it also cautions that there are many factors—cultural and social, as well as legal—that can motivate interventions on intersex people.

The other approach discussed in this chapter is *recognition*. In such a model, the demands of intersex people are acknowledged. Standardizing medical interventions are restricted or banned. Germany and Colombia, each in its own way, exemplify this dynamic. The German Parliament passed legislation imposing limits on intersex medical treatments in 2021.[7] The 2021 law is connected to the 2017 decision of the Federal Constitutional Court (FCC) granting recognition to nonbinary gender identity.[8] The 2017 decision of the FCC is silent about medical interventions on intersex children. However, it contributed to a legal and political process that eventually culminated in protecting intersex physical characteristics. The Colombian Constitutional Court, for its part, had already developed a doctrine restricting involuntary treatments on intersex children in the 1990s. This development took place in a jurisdiction where binary sex registration was required at birth and nonbinary recognition was absent. Yet the narrative and values protecting intersex characteristics transformed the Colombian binary system and opened it up to the recognition of gender diversity.[9]

This chapter examines a wide range of laws, including soft law, administrative regulations, and constitutional jurisprudence. In all of the jurisdictions discussed here, whether intersexuality is perceived as a challenge to be overcome or a source of diversity worthy of protection, sexual anatomy is relevant to the system of sex categories and its constitutional implications. Even when public law considerations are not apparent—for example, in tort law—courts define the contours of the acceptable legal subject on the basis of human anatomy. The definition of

[7] Gesetz zum Schutz von Kindern mit Varianten der Geschlechtsentwicklung, 21 May 2021, Art. 1, adding § 1631e and following to the Civil Code [BGB].

[8] Bundesverfassungsgericht [BVerfG] [German Federal Constitutional Court], 10 Oct. 2017, 1 BvR 2019/16.

[9] Stefano Osella, *Come Evolve il Diritto all'Identità di Genere? Fattori Strutturali, Culturali, e Dogmatici nella Giurisprudenza Costituzionale Italiana e Colombiana. Un'Analisi Comparata*, DIRITTI COMPARATI 1, 16 (2023), https://www.diritticomparati.it/bozza-automatica-170/.

this acceptable legal subject has widespread implications for how intersexuality is understood and then treated.

Some caveats are in order at the outset. First, when I mention 'intersex treatments', I refer exclusively to those that are culturally motivated and intended to bring the subject into conformity with a purported 'standard'. I do not refer to those therapies intended to restore the physical health of the person. I also acknowledge that scholars and activists have criticized the use of terms such as 'normalizing' or 'standardizing' treatments.[10] This terminology, it is argued, implies the abnormality of intersex people. Furthermore, it whitewashes the grievousness of some treatments. Some activists prefer instead the much more evocative term 'intersex genital mutilation' (IGM). I nevertheless use the terms 'normalizing' and 'standardizing' treatments and IGM somewhat interchangeably. I do so to reflect the prevalent terminology in the scholarly discourse and stress that the medical and surgical interventions discussed in this chapter may be performed to align the anatomy of intersex people to the gender norms that are presupposed in the law. In no way do I use 'normalizing' or 'standardizing' with a trivializing or derogatory intent.

Second, the following discussion is limited to the connections between physical diversity and identity diversity. The chapter does not aim to offer an exhaustive discussion of intersexuality in the law. Some aspects—for example, the human rights implications of the treatments and the remedies that are necessary to safeguard the physical integrity of intersex people—will not be examined.

Third, this chapter makes no empirical argument about the political and legal preconditions that are needed to protect or entail the protection of the physical integrity of intersex people. As noted above, nonbinary recognition does not necessarily lead to safeguarding intersex characteristics. A variety of contextual factors influence the success of the advocacy for intersex human rights. Hence, I do not offer any strategic advice on the protection of the rights of intersex people. Instead, I acknowledge that intersex people alone have the political legitimacy to decide how best to advance their agenda.

2. Erasure, literal and figurative

2.1. Erasing intersexuality, literally: Italy[11]

Italian law offers a prime example of the erasure of intersexuality. The reason behind this erasure is to be found in how stigma and legal unintelligibility combine.

10 Bauer, Truffer & Crocetti, *supra* note 3, at 741.

11 This section draws on and expands: Stefano Osella, The Legal Regime of Gender Identity: A Comparative Enquiry 125–129 (European University Institute, May 7, 2019). *See also*: Stefano Osella, *"Harmonic Bodies": Intersex Persons, Corrective Treatments, and Gender Violence in Italian Law.*

Italian authorities have consistently devalued intersexuality from a cultural point of view, painting it as a source of unhappiness and shame. In addition, and central to the argument presented in this chapter, they have used the understanding of intersexuality as a pathological condition to legitimize normalizing medical treatments, which, in turn, have been promoted to legally assign and stabilize sex.

Every child must be registered at birth.[12] Even though the law does not specify it, sex is binary.[13] Legal registration must in principle reflect biological markers, assuming that they are unequivocal. If they are not, and if an entry is 'incorrectly' recorded, Italian law provides a specific procedure for correcting civil registries.[14] This procedure applies when the sex legally assigned to a child turns out to be mistaken, which can happen when, for example, sex characteristics at birth are different from the standard. This procedure was not envisioned to protect the identity of the person—even though its reappropriation for this purpose has been imagined.[15] Rather, it was introduced to avoid mistaken classifications and thus safeguard the public order,[16] with its gender implications. It is revealing that this correction is not necessarily requested by the intersex person themselves, but may be initiated by the public prosecutor autonomously.

There is a distinctive public and constitutional law dimension to the legal treatment of intersexuality. As Anna Lorenzetti suggests, early treatments on sex characteristics are formally motivated by the need to attribute a legal sex and a corresponding gendered name.[17] Barbara Pezzini in turn shows that sex assignment has the purpose of predetermining the role of each person in society and favouring the 'complementarity' that relegates women to the private sphere.[18] Pezzini further argues that intersex people challenge the legal (and social) binary and thus question the relational and hierarchical gender system that informs the law.[19] This is evident when we consider that the Constitutional Court has repeatedly ruled that

A Research Proposal, in LGBTI Persons and Access to Justice (Anna Lorenzetti & Maria Federica Moscati eds., 2015) (offering an overview of Italian law and discussing it the possibility of using the framework of gender violence to describe the treatments of intersex people in the jurisdiction).

[12] Arts. 30(1) and 35, Decreto del Presidente della Repubblica [Decree of the President of the Republic][D.P.R] 396/2000.

[13] Corte Costituzionale [Constitutional Court] [Corte Cost.], 23 luglio 2024, n. 143. On the rejection of nonbinary identity in Italy, refer to Chapter 4.

[14] Art. 95, D.P.R. 396/2000.

[15] The procedure is indeed quicker than the standard procedure for gender identity recognition: Giacomo Cardaci, *Il Processo di Rettificazione dell'Atto di Nascita della Persona Intersex*, GenIUS 40 (2018).

[16] *See* Chapter 4.

[17] Anna Lorenzetti, *Frontiere del Corpo, Frontiere del Diritto: Intersessualità e Tutela della Persona*, BioLaw Journal 109, 116 (2015), https://teseo.unitn.it/biolaw/article/view/1720..

[18] Barbara Pezzini, *La Condizione Intersessuale in Italia: Ripensare la Frontiera del Corpo e del Diritto*, Reponsabilita Medica 444 (2017); Barbara Pezzini, *Costruzione del Genere e Costituzione, in* La Costruzione del Genere. Norme e Regole 17 (Barbara Pezzini ed., 2012).

[19] Barbara Pezzini, *Il Binarismo di Genere come Problema di Bio-diritto*, BioLaw Journal 59 (2023), https://teseo.unitn.it/biolaw/article/view/2618.

binary sex categories are connected to the preservation of the heterosexuality of marriage and, more recently, to family law in general, labour law, sport law, and to the right to intimacy (e.g., by maintaining sex-segregated facilities).[20] Giacomo Mingardo has argued that several provisions in the Italian constitution seem to presuppose a binary understanding of sex/gender, for example, those pertaining to the equality between men and women.[21] In short, it seems clear that maintaining the binary is crucial to central aspects of gender constitutionalism and to pursuing public interests and protecting fundamental rights of constitutional status. As treatments intended to erase the bodily diversity of intersex children have been seen as crucial to the stability of the binary, we can understand why it has been argued that 'power creates bodies' in Italian law.[22]

Scholars have voiced concerns about intersex medical treatments and surgeries in Italy. Not only has it been pointed out that such treatments might lead to financial and criminal liability on the part of those who perform them,[23] but they also appear to contradict principles in the Italian Constitution that protect diversity (*principio pluralista*), the uniqueness of each individual person (*principio personalista*),[24] and the fundamental right to health.[25]

The legal sources that explicitly deal with intersexuality in Italian law are scarce, relatively old, and limited to non-binding guidelines of an advisory body to the government and to the case law of lower courts. Yet they are consistent and still in force, and favour early medical treatments. In 1993, a court was called on to decide on the treatment of an intersex child.[26] The parents were reluctant to authorize early surgery, yet the doctors successfully sought judicial authorization to proceed with it. The court granted the authorization, as it reasoned that the child's intersexuality would expose them to bullying and ostracism. Considering that this decision was rendered in the very early days of intersex activism,[27] the court did

[20] Corte Cost., 143/2024. The Court added that even rules concerning names will have to be adapted. Italian law requires consistency between a person's name and their legal sex (Art. 35.1, DPR 396/2000); in Italian however, gender-neutral names are rare.

[21] Mingardo refers to Arts. 3, 31, and 37 of the Italian Constitution: Giacomo Mingardo, *Il Riconoscimento delle Nuove Soggettività e il Limite del Binarismo di Genere nella Prospettiva Costituzionale*, GENIUS 11–14 (2024) (online first, 19 Sept. 2024), https://www.geniusreview.eu/2024/il-riconoscimento-delle-nuove-soggettivita-e-il-limite-del-binarismo-di-genere-nella-prospettiva-costituzionale/.

[22] Paolo Veronesi, *Se il Potere Plasma i Corpi: Le Persone Intersex tra Antidiscriminazione e Antisubordinazione*, *in* 70 ANNI DOPO TRA UGUAGLIANZA E DIFFERENZA. UNA RIFLESSIONE SULL'IMPATTO DEL GENERE NELLA COSTITUZIONE E NEL COSTITUZIONALISMO 181 (Barbara Pezzini & Anna Lorenzetti eds., 2019).

[23] Ginevra Cerrina Feroni, *Intersessualismo: Nuove Frontiere*, DIRITTO PUBBLICO COMPARATO ED EUROPEO 303, 336 (2015).

[24] Paolo Veronesi, *Corpi e Questioni di Genere: Le Violenze (Quasi) Invisibili*, GENIUS 8, 19 (2021).

[25] Lorenzetti, *supra* note 17, at 119; Mingardo has similarly highlighted the importance attached to personal differences within the Italian constitution (*supra* note 21).

[26] Tribunale [Court of First Instance] [Trib.] Potenza, 29 luglio 1993.

[27] We should consider that the birth of intersex activism is conventionally dated to the early 1990s, when Bo Laurent—also known as Cheryl Chase—established the International Society of North America in 1994. *See* Chapter 2.

not discuss the potential adverse effects of medical interventions or the actual lived experiences of intersex people. While bullying and ostracism are valid concerns per se, subjecting a child to invasive treatments to avoid them reveals a cultural depreciation of sexual diversity—as if the problem to be removed were in the intersex body and not in the toxic social environment.

Intersexuality has been understood as a source of distress for the family as well. In 2013, a court found a team of doctors liable for damages to be paid to the parents of an intersex child because the doctors had failed to identify an intersex condition and had *not* subjected the child to treatments intended to modify their appearance.[28] When the child reached the age of two, and their intersexuality became apparent, doctors performed surgeries and reassigned their sex/gender. The court described the distress and the shame suffered by the parents. They had announced the birth of a *son* and were then bound to backtrack and clarify to their social circle in a small town that they had been mistaken. The doctors could have avoided this distress, the court reasoned, if they had correctly recognized the intersexuality of the child and intervened at once. Again, no consideration is given to the rights of the infant.

Stigma and legal hostility also emerge from a careful reading of the 2010 guidelines of the *Comitato Nazionale di Bioetica* (National Committee for Bioethics, CNB)—an advisory body to the Italian government.[29] In these guidelines, this cultural attitude is also used to stabilize binary legal categories. Ostensibly, the CNB was pursuing the well-being of intersex children. Indeed, several passages of this document advise a cautious attitude.[30] The CNB emphasized the importance of informed consent, which should be based on clear information sensitively conveyed,[31] as well as the psychological support of the child, who, when mature enough, is to be involved in the decision.[32] To a limited extent, the CNB acknowledged the demands of intersex people[33] and the position of healthcare professionals who were critical of normalizing surgeries and medicalization.[34] Some critical literature on intersex treatments is also cited.[35]

[28] Trib. Bari, 25 giugno 2012, n. 2295.

[29] Comitato Nazionale di Bioetica [National Committee of Bioethics] [CNB], I Disturbi della Differenziazione Sessuale nei Minori: Aspetti Bioetici (25 Feb. 2010), https://bioetica.governo.it/it/documenti/pareri/i-disturbi-della-differenziazione-sessuale-nei-minori-aspetti-bioetici/. Further research is needed to determine the extent to which such guidelines are effectively followed by medical professionals. For example, some in this category have called for their practice to be informed by the human rights of intersex people. *See* Marco De Santis et al., Istituto Superiore di Sanità, Le Persone Intersex in Italia: I Dati del Registro Nazionale Malattie Rare e delle Schede di Dimissione Ospedaliera 2, 53 (2024).

[30] CNB, ¶ 6.2.

[31] CNB, ¶ 6.3. The need to soften potentially distressing information has been deemed by some to be a central aspect of any genuine consent procedure. J. David Hester, *Intersex(es) and Informed Consent: How Physicians' Rhetoric Constrains Choice*, 25 Theoretical Medicine and Bioethics 21 (2004).

[32] CNB, ¶ 6.4.

[33] CNB, ¶ 5.3.

[34] CNB, ¶¶ 5.2–5.4.

[35] For example, the CNB refers to the works of Judith Butler (¶ 6.5) and to the case law of the Colombian Constitutional Court (¶ 5.5): Section 3.2 below.

Nevertheless, the guidelines adopt a controversial understanding of well-being to which the notion of 'harmonious development' is central.[36] The introduction to the guidelines insists on preserving 'harmony' among biological characteristics, which may in turn influence gender identity and role.[37] 'Harmonious development' is not clearly defined, yet it appears to index concordance between sex characteristics (hormones, anatomy, etc.) and identity. In other words, on close reading, the CNB guidelines still appear to conflate well-being with a cis identity. This reading of 'harmonious development' seems to be in line with some definitions given by the coordinator of the working group that eventually produced the CNB's guidelines.[38] In this scholarship, 'cisgender' people are defined as those who 'live in harmony the sexual difference on the bodily-psychological-social level'.[39] Furthermore, although great emphasis is placed on informed consent and 'rushed' treatments are discouraged, a prompt assignment of a 'sexual identity' is deemed 'indispensable' to avoid 'disharmony'.[40] Since 'cis' identity is associated with 'harmony', this 'disharmony', I contend, could be read as trans identity. This approach echoes the long-standing mainstream attitude to intersexuality.

In short, despite emphasizing the importance of well-being and consent, the CNB controversially appears to assume that being different is detrimental per se to the person. The otherwise laudable pursuit of well-being does not necessarily lead to defending the physical integrity of people, but rather to promoting standard embodiments.[41] Incidentally, as Paolo Veronesi suggests, this seems to be a rather common occurrence in Italian law, where the interests of the child might be defined not on their real needs, but rather to reaffirm 'assumptions, expectations, and habits of society'.[42]

The conclusion made explicit by the CNB is that early treatments are 'not only lawful, but legally required' if they favour 'a harmonious sexual identification' and '[harmonious] future sexual activity'—which arguably refers to cis identity and heterosexuality.[43] In fairness, the CNB emphasized the need to justify irreversible treatments with 'medical reasons' and to avoid 'unnecessary mutilations'. However, what is medically necessary in this discourse is hazily defined, and this lack of precision might potentially be harmful to intersex people—especially because, as outlined in Chapter 2, the well-being of intersex children has ostensibly been at the core of the traditional approach to intersex medical treatment, too. The

[36] CNB, ¶ 6.1.
[37] CNB, ¶ 1.
[38] CNB, in the foreword (identifying the coordinator of the project).
[39] Laura Palazzani, *Identita di Genere come Problema Biogiuridico*, IUSTITIA 7, 14 (2012).
[40] *Id.* at 20.
[41] On this reading of the traditional understanding of well-being: Lorenzetti, *supra* note 17, at 119–22.
[42] Veronesi, *supra* note 24, at 193.
[43] CNB, ¶ 6.2. The meaning of 'harmonious sexual activity' is not specified, although a heteronormative overtone can be detected. After all, a preference for heterosexual, penile–vaginal intercourse has been central to the standard medical treatments of intersex children, as explained in Chapter 2.

significance of these recommendations for the binary categories in public law must be clearly flagged. The identities that the CNB seems to promote indeed fit with the 'traditional' understanding of the presumably 'natural' and heterosexual family that the Constitutional Court of Italy has repeatedly endeavoured to protect.[44]

The guidelines discourage early interventions only exceptionally, namely, 'in the most difficult cases ... that is, when objective data to assign a sex do not emerge'. In such cases, when surgeries and treatments are postponed, the CNB recommends that it may be useful to involve the child as well, if aware enough.[45] Even though intersex advocates might welcome the suggestion of delaying treatments and involving the child, it appears far too evident that this caution is motivated by the objective of avoiding 'mistaken' assignments—and the 'gender trouble' that they create. Indeed, as discussed in Chapter 4, a mistaken sex assignment and the subsequent trans identity might ultimately lead to applications for gender recognition, which might, in turn, disrupt the heterosexuality of family law.

Finally, the CNB weaves together pathologizing discourses, the erasure of intersex bodies, and the stability of legal principles to deny any legitimacy to requests for recognition of nonbinary identity, and thus prevent the feared constitutional complications that any deviation from the binary would create:

> [The proposal to register intersex children as such] cannot be accepted. First, it would legally institutionalize ... a third legal sex that is not recognized in our legal system, and that will have significant consequences for its balance .... [Such recognition, no matter how well intended] would entail a legal stigmatization of the person [registered as nonbinary] with social and psychological consequences hard to foresee but surely highly risky. ... Finally, these disorders, pathologies and anomalies are a not a specific gender identity, but rather manifest a position of uncertainty in sexual assignment, and it does not make sense to create an identity based on uncertainty.[46]

To put it more succinctly, the CNB states first that a third sex would adversely impact the legal system; second, that it would negatively affect the person; and third, that recognition cannot be granted to what is considered a pathological status and a situation of uncertainty. Pathologization, medical treatments, and the binary order are yoked together. In all fairness, it should be noted that the CNB does suggest annotating the birth certificate to indicate the 'pathology' from which the intersex child suffers,[47] so that future changes of legal sex may be facilitated. In this

[44] Stefano Osella & Graziella Romeo, *Something's Wrong with Traditionalism: LGBTQI+ Rights in Comparative Perspective*, Asian Journal of Comparative Law (2026), https://doi.org/10.1017/asjcl.2025.10005. *See* Chapter 4.

[45] CNB, ¶ 6.4.

[46] CNB, ¶ 6.5.

[47] CNB, ¶ 6.5.

context, however, I contend that this suggestion appears less intended to protect the identity of the child, and more so to assure conformity to and consistency in public registries.

2.2. Erasing intersexuality, figuratively: France

France offers yet another example of how medicalization can be used to erase intersexuality and promote the legal assignment of a binary sex at birth. The French case also demonstrates that the interplay between law and medicine to preserve the legal binary does not necessarily require medical and surgical interventions.[48] Indeed, IGM is not officially encouraged in France, and sex characteristics enjoy, at least on paper, a modest level of protection.[49] Medico-legal erasure can be figurative.

Article 57 of the Civil Code requires the registration of all newborn children. Several details must be recorded. Sex is among them. The law does not list the sexes that can be assigned. Yet, in 2017, the Court of Cassation stated that the binary system of sex categories is 'necessary for the social and legal order, of which [it] represents a fundamental [*fondateur*] element' and that 'the judicial recognition of a "neuter sex" would have far-reaching consequences' for French law.[50] As of 2021, the newly added Article 57, *alinea* 2, of the Civil Code allows for a three-month delay in the specification of the sex of the child in cases where immediate sexual assignment is medically impossible, and only under strict procedural supervision.[51] Once three months have elapsed, the medically ascertained sex must be registered. The administrative guidelines—*circulaire*—of 8 September 2023, which details the concrete application of the law, also specify that the sex must be male or female, and that alternative designations 'are proscribed'.[52]

[48] Cultural attitudes can partly explain the hostility against intersexuality in France, too: Anne Saris & Benjamin Moron-Puech, *La Lutte pour la Reconnaissance des Droits des Personnes Intersexuées*, 104 COMMUNICATIONS 131, 134–35 (2019).

[49] Arrêté du Ministère de la Santé et de la Prévention fixant les règles de bonnes pratiques de prise en charge des enfants présentant des variations du développement génital en application de l'article L. 2131-6 du code de la santé publique (NOR: SPRP2232078A) (15 Nov. 2022).

[50] Cour de Cassation [Supreme Court for Criminal and Civil Matters][Cass.], 1e civ., 4 Mai 2017, n. 16-17.189. In 2023, the European Court of Human Rights found the position of the French Court of Cassation to comply with the European Convention on Human Rights (Y v. France, App. No. 76888/17 (31 Jan. 2023), https://hudoc.echr.coe.int/eng?i=001-223027). For further details, refer to Chapter 5. For an overview inclusive of constitutional aspects: Aude Mirkovic, *La Dualité des Énonciations Relatives au Sexe dans les Actes de l'État Civil Constitue-t-Elle «un Element Fondateur de l'Organisation Sociale et Juridique»?*, *in* LE(S) DROIT(S) À L'ÉPREUVE DE LA NON-BINARITÉ 71 (Olivia Bui-Xuan ed., 2023).

[51] Art. 30, Loi [L] n° 2021-1017 du 2 août 2021 relative à la bioéthique. introducing alinea 2 of Article 57 of the Civil Code [C. civ.].

[52] Circulaire du Ministere de la Justice de présentation des dispositions relatives à l'état civil des personnes présentant une variation du développement génital issues de la loi n° 2021-1017 du 2 août 2021 relative à la bioéthique, ainsi que des dispositions particulières du décret n° 2017-890 du 6 mai

The 2021 law of bioethics, which added a new procedure to Article 99 of the Civil Code to amend the legal sex of intersex people, should also be referenced in this context. This provision states that sex registration is to be corrected upon the request of the registered person or their parents 'if it is medically established that their sex does not align with that stated on their birth certificate'. This provision in the substance requires an administrative procedure based on medical evidence. As Amélie Gogos-Gintrand argues, this procedure appears to be concerned with the registration of the 'true sex' of each person, thereby avoiding a situation in which a person is assigned the legal positions of the 'other' sex.[53] After all, registration can be corrected upon the request of the legal representative of the intersex person, if they are a child, and all that is required is medical documentation. The voice of the intersex person is, in other words, optional.

As Benjamin Moron-Puech points out, the legal approach to intersexuality in France is characterized by a mix of pathologization and overmedicalization. Medical expertise is indeed relied on to legally assign a sex based on biological criteria and to reassign it if need be.[54] To borrow the words of Marie-Xavière Catto, the law establishes a 'medical monopoly on sex determination', and assumes 'every person [to be], biologically, either male or female'.[55] In other words, the law appears to use medical expertise to reject any suggestion that intersexuality could possibly be a healthy variation of human anatomy, and does so to preserve binary categories.

In fairness, the current state of the law represents a step forward vis-à-vis the previous legal framework. Although prior to 2021 the Civil Code was silent on intersexuality,[56] a now-repealed 2011 *circulaire* from the Ministry of Justice recommended assigning a binary sex at birth and avoiding annotations such as 'indeterminate sex'.[57] Crucially, the *circulaire* encouraged the registrar to advise parents to consult with doctors to determine the foreseeable sex of the child after medical treatment. In some exceptional cases—when doctors could not determine sex at

2017 modifié relatif à l'état civil applicables en matière de délivrance de copies intégrales et d'extraits d'actes de l'état civil expurgés de certaines mentions (CIV/05/23) ¶ 1.1 (8 Sept. 2023).

[53] Amélie Gogos-Gintrand, *L'Inscription du Sexe à l'État Civil en Cas d'Intersexuation ou la recherche du «Vrai Sexe»*, *in* IDENTITÉ ET ÉTAT CIVIL. ÉVOLUTIONS CONTEMPORAINES 73 (Amélie Gogos-Gintrand & Stéphanie Moracchini-Zeidenberg 2024) (in particular, *Id.* at 84, underlining how this procedure is crucially aimed at ensuring the registration of the medical sex).

[54] Benjamin Moron-Puech, *Loi de Bioéthique et Intersexuation. Commentaire d'un Article Précaire*, REVUE DE DROIT SANITAIRE ET SOCIALE 827, 832–33 (2021).

[55] Marie-Xavière Catto, *Personnes Intersexuées: La Binarité des Sexes Confortée par les Actes d'État Civil*, DALLOZ ACTUALITÉ (8 Nov. 2023), https://www.dalloz-actualite.fr/flash/personnes-intersexuees-binarite-des-sexes-confortee-par-actes-d-etat-civil.

[56] I have examined the previous state of the law on intersexuality in France in my doctoral dissertation: Osella, *supra* note 11, at 78–84.

[57] Circulaire du 28 octobre du Ministere de la Justice 2011 relative aux règles particulières à divers actes de l'état civil relatifs à la naissance et à la filiation (NOR: JUSC1119808C).

birth but felt they would be able to do so within two years following treatments—the sex designation could temporarily be left blank, with the approval of the public prosecutor.[58] As Catto forcefully argued, the law essentially relied on 'mutilation' to preserve the binary and the legal structures grounded in it.[59]

Understandably, this 2011 *circulaire* was much criticized in France. In 2017, following the resolution on the rights of intersex children passed by the Parliamentary Assembly of the Council of Europe[60] and the then-ongoing case on the recognition of a third sex in the law, the Senate produced a report and acknowledged the psychosocial rationales justifying early treatments on intersex children. The pressure to conform to the binary—including the need to assign a binary legal sex—was mentioned by the Senate as a reason for treatments. The Senate also stated that the system of registration (*état civil*)—which guarantees precision and certainty in the determination of the legal position of each person—is an instrument of social control.[61] Nevertheless, the Senate was cautious regarding intersex treatments. It limited itself to encouraging a precautionary approach and assessing *real* medical necessity and urgency before undertaking any surgical interventions. Modifications to the system of registration—for example, allowing more time to record the sex of the child—were also called for.[62]

In 2017, the *Défenseur des Droits*—the French ombudsperson—acknowledged both the cultural imperatives and the legal pressure on parents and medical professionals that comes from the need to assign children to a (binary) sex in order to complete the proper registration of their civil status.[63] He recommended flexible mechanisms for sex reclassification and the introduction of a legal sex corresponding to the identity of the person.[64] Concomitantly, he called for a new approach, with clear information for the child and the support of an interdisciplinary team.[65] In a 2018 study concerning the draft bill on bioethics (which was eventually adopted in 2021), the *Conseil d'État* targeted the 2011 *circulaire*, arguing that interpreting it as a suggestion to use medical treatments and the legal

[58] *Id.* ¶ 55.

[59] Marie-Xavière Catto, *La Mention du Sexe à l'État Civil*, *in* La Loi et le Genre: Études Critiques de Droit Français 29, 35–39 (Marc Pichard, Stéphanie Hennette-Vauchez & Diane Roman eds., 2014). *See* also the analysis of Catto, explaining the reproduction of bodies that are useful to the legal order in: Catto & Osella, *supra* note 6, at 37–39.

[60] Parliamentary Assembly of the Council of Europe, Resolution 2191, Promoting the Human Rights of and Eliminating Discrimination against Intersex People (12 Oct. 2017).

[61] Maryvonne Blondin & Corinne Bouchoux, Sénat-Session Ordinaire 2016–2017. Rapport d'information Fait Au Nom de La Délégation Aux Droits Des Femmes et à l'égalité Des Chances Entre Les Hommes et Les Femmes (1) Sur Les Variations Du Développement Sexuel: Lever Un Tabou, Lutter Contre La Stigmatisation et Les Exclusions 76–82 (23 Feb. 2017).

[62] *Id.* at 80 (referring to the need for more time to register the newborn's sex). *See* also *Id.*, at 28–64 (offering a broader discussion of the proper medical approach to intersexuality).

[63] Avis du Défenseur des Droits n. 17-04, 9 (20 Feb. 2017).

[64] *Id.* at 10–15.

[65] *Id.* at 7–9.

assignment of sex was 'awkward' (*maladroite*).[66] It further critically assessed the pathological understanding of intersexuality and the therapeutic function of intersex treatments. It stated that the 'therapeutic purpose' of such treatments 'cannot be recognized independently of the expression of the will of the person concerned'.[67] Further criticisms against intersex treatments came from the *Comité Consultatif National d'Éthique*, yet again falling short of demanding a moratorium on intersex treatments.[68]

The 2021 law on bioethics somewhat improved the protection of intersex people.[69] To be clear, the law does not appear to forbid normalizing treatments,[70] but does order the creation of specialized centres operated by multidisciplinary teams to take care of intersex children.[71] The law also emphasizes the protection of informed consent.[72] In 2022, the Ministry of Health and Prevention passed a decree to define the 'good practices for the care of children with variations of genital development'.[73] The decree orders concrete measures to enable parents—and, if aware enough, children—to make informed decisions about medical treatments. For example, counselling must be provided.[74]

Fundamentally, the decree specifies that making atypical genitalia conform to 'representations of the female or male sex/gender [*du féminin et du masculin*]' is not a medical necessity per se. In such cases, the decree continues, 'it is appropriate [*il convient*] to wait until the minor can participate in the decision'.[75] Although providing a critique of this legal development from a human rights perspective is not the objective of this chapter, it should be noted that the reactions to this decree have been mixed. Laurence Brunet and Amélie Gogos-Gintrand, for example,

[66] Conseil d'État, Révision de la Bioéthique: Quelles Options Pour Demain? 129–40 (11 July 2018), https://www.conseil-etat.fr/publications-colloques/etudes/etudes-a-la-demande-du-gouvernement/revision-de-la-loi-de-bioethique-quelles-options-pour-demain.

[67] *Id.* at 135.

[68] Comité Consultatif National d'Êthique Pour les Sciences de la Vie et de la Santé, Opinion 132 Ethical Issues Raised by the Situation of People with Variations in Sexual Development (27 Nov. 2019), https://www.ccne-ethique.fr/en/publications/opinion-132-ethical-issues-raised-situation-people-variations-sexual-development-0?taxo = 67.

[69] For a critical discussion of the law and the developments that led to its passing: Marie-Xavière Catto, *La Loi de Bioéthique et les Intersexes*, 25 Journal du Droit de la Santé et de l'Assurance - Maladie (JDSAM) 64 (2020); Audrey Boisgontier, *Neutralité Scientifique, Neutralité Juridique? La Prise en Charge de l'Intersexuation Appréhendée dans le Cadre de la Loi de Bioéthique*, 4 Revue de Droits de l'Homme ¶ 8 (online) (2023), https://journals.openedition.org/revdh/17556.

[70] Sophie Paricard, *La Loi Bioéthique Encadre la Situation des Enfants Intersexes*, Dalloz Actualité (13 Sept. 2021), https://www.dalloz-actualite.fr/flash/loi-bioethique-encadre-situation-des-enfants-intersexes; Moron-Puech, *supra* note 54.

[71] Art. 30, L. n° 2021-1017 du 2 août 2021 relative à la bioéthique, adding Article 2131-6 to the Code de la Sante Publique.

[72] *Id.*

[73] Arrêté du Ministère de la Santé et de la Prévention fixant les règles de bonnes pratiques de prise en charge des enfants présentant des variations du développement génital en application de l'Article L. 2131-6 du Code de la Santé Publique (NOR: SPRP2232078A) (15 Nov. 2022).

[74] *Id.* ¶ I.2.

[75] *Id.* ¶ II.3.

argue that these protections represent a paradigmatic change to the approach to intersexuality in France.[76] Yet activists, though welcoming the improvement, have also criticized the mild phrasing of the decree, which speaks of appropriateness instead of imposing a moratorium on IGM.[77]

Be that as it may, even in a system where the rights of intersex people have received a degree of attention, intersexuality can still be seen as a source of 'gender trouble', to echo Judith Butler. The medico-legal apparatus can here be mobilized—though in a gentler fashion—to erase intersexuality by still treating it as a pathology. Indeed, French law employs medical expertise to ensure every person is, so to speak, biologically understood as binary—a very convenient solution when the binary is a 'founding element' of the system.

2.3. Erasure in a system that went beyond the binary: A cautionary tale from Belgium

Before we rush to conclude that infringements on intersex physical integrity are only due to the lack of nonbinary recognition, I should clarify that legal recognition of a third sex does not necessarily guarantee the prevention of IGM. To this purpose, a brief foray into Belgian law is instructive, as it cautions against simplistic explanations of the development of intersex human rights and pays respect to those intersex activists who have argued that LGBTQ+ advocates can sometimes politically appropriate their cause.[78]

The Belgian Constitutional Court granted recognition of nonbinary and gender-fluid identities in 2019.[79] To date, the decision of the Belgian Constitutional Court is likely one of the most progressive ever rendered on these issues. Belgian law, in other words, is not as constrained as its French and Italian equivalents when

[76] Laurence Brunet & Amélie Gogos-Gintrand, *Changement de Paradigme dans la Prise en Charge Médicale des Enfants Présentant une Variation du Développment Génital*, REVUE DE DROIT SANITAIRE ET SOCIAL 258 (2023).

[77] Sarita-Vincent Guillot et al., NGO Report (for Session) to the 6th to 7th Report of France on the Convention on the Rights of the Child (CRC) (Dec., 2022) https://intersex.shadowreport.org/public/2022-CRC-France-NGO-Intersex-IGM.pdf.

[78] Chapter 2 and Bauer, Truffer & Crocetti, *supra* note 3.

[79] C.C. [Constitutional Court], 19 June 2019, n. 99/2019. *See also*: Loi modifiant des dispositions diverses concernant la modification de l'enregistrement du sexe (20 July 2023). For a detailed analysis: Nicole Gallus, *La Modification des Actes de l'État Civil en Droit Belge: Regard Comparatiste, in* IDENTITÉ ET ÉTAT CIVIL. ÉVOLUTIONS CONTEMPORAINES 193 (Amélie Gogos-Gintrand & Stéphanie Moracchini-Zeidenberg 2024). Refer also to: Stefano Osella, *When Comparative Law Walks the Path of Anthropology: The Third Gender in Europe*, 23 GERMAN LAW JOURNAL 920, 940–41 (for an argument of how to use anthropology to understand the constitutional case); Stefano Osella & Ruth Rubio-Marín, *Gender Recognition at the Crossroads: Four Models and the Compass of Comparative Law*, 21 INTERNATIONAL JOURNAL OF CONSTITUTIONAL LAW 574, 598 (2023) (for a discussion of how to understand this form of recognition as 'nonbinary elective' in comparative constitutionalism). 'Gender-fluid' people may need to change their legal status multiple times during their life.

it comes to preserving the legal assignment of a binary sex. Nevertheless, intersexuality remains largely invisible in the jurisdiction.[80]

Children must be legally registered at birth in a binary sex, despite the constitutional recognition of a nonbinary identity.[81] When medically certified as 'ambiguous', sex can be registered with a delay of three months.[82] During this time, it has been argued, medical and surgical treatments can be carried out.[83] The status of intersex treatments is unclear in Belgian law. On the one hand, general rules of medical law may provide some protection. In 2023, the Court of Appeals of Brussels found doctors liable for damages for having subjected an intersex child to invasive treatments motivated by cultural considerations.[84] Furthermore, Article 22-bis of the Belgian Constitution protects the moral, physical, and sexual integrity of children. This constitutional provision can be used to ground political demands for intersex rights.[85] The law also explicitly forbids discrimination against intersex people.[86] Nevertheless, Belgian law provides no specific protection against intersex medical treatments.[87]

In fairness, Parliament and the government have put forward soft-law initiatives. It is not entirely clear, however, what role the opening up to nonbinary identity and gender fluidity determined by the 2019 constitutional decision has played. For example, a draft resolution—which was ultimately not passed—was presented before the Belgian Parliament in 2020. While the 2019 decision was not cited in this proposal, the demand for a moratorium on interventions on intersex children[88] was accompanied by a call for the introduction of multiple sex options and

[80] For an introduction: Lisa Guillaume, Amnesty International, Garantir les Droits des Personnes Intersex: Un Défi pour la Belgique (2 Sept. 2024), https://www.amnesty.be/infos/notre-magazine-le-fil/2024/article/garantir-droits-intersexes-defi-belgique.

[81] Art. 44 Old Code Civil [Civil Code][C. Civ.], as replaced by: Art. 4, Loi portant dispositions diverses en matière de droit civil et des dispositions en vue de promouvoir des formes alternatives de résolution des litiges (12 June 2018). Refer to: Geoffrey Willems, *Les Personnes Intersexes: À la Croisée des Genres, in* L'ÉTRANGER, LA VEUVE, ET L'ORPHELIN ... LE DORIT PROTÈGE-T-IL LES PLUS FAIBLES? LIBER AMICORUM JACQYES FIERENS 485 (Géraldine Mathieu et al. eds., 2020).

[82] Art. 48 Old C.civ., as replaced by: Art. 4, Loi portant dispositions diverses en matière de droit civil et des dispositions en vue de promouvoir des formes alternatives de résolution des litiges (12 June 2018).

[83] For a discussion: Géraldine Mathieu, Anne Catherine Rasson & Mathieu Rolain, *L'Appréension des Violence Subies par les Personnes Trans* et Intersexes au Prisme des Droits Humains: Une Révolution Douce, in* LES VIOLENCES DE GENRE AU PRISME DU DROIT (Stéphanie Wattier ed., 2020).

[84] Cour d'Appel [Court of Appeal][App] Bruxelles, 7 Feb. 2023, n. 2019/AR/159. For a commentary: Isabelle Rorive, Anne-Catherine Rasson & Céline Derave, *La Cour d'Appel de Bruxelles Met un Coup d'Arrêt à la Normalisation des Corps des Enfants Intersexués*, JOURNAL DES TRIBUNAUX 6982, 310 (2024). For an overview of medical law as applicable to intersex people in Belgium: Pieter Cannoot, *Do Parents Really Know Best? Informed Consent to Sex Assigning and 'Normalising' Treatment of Minors with Variations of Sex Characteristics*, 23 CULTURE, HEALTH, AND SEXUALITY 564, 569 (2021).

[85] Art. 22-bis of the Belgian Constitution.

[86] Loi modifiant la loi du 10 mai 2007 modifiant, en ce qui concerne l'interdiction de discrimination relative à la paternité ou à la comaternité, la loi du 10 mai 2007 tendant à lutter contre la discrimination entre les femmes et les hommes (4 Feb. 2020) Art. 2(2).

[87] Willems, *supra* note 81, at 481–85.

[88] Proposition de résolution visant à établir un cadre juridique en vue de garantir la protection des droits fondamentaux des personnes intersexes 0974/001(28 Jan. 2020).

procedures of gender self-determination.[89] Similar initiatives have followed at the regional level, and in those cases as well the 2019 decision is not mentioned.[90]

This is not to say that the 2019 decision had no influence at all on the protection of intersexuality. In 2021, a resolution was passed by the Belgian Parliament urging the government to delineate a legislative framework to ban all involuntary interventions on intersex children, including those that are socially, psychosocially, culturally, or aesthetically motivated.[91] The only envisioned exception would be urgent medical situations that make any postponements impossible.[92] The Belgian Parliament contested the pathological understanding of intersexuality and the therapeutic purpose of standardizing medical treatments.[93] Parliament also invited the government to reform the system of sex registration. The 2019 decision is in this context relied on to demand a more flexible form of registration. The 2021 resolution seems also to be grounded in numerous international and comparative documents. Legal developments taking place before the Parliamentary Assembly of the Council of Europe,[94] in multiple UN bodies,[95] as well as in other jurisdictions such as France and Malta, were cited.

It should also be noted that the 2019 decision may help to generate momentum in advancing the rights of intersex people. In this sense, it has been defined as a 'change of paradigm'.[96] As a federation of activists said in the *Code—Coordination des ONG pour le Droits des Enfants*, the 2019 decision

> opens a door for the rights of intersex children. If we remove the obligation to choose a male or female designation on the birth certificate, resorting to normalizing medical treatments without medical necessity will no longer make sense.[97]

[89] *Id.* ¶¶ I.26–I.28.

[90] Voorstel van resolutie Voorstel van resolutie van Orry Van de Wauwer, Elke Sleurs, Freya Saeys, Freya Perdaens, Katrien Schryvers en Katja Verheyen over de Betere Ondersteuning en een Betere Zorg voor Mensen met een Interseksecondititie 1850 (2023–2024) nr.1, https://www.vlaamsparlement.be/nl/parlementaire-documenten/parlementaire-initiatieven/1771652.

[91] Résolution visant à reconnaître le droit à l'intégrité physique des mineurs intersexes 55 0043/008 (11 Feb. 2021).

[92] *Id.* ¶ n. 1.

[93] *Id.* ¶ J (a)(b).

[94] The Resolution of the Belgian Parliament (*Id.*) recalls Resolution 2191 (2017) Promoting the Human Rights of and Eliminating Discrimination Against Intersex People (¶ A).

[95] *Id.* ¶¶ B–E.

[96] Marie-Pascale Allard, Géraldine Mathieu & Anne-Catherine Rasson, *L'Invisibilité des Enfants Intersexes en Droit Belge: Vers un Changement de Paradigme?*, *in* L'Enfant et le Sexe 57, 65 (Blandine Mallevaey & Alice Fretin eds., 2021).

[97] Code—Coordination des ONG pour les Droits de l'Enfant, Les Droits des Enfants Intersexes 6 (Dec. 2021), https://lacode.be/wp-content/uploads/2022/09/Analyse-CODE-Les-droits-des-enfants-intersexes-PUBLI.pdf.

3. Recognition

3.1. Multiple legal sexes, multiple bodies?

Germany takes an entirely different approach to intersexuality. The rights of intersex people to gender recognition and physical integrity have been protected by the Constitutional Court and by the legislature respectively. Indeed, the constitutional right to nonbinary recognition arguably contributed to the legal and political conditions that led to legislating the protection of intersex physical integrity.

German law requires sex registration at birth.[98] As of 2018, following the Law on Amending the Information to be Entered in the Birth Registry,[99] which modified the Personal Status Law,[100] children should be registered as either male or female. However, if they cannot be assigned to either sex, they can either be registered without 'ticking the box' or with the designation *divers* ('other'). Although the law does not require medical evidence, in 2023 the *Oberlandesgericht* in Munich ruled out the possibility of registering a child as *divers* or without ticking the box without a supporting medical opinion.[101] Following the 2024 law on gender self-determination,[102] no special procedures are envisioned to correct the legal sex of an intersex child, even though Section 47 of the Personal Status Law details an administrative procedure to fix clerical mistakes.

Intersex interventions are restricted by the 2021 law 'On the Protection of Children with Variations of Sex Development',[103] which added § 1631e to the Civil Code (BGB). Parents can no longer consent to treatments—be they medical or surgical—when their *sole purpose* is to ensure conformity to the male or female standards. Intention, Rainer Kemper points out, is the determining factor here.[104] Urgent 'life-saving' treatments may be authorized by parents. Less well-defined is the status of a third category of interventions, namely, 'urgent'—that is, not postponable—treatments intended to eliminate a 'functional disorder' which may *also* result in the approximation of genital anatomy to the male or female standards. Parental consent in such cases must be vouchsafed by a family court, which is called on to assess whether subjecting the intersex child to medical or surgical treatment is in their best interests. Parents may also submit to the court a detailed opinion by an interdisciplinary committee, composed of at least two medical

[98] Personnenstandsgesetz [PStG] § 22(3).
[99] Gesetz zur Änderung der in das Geburtenregister einzutragenden Angaben, 18 Dec. 2018, § 1.
[100] PStG § 22(3).
[101] OLG München, 1 Sept. 2023, n, 31 Wx 210/23 e, BeckRS 2023, 32675.
[102] Gesetz über die Selbstbestimmung in Bezug auf den Geschlechtseintrag [SBGG], 19 June 2024.
[103] Gesetz zum Schutz von Kindern mit Varianten der Geschlechtsentwicklung, 21 May 2021.
[104] Rainer Kemper, *Die Behandlung von Kindern mi Varianten des Geschlechtsentwicklung*, FAMRB—FAMILIENRECHTS BERATER 396 (2021). *See also*: Dagmar Coester-Waltjen & Wolframm Henn, *Das Gesetz zum Schutz von Kindern mit Varianten des Geschlechtsentwicklung*, FAMRZ—ZEITSCHRIFT FÜR DAS GESAMTE FAMILIENRECHT 1589 (2021).

doctors—one of which must be a paediatrician—a mental health professional, and an expert in medical ethics. When parents do so, the law states that 'it shall be assumed' by the Court that the intervention is in the child's best interests.

Although the assessment of the law itself is not the objective of this chapter, it is interesting that it has attracted both praise and criticism from different sources. For example, the Federal Association of Medical Doctors (*Bundesärztekammer*) underlined that a blanket ban does not do justice to the targeted approach that—they argue—is preferable for protecting children with variations of sex development,[105] especially after the *Bundesärztekammer*'s official statement on the 'optimum gender of rearing' model.[106] On the other hand, the Organization Intersex International (OII) Europe, an NGO for the protection of intersex rights, lamented that the law left grey areas that could be exploited, such as the possibility of correcting 'functional disorders'.[107] Furthermore, it was underlined in the scholarship that the notion of urgency is not well defined in the law.[108] It was also pointed out that treatments intended *solely* to ensure conformity to the binary tend to be exceptional,[109] thus arguably making the ban ineffective in many less defined cases, where functional and cosmetic concerns may combine.

Be that as it may, what is relevant for the argument presented here is that the law is the outcome of a nearly twenty-year-long process during which the protection of intersex physical integrity and the opening of the legal order to gender diversity proceeded jointly.[110] As detailed by Angelika von Wahl, on whose account this section substantially draws, intersex associations mobilized at the international level to denounce violations of their rights at least as early as 2007.[111] Thanks to an

[105] Stellungnahme des Bundesartzkammer zum Regierungsentwurf eines Gesetzes zum Schutz von Kindern mit Varianten des Geschlechtsentwicklung (BT-Drs. 19/24686), (8 Jan. 2021) https://www.bundesaerztekammer.de/politik/stellungnahmen-gesetzgebung.

[106] The Association of Medical Doctors criticized the 'optimum gender of rearing' model in 2015: Stellungnahme der Bundesärztekammer 'Versorgung von Kindern, Jugendlichen und Erwachsenen mit Varianten/Störungen der Geschlechtsentwicklung (Disorders of Sex Development, DSD)' (30 Jan. 2015), https://www.bundesaerztekammer.de/fileadmin/user_upload/_old-files/downloads/pdf-Ordner/Stellungnahmen/BAeK-Stn_DSD.pdf.

[107] OII Europe, A Good First Step: Germany Adopts Law Banning IGM. But There Is Still Room for Improvement (Mar. 30, 2021), https://www.oiieurope.org/a-good-first-step-germany-adopts-law-banning-igm/.

[108] Nina Schrott, *Beiträge Autonomie in und durch Repräsentation? Möglichkeiten und Grenzen elterlicher Einwilligung in geschlechtsbestimmende Maßnahmen bei Kindern mit Varianten der Geschlechtsentwicklung Zum neuen § 1631e BGB als Prüfstein aktueller Kindeswohlkonzepte und der Zulässigkeit stellvertretender Einwilligung (auch) bei unklarer medizinischer Indikation,* JURIS 358 (2021).

[109] *Id.*

[110] The legal treatment of intersexuality is not a new problem in German law. For a history: Geertje Mak, *Doubtful Sex in Civil Law: Nineteenth and Early Twentieth Century Proposals for Ruling Hermaphroditism*, 12 CARDOZO JOURNAL OF LAW & GENDER 197 (2005); SUSANNA ROSSBACH, DAS PERSONENSTANDSRECHTLICHE GESCHLECHT ZU VERGANGENHEIT, GEGENWART UND ZUKUNFT DES GESCHLECHTSEINTRAGS IN DEN PERSONENSTANDSREGISTERN 19 (2025).

[111] Angelika von Wahl, *From Object to Subject: Intersex Activism and the Rise and Fall of the Gender Binary in Germany*, 28 SOCIAL POLITICS 755, 767–73 (2021); Angelika von Wahl, *From Private Wrongs to Public Rights: The Politics of Intersex Activism in the Merkel Era*, 31 GERMAN POLITICS 59, 64–73 (2022).

alliance with the National Council of German Women's Associations (*Deutscher Frauenrat*), intersex activists filed a shadow report to the CEDAW Committee in Geneva, denouncing infringements of intersex bodily integrity.[112] The report also contains references to the importance of flexible rules for amending legal identity.[113] In addition to the demands for physical integrity, intersex activists called for the possibility 'to have gender-neutral names' and to legally register sex 'preliminarily'—that is, with the possibility of subsequent facilitated changes.[114] In 2009, the CEDAW Committee 'regret[ted], however, that the call for dialogue by non-governmental organizations of intersexual and transsexual people has not been favourably entertained by the State party',[115] and called on it to enter into a conversation with such associations to 'better understand their claims and to take effective action to protect their human rights'.[116] As von Wahl argues, the Concluding Observations of the CEDAW Committee were one reason why the German government charged the national Ethics Council (*Deutscher Ethikrat*) with elaborating guidelines to protect intersex people.[117]

The Ethics Council linked together identity recognition and the protection of physical integrity.[118] It first clarified how intersexuality had long been perceived as legal trouble (my words). The report of the Ethics Council details an ancient history of the legal questions posed by intersexuality from Roman times to the present day.[119] It also explains how the illegibility of intersex people has often caused difficulties in identifying the person,[120] resulting in legal uncertainty. On the other hand, the Ethics Council argued that the lack of a third option affects the rights to self-determination and personality, as well as gender equality.[121] The Ethics Council also seemed to suggest that the legal and constitutional importance of sex registration at birth was losing relevance due to the increased gender equality—that is, because of the transformation of the gender legal order. Except for preserving the heterosexuality of marriage,[122] the report arguably identified no legal interests in tension with nonbinary recognition.[123] The classificatory difficulties presented

[112] Lucie Veith, Sarah Hassel-Reusing & Claudia Kreuzer, Intersexuelle Menschen e.V./XY-Frauen, Schattenbericht zum 6. Staatenbericht der Bundesrepublik Deutschland zum Übereinkommen der Vereinten Nationen zur Beseitigung jeder Form der Diskriminierung der Frau (CEDAW) (2008), https://www.im-ev.de/pdf/Schattenbericht_CEDAW_2008-Intersexuelle_Menschen_e_V.pdf.

[113] *Id.* ¶ 4.3.

[114] *Id.* ¶ 6.1. n. 17.

[115] Committee on the Elimination of Discrimination Against Women, Concluding Observations, UN Doc. CEDAW/C/DEU/CO/6, ¶ 61 (12 Feb. 2009), https://docs.un.org/CEDAW/C/DEU/CO/6.

[116] *Id.* ¶ 61.

[117] Von Wahl, *From Private Wrongs to Public Rights*, *supra* note 111, at 67.

[118] Ethikrat [German Ethics Council], Intersexuality (Philip Slotkin trans., 23 Feb. 2012).

[119] *Id.* at 113.

[120] *Id.* at 115.

[121] *Id.* at 120. Arts. 1 and 3 of the German Constitution [GG].

[122] *Id.* at 132. Maintaining the heterosexuality of marriage is no longer a public interest in Germany. Same-sex marriage was introduced in this jurisdiction in 2017: Gesetz zur Einführung des Rechts auf Eheschließung für Personen gleichen Geschlechts, 20 July 2017.

[123] Ethikrat, *supra* note 118, at 130.

by intersexuality could be solved, the Ethics Council seems to suggest, by changing the way people are classified. The Ethics Council also described the nonbinary option in the personal civil status as a step towards greater social acceptance and a non-pathological understanding of intersexuality.[124] Finally, the Ethics Council condemned involuntary treatments on intersex people. In addition to being a criminal offence and cause for civil liability, the Ethics Council characterized such treatments as an infringement on the constitutional rights to physical integrity[125] and personality.[126]

Following the 2012 opinion of the German Ethics Council, the German legislature passed an initial reform of the personal status law in 2013.[127] This reform offered the possibility of leaving the sex designation in a person's civil status registration blank when the anatomy of the child was unclear, which would effectively render the child 'sexless'; it did not, however, say anything about intersex treatments. The law did not introduce a third, positive, sex entry.[128] Furthermore, the legal status of 'sexless' children—that is, their set of legal positions vis-à-vis the state and other individuals—remained unclear.[129] Ultimately, the law was aimed at decreasing the pressure on parents to legally assign a sex. The underlying idea was that, without the urgency of assigning a legal sex within a stringent deadline, parents would be less inclined to agree to normalizing treatments.[130] It should be acknowledged that the effectiveness of this measure is questionable, as intersex normalizing treatments apparently remained common even after the introduction of the 'sexless' option.[131] On the other hand, in 2015, the Federal Association of Medical Doctors condemned involuntary medical treatments as a violation of the right to personality. Citing the 2013 Personal Status Law, the *Bundesärztekammer*

[124] *Id.* at 130–31.

[125] Art. 2(2) GG. *See* Ethikrat, *supra* note 118, at 137.

[126] Art. 2(1) in conjunction with Art. 1(1) GG. *See* Ethikrat, *supra* note 118, at 137.

[127] As noticed by von Wahl, *From Private Wrongs to Public Rights*, *supra* note 111, at 69. As for the law: Gesetz zur Änderung personenstandsrechtlicher Vorschriften, 7 May 2013, which reformed § 22(3) PStG as follows: 'Kann das Kind weder dem weiblichen noch dem männlichen Geschlecht zugeordnet werden, so ist der Personenstandsfall ohne eine solche Angabe in das Geburtenregister einzutragen' ['If the child cannot be assigned to either the female or male gender, civil status must be entered in the birth register without such information'].

[128] That was not legislated until 2018 (Gesetz zur Änderung der in das Geburtenregister einzutragenden Angaben, 22 Dec. 2018). This law followed the 2017 decision of the Federal Constitutional Law (BVerfG, 1 BvR 2019/16). For a thorough discussion: Chapter 5.

[129] Tobias Helms, *The 2013 German Law: Analysis and Criticism*, *in* THE LEGAL STATUS OF INTERSEX PERSONS 369, 375 (Jens M. Scherpe, Anatol Dutta & Tobias Helms eds., Intersentia 2018).

[130] *Id.* at 372.

[131] StopIGM.org/Zwischengeschlecht, Intersex Genital Mutilations: Human Rights Violations of Children with Variations of Reproductive Anatomy, NGO Report (for Session) to the 6th Report of Germany on the Convention against Torture (CAT) (Jan. 2019), https://intersex.shadowreport.org/public/2019-CAT-Germany-NGO-Intersex-StopIGM.pdf; Ulrike Kloppel, *Zur Aktualitat kosmeticher Operationen 'uneindeutiger' Genitalien im Kidesalter*, 42 BULLETTIN-TEXTE/ZENTRUM FUR TRANSDIZIPLINARE GECHLECTHERSTUDIEN, HUMBOLD UNIVERSITAT ZU BERLIN 3–85 (2016), https://www.gender.hu-berlin.de/de/publikationen/gender-bulletin-broschueren/bulletin-texte/texte-42/kloeppel-2016_zur-aktualitaet-kosmetischer-genitaloperationen.

stated that immediate sex assignment at birth was not necessary under the new law.[132]

As I will discuss in greater detail in Chapter 7, the FCC declared unconstitutional the lack of a third, positive, sex entry in the Personal Status Law on 10 October 2017. The FCC determined that the lack of a third *positive* option for people with variations of sex characteristics who permanently identify as nonbinary was a violation of the rights to identity and equality. This ruling was silent on intersex treatments. Even though the litigation had been initiated by an activist group in support of an intersex nonbinary-identifying person (the *Dritte Option* campaign), the question of involuntary medical treatments was not part of the litigation.[133]

As I have argued elsewhere,[134] how this decision related to intersex rights was the object of some controversy. Some intersex activists pointed out that the FCC's decision could shift the focus of the debate to a 'non-issue', or, at best, a 'marginal' question for most intersex people, i.e. the lack of a third positive option.[135] They felt that it diverted attention away from involuntary medical treatments and might, therefore, do 'more harm than good'.[136] Other NGOs for trans and intersex rights were more sanguine, describing the case as 'a beacon of hope for anyone outside the norms of sex and gender in Germany and Europe'.[137] Regardless, it can be argued that the case law of the FCC brought sexual diversity into the limelight. As von Wahl underlines, the political parties negotiating the 2018 *Koalitionsvertrag*—the agreement between political parties with a view to forming a majority coalition to support a government—were influenced by the constitutional jurisprudence on anti-discrimination and 'promised reform in response to the recent ruling of the Constitutional Court'.[138] The *Koalitionsvertrag* expressly cites the case law of the FCC as one motivator behind the choice to protect gender diversity, and, in this context, the political parties subscribing to the agreement committed to safeguarding the physical integrity of intersex children.[139] This promise was eventually

[132] Bundesärztekammer, *supra* note 106.

[133] *See* BVerfG, 1 BvR 2019/16. One wonders whether the FCC could have seized this opportunity to condemn involuntary treatments on intersex people. The Constitutional Court of Austria, in a 'twin' decision rendered just a few months later, indeed followed this path, though as a obiter dictum (Verfassungsgerichtshof [VfGH] [Constitutional Court], 19 June 2018, G-77/2018, ¶ 3).

[134] Osella, *supra* note 79, at 938–39.

[135] Zwischengeschlecht/StopIGM, Stellungnahme zum BVG-Urteil für einen 3. Geschlechtseintrag (10 Nov. 2017) http://blog.zwischengeschlecht.info/post/2017/11/10/Stellungnahme-zum-BVG-Urteil-3-Geschlechtseintrag.

[136] *Id.* For a broader discussion of nonbinary recognition as 'harmful' and as a 'misrepresentation', *see* Fae Garland & Mitchell Travis, Intersex Embodiment: Legal Frameworks beyond Identity and Disorder 60–74 (2023).

[137] OII Europe, IVIM-OII Germany, TGEU and the German Trans* Association (Bundesvereinigung Trans*), Joint Statement: Civil Society Welcomes German Constitutional Court Demand for a New Regulation of Sex Registration as Ground-Breaking (8 Nov. 2017), https://oiieurope.org/wp-content/uploads/2017/11/press_release_OIITGEUBVT2017.pdf.

[138] Von Wahl, *From Private Wrongs to Public Rights*, *supra* note 111, at 71.

[139] It should be noted that the *Koalitionsvertrag* does not exclusively refer to the 2017 judgment of the FCC, but rather to *all* the case law of the FCC concerning anti-discrimination of sexual minorities. Nevertheless, the 2017 decision on the third option was the most recent at the time of the

granted by the 2021 law 'On the Protection of Children with Variations of Sex Development', which was also influenced by broader human rights developments concerning the physical integrity of intersex children, as is evident from the relation accompanying the law.[140] It should be noted, however, that doubts have recently been raised about the practical effectiveness of the law in meaningfully restricting operations on intersex children. Anna Katharina Mangold and Nick Markwald have conducted research into the decisions courts must make when interventions are urgently needed to eliminate a 'functional disorder', which may also lead to the approximation of genital anatomy to male or female standards.[141] Their findings suggest a lack of meaningful critical engagement with the recommendations made by multidisciplinary panels. Concerningly, Mangold and Markwald underline that references to 'gender normality' and 'normal' sexual intercourse are all but uncommon. Reasoning on intersex rights, on the other hand, appears rare.

To conclude, the evolution of German law highlights that the recognition of nonbinary gender identities and the protection of physical diversity are connected in the legal discourse. Although the introduction of a nonbinary category may not stop involuntary intersex treatments in practice, it nonetheless changes the need for the legal system to categorize each person as either male or female. What is an unbearable uncertainty that must be erased in systems grounded in the binary becomes a common human variation in systems that recognize gender diversity. The legal pressure to erase intersexuality—either figuratively or literally—fades away. Although the progress for intersex people might be challenged in practice, the law still represents a considerable step forward for the rights of intersex people.

3.2. Multiple bodies, multiple identities: Colombia[142]

Transforming the sexed subject

The Constitutional Court of Colombia has produced a body of case law concerning the physical integrity of intersex people whose abundance has not seen the likes in

Koalitionsvertrag and was the only one specifically referring to intersex people: Ein neuer Aufbruch für Europa. Eine neue Dynamik für Deutschland. Ein neuer Zusammenhalt für unser Land. Koalitionsvertrag zwischen CDU, CSU und SPD 21 (7 Feb. 2018), https://www.csu.de/politik/beschluesse/koalitionsvertrag-von-cdu-csu-und-spd-2018/.

[140] Begründung (Accompanying Relation), 13 https://dserver.bundestag.de/btd/19/246/1924686.pdf.

[141] This research has not been published in a scientific journal yet. Nevertheless, it constituted the core of a report submitted by the Authors to the ministry of Justice: Anna Katharina Mangold and Nick Markwald, Letter to the Bundesministerium der Justiz, Referat I A 2—Kindschaftsrecht (Flensburg, 17 June 2025), on file with the author. I thank Mangold and Markwald for kindly sharing this letter with me.

[142] Section 3.2 is indebted to and expands: Ruth Rubio-Marín and Stefano Osella, *Between Rights and Pragmatism: Intersexuality before the Colombian Constitutional Court, in* THE LEGAL STATUS OF

comparative law. The Court relied on several constitutional principles to shape a specific form of informed consent and offered a positive account of intersexuality. Involuntary intersex treatments have thus been meaningfully restricted. By doing so, the Court has revolutionized the narrative around intersexuality and challenged the cultural and socio-juridical justifications of normalizing treatments on infants. The Constitutional Court has, moreover, linked the protection of intersex physical characteristics to the gender identity of intersex people.

This case law, I argue, has profoundly transformed the relationship between gender diversity and public law in Colombia. To start with, once acknowledged that intersexuality is a benign variation of human anatomy and that normalizing treatments are culturally motivated, preserving a legal system based on the binary becomes theoretically untenable.[143] Furthermore, as Lina Céspedez-Báez and Jorge Sarmiento-Forero argue, the jurisprudence on intersex rights has reshaped the idea of the legal subject in the jurisdiction, clearly detaching it from more traditional understandings of sex/gender.[144] Finally, despite acknowledging that intersexuality might be seen as a challenge to a legal and constitutional system based on the binary, the Colombian Court has determined that protecting human diversity is a fundamental obligation of the state.

It should be underlined that the jurisprudence on intersex rights emerged in the decades before the 2015 decision on gender self-determination[145] and the 2022 judgment on nonbinary recognition.[146] Furthermore, to this day, children must in principle be registered with a sex at birth, pursuant to Article 52 of *Decreto* 1260 of 1970, which regulates the system of personal registration. Despite this, normalizing treatments on intersex children have been significantly restricted since the mid-1990s, when the Constitutional Court rendered its first decision on intersexuality. This sequence of events confirms that intersex physical integrity may be protected before, or even without, the right to nonbinary recognition: a consideration of great practical importance for intersex people.

As said, the first decision on intersex rights dates to 1995, when the Constitutional Court banned the involuntary gender reassignment of intersex children.[147] The case concerned a child who, the parents reported, lost his penis after a domestic

INTERSEX PERSONS 319 (Jens Scherpe, Anatol Dutta & Tobias Helms 2018) (presenting a doctrinal analysis of the rules concerning the protection of intersex children in the Colombian constitutional jurisprudence).

[143] Catto & Osella, *supra* note 6, at 44.

[144] Lina Céspedez-Báez & Jorge Sarmiento-Forero, *¿Cómo Mira el Estado? Constitución de 1991 y Compromisos de Género del Estado Colombiano*, 13 REVISTA ESTUDIOS SOCIO-JURÍDICOS 389, 413 (2011).

[145] Corte Constitucional [Constitutional Court][C.C.], 13 febrero 2015, Sentencia T-063/15. Henceforth, all decisions already cited in full will be reported with the number and year only. *See* Chapter 6.

[146] C.C., 4 febrero 2022, Sentencia T-033/22. *See* Chapter 7.

[147] C.C., 23 octubre 1995, Sentencia T-477/95.

accident. Following the seemingly standard practice of the optimum gender of rearing, medical professionals reassigned the boy to the female sex/gender and advised his caretakers to raise him accordingly.[148] Later in life, having learned of the reassignment, the boy reaffirmed his male identity and lodged a *tutela* for the protection of his constitutional rights.[149] The Court found that the value of human dignity, which grounds the right to free development of personality,[150] forbids involuntary sex/gender reassignments.

This decision has been criticized for displaying a contradictory, and even arguably an essentialist, understanding of sex/gender in a few passages.[151] For example, as Céspedez-Báez and Sarmiento-Forero observe, the Court stated that 'sex' is an 'unmodifiable' element of human identity.[152] Nevertheless, the same authors continue, the Court also added that sex is unmodifiable *by others*,[153] implying the right of the person concerned to change it. The Court, in practice, asserted the sovereignty of the individual over their own identity. Although intended to stop the medical practice of involuntary reassignment of intersex children, this ruling also laid the legal foundation for the right to gender recognition. Grounding this right in dignity is especially significant in Colombian law. As Manuel José Cepeda Espinosa and David Landau explain, the preservation of human dignity is among the objectives of the Colombian state.[154] This is, after all, the content of Article 1 of the Constitution.

In 1999, the Constitutional Court went beyond involuntary reassignment with decision SU-337/99.[155] It developed a heightened standard of substituted consent that applies to all other normalizing treatments on intersex children. The case concerned a girl whose clitoris was considered by her mother to be too large according to established cultural standards. In light of the 1995 decision of the Constitutional Court mentioned above, the doctors refused to reduce the size of the clitoris surgically. The mother lodged a *tutela*, claiming that this refusal infringed on her daughter's rights to equality,[156] free development of personality,[157] and special protection of childhood.[158]

In deciding the case, the Court determined that ordinary parental consent is insufficient to authorize normalizing treatments on intersex children. Instead, it

[148] For an overview: Chapter 2.
[149] A *tutela* is a specific writ allowing every person to seek judicial protection of their human rights. It is regulated by Art. 86 Constitucion Politica [C.P.].
[150] Art. 16 C.P.
[151] Céspedez-Báez & Sarmiento-Forero, *supra* note 144, at 406.
[152] C.C., T-477/95, ¶ 13.1.
[153] Céspedez-Báez & Sarmiento-Forero, *supra* note 144, at 406.
[154] Manuel José Cepeda Espinosa & David Landau, Colombian Constitutional Law. Leading Cases 7 (2017).
[155] C.C., 12 mayo 1999, Sentencia SU-337/99.
[156] Art. 13 C.P.
[157] Art. 16 C.P.
[158] Art. 44 C.P.

required an 'informed, qualified, and persistent consent', as intersex treatments were considered serious, irreversible, and, in many cases, distressing.[159] This form of consent, the Court clarified with the subsequent decision T-551/99, which was rendered just a few months later, entails full information to the parents, special formalities (such as consent in writing), and must be repeated on several occasions.[160] While decision SU-337/99 has been criticized for a few passages where intersexuality is labelled an 'abnormality',[161] the light that it projects on bodily diversity is, overall, very positive. In this decision, the Court affirmed the cultural origin of the binary.[162] Furthermore, it observed that the 1991 Constitution aims to create a society where diversity is not met with 'violence and exclusion', and understood constitutional law as a shelter for diversity and pluralism. In the words of the Constitutional Court: 'we all must listen to [intersex people] and not only learn to live with them, but also to learn from them.'[163]

This approach was confirmed in a few later decisions. For example, in *sentencia* T-551 of 1999, not only did the Constitutional Court reaffirm the 'informed, qualified, and persistent' consent, but also pointed at the discrimination directed to intersex people—including within the family—due to the binary-normative cultural understandings of sex/gender.[164] In decision T-692 of 1999, the Constitutional Court judged normalizing treatments on intersex children to be in violation of the right to life and physical integrity of the person.[165] This doctrine, it should be specified, did not entirely ban medically unnecessary treatments on intersex people. If the consent given by the child's guardians met the standards set by the Court, such treatments remain lawful—except for gender reassignment, which the Court banned with decision T-477/95. For example, in 2003, the Constitutional Court considered early intervention on a child legitimate and ordered that the costs of the operation should be covered by public funding.[166]

In sum, despite all legitimate criticism, this doctrine has rejected the notion that only two sexes/genders exist, with all others being negligible exceptions for which no place can be made in the law. The Court did not establish that the difficult classification of intersex people is a valid reason to erase them, nor has it taken advantage

[159] C.C., SU-337/99, ¶ 40 (Fundamentos juridicos). The Court speaks of an 'informed, qualified, and persistent consent' at ¶ 83.

[160] C.C., 2 agosto 1999, Sentencia T-551/99, ¶ 20.

[161] C.C., SU-337/99, ¶ 51 (Fundamentos juridicos). Javier Enrique García León & David Leonardo García León, *Sujetos Intersexuales y Matriz Heterosexual: Los Cuerpos que le Importan a la Jurisprudencia Colombiana. Una Lectura Queer*, 52 LATIN AMERICAN RESEARCH REVIEW 124, 127–30 (2017). However, the Court placed the word 'abnormality' in quotation marks, possibly to distance itself from the term's normative implications.

[162] C.C., SU-337/99, ¶ 32 and ¶¶ 45–54 (Fundamentos juridicos).

[163] C.C., SU-337/99, ¶ 91 (Fundamentos juridicos).

[164] García León & García León, *supra* note 161, at 128. *See* C.C., T-551/1999, ¶ 20 (Fundamentos juridicos). This decision was largely restated in C.C., 16 septiembre 1999, Sentencia T-692/1999; C.C., 12 octubre 2000, Sentencia T-1390/00.

[165] C.C., T-692/1999, ¶ 3.

[166] C.C., 30 octubre 2003, Sentencia T-1021/03.

of a pathologizing description of intersexuality to entrench binary categories in the law. Quite the contrary, the Court has insisted that the legal system must welcome and protect gender diversity. This jurisprudence establishes that individuals do not need to be 'normalized' to match the legal system's assumptions about sex/gender corporeality. This approach stands in contrast, for example, to that of the Italian and French authorities. While the latter erase intersexuality to uphold the consistency of sex categories, the Colombian Court accepts it, regardless of the consequences for the consistency of sex registration.

When protecting physical diversity leads to challenging the binary order

Over time, the Constitutional Court coupled the protection of intersex characteristics with the recognition of gender identity, thus determining a further transformation of the gender order in public law. In a 2002 decision, the Constitutional Court authorized virilizing treatments aimed at reinforcing the gender identity of an eight-year-old intersex child who self-identified as a boy.[167] The Court reaffirmed the doctrine expressed in the SU-337/99 judgment. However, it observed that substitute consent—no matter how 'informed, qualified, and persistent'—cannot apply when the child has sufficient awareness and capacities and when gender identity has developed. In such cases, the autonomous, yet adequately supported, consent of the child was deemed necessary.[168] In particular, the Court considered intersex treatments acceptable as long as they were accompanied by the consent of the capable child, the agreement of the parents, and the favourable consensus of a multidisciplinary team of healthcare professionals.[169] This approach is grounded in the right to free development of personality (Article 16 of the Colombian Constitution), which in turn grounds the rights to self-determination[170] and (gender) identity.[171]

Admittedly, as Javier Enrique García León and David Leonardo García León point out, the language of this 2002 decision is not as accepting of intersexuality as its precedents were: it refers to sexual ambiguity as a 'hindrance to a dignified life' and as an 'oddity' (*extraña*).[172] Furthermore, the Court stated that 'it is mandatory ... to assign each person a clear sex at birth or, when their pathological condition does not allow it, as soon as possible'.[173] As Octavio Caro Garzón provocatively contended, the Court seemed to emphasize the 'right' of intersex children to be 'a man or a woman'.[174] This approach, while incontestable per se, seems

[167] C.C., 27 noviembre 2002, Sentencia T-1025/02.
[168] C.C., T-1025/02, ¶ 41.
[169] C.C., T-1025/02, ¶ 67.
[170] C.C., T-1025/02, ¶ 17.
[171] C.C., T-1025/02, ¶ 19.
[172] García León & García León, *supra* note 161, at 129. *See* C.C., T-1025/02, ¶ 36 and ¶ 66.
[173] C.C., T-1025/02, ¶ 12.
[174] Octavio Caro Garzón, *Hermaphroditas en Colombia: Estudio de la Jurisprudencia Constitucional*, 5 Revista Eletrônica Direito e Política 218, 243 (2010).

to imply hostility towards intersexuality and could be seen as a restrictive reinterpretation of the earlier case law. In this 2002 decision, whose language remains exceptional in the Colombian jurisprudence, normalizing treatments were therefore seen as more benign.[175] Regardless of the language, however, these treatments were judged to be acceptable as the person had consented to them to reinforce their gender identity.

A similar connection between gender identity and intersex characteristics can be found in a 2008 decision.[176] In this case, the Court considered whether to allow normalizing treatments on a self-identified boy whose chromosomal pattern was feminine, but whose genitals included both a phallus and a vagina. The parents requested the interventions; the doctors were hesitant. The Court, hearing the claim lodged by the parents, recalled its previous jurisprudence on informed consent. It also added that, ultimately, it was up to the boy to decide, in conformity with his dignity, and, crucially, his right to free development of personality, as prescribed by the Constitution at Articles 1 and 16.

Once the restrictions on intersex treatments were coupled with the protection of gender identity, questioning binary sex categories in the law was only a matter of time. The Court indeed problematized the binary with great clarity in two decisions in 2013 and 2014.[177] The former seems to be particularly significant,[178] as it concerned the inscription in the birth registry of a newborn intersex child who had been refused registration because doctors could not determine their sex/gender, and the sex box on the birth certificate could not be ticked. The consequences were serious. The child was unable to receive medical care, a situation that put their life at risk. The parents first filed an action for an interim measure to obtain the prompt protection of the rights of their child.[179] After granting it, the Constitutional Court judged on the substantive issues of the case.

At a doctrinal level, the Constitutional Court referred to constitutional[180] and international human rights provisions[181] that require the prompt registration of all children. The Court acknowledged that requiring sex registration 'is legitimate and necessary to achieve the purposes set out in the Constitution'.[182] Sex registration, the Court continued, allows the protection of individual identity but also enables public authorities to clearly identify each person. Despite having declared that same-sex couples have a right to marry in 2011,[183] the Court held that sex

[175] *E.g.*: C.C., T-1025/02, ¶ 66.
[176] C.C., 18 septiembre 2008, Sentencia T-912/08.
[177] C.C., 16 julio 2013, Sentencia T-450A/13 and C.C., 28 agosto 2014, Sentencia T-622/14.
[178] C.C., T-450A/13.
[179] C.C., 27 julio 2012, A-178/12.
[180] Art. 14 C.P.
[181] Art. 24(2), International Covenant on Civil and Political Rights, 16 Dec. 1966, 999 U.N.T.S. 171.
[182] C.C., T-450A/13, ¶ 4.5.3.
[183] C.C., 26 julio 2011, Sentencia C-577/11. Previously, the Court had held that same-sex couples were entitled to enter *de facto* marital unions on equal terms with heterosexual couples (C.C., 7 febrero

registration was required for the purposes of (heterosexual) marriage, as well as for gender equality.[184] The Court also acknowledged that 'there are intersex people who cannot be classified as male or female at birth for medical and biological reasons'.[185] With this statement, the Court essentially recognized the challenge of intersex diversity for a constitutional system based on the binary.[186]

At the same time, the Court observed that intersex people, despite not always being classifiable as 'men or women [*hombres o mujeres*] at birth', should not be denied their constitutional guarantees.[187] Sex/gender indeterminacy, the Court continued, does not justify the refusal of *any* registration whatsoever.[188] In other words, although they may present a puzzle for the legal system, intersex people cannot be excluded from it. The Court invited the legislature to solve the tension between the need of the state to identify citizens and clarify their legal status, and the right to identity of every person.[189] While waiting for legislative solutions, the Court established some temporary rules. It allowed intersex children to be registered without a sex being immediately assigned to them, while recommending a separate annotation of their intersexuality.[190]

Admittedly, as García León and García León argue, the Court failed to give 'real visibility to queer bodies and plac[e] them on the same level as dominant corporealities' and thus to bring about 'a radical transformation of the cisnormative heterosexual regime'.[191] Nonetheless, this judgment, despite not introducing a positive nonbinary legal identity, opened up the system to the possibility of a registration outside the male-female dyad. The Court explicitly acknowledged that sex classification pursues constitutionally grounded public interests. Nevertheless, it also recognized that intersexuality cannot simply be erased.

In decision T-622/14, after reaffirming the doctrine on informed consent, the Court confirmed that the birth of an intersex child can be seen as a legal problem due to the need to register each child in a binary sex.[192] It further stressed that the legal assignment of a binary sex puts pressure on doctors and parents, leading to unnecessary surgeries that do not serve the health or the best interests of intersex children. Hence, the Court concluded, the course of action that is most respectful

2007, Sentencia C-075/07). The Court ultimately ordered the introduction of same-sex marriage in 2016 (C.C., 28 abril 2016, Sentencia SU-214/16). *See* Cepeda Espinosa & Landau, *supra* note 154, at 85.

[184] C.C., T-450A/13, ¶ 4.5.3.
[185] C.C., T-450A/13, ¶ 4.5.3.
[186] Marriage is protected at Art. 42 C.P.; equality is protected at Art. 13 C.P. and gender equality at Art. 43 C.P.
[187] C.C., T-450A/13, ¶ 4.5.3.
[188] C.C., T-450A/13, ¶ 4.6.1.
[189] C.C., T-450A/13, ¶ 4.5.5.
[190] C.C., T-450A/13, ¶ 4.5.5.
[191] García León & García León, *supra* note 161, at 132.
[192] C.C., T-622/14, ¶ 2.3.

of intersex rights is to wait before assigning a legal sex to the child.[193] In short, the Court appeared to be suggesting options of nonbinary registration.

Decision T-450A/13 was subsequently implemented by a *circular* of the *Registraduría Nacional del Estado Civil*.[194] This administrative guideline clarified that, when a newborn is intersex, their parents had to indicate the sex in which they wanted the child to be recorded.[195] It further specified that sex registration could be changed by the child later in life, when aware enough to decide. Rectifications of legal sex had to be supported by medical documentation proving the intersexuality at birth.[196] Considering the transformation of the right to gender identity recognition in Colombia, this *circular* is clearly no longer in force.[197] Nevertheless, it signalled a sensitivity to protecting the self-expressed diversity of the person. This is evident if we compare this document to the procedures for amending the civil registration of intersex people in France and Italy. The main purpose of the latter is supposedly the faithful representation of the biological status in civil registries. In Colombia, the procedure required the involvement of the person to reflect their identity.

In fairness, it should be noted that the legislative and administrative implementations of the case law on intersexuality have been somewhat disappointing. In 2018, questioned by a group of activists, the Colombian Ministry of Health stated that there are no national administrative guidelines concerning intersexuality. The management of medical treatments is remanded to each hospital individually[198]—which must, obviously, respect the rules developed in the case law of the Constitutional Court. To the best of my knowledge, this is still the case at the time of writing (2025). It is worth mentioning that the 2024 bill (*Proyecto de ley*) that introduces legislative mechanisms to protect gender identity in Colombia refers to 'intersexuality' in non-pathological terms as a biological condition 'that does not correspond to the socially established notions of male or female bodies'.[199] Crucially, Article 26 of the bill provides that the Ministry of Health shall adopt guidelines 'to forbid all procedures and practices in the health system aimed at changing, reducing, preventing or repressing diverse gender identities' and to 'guarantee and guide access to health care for persons with diverse gender identities and intersex persons'.

[193] C.C., T-622/14, ¶ 2.5.3.
[194] Registraduría Nacional del Estado Civil, Circular 033/2015 (24 Feb. 2015).
[195] *Id.* ¶ 1.
[196] *Id.* ¶ 2.
[197] As clarified in Chapter 6, indeed, the Colombian Court has now introduced a fully self-determined system of gender recognition, inclusive of a nonbinary option.
[198] Ministerio de la Salud, Respuesta Derecho de Petición sobre la Población Intersexual (Radicado No.: 201821001198481) (20 Sept. 2018).
[199] Art. 3, Proyecto de ley de 31 julio 2024 n. 122/2024C, https://www.camara.gov.co/ley-de-identidad-de-genero.

To wrap up, the Colombian Constitutional Court acknowledged that intersex people might be a puzzle for the legal system; nevertheless, it also stressed that they cannot be excluded from it. It protected physical diversity and acknowledged intersexuality as a benign variation of human anatomy. It allowed normalizing treatments, but only as long as they were supported by a reinforced informed consent. This consent led, in turn, to the recognition of gender diversity. By so doing, the Colombian Court disarticulated the idea that the binary order is grounded in a biological foundation and opened the legal system up to gender diversity.

4. Conclusion

Intersexuality challenges the gender order in public and constitutional law. Indeed, it obliges authorities to make explicit what might otherwise remain silent—namely, the centrality of sexual anatomy to the very make-up of the legal system. Read together, the models identified in this chapter—erasure and recognition—show the very close connection between physical diversity, the system of sex categories in the law, and the pursuit of interests and rights, at times of constitutional status.

With the erasure model, intersexuality is perceived as a problem for the system of sex categories. Recognition of an irregular sex/gender anatomy complicates sex assignment at birth and may be perceived as favouring trans identities—thus as a source of destabilization for the system of civil registration and the binary, which is, in the words of the French Court of Cassation in 2017, 'a fundamental element of the legal system'. In such cases, medicalization and pathologization can be invoked and/or relied on by legal authorities to assign and stabilize a binary sex, including via IGM if necessary. In this sense, intersexuality is seen as a public law problem that a strategic combination of law and medicine can erase. Of course, the erasure of intersex characteristics can be due to a multiplicity of social and cultural factors, well beyond the needs of legal categorization. As the Belgian case proves, a constitutional shift of the legal system from two to three sexes does not ensure the protection of intersexuality. The Italian and the French cases, it is worth emphasizing, show that the idea that legal categories are simply based on a biological, pre-legal, sex is questionable, as legal authorities are active contributors to the creation of the fundament that the legal system needs.

The recognition model shows the other side of the coin. In Germany, the debate on intersexuality was strictly tied to nonbinary recognition and to the transformation of the gender order. The jurisprudence of the Constitutional Court was influential in establishing the 2021 legislative protection of sex characteristics. In a way, the protection of gender diversity and the opening of the system to a nonbinary category contributed to creating the conditions for acknowledging and safeguarding intersex physical diversity. Colombia is a spectacular example in terms of comparative law, with intersex physical integrity being protected before nonbinary identities. Intersexuality is mostly defined as normal, healthy, and acceptable—in fact, as an opportunity for learning. The binary is consistently understood as a cultural construction, and constitutional law is conceived as a means to safeguard diversity and pluralism. Protecting intersexuality led, over time, to recognizing gender identity and to transforming the legal system based on the binary. When we take a step back and view all of this more holistically, it seems evident that the preservation of the legal binary is strengthened when grounded in the erasure of intersexuality, and that the protection of intersexuality is strictly tied to the welcoming of gender diversity in public law.

4
The Medico-Behavioural Model
Italy*

1. The medico-behavioural model: An introduction

Since 1972, when Sweden broke new ground and became the first jurisdiction in the world to grant 'transsexual' people the possibility to change their sex status in civil registries and identity documents,[1] the right to gender recognition has often been tied up with medical preconditions. Laws on gender recognition often require applicants intending to change their legal sex to undergo treatments of varying natures, including psychiatric diagnosis, aesthetic surgery, or sterilization.[2] Courts and legislatures have persistently treated medical transformation and trans identity—or 'transsexuality'—as coextensive, as trans people have often been understood as overwhelmed by the need to acquire the features of *the* other gender. However, not all display these characteristics. Unsurprisingly, mandatory medical interventions have been contested by scholars and activists as intrusive, coercive, cruel, and humiliating.[3] They have been condemned in international soft law.[4] Mandatory sterilization has been found in violation of the fundamental right to physical integrity by the European Court of Human Rights (ECtHR)[5] and

* This chapter is indebted to, partly reproduces, and expands: Stefano Osella, *Reinforcing the Binary and Disciplining the Subject: The Constitutional Right to Gender Recognition in the Italian Case Law*, 20 International Journal of Constitutional Law 454 (2022). Section 3, in particular, substantially reproduces and updates *Id.* at 466–73. The chapter also draws on, partly reproduces, and expands: Stefano Osella, *When Comparative Law Walks the Path of Anthropology: The Third Gender in Europe*, 23 German Law Journal 920 (2022); Stefano Osella, The Legal Regime of Gender Identity. A Comparative Enquiry 121–63 (7 May 2019) (Ph.D. Dissertation, European University Institute).

[1] Lag (1972:119) om fastställande av könstillhörighet a fall (Act (1972: 119) on the Determination of Gender Identity in Certain Cases). *See also*: Jameson Garland, *The Legal Status of Transgender and Transsexual Persons in Sweden*, *in* The Legal Status of Transsexual and Transgender Persons 281 (Jens Scherpe ed., 2015). In this context, I use the term 'transsexual' advisedly, as gender recognition was granted only to people who were understood to transform their bodies medically.

[2] Medical preconditions for gender recognition vary. For an overview: Scherpe, *supra* note 1.

[3] *Id.*; Peter Dunne, *Transgender Sterilisation Requirements in Europe*, 25 Medical Law Review 554 (2017); Anne E. Silver, *An Offer You Can't Refuse: Coercing Consent to Surgery Through the Medicalization of Gender Identity*, 26 Columbia Journal of Gender and the Law 488 (2014).

[4] Parliamentary Assembly of the Council of Europe, Resolution 2048 (2015), Discrimination against Transgender People in Europe (22 Apr. 2015); Opinión Consultiva sobre Identidad de Género, e Igualdad y No Discriminación a Parejas del Mismo Sexo, Advisory Opinion OC-24/17, Inter-American Court of Human Rights, (Ser. A) No. 24 (24 Nov. 2017).

[5] Notably in: A.P., Garçon, and Nicot v. France, Apps. No. 79885/12, 52471/13, and 52596/13 (6 Apr. 2017), https://hudoc.echr.coe.int/eng?i=001-172913.

Gender Diversity in Public Law. Stefano Osella, Oxford University Press. © Stefano Osella 2026.
DOI: 10.1093/9780198935070.003.0004

condemned at the national level by several courts.[6] The ongoing trend towards recognizing self-determination similarly underlines the increasingly critical stance on medical requirements.[7] Yet, medical preconditions are still widespread. For example, in 2024, of the forty-one states in Europe and Central Asia that allow gender recognition, twenty retain medical preconditions that are defined as abusive, including medical, surgical, and diagnostic requirements.[8] In eleven states, sterilization is included.[9]

Italy is a case in point. Law 164 of 1982 ensures the right to 'sexual identity' (*identità sessuale*)[10]—that is, to gender recognition. The Constitutional Court and the Court of Cassation have grounded this right principally in the constitutional rights to personality[11] and health.[12] The law specifies that every person can amend their sex in the civil registries following the 'modification of sex characteristics'.[13] Until 2015, this requirement was interpreted as including gender confirmation surgeries on secondary characteristics and primary sex characteristics[14]—the latter being a euphemism for surgical sterilization.[15] In 2015, both the Constitutional Court and the Court of Cassation ruled out the surgical sterilization requirement. However, they insisted that recognition can *only* be granted after an irreversible and medically supervised transformation of the 'physical, behavioural, and psychological' characteristics of the applicant.[16] Despite its silence, the law has been

[6] Dunne, *supra* note 3. For example: Bundesverfassungsgericht [BVerfG] [German Federal Constitutional Court], 11 Jan. 2011, 1 BvR 3295/07; Verwaltungsgerichtshof [VwGH] [Austrian Administrative Court], 27 Jan. 2009, No. 2008/17/0054; Verfassungsgerichtshof [VfGH] [Austrian Constitutional Court], 3 Dec. 2009, B 1973/08-13; Stockholm Administrative Court of Appeals, Case No. 1968–12, 19 Dec. 2012. Outside Europe, for example: National Legal Service Authority v. Union of India (2014) 5 SCC 438 (India) (*see* Chapter 7).

[7] On self-determination: Chapter 6.

[8] LGR Cluster (TGEU 2025), https://transrightsmap.tgeu.org/home/legal-gender-recognition/cluster-map.

[9] Sterilisation (TGEU 2025), https://transrightsmap.tgeu.org/home/legal-gender-recognition/sterilisation.

[10] Law [L.] 14 aprile 1982, n. 164 [henceforth, 164/1982].

[11] Art. 2 Italian Constitution [Cost.] and Art. 8 of the European Convention on Human Rights [ECHR].

[12] Art. 32 Cost.

[13] Medical treatments on primary sex characteristics were to be authorized by a court (Art. 3, L. 164/1982). The analysis of this aspect of the evolution of the law on gender recognition in Italy is not immediately related to sex reclassification and cannot be discussed here. Anna Lorenzetti, Diritti in Transito. La Condizione Giuridica delle Persone Transessuali (2013) (offering a detailed constitutional analysis of the case law prior to 2013).

[14] For a previous discussion, please *see* Ruth Rubio-Marín & Stefano Osella, *Le Precondizioni per il Riconoscimento dell'Identità Sessuale,* Quaderni Costituzionali 66 (2015) (presenting and discussing the preconditions on gender recognition in terms of human rights law until 2015). Secondary sex characteristics refer to the general appearance of the person: they include body hair, facial hair, and breasts. Primary sex characteristics are connected to reproductive organs such as genitalia, the uterus, and gonads.

[15] *Id.* Refer also to: Francesco Bilotta, *Transessualismo*, in Digesto delle Discipline Privatistiche 732, 760 (2013); Paolo M. Vecchi, *Transessualismo*, in Enciclopedia del Diritto Treccani; Salvatore Patti, *Transessualismo, in* Digesto delle Discipline Privatistiche 416 (1999).

[16] Corte Costituzionale [Constitutional Court] [Corte Cost.], 21 ottobre 2015, n. 221. All decisions of the Italian Constitutional Court are available at: www.cortecostituzionale.it. For brevity, decisions

applied to adults and underage people alike.[17] Married applicants, moreover, will have their marriage transformed into a same-sex civil union—unless the spouses are determined to divorce.[18] If the applicant is already in a same-sex civil union, this status will continue for a limited period of time, until the applicant and their partner fulfil all necessary formalities to marry[19]—unless they are determined to dissolve the union.

Why do the Italian legislature and Italian courts impose these medico-behavioural requirements? How is the medicalization of trans identity invoked in public law, and why is such importance attached to it? How do such preconditions impact the creation of the sexed subject in constitutional law? In this chapter, I address these questions. First, I assert that this right, as granted in Italian law, represents a model of gender identity based on 'ascription'.[20] Indeed, individuals do not have the final word on their own identity; instead, it must be 'certified' by a third-party authority, namely a court, with medical support.

Second, I contend that courts and Parliament have imposed medico-behavioural preconditions to safeguard the 'certainty of legal relations'. In the Italian context, this principle primarily relates to the preservation of traditional and heterosexual family law.[21] Italian law therefore confirms the relationship between heteronormativity and the sexual binary,[22] especially at the constitutional level. More recently, asserting control over the binary has been motivated by needs relating to regulating athletic competitions and intimacy in public establishments, too.[23] To be clear, the presence of sex categories may also serve admirable goals in the field of gender equality.[24] Nevertheless, to borrow the words of Ruth

previously cited will hereinafter be referred to only by jurisdiction, number, and year (*E.g.* Corte Cost., 221/2015).

[17] The Constitutional Court and the Court of Cassation have not discussed the right to gender recognition of trans children. For an overview: Anna Lorenzetti, *La Condizione Giuridica del Bambino e dell'Adolescente Transgenere tra Diritto alla Salute, Autodeterminazione e (In)certezza del Diritto*, Ragion Pratica 533 (2020); Giacomo Mingardo, *Il Diritto Vissuto per il Riconoscimento dell'Identità di Genere. Una Rassegna della Giurisprudenza di Merito (2015–2024)*, 3 Biolaw Journal 100 (2024), https://teseo.unitn.it/biolaw/article/view/3190.

[18] Corte di Cassazione [Court of Cassation] [Cass.]. 20 luglio 2015, n. 15138, https://www.federalismi.it/nv14/articolo-documento.cfm?Artid=30132; Corte Cost., 11 June 2014, n. 170.

[19] Art. 2, L. n. 164/1982. Now: Art. 31, co. 6 D.lgs. n. 150/2011 and Arts. 1(26) and 27, L. 20 maggio2016, n.76.

[20] The terms to refer to identity (ascriptive and elective) are borrowed from: Jessica A. Clarke, *Identity and Form*, 103 California Law Review 743, 757–58 (2015).

[21] The Constitutional Court has denied same-sex couples the right to marry and to access assisted reproductive technologies. Stefano Osella & Graziella Romeo, *Something's Wrong with Traditionalism: LGBTQI+ Rights in Comparative Perspective*, Asian Journal of Comparative Law (2026), https://doi.org/10.1017/asjcl.2025.10005.

[22] *See* Chapter 2.

[23] Corte Cost., 23 luglio 2024, n. 143. *See*: Sul Non-Binarismo di Genere e sull'Autorizzazione Giudiziaria a Effettuare gli Interventi Chirurgici di Affermazione di Genere. La Sentenza 143 del 2024 (Nicola Posteraro & Benedetta Liberali eds., 2025).

[24] For an overview from a constitutional standpoint, *see*: Barbara Pezzini, *Costruzione del Genere e Costituzione*, *in* La Costruzione del Genere. Norme e Regole. Corso di Analisi di Genere e Diritto Antidiscriminatorio (Barbara Pezzini ed., 2012); Barbara Pezzini, *Tra Uguaglianza e*

Rubio-Marín, the Italian case shows concretely how 'modern constitutionalism was superimposed on an extractive and reproductive and heteronormative family structure with racist undertones, which was naturalized and even romanticized'.[25] Adding to these primary explanations, other factors weigh in. Courts have associated medicalization with the 'seriousness' of the intention driving the application for gender recognition. While a detailed analysis of the relations between medical science and sexuality is beyond the scope of this study, it should be recalled that the production of *scientia sexualis* has long been used to control those who were seen as 'deviants'.[26] Finally, the doctrinal construction around the right to health favours a medical understanding of gender recognition as the 'final step' of a medicalized process.

The third prong of my argument addresses how this mechanism operates. I suggest that the right to 'sexual identity' works in an ambivalent, or even paradoxical, way.[27] Leading Italian trans activist and theorist Porpora Marcasciano has argued that gender recognition in Italy simultaneously allows trans people to obtain recognition while forcing them to situate themselves within the bounds of a strictly defined binary sex/gender.[28] Elaborating on this analysis, I claim that the right to gender recognition functions as a normalizing mechanism that disciplines and controls individuals—clearly, to safeguard the stability of sex categories in the law.

The choice of Italy as an example of the medico-behavioural model is based on several factors. First, the Italian case is characterized by an abundant jurisprudence examining this constitutional right, as well as ample case law from lower courts applying it. Second, a rich body of literature has developed on the matter. Third, the virtually exclusive focus of Italian courts and Parliament on the heterosexuality of family law as the main public interest in conflict with gender recognition is conducive to a queer-based analysis. Finally, with its requirements of psychiatric supervision and transformation of secondary sexual characteristics—often through

Differenza: Il Ruolo della Corte Costituzionale nella Costruzione del Genere, in Per i 60 Anni della Corte Costituzionale. Convegno Scientifico, 19–20 Maggio 2016 (Barbara Pezzini ed., 2017); Barbara Pezzini, *La Costituzione al Femminile. Donne e Assemblea Costituente, in* 70 Anni Dopo tra Ugualglianza e Differenza. Una Riflessione sull'Impatto del Genere nella Costituzione e nel Costituzionalismo (Barbara Pezzini & Anna Lorenzetti eds., 2019).

[25] Ruth Rubio-Marín, Global Gender Constitutionalism and Women's Citizenship: A Struggle for Transformative Inclusion 79 (2022). The racist undertones are not manifested in the Italian case law. Nevertheless, as we shall see in Chapters 6 and 7, the connections between Eurocentrism, colonization, and the binary are unmistakable.

[26] Michel Foucault, History of Sexuality. Volume I: An Introduction 53 (Robert Hurley trans., 1990); Dagmar Herzog, Sexuality in Europe: A Twentieth-Century History (2004).

[27] Ben Golder, Foucault and the Politics of Rights 89–113 (2015); Philippe Chevallier, *Michel Foucault and the Question of Right, in* Re-reading Foucault: On Law, Power, and Rights (Ben Golder ed., 2013).

[28] Stefania Voli, *«Il Parlamento Può Fare Tutto, Tranne che Trasformare una Donna in un Uomo e un Uomo in una Donna». (Trans)sessualità, Genere, e Politica nel Dibattito Parlamentare della Legge 164/1982*, 287 Italia Contemporanea 75, 101 (2018).

surgery—the Italian case involves many different forms of medicalization, from the least to the most intrusive, thus offering useful lessons for other systems where only some of such forms may be established.

2. Medico-behavioural requirements and gender constitutionalism

2.1. Sex categories and the early application for gender recognition

As specified in the previous Chapter, Italian law prescribes that the sex of newborns must be registered in civil registries.[29] Sex is presumed to be either male or female—a practice that has been confirmed by the Constitutional Court's 2024 denial of nonbinary recognition. Sex is normally assigned on the basis of genital examination.[30] All corrections to a person's civil status—including sex—fall under judicial competence.[31] This exclusive jurisdiction is intended to safeguard the certainty of registration, which is ostensibly meant to reflect reality[32] and is deemed essential to determine the individual's legal position.[33] Clear identification and the stability of the legal status[34] have also long been presumed to be preconditions for protecting rights, for example, with regard to affirmative equality.[35] Moreover, the 'certainty of legal relations' is an organizational principle: the certainty of each person's complex of legal positions is relied on by the state to pursue public interests.[36]

This is the framework that the first applicants for sex change met when they reached Italian courts in the late 1960s.[37] Lacking a specific rule, applicants would rely on the general judicial procedure to make changes in the civil registry.[38] They

[29] Art. 30, Decreto del Presidente della Repubblica [D.P.R.] 3 novembre 2000, n. 396.

[30] *See*: Comitato Nazionale di Bioetica [National Committee of Bioethics], I Disturbi della Differenziazione Sessuale nei Minori: Aspetti Bioetici (25 Feb. 2010), https://bioetica.governo.it/it/documenti/pareri/i-disturbi-della-differenziazione-sessuale-nei-minori-aspetti-bioetici/.

[31] Art. 96 DPR 396/2000.

[32] Giuseppe Marziale, *Stato Civile*, *in* ENCICLOPEDIA GIURIDICA TRECCANI ¶ 5. *See also*: Maria Claudia Andrini, *Commento sub Art. 454 e 455 del Codice Civile*, *in* COMMENTARIO AL CODICE CIVILE 825 (Paolo Cendon ed., 1991) (offering a more detailed comment of the earlier form of gender recognition under the discipline of the civil code).

[33] Marziale, *supra* note 32, ¶ 1.2.

[34] On the notion of status, *see*: Aldo Corasaniti, *Stato delle Persone*, in 43 ENCICLOPEDIA DEL DIRITTO 938, 952 (1990).

[35] GUIDO ALPA, STATUS E CAPACITÀ. LA DIFFERENZA GIURIDICA DELLE DIFFERENZE INDIVIDUALI 143 (1993); Marta Cartabia, *Le Avventure Giuridiche della Differenza Sessuale*, IUSTITIA 285 (2011).

[36] Corasaniti, *supra* note 34, at 948–52.

[37] Francesco Carnelutti, *Rettificazione del Sesso*, RIVISTA DI DIRITTO PROCESSUALE 492 (1962); Pasquale Antignani, *Sulla Natura delle Diagnosi di Sesso (A Proposito di Alcune Sentenze)*, DIRITTO E GIURISPRUDENZA 513 (1970).

[38] Art. 454 Civil Code [C.c.].

did not frame their demands as a right. Rather, they would argue that their legal sex no longer represented their real identity.[39] Such demands were routinely rejected. Courts held that there had been no 'sex change'.[40] 'Psychological sex'—as gender identity was called—was not considered a relevant factor,[41] even after attentive investigations into the anatomy, behaviour, and sexuality of the applicants.[42] Emphasis was placed on the biological immutability of sex. At the same time, this immutability was not detached from public law judgments. Courts also justified these rejections by referencing the different roles of each of the sexes in reproduction and the family.[43] For example, the Court of Cassation held that preserving birth-assigned sex in the legal status preserved the certainty of legal relations.[44]

In 1974, with a narrative that evokes the 'politics of disgust' described by Martha Nussbaum with reference to US law, the Court of Cassation stated:[45]

> [T]he protection of the applicant finds its limit in the protection of those who come into, or may come into, contact with him. It is undeniable that, in the current state of our culture ... personal relations between individuals of the opposite sex, when they are sufficiently intimate, are commonly perceived in the social conscience as profoundly different from those between persons of the same sex. ... This indisputable consideration must be acknowledged by the legal order, so that it may protect members of society from all possible misunderstandings that may stem from artificial sex modification ... [T]he surgical construction of a vagina instead of a penis is perceived in the [common] conscience as *repulsive* [*un fatto ripugnante*] and completely incapable of allowing the person with this artificial organ to be treated as a woman or to form with him a genuine heterosexual relationship. ... One cannot doubt the need to protect those who come into contact with [a transsexual person] from being tricked [*ingannati*] into this kind of relationship, as this will have the most serious [*gravissime*] consequences for the moral order.[46]

[39] *E.g.*: Cass., 13 giugno 1972, n. 1847, Foro Italiano I, I, 2399 (1972); Cass., 3 dicembre 1974, n. 3948, Diritto di Famiglia e delle Persone 127 (1974).

[40] *See* Luigi Ferri, *Commento sub art. 454 del Codice Civile, in* Commentario al Codice Civile (Antonio Scialoja & Giuseppe Branca eds., 1971); Massimo Garutti & Francesco Macioce, *Il Diritto all'Identità Sessuale*, Rivista di Diritto Civile 273 (1981).

[41] Cass., 3948/1974, 135.

[42] Cass., 1847/1972, 2401.

[43] Cass., 9 marzo 1981, n. 1315; Cass., 2161/1980, 1516.

[44] Cass., 3948/1974, 132.

[45] Martha C. Nussbaum, From Disgust to Humanity: Sexual Orientation and Constitutional Law (2010).

[46] Cass., 3948/1974, 135–36 (emphasis added).

2.2. The law on 'amending legal sex'

A breakthrough came with decision 98 of 1979. A post-operative trans woman claimed a fundamental right to 'sexual identity' and grounded it in the protection of fundamental rights and in the duty of solidarity, a general clause enshrined in the Italian Constitution.[47] The Court of First Instance referred the claim to the Constitutional Court. The Constitutional Court denied that this general clause protected 'sexual identity'.[48] Nevertheless, it considered that Parliament could provide protection by way of legislation. At the same time, the Court warned the legislature of the limits posed by 'marriage, which the Constitution defines [at Article 29] as the foundation of the family as a natural institution'.[49]

As noted by Stefania Voli, whose historical account informs the discussion of the legislative evolution presented here, this decision served as a catalyst for activism.[50] A group of trans people started to mobilize and formed the *Movimento Italiano Transessuali*[51] (*Mit*; today, *Movimento di Identità Trans*),[52] in coalition with the *ante litteram* queer collective *F.u.o.r.i.!*.[53] This group of activists liaised with legislators from the libertarian Radical Party, who presented a bill in the lower house of Parliament. From the beginning, the legislators intended to protect 'transsexual' people only, whom they understood as 'trapped in the wrong body'. In the debates, they presented trans identity as a psychiatric condition, hardly freely chosen by the 'transsexual' person.[54] As Voli argues, legislators saw the right of 'transsexual' people to change legal sex as a way of safeguarding the 'standards of propriety' and the 'continuity of the human species'.[55] They pragmatically perceived the recognition of 'transsexual' people as an inevitability to be governed. Being ostensibly sympathetic to the hard conditions lived by unrecognized 'transsexual' people,

[47] Corte Cost., 12 luglio 1979, n. 98. *See*: Art. 2 Cost. Emanuele Rossi, *Commento all'Articolo 2, in* Commentario alla Costituzione 38 (Vol. 1, Raffaele Bifulco, Alfonso Celotto & Marco Olivetti eds., 2006).

[48] Roberto Romboli, *Commento Sub Art. 5 del Codice Civile, in* Commentario del Codice Civile Scialoja Branca. Art. 1-10 225, 261 (Alessandro Pizzorusso, Roberto Romboli, Umberto Breccia & Anna De Vita eds., 1988).

[49] Corte Cost., 98/1979, ¶ 2 (in diritto) [legal grounds]. Following the 2023 translation of the Constitution offered by the Constitutional Court, I translate '*società*' as 'institution', https://www.cortecostituzionale.it/documenti/download/pdf/The_Constitution_of_the_Italian_Republic.pdf.

[50] Stefania Voli, *(Trans)gender Citizenship in Italy: A Contradiction in Terms? From the Parliamentary Debate About Law 164/1982 to the Present*, 23 Modern Italy 205 (2018).

[51] Italian Transsexuals Movement, https://mit-italia.it/chi-siamo/. For a history of the movement: Stefania Voli, *Broadening the Gendered Polis: Italian Feminist and Transsexual Movements, 1979–1982*, 3 TSQ: Transgender Studies Quarterly 235 (2016) and Porpora Marcasciano, L'Aurora delle Trans Cattive 167 (2018).

[52] 'Italian Movement for Trans Identity.'

[53] '*Fuori!*' literally means 'Out!'. The acronym stands for *Fronte Unitario Omosessuale Rivoluzionario Italiano* (Unitary Revolutionary Homosexual Italian Front). For an overview: Gianni Rossi Barilli, Il Movimento Gay in Italia (1999).

[54] Voli, *supra* note 28, at 83–84. Chamber of Deputies, Proposta di legge De Cataldo et al., 27 Feb. 1980. All parliamentary debates are available at <www.camera.it>.

[55] Voli, *supra* note 50, at 205–06.

legislators eventually passed Law 164 of 1982. This law grants gender recognition, but only after the 'modification of sex characteristics' of the applicants.[56] It requires prior judicial authorization for surgery to modify primary sex characteristics.[57] It also includes a clause of 'automatic divorce' to ensure that married applicants can no longer remain in what would, following recognition, become a same-sex marriage.[58]

Although Law 164 of 1982 was a victory for 'transsexual' people,[59] only those who identified with a binary sex/gender and wished to undergo physical transformation benefitted from the newly legislated right.[60] For this reason, Marcasciano defined the law as a generalized 'regularization' (*sanatoria*) for unrecognized trans people.[61] Voli argued that Law 164 of 1982 is a 'compensatory mechanism' that is ultimately aimed at negating any ambiguity that trans people might embody.[62] As Francesco Bilotta put it:

> The law [i.e. Law 164 of 1982] rests on two assumptions. The first is that, within [the Italian] legal system, people must be classified as either male or female. This distinction is so deeply entrenched in [the Italian] culture that it prevents ... the conceptualization of additional genders or the possibility of recognizing a right to gender indeterminacy. The second assumption is that public interests are tied to the certainty in legal relationships, and to categorizing individuals according to

[56] Art. 1, L. 164/1982.

[57] Art. 3, L. 164/1982. Over time, it became possible to obtain this authorization as part of the same decision granting recognition. As of 2024, this authorization is no longer necessary when the applicant already meets the requirements for gender recognition (Corte Cost., 143/2024). This question has been largely debated in the Italian context but is not immediately relevant for the argument present in this chapter. On the innovations brought by decision 143 of 2024, *see*: Nicola Posteraro, *La Corte Costituzionale Interviene sui Diritti delle Persone Trans: Cosa Cambia?*, LACOSTITITUZIONE.INFO (5 Aug. 2024), https://www.lacostituzione.info/index.php/2024/08/05/la-corte-costituzionale-interviene-sui-diritti-delle-persone-trans-cosa-cambia/; Roberta Parigiani, *Il diritto al Compimento degli Interventi Chirurgici di Affermazione di Genere dopo la Pronuncia n. 143/2024 della Corte Costituzionale: Prime Riflessioni alla Luce delle Pronunce di Merito*, *in* SUL NON-BINARISMO DI GENERE E SULL'AUTORIZZAZIONE GIUDIZIARIA A EFFETTUARE GLI INTERVENTI CHIRURGICI DI AFFERMAZIONE DI GENERE. LA SENTENZA 143 DEL 2024 (Nicola Posteraro & Benedetta Liberali eds., 2025). This chapter does not expand on the procedural aspects of the process for gender recognition. On the procedure to obtain the recognition before decision 143 of 2024: Bilotta, *supra* note 15, at 758; Giacomo Cardaci, *Per un 'Giusto Processo' di Mutamento di Sesso*, IL DIRITTO DI FAMIGLIA E DELLE PERSONE 1459 (2015). For the most recent innovations concerning the procedure for gender recognition: Paola Widmann, *Il Procedimento per la Rettificazione di Attribuzione di Sesso dopo la Riforma Cartabia: Cenni Introduttivi*, *in* IDENTITÀ DI GENERE E DIRITTO: PERCORSI DI RICERCA 155 (Nicola Posteraro, Lucia Busatta & Andrea Magliari eds., 2025).

[58] Art. 4, L. 164/1982.

[59] MARCASCIANO, *supra* note 51, at 184 (offering a point of view of the stakeholders).

[60] Voli, *supra* note 28, at 101–02.

[61] As reported by Voli (*Id.*).

[62] *Id.*

one's sex, since the organization of the entire social structure ... rests on the male/female binary.[63]

2.3. The constitutional right to gender recognition

The ambivalent—at once emancipatory and regulatory—dimension of Law 164 of 1982 is manifested in the decision of the Constitutional Court that grounded the right to 'sexual identity'. In 1983, the Court of Cassation challenged Law 164 of 1982 with a preliminary reference to the Constitutional Court. First, the Court of Cassation suspected that the law infringed on the principle of bodily integrity.[64] The law seemed to favour gender confirmation surgeries, which the Court of Cassation considered a form of self-mutilation.[65] Additionally, the Court was concerned about gender recognition because it feared its possible social consequences, which it clearly saw as bizarre. For example, the Court worried about threats to family life, such as in the hypothetical case of a man who is at once the father of some children and the mother of others. These situations were allegedly in conflict with the protection of the family.[66] Furthermore, the Court of Cassation argued that changing legal sex jeopardized the institution of heterosexual marriage, as the medical treatments could not enable recognized trans people to perform the 'nature-based copulative and generative' functions.[67]

The Constitutional Court rejected this preliminary reference and declared a right to 'sexual identity'.[68] It ruled that such a right was a manifestation of an evolving legal culture capable of protecting minorities, regardless of how small or different from the standard those minorities might be.[69] This powerful statement extended the protection of constitutional law to gender diversity, at least to some extent. Indeed, the Constitutional Court defined the right to gender recognition in a way that limited it to 'transsexual' people, whom the Court described as always

[63] Bilotta, *supra* note 15, at 732. *See also*: Barbara Pezzini, *Il paradigma eterosessuale del matrimonio di nuovo davanti alla Corte costituzionale: la questione del divorzio imposto ex lege a seguito della rettificazione di sesso (ordinanza n. 14329/13 Corte di cassazione)*, (1) GenIUS 21 (2014).

[64] Art. 5 C.c.; Art. 32 Cost.

[65] Cass., 15 aprile 1983, ord. n. 783, (60) Gazzetta Ufficiale della Repubblica Italiana (G.U.) 1755, 1759 (29 febbraio 1984).

[66] Art. 29 Cost. *See* Cass., 783/1983, 1759.

[67] Cass., ord. 783/1983, 1758.

[68] Corte Cost., 6 maggio 1985, n. 161. *See* Mario Dogliotti, *La Corte Costituzionale Riconosce il Diritto all'Identità Sessuale*, Giurisprudenza Italiana 235 (1987). On this decision, *see* also a previous discussion in: Rubio-Marín & Osella, *supra* note 14. For one more examination of the Italian constitutional jurisprudence, refer to: Barbara Pezzini, *L'Intreccio Complesso tra Identità di Genere, Identità Sessuale e Diritto alla Salute nella Chiave della Giurisprudenza Costituzionale*, *in* Identità di Genere e Diritto: Percorsi di Ricerca 185 (Nicola Posteraro, Lucia Busatta & Andrea Magliari eds., 2025).

[69] Corte Cost., 161/1985, ¶ 4 (in diritto).

longing for bodily transformations.[70] Gender recognition, therefore, was predicated on an ascriptive basis and linked to externally ascertainable indicia.[71]

The Court rooted this right in the principles of solidarity, dignity and liberty,[72] and, centrally, in the right to health.[73] Health was given particular importance because it is connected to the transsexual person's quest to achieve well-being by aligning mind and body.[74] The Constitutional Court saw gender recognition as the last step in a process of social and physical transformation towards a happier life. Some scholars welcomed the doctrinal grounding in the right to health because of the high status of such a right in the Italian Constitution.[75] Indeed, this grounding would in theory allow the right to 'sexual identity' to trump conflicting interests—something that, as I will show, however failed to materialize. Yet, this focus on health also defined a right where physical transformation and gender identity were largely coterminous.[76] Arguably, the right to health favoured a medicalized understanding of gender recognition.

As for the threats to the constitutional protection of the heterosexual family feared by the Court of Cassation, the Constitutional Court appeared to align with the government's position. As Roberto Romboli observed, an opinion submitted by the Minister of Justice to the President of the Council of Ministers (the Italian 'prime minister') shortly before the judgment stated that social relations are not disrupted by gender recognition. The Ministry considered that applicants for gender recognition already normally display the appearance and behaviour of the 'other' sex/gender. It thus considered that the certainty of legal relations was maintained by allowing the change of legal sex, rather than by denying it.[77] Along these lines, the Constitutional Court held that ensuring 'the coincidence between the sex recorded in public registries and physical appearance [favours] the clarity of social relations, and, hence, also the certainty of legal relations'.[78] With specific reference to family law, the Court considered that 'the natural order of the family' is not altered by changes of legal sex, but by the 'transsexual syndrome'. The Constitutional Court went on to say that Parliament had simply regulated an existing reality,[79] thus arguably demonstrating a pragmatic approach to the matter. In summary, the

[70] Corte Cost., 161/1985, ¶ 4 (in diritto).

[71] About the notion of 'gender ascription', see Clarke, *supra* note 20, at 757–58.

[72] Art. 2 Cost.

[73] Art. 32 Cost.

[74] Lorenzetti, *supra* note 13, at 35–36.

[75] This was prominently theorized by: Barbara Pezzini, *Transessualismo, Salute, e Identità Sessuale*, Rassegna di Diritto Civile 461 (1984).

[76] For a discussion of the right to health in relation to trans identity, *see* Lorenzetti, *supra* note 13, at 32–36. Lorenzetti also argues that the right to health can be the starting point to rule out those treatments that are not necessary to the well-being of the trans person (*Id.* at 59–61).

[77] Opinion of the Ministry of Justice, 30 Aug. 1983, as cited by Romboli, *supra* note 48, at 265 and 267, footnotes 28 and 33.

[78] Corte Cost., 161/1985, ¶ 10 (in diritto).

[79] Corte Cost., 161/1985, ¶ 12 (in diritto).

Court's judgment can be read as an acknowledgement that trans identity could enter into tension with social relations and the 'natural' family protected by the Constitution. Nevertheless, it also considered that more clarity follows from the recognition of 'transsexual' identity rather than from its denial. In conclusion, it could be argued that, *de facto*, the Court balanced gender recognition with the certainty of legal positions by identifying a specific beneficiary of the right. Although it did not explicitly frame its reasoning in terms of balancing, the public interest at stake was preserved by the fact that the 'transsexual' person possessed certain characteristics. These characteristics will then be read and applied by courts as preconditions for gender recognition. They could be viewed—and indeed will be treated—as limits on the right, intended to preserve competing interests.

2.4. The constitutional entrenchment of the medico-behavioural model

Over time, one specific precondition—surgery to modify primary sex characteristics, which, in practice, amounted to surgical sterilization[80]—began to be perceived as untenable.[81] This perception appeared first at the domestic level. Until 2015, the right to gender recognition was, generally speaking, operationalized consistently.[82] Trans people would lodge their application for recognition before a court after having modified their genitalia and secondary sex characteristics[83] and having acquired the behaviour associated with the claimed sex status.[84] This transition had to be irreversible.[85] Nevertheless, despite this uniformity, the requirement of surgery on genitalia was at times successfully contested, but no generalized rejection thereof was sanctioned.[86] To be sure, trans people seeking recognition were still required to undergo the transformation of secondary sex characteristics, behave according to pre-established gendered standards, and submit to psychological supervision.[87] That said, the principles underlying the law went unchallenged, as these claims were mostly framed as an interpretation of the literal ambiguities

[80] Vecchi, *supra* note 15, at 5; Patti, *supra* note 15, at 423; Bilotta, *supra* note 15, at 760.
[81] For a discussion of the case law of lower courts, *see*: LORENZETTI, *supra* note 13, at 62–65.
[82] For an earlier discussion of the jurisprudence of lower courts, *see* Rubio-Marín & Osella, *supra* note 14.
[83] This chapter does not expand on the authorization that was necessary to proceed to the surgery to modify primary sex characteristics, as first required by Art. 3, L. 164/1982 and subsequently by Art. 31(4), D. Lgs. 150/2011.
[84] Rubio-Marín & Osella, *supra* note14, at 69–70; LORENZETTI, *supra* note 13, at 62–65.
[85] Alberto Venturelli, *Volontarietà e Terapeuticità nel Mutamento dell'Identità Sessuale*, RASSEGNA DI DIRITTO CIVILE 732, 752 (2008).
[86] LORENZETTI, *supra* note 13, at 62.
[87] *Id.* at 62; Francesco Bilotta, *Identità di Genere e Diritti Fondamentali della Persona. Nota sub. Tribunale di Rovereto, 3 maggio 2013*, LA NUOVA GIURISPRUDENZA CIVILE COMMENTATA 1116 (2013). Tribunale [Court of First Instance][Trib.] Rovereto, 25 febbraio 2013, n. 194 (unreported); Trib. Siena, 12 giugno 2013, n. 412 (unreported); Trib. Messina, I sezione civile, 4 novembre 2014 (unreported).

contained in the existing law, and not as a challenge to the deeper principles thereof.[88]

In addition, courts in various European jurisdictions had begun to outlaw compulsory sterilization.[89] At the supranational level, the Commissioner for Human Rights had spoken out against it in 2009.[90] In March 2015, the European Court of Human Rights, albeit in an *obiter dictum* and possibly in ambiguous terms, questioned the conformity of sterilization requirements to Article 8 of the ECHR.[91] A month later, the Parliamentary Assembly of the Council of Europe invited Member States to 'develop quick, transparent and accessible procedures, based on self-determination, for changing the name and registered sex of transgender people' and to abolish 'sterilisation and other compulsory medical treatment, as well as a mental health diagnosis' as preconditions for recognition.[92]

When two cases reached the Court of Cassation and the Constitutional Court in 2015, the time was ripe.[93] In July 2015, the Court of Cassation granted the claim of a trans woman who, for medical reasons, could not undergo surgery to modify her primary sex characteristics.[94] It ruled that the 'modifications of sex characteristics' required by Law 164 of 1982 did not include surgical sterilization. Reading such a requirement into the law, the Court of Cassation reasoned, would disproportionately limit the right to gender recognition,[95] interpreted in light of the jurisprudence of the ECtHR.[96]

[88] Art. 3, L. 164/1985 specifies that individuals should apply for judicial authorization to undergo gender reassignment surgery on their primary sex characteristics 'when necessary'. Since it was framed as 'when necessary', this led some applicants to argue that gender confirmation surgery was not necessary in all cases. *See*, Bilotta, *supra* note 87, at 1120. Furthermore, it was stressed that, even though Art. 1, L. 164/82 demands 'modifications' of sex characteristics, it does not specify the kind of intervention that is required. PAOLO VERONESI, IL CORPO E LA COSTITUZIONE 71–74 (2007).

[89] BVerfG, 10 Oct. 2017, 1 BvR 3295/07 (Germany); VwGH, 27 Jan. 2009, n. 2008/17/0054 (Austria); VfGH, 3 Dec. 2009, 1973/08-13 (Austria); Stockholm Administrative Court of Appeals, Case No. 1968–12, 19 Dec. 2012 (Sweden).

[90] Commissioner for Human Rights of the Council of Europe, Human Rights and Gender Identity, CommDH/IssuePaper (2009) (29 July 2009).

[91] Y.Y. v. Turkey, App. No. 14793/08 (10 Mar. 2015), https://hudoc.echr.coe.int/eng?i=001-153134.

[92] Parliamentary Assembly of the Council of Europe, *supra* note 4. These developments would lead the ECtHR to find sterilization in violation of the ECHR: A.P., Garçon, and Nicot v. France, Apps. No. 79885/12, 52471/13, and 52596/13 (6 Apr. 2017), https://hudoc.echr.coe.int/eng?i=001-172913.

[93] For an earlier discussion, *see* Rubio-Marín & Osella, *supra* note 14. *See* also Chiara Angiolini, *Transessualismo e Identità di Genere. La Rettificazione del Sesso tra Diritti della Persona e Interesse Pubblico*, (1) EUROPA E DIRITTO PRIVATO 263 (2017) (offering a detailed reconstruction of the cases); Stefano Osella & Ruth Rubio-Marín, *Gender Recognition at the Crossroads: Four Models and the Compass of Comparative Law*, 21 INTERNATIONAL JOURNAL OF CONSTITUTIONAL LAW 574, 583 (2023) (for a comparative analysis).

[94] Cass., 15138/2015.

[95] Cass., 15138/2015, 28–36.

[96] Cass., 15138/2015, 21 (stating that the legal principles at stake must be interpreted in conformity with the Constitution and the ECHR, as defined by the jurisprudence 'of Strasbourg') and 25 (Y.Y. v. Turkey, App. No. 14793/08, ¶ 119 (10 Mar. 2015), https://hudoc.echr.coe.int/eng?i=001-153 134). References to Art. 8 ECHR are disseminated throughout the judgment.

Tensions are evident in this decision. On the one hand, the Court stated that medical treatments should serve the well-being of the person.[97] This could be read as an opening to autonomy and self-determination. Indeed, only the individual can ultimately determine their own well-being and, therefore, whether any medical treatment is needed. On the other hand, the Court of Cassation repeatedly emphasized that legal recognition can only follow a medically supervised transition, including the transformation of (secondary) sex characteristics.[98] The Court acknowledged that preserving a clear distinction between the two sexes—in other words, the clear preservation of the binary—does not require surgery on primary sexual characteristics. It does, however, require—as the Court emphasized—a medical transition (mainly concerning secondary characteristics) and psychological supervision.[99] Furthermore, the Court of Cassation arguably considered that bodily modifications ensure the 'seriousness' and 'irreversibility' of the transformation, which must be ascertained by a court for the purposes of amending the sex legal status.[100] Finally, the Court of Cassation pointed out that the specific trans applicant was virtually sterile because of her protracted hormone therapy and that she looked and behaved in a feminine manner. Therefore, the Court granted recognition.

In November 2015, the Constitutional Court adjudicated a similar case and endorsed the July 2015 decision by the Court of Cassation.[101] On the one hand, the Constitutional Court emphasized the duty of solidarity enshrined in Article 2 of the Constitution, and confirmed gender recognition as a fundamental right. On the other hand, it balanced the fundamental rights to personal identity[102] and health,[103] on which the right to gender recognition is based, with the principle of certainty of legal relations.[104] While it established that surgical sterilization cannot be a requirement for recognition, it also established that a complete transformation of the 'psychological, behavioural and physical' characteristics is necessary to preserve the constitutional principles at stake.[105] With two judgments released in June 2017, the Constitutional Court reaffirmed its stance. In both decisions, the Constitutional Court ruled that surgery on primary sex characteristics was no

[97] Cass., 15138/2015, 31–33, where the Court emphasizes that the endpoint of medical treatments must be determined by the trans person. For a discussion of this concept (prior to the decision, *nota bene*): LORENZETTI, *supra* note 13, at 59–61.

[98] Cass., 15138/2015, 29. For a critique: Salvatore Patti, *Trattamenti Medico-Chirurgici e Autodeterminazione della Persona Transessuale. A Proposito di Cass., 20.7.2015, n. 15138*, (11) NUOVA GIURISPRUDENZA CIVILE COMMENTATA 643, 648–50 (2015); Rubio-Marín & Osella, *supra* note 14.

[99] Cass., 15138/2015, 34–35.

[100] Cass., 15138/2015, 35.

[101] Corte Cost., 221/2015, ¶ 4.1 (in diritto).

[102] Art. 2 COST. and Art. 8 ECHR.

[103] Art. 32 COST.

[104] Corte Cost., 221/2015, ¶ 4.1 (in diritto).

[105] Corte Cost., 221/2015, ¶ 4.1 (in diritto).

longer required. At the same time, it underlined the importance of ascertaining the 'objective' and 'univocal' transition.[106]

In summary, Italian top courts have answered a central need of trans people, who no longer need to undergo surgical sterilization to obtain recognition. In so doing, they have confirmed that gender recognition is a fundamental right and that trans people deserve protection. They have also affirmed the value of diversity. For this reason, several scholars have positively welcomed these developments.[107] At the same time, however, the courts have defined the beneficiary of the right as the medicalized transsexual binary person. Courts have endeavoured to maintain two mutually exclusive legal sexes to guarantee the certainty of legal relations, specifically, the stability of the heterosexual family ('as a natural institution'),[108] the 'continuation of the species',[109] 'natural' marriages,[110] the 'natural order of the family',[111] and the existing system of family law.[112]

2.5. Rejecting nonbinary recognition and affirming the centrality of the binary to the constitutional gender order

The Constitutional Court's willingness to protect the binary, while arguably visible in the 2015 decision, became even more apparent in *ordinanza* 185 of 2017.[113] In this ruling, the Constitutional Court rejected a preliminary reference with which a court of first instance had questioned the constitutionality of the decision to remove the sterilization requirement.[114] The referring court of first instance worried that the possibility of recognition without sterilization could be the first step on a slippery slope that would eventually lead to forms of gender self-determination. This, in turn, was seen as a threat to the 'right of society' (*consociati*) to preserve the male-female binary. Any deviations from the binary, the referring court argued, would clash with a 'centuries-old' Italian tradition.[115] The referring court of

[106] Corte Cost., ord. 13 luglio 2017, n. 180; Corte Cost., ord. 13 luglio 2017, n. 185. For a comment: Anna Lorenzetti, *Il Cambiamento di Sesso Secondo la Corte Costituzionale: Due Nuove Pronunce (180 e 185 del 2017)*, STUDIUM IURIS 446 (2018).

[107] Angiolini, *supra* note 93; Patti, *supra* note 98; LORENZO BERNINI, LE TEORIE QUEER. UN'INTRODUZIONE 101 (2017).

[108] Corte Cost., 98/1979, ¶ 2 (in diritto).

[109] Voli, *supra* note 28, at 101.

[110] Cass., ord. 783/1983.

[111] Corte Cost., 161/1985, ¶ 12 (in diritto).

[112] Cass., 15138/2015.

[113] This comment on Corte Cost., ord. 185/2017 draws on: Stefano Osella, *When Comparative Law Walks the Path of Anthropology: The Third Gender in Europe*, 23 GERMAN LAW JOURNAL 920, 932 (2022).

[114] Trib. Avezzano, ord. 12 gennaio 2017, (17) GAZZETTA UFFICIALE (SERIE SPECIALE) (2017), https://www.gazzettaufficiale.it/atto/corte_costituzionale/caricaDettaglioAtto/originario?atto.dataPubblicazioneGazzetta=2017-04-26&atto.codiceRedazionale=17C00099.

[115] Anthropological research has documented long-present nonbinary identities in Italy: MARIA CAROLINA VESCE, ALTRI TRANSITI. CORPI, PRATICHE, RAPPRESENTAZIONI DI FEMMINIELLI E TRANSESSUALI (2017) (discussing the case of *femminielli* from Naples).

first instance also lamented the risks in segregated spaces and police searches. The judge, vividly enough, referred to 'the beach', where trans people (obviously trans women) might wear 'a typically female swimsuit' and where 'the primary sex characteristics present from birth would become clearly and visibly prominent', with 'minors' experiencing 'difficulties in coping' (with the view, apparently).[116]

The Court rejected the preliminary reference with an ordinance of *manifesta inammissibilità* (clear inadmissibility)—a choice that, it has been argued, suggested that the Court found no merit in the question raised by the referring court.[117] The Constitutional Court further bolstered its decision by considering that the right to gender recognition as devised by the Constitutional Court and the Court of Cassation was already a strong enough instrument to avoid the concerns of the referring court of first instance—or, in other words, to preserve the binary. The Court wrote that

> The interpretation adopted [in the 2015 decisions] gives adequate weight to the needs highlighted by the referring court, especially in acknowledging that, under Law 164 of 1982, [the right to gender recognition] is granted through a judicial procedure that simultaneously safeguards both the right of the person and the public interest in preserving the certainty of legal relations.[118]

While not endorsing it, the Constitutional Court did not explicitly push back on the more claimed-than-demonstrated 'centuries-old tradition' discourse. This silence might be interpreted as confirmation that tradition could be a valid reason to limit gender recognition. To its credit, the Court did push back on the most imaginative aspects of the preliminary reference—clarifying, for instance, that the awkward situations envisioned by the referring Court had nothing to do with gender recognition and that, at any rate, solidarity and protection of minorities, regardless of how different they are, is a constitutional duty.

This entrenchment became more explicit in decision 143 of 2024. The case concerned whether Article 1 of Law 164 of 1982, which does not contemplate nonbinary recognition, conformed to the Constitution.[119] The Court declined

[116] Trib. Avezzano, ord. 12 gennaio 2017.

[117] Federico Mannella, *Sulla Tecnica Decisoria Adottata dalla Corte Costituzionale in Occasione di Due Recenti Pronunce in Tema di Rettificazione di Attribuzione di Sesso*, GIURISPRUDENZA COSTITUZIONALE 1680, 1689 (2017).

[118] Corte Cost., 185/2017.

[119] For a comment on the decision: Anastasia Granato, *Corte e Legislatore di Fronte al Riconoscimento delle Identità non Binarie: Una Lettura in Parallasse. Nota a Corte Costituzionale, sentenza n. 143 del 2024*, OSSERVATORIO AIC (2025) https://www.osservatorioaic.it/it/osservatorio/ultimi-contributi-pubblicati/anastasia-granato/corte-e-legislatore-di-fronte-al-riconoscimento-delle-identita-non-binarie-una-lettura-in-parallasse-nota-corte-costituzionale-sentenza-n-143-del-2024; Giulio Farronato & Giacomo Giorgini Pignatiello, *La Sentenza n. 143 del 2024 della Corte Costituzionale Italiana nel Prisma del Diritto Comparato ed Internazionale*, SUL NON-BINARISMO DI GENERE E SULL'AUTORIZZAZIONE GIUDIZIARIA A EFFETTUARE GLI INTERVENTI CHIRURGICI DI AFFERMAZIONE DI GENERE. LA SENTENZA 143 DEL 2024 127 (Nicola Posteraro & Benedetta Liberali eds., 2025).

jurisdiction and deferred to Parliament. In fairness, the Court reaffirmed the most progressive aspects of its own jurisprudence, such as the protection of diversity and well-being, as well as the duty of all consociates to support individual identities.[120] It acknowledged the constitutional ramifications of nonbinary recognition,[121] recalling the 2017 decision of the German Federal Constitutional Court and the 2019 decision of the Belgian Constitutional Court.[122] The Court further conceded that misrecognition of nonbinary identity could generate 'significant discomfort' and thus present constitutional questions, given the pre-eminence of the protection of the individual under the Italian constitution. Furthermore, when misrecognition generates 'differential treatment' or 'undermine[s] the psycho-physical well-being', the Court stated that it may 'raise an issue' in relation to the rights of equality and health.[123]

On the other hand, no constitutional violation was found. The Constitutional Court underlined the importance of objectivity and the seriousness of the applicant's intention,[124] and adopted a medicalized understanding of nonbinary identity, making explicit reference to the DSM5, the diagnostic manual of the American Psychiatric Association.[125] The Court also cited the 2023 decision of the ECtHR in *Y v France* to underline the lack of consensus on nonbinary recognition. Finally, it recalled that the gender binary is central to areas of constitutional status, such as:

> family law (as marriage and civil unions are reserved respectively to people of different and same sex), labour law (affirmative actions to support women workers), sport law (to differentiate between competition categories), and the right to intimacy (places where human contact may develop, such as prisons or hospitals, are normally gender segregated).[126]

[120] Corte Cost., 143/2024, ¶¶ 4.2–4.4 (in diritto).
[121] Corte Cost., 143/2024, ¶ 5 (in diritto).
[122] Corte Cost., 143/2024, ¶ 5.2 (in diritto).
[123] Corte Cost., 143/2024, ¶ 5.4 (in diritto); Arts. 3 and 32 Cost.
[124] Corte Cost., 143/2024, ¶ 4.4 (in diritto).
[125] Corte Cost., 143/2024, ¶ 5.1 (in diritto). Note that decision 143 of 2024 does not break with its pathologizing attitude to trans and nonbinary identities: Miriana Chiricò, *Patologizzazione delle Persone Trans+: Unica Via per il Loro Riconoscimento Giuridico?*, *in* Sul Non-Binarismo di Genere e sull'Autorizzazione Giudiziaria a Effettuare gli Interventi Chirurgici di Affermazione di Genere. La Sentenza 143 del 2024 95, 104–05 (Nicola Posteraro & Benedetta Liberali eds., 2025).
[126] Corte Cost., 143/2024, ¶ 5.5 (in diritto). The Court added that rules concerning names would have to be adapted, too. Italian law requires consistency between name and legal sex (Art. 35.1., DPR 396/2000) and, in Italian, gender-neutral names are exceedingly rare. The reference to the jurisprudence of the European Court of Human Rights is at: Corte Cost., 143/2024, ¶ 5.3 (in diritto). For a reflection on the constitutional implications of nonbinary recognition: Benedetta Liberali, *Alla Ricerca del Fondamento Costituzionale dell'Identità di Genere: il Transessualismo e il Non Binarismo fra Diritto alla Salute, Dignità Umana e Identità personale*, 3 BioLaw Journal (2024) https://teseo.unitn.it/biolaw/article/view/3179; Giacomo Mingardo, *Il Riconoscimento delle Nuove Soggettività e il Limite del Binarismo di Genere nella Prospettiva Costituzionale*, GenIUS 11–14 (online first, 19 Sept. 2024), https://www.geniusreview.eu/2024/il-riconoscimento-delle-nuove-soggettivita-e-il-limite-del-binarismo-di-genere-nella-prospettiva-costituzionale/; Pezzini, *Costruzione del Genere e Costituzione*, *supra*

In short, the Court seemed to signal that legislation recognizing nonbinary identity could be constitutional under certain circumstances, but it went out of its way to draw clear boundaries around nonbinary recognition, ensuring its medicalization and 'seriousness'.

2.6. The effects of gender recognition on family life

The conflict between constitutional heteronormativity and gender recognition is also apparent in the consequences on the marriage or civil union of the applicant. The pre-existing heterosexual marriage of the applicant that becomes same-sex following gender recognition can either be transformed into a civil union or terminated through divorce. Up until 2024, civil unions, which are reserved for same-sex couples, were automatically and immediately dissolved upon the gender recognition of one of the partners.[127] In April 2024, following a decision of the Constitutional Court, civil unions are allowed to persist for a limited time—just enough to allow the partners in the civil union to take care of all formalities and marry.

Before the introduction of the law on civil unions,[128] married trans people would see their marriage terminated with an 'automatic divorce'.[129] Based on the judgment that granted recognition, the registrar would mark the marriage as terminated in the civil registry without requiring a separate application.[130] This represented an exception in the Italian context, where divorce normally requires an application from the person. Despite lively scholarly debate, the consensus was that this form of 'automatic' divorce was needed.[131] If trans people had to seek a divorce through a separate procedure, this would occur at some indefinite point in the future. Possibly, it may not occur at all. Either way, the now-same-sex couple would be married, a situation that would conflict with the heterosexual monopoly on marriage.[132] As the Court of Cassation stated, this automatic divorce clause confirmed that Law 164 of 1982 is 'entirely aimed' at balancing the right to gender recognition with the 'existing' (read 'heterosexual') forms of family law.[133]

note 24; Barbara Pezzini, *Il Binarismo di Genere come Problema di Bio-diritto*, BioLaw Journal 59 (2023), https://teseo.unitn.it/biolaw/article/view/2618.

[127] Arts. 1(26) and 27, L. 76/2016.

[128] L. 76/2016.

[129] Art. 4, L. 164/1982; now: Art. 31 (6), D. lgs. 150/2011.

[130] This practice was made official by the guidelines of the Ministry of Interiors, Massimario per l'Ufficiale dello Stato Civile—Guida all'Applicazione, ¶ 11.5 (2011) http://www.articolo29.it/2393-2/.

[131] For a summary: Marco Gattuso, *Matrimonio, Identità e Dignità Personale: Il Caso del Mutamento di Sesso di Uno dei Coniugi*, Diritto di Famiglia e delle Persone 1076 (2012).

[132] Cesare Massimo Bianca, La Famiglia 272 (2005).

[133] Cass., ord. 6 giugno 2013, n. 14329, 20, http://www.articolo29.it/cassazione-ordinanza-n-14329-del-2013.

The automatic divorce clause was, however, challenged by a couple, composed of a cis woman and a trans woman, who had married before the transition of one of the spouses and did not intend to divorce. After varying results before lower courts, the case was referred to the Constitutional Court by the Court of Cassation.[134] The Constitutional Court found it that the 'automatic divorce' clause violated the general protection of fundamental rights of the person, as the applicants represented a 'social formation' (*formazione sociale*) through which human personality is expressed.[135] The characteristics of the relationship of the applicants, which the Court deemed to be different from those of an unwed same-sex couple intending to marry, were decisive in this case. They had already been married, developed reciprocal rights and duties, and had a previous family life.[136] From this point of view, the case could be seen as a reinforcement of the rights of gender-diverse people.

However, the Constitutional Court denied the applicants the right to preserve their marital union and stressed that their relationship *could not* continue as a marriage.[137] For good measure, the Court also ruled that the couple enjoyed neither the constitutional protection granted to family life and marriage,[138] in which heterosexuality is an 'essential component',[139] nor the ECHR rights to marry[140] and to privacy and family life,[141] as a European consensus on same-sex marriage is lacking.[142] Ultimately, the Court deferred to Parliament, which was invited to provide some form of recognition.[143]

When the case was resumed by the couple before the Court of Cassation to apply the Constitutional Court's ruling to the specific controversy, the Court of Cassation held that it could not simply declare the spouses' divorce to be automatic.[144] Instead, it determined that their marriage would remain valid until the legislature granted some legal recognition to same-sex couples—a step it ultimately took with the enactment of Law 76 of 2016, which legalized same-sex unions in Italy. For a brief moment, then, the Court of Cassation had effectively created a 'temporary' same-sex marriage within the legal order. Leaving aside the creativity

[134] Trib. Modena, 27 ottobre 2010 (unreported); App. Bologna, 18 maggio 2011 (unreported); Cass., 14329/2013.

[135] Corte Cost., 170/2014, ¶ 5.5 (in diritto); *see* Art. 2 Cost. For a comment: Antonio D'Aloia, *Lo Scioglimento del Matrimonio del Transessuale: Una Incostituzionalità per «Mancanza di Alternative»*, Quaderni Costituzionali 672 (2014); Roberto Romboli, *La Legittimità Costituzionale del 'Divorzio Imposto': Quando la Corte Dialoga con il Legislatore, ma Dimentica il Giudice*, Il Foro Italiano 2680 (2014).

[136] Corte Cost., 170/2014, ¶ 5.1 (in diritto).

[137] Corte Cost., 170/2014, ¶ 5.1 (in diritto).

[138] Art. 29 Cost.

[139] Corte Cost., 170/2014, ¶ 5.1 (in diritto).

[140] Art. 12 ECHR.

[141] Art. 8 ECHR.

[142] Corte Cost., 170/2014, ¶ 5.3 (in diritto).

[143] Corte Cost., 170/2014, ¶ 5.5 (in diritto).

[144] Cass., I sez., 21 aprile 2015, n. 8095, https://www.articolo29.it/2015/vittoria-delle-alessandre-donne-restano-sposate-sino-allentrata-in-vigore-legge-sulle-unioni-civili/. For a comment, refer to the Special Issue 1 of 2015 volume of the Journal 'Genius', https://www.geniusreview.eu/2015/06/.

of the remedy (and arguably its brilliance in a context where the legislature was largely inert), the case once again confirmed the close connection between gender recognition and same-sex marriage.

This connection between gender recognition and heteronormativity was arguably confirmed in a 2024 decision, where the Constitutional Court decided on the consequences of gender recognition of one of the partners of a same-sex civil union.[145] At stake in this case was the heterosexuality of marriage, albeit in disguise. A different-sex civil union—which follows the gender recognition of one of the originally same-sex partners—would threaten the separate(-and-unequal) system of family law entrenched in Italian constitutional law, and, by implication, the heterosexuality of marriage. From an empirical perspective, it might also be interesting to notice, as Jens Scherpe did, that equality in civil unions might eventually lead to equality in marriage, as has happened in comparable situations in other countries.[146]

The plaintiff in the case referred to the Constitutional Court was a trans person seeking recognition. They were in a same-sex civil union with their partner and lamented the lack of protection following the automatic dissolution of their family status. Indeed, between the time of the decision granting gender recognition and the moment when the couple could celebrate a (then-heterosexual) marriage, the plaintiff and their partner would not have been in any legally recognized relationship. The plaintiff claimed that this legal void violated their right to live as a couple with their partner.[147] Furthermore, they complained of a violation of their right to equality, given the different treatment vis-à-vis married couples when one of the spouses transitions.[148]

The Court ruled that the Constitution protects same-sex couples. It also held that the applicant could not be forced to choose between their identity and their family.[149] However, the Court found no discrimination vis-à-vis married people and considered the two institutions—same-sex unions and heterosexual marriage—as not comparable.[150] For the same reason, the Constitutional Court wrote that the remedy *could not* be to extend the protection enjoyed by married couples to couples in civil unions. Instead, the constitutional judges envisioned the possibility of suspending the effects of gender recognition on civil unions until

[145] Corte Cost., 22 febbraio 2024, n. 66. For a comment: Giacomo Mingardo, *Affermazione di Genere e Scioglimento Imposto dell'Unione Civile. Nota a Corte Cost., Sentenza n. 66 del 2024*, OSSERVATORIO AIC (5 Nov. 2024) https://www.osservatorioaic.it/images/rivista/pdf/2024_6_04_Mingardo.pdf; Giuseppe Ugo Rescigno, *Sul Passaggio da Matrimonio a Unione Civile e da Unione Civile a Matrimonio a Causa di Mutamento di Sesso*, 67 GIURISPRUDENZA COSTITUZIONALE 2953 (2022).

[146] Jens Scherpe, *The Past, Present and Future of Registered Partnerships*, *in* THE FUTURE OF REGISTERED PARTNERSHIPS: FAMILY RECOGNITION BEYOND MARRIAGE? 561, 573 (Andy Hayward & Jens Scherpe eds., 2017).

[147] Art. 2 COST.

[148] Art. 3 COST.

[149] Corte Cost., 66/2024, ¶ 4.3 (in diritto).

[150] Corte Cost., 66/2024, ¶ 3 (in diritto).

marriage can be celebrated. To prevent the indefinite duration of a different-sex civil union, the Court granted a fixed term for the partners to marry.[151]

3. 'Physical, behavioural, and psychological transformations' in practice: The normalization of a subject of recognition

As suggested by Marcasciano, while allowing for the possibility of changing legal sex on certain preconditions, the right to gender recognition in the Italian context actually forces the gender binary on trans applicants.[152] Anthropologists Simona Grilli and Maria Carolina Vesce have pointed out that courts still require individuals to narrate themselves according to established binary and stereotyped patterns.[153] Both the Court of Cassation and the Constitutional Court have indeed laid down standards for gender recognition that enforce a specific understanding

[151] Corte Cost., 66/2024, ¶¶ 4.5–4.6 (in diritto).

[152] Section 3 is based on the examination of sixty-nine decisions. These were all the decisions that I could find on *dejure.it* or, when specified, *leggiditaliaprofessionale.it* (henceforth, LI). Nota bene: more decisions may have been added to the databases since my last access (Aug. 2024). The decisions reported here do not represent the entirety of the cases on gender recognition in Italy, but rather a subset. Nevertheless, they still are helpful to illustrate the application of the doctrine of the Constitutional Court by lower courts. The decisions are: Trib. Padova, 17 giugno 2024 (LI); Trib. Padova, Sez I, 23 maggio 2024 (LI); Trib. Ferrara, 20 maggio 2024 (LI); Trib. Torino, 27 marzo 2024 (LI); Trib. Pavia, 1 marzo 2024 (LI); Trib. Trieste, 13 febbraio 2024 (LI); Trib. Cuneo, 23 febbraio 2024 (LI); Trib. Ascoli Piceno, 16 gennaio 2024 (LI); Trib. Pisa, 17 Ottobre 2023, Sez. Civile (LI); Trib. Novara, 9 settembre 2023; Trib. Milano, 26 April 2023 (LI); Trib. Milano, 24 Aprile 2023 (LI); Trib. Santa Maria Capua Vetere, 26 luglio 2023 (LI); Trib. Roma, 24 luglio 2023 (LI); Trib. Messina, 3 gennaio 2023; Trib. Benevento, 10 novembre 2022 (LI); Trib. Santa Maria Capua Vetere, Sez. I, 27 ottobre 2022 (LI); Trib. Torino, 15 settembre 2022 (LI); Trib. Savona, 4 maggio 2021 (LI); Trib. Civitavecchia, 8 febbraio 2022 (LI); Trib. Rimini, 21 gennaio 2022 (LI); Trib. Agrigento, 12 gennaio 2021 (LI); Trib. Monza, 4 gennaio 2021 (LI); Trib. Genova, 15 dicembre 2020, n. 2112; Trib. Perugia, 21 settembre 2020, n. 994; Trib. Vicenza, 7 agosto 2020, n. 1342; Trib. Vicenza, 26 giugno 2020 (LI); Trib. Civitavecchia, 25 giugno 2020, n. 540; Trib. Busto Arsizio, 11 marzo 2020 (LI); Trib. Milano, 17 febbraio 2020, n. 1479; Trib. Pavia, 8 gennaio 2020, n. 13; Trib. Milano, 5 dicembre 2019, n. 11278; Trib. Milano, 11 luglio 2019, n. 6914; Trib. Milano, 10 maggio 2019, n. 4538; Trib. Torino, 7 maggio 2019, n. 2156; Trib. Milano, 6 marzo 2019, n. 2295; Trib. Milano, 1 marzo 2019, n. 2081; Trib. Milano, 1 marzo 2019, n. 2072; Trib. Milano, 13 febbraio 2019, n. 1431; Trib. Bari, 7 febbraio 2019, n. 585; Trib. Lamezia Terme, 29 gennaio 2019 (LI); Trib. Trani, 6 dicembre 2018, n. 2461; Trib. Novara, 27 novembre 2018, n. 1087; Trib. Frosinone, 19 luglio 2018 (LI); Trib. Nola, 4 maggio 2018 (LI); App. Torino, 28 marzo 2018, n. 569; Trib. Perugia, 23 gennaio 2018, n. 116 (unreported, on file with author); Trib. Pavia, 16 gennaio 2018; Trib. Trento, 29 settembre 2017; Trib. Roma, 4 agosto 2017, n. 15902; Trib. Prato, 11 luglio 2017, n. 2; Trib. Roma, 5 luglio 2017, n. 13618; Trib. Roma, 7 giugno 2017, n. 80; Trib. Genova, 23 maggio 2017 (LI); Trib. Bari, 22 maggio 2017, n. 2642; Trib. Pordenone, 18 maggio 2017; Trib. Santa Maria Capua Vetere, 12 maggio 2017, n. 1617; Trib. Reggio Emilia, 27 aprile 2017, n. 435; Trib. Roma, 13 aprile 2017, n. 7518; Trib. Mantova, 21 aprile 2017; Trib. Roma, 4 aprile 2017, n. 6734; Trib. Pistoia, 9 febbraio 2017, n. 133; Trib. Bari, 11 ottobre 2016, n. 5079; Trib. Vicenza, 4 ottobre 2016 (LI); Trib. Bari, 27 settempre 2016, n. 4801 (unreported, on file with author); Trib. Reggio Emilia, 27 luglio 2016 (LI); Trib. Foggia, 6 luglio 2016 (LI); Trib. Genova, 20 giugno 2016; Trib. Bari 10 maggio 2016, n. 1335; Trib. Bari, 14 dicembre 2015, n. 5467. For a further analysis of the jurisprudence of the lower courts: Mingardo, *supra* note 17.

[153] Simonetta Grilli & Maria Carolina Vesce, *Genitalia Out of Scope. Riflessioni Intorno a Pratiche di Cura e Cittadinanza Trans nelle Sentenze di Rettifica e di Attribuzione di Sesso*, DADA—RIVISTA DI ANTROPOLOGIA POST-GLOBALE 91 (2020).

of trans identity and define a sexed subject: a binary, medicalized, 'transsexual person'. The abundant case law that assesses the 'physical, behavioural, and psychological' transformations achieved by the applicants shows how this subject is 'shaped' in practice.

The analysis of the case law indicates that the requirement that applicants for gender recognition must undergo 'psychological, behavioural, and physical' transformations makes courts more likely to impose gender norms on individual applicants through a mechanism showing the characteristics of 'disciplinary power'.[154] This notion, which is central to the thinking of Michel Foucault, refers to a special type of power that constructs and defines subjectivities. Disciplinary power impacts individual bodies and 'moulds [them] into useful components of larger social machines'.[155] Individuals are turned into useful subjects to serve a more general purpose: a good soldier in the army, a good worker on the factory floor, etc. The notion of disciplinary power has been frequently invoked in the field of gender studies to explain how standards are imposed on cis men and women as well as on trans people in different social and medical settings.[156]

Disciplinary power is commonly schematized as consisting of three central components, all of which can be traced in the application of the Italian courts' doctrine of gender recognition: hierarchical observation or surveillance; examination through norms; and a system of penalties and rewards.[157] In the cases examined here, the courts (i) engage in a hierarchical observation or surveillance of the trans applicant and (ii) minutely examine their compliance with standards or norms. (iii) Finally, the application can either be welcomed (and thus the compliance with the norms rewarded) or rejected (hence subjected to a micro-penalty).[158]

It should be noted that I did not encounter any cases where gender recognition was denied.[159] This does not, however, undermine the analysis. Indeed, failing to achieve the transformation required by the doctrine of the Court of Cassation and Constitutional Court is grounds for denying the application.[160] It should also

[154] Michel Foucault, Discipline and Punish. The Birth of the Prison (Alan Sheridan trans., 1977); Foucault, *supra* note 26, at 135–39.

[155] Devonya D. Havis, *Discipline*, *in* The Cambridge Foucault Lexicon 110 (Leonard Lawlor & John Nale eds., 2014).

[156] Sandra L. Bartky, *Foucault, Femininity, and the Modernization of Patriarchal Power*, *in* The Politics of Women's Bodies. Sexuality, Appearance, and Behaviour (4th ed., Rose Weitz & Samanthan Kwan eds., 2013); Ellen K. Feder, Family Bonds. Genealogies of Race and Gender (2007); Dean Spade, *Mutilating Gender*, *in* The Transgender Studies Reader (Susan Stryker & Stephen Whittle eds., 2006).

[157] Foucault, *supra* note 154, at 170–94. For a systematization: Alan Hunt & Gary Wickham, Foucault and Law: Towards a Sociology of Law as Governance 20–22 (1994); Hubert L. Dreyfus & Paul Rabinow, Michel Foucault. Beyond Structuralism and Hermeneutics 153–60 (2d ed. 1983); Havis, *supra* note 155.

[158] Hunt & Wickham, *supra* note 157, at 21.

[159] Mingardo (*supra* note 17, at 94) points out that we cannot find cases where secondary sex characteristics have not been modified, at least through hormonal treatments.

[160] Mingardo (*supra* note 17, at 94) argues that the lack of decisions denying recognition for the failure of the applicant to meet the requirement of the transformation of secondary sex characteristics does not allow to reach a definitive conclusion concerning the necessity of such transformations.

be clarified that there is no reason why disciplinary power cannot be articulated in legal terms and exerted through judicial institutions.[161] Normalization can also occur through the implementation of rights, which, while expanding the entitlements of individuals, may also constrain them within predetermined notions of subjecthood.[162]

3.1. Hierarchical observation

First, the applicant faces a number of different authorities, in whose hands lies the power to determine whether they are 'fit' for recognition. In fairness, it should be specified that courts oftentimes express a sympathetic attitude towards trans applicants, and hardly appear to be hostile to them. Nevertheless, the power balance is skewed in favour of the court that is called on to assess the application, with the applicant undergoing the examination.[163] The judge is assisted in their decision-making by one or more health professionals, who are also arguably in a hierarchically ascendant position vis-à-vis the applicant.[164] These professionals might *de facto* have the power to terminate medical transition, and thereby to stop, delay or re-initiate the process of legal recognition. The opinion of health professionals is decisive, and it would be reasonable to regard them as the gatekeepers of the procedure.

3.2. Assessing through (fussy and stereotyped) norms

The control is exercised by courts through the application of '"standards" that the subject of a discipline must internalize or manifest in behaviour'.[165] On the basis of such norms, individuals are examined and moulded into precise shapes.[166] It has been argued that gender is primarily a network of norms of intelligibility, an approach that articulates well with Foucauldian philosophy. Bartky, for example,

[161] François Ewald, *Norms, Discipline, and the Law*, 30 Representations 138, 138–39 (1990).

[162] Golder, *supra* note 27, at 89–113.

[163] Trans applicants should not be viewed as victims of the system. They are capable of adopting strategic narratives that influence the power dynamics between the applicant and the examiner. Zowie Davy, *Transsexual Agent: Negotiating Authenticity and Embodiment Within the UK's Medicolegal System*, *in* Transgender Identities: Towards a Social Analysis of Gender Diversity (Sally Hines & Tam Sanger eds., 2010); Tamar Klein, *Technologies of Trans* Citizen Configuration: The Case of South Africa, Max Planck Institute for Social Anthropology* Working Paper 119/2009 (2009), https://www.eth.mpg.de/pubs/wps/pdf/mpi-eth-working-paper-0119.

[164] Spade, *supra* note 156; Stefania Voli, Modificazioni Corporee e Cittadinanza Transgender. Il Caso del Movimento Identità Transessuale (MIT) di Bologna (University of Milano-Bicocca, 2016) https://boa.unimib.it/handle/10281/111649.

[165] Alan Hunt, *Foucault's Expulsion of Law: Towards a Retrieval*, 17 Law and Social Inquiry 1, 21 (1992).

[166] Havis, *supra* note 155, at 110–11.

has shown how femininity is pressed on women through an attentive and minute breakdown of norms establishing body shape, gestures, and ornamental standards.[167] Similarly, Feder has discussed how masculinity can be imprinted on boys through the 'courtyard tribunal' in the school setting.[168] Spade has argued how specific personal feelings of being 'trapped in the wrong body' are expected from and imposed on trans people seeking sex/gender confirmation treatments.[169]

A similar attitude can be identified among Italian courts when they apply the doctrine established by the Constitutional Court and the Court of Cassation. These decisions vary in length, intrusiveness, and the degree of detail of the examination of the applicant. For this reason, the analysis presented here paints a general picture. It should also be noted that courts often recall the progressive statements of the Court of Cassation and of the Constitutional Court. Nevertheless, a fussy, detailed, and careful application of norms is found in virtually all cases. First, courts must assess whether the application is 'serious' and the transition 'irreversible'. Applicants who have undergone a long and complex medical process are often considered 'serious'.[170] 'Serious' also implies stable identification in a binary sex/gender,[171] perhaps since childhood[172] (as manifested in the preferences of toys, for example).[173] Seriousness and medicalization relate to irreversibility. For example, several courts have accepted as proof only bodily transformations that are unlikely to be reversed, such as modifications in physical appearance[174] or the loss of reproductive capacity.[175]

A similar attentiveness can be detected in the search for psychological, physical, and behavioural transformations. As to the examination of the *psychological transformation*, courts may consider psychiatric or psychological reports. Invariably, they have positively valued a diagnosis of gender dysphoria.[176] In some cases, courts have been swayed by findings that exclude the presence of mental illness (presumably an indication that the applicant is of sound mind).[177]

[167] Bartky, *supra* note 156, at 97–98.
[168] FEDER, *supra* note 156, at 45–68.
[169] Spade, *supra* note 156.
[170] The association between medicalization and 'seriousness' can be discerned in all cases in this study, *e.g.* is evident in: Trib. Pavia, 16 gennaio 2018 and, especially, Trib. Bari, 22 maggio 2017 (where medical treatments ensure that the applicant is not simply 'noncomformist').
[171] In all cases under study, the applicant was binary in their identification.
[172] *E.g.*: Trib. Trieste, 13 febbraio 2024 (LI); Trib. Ascoli Piceno, 16 gennaio 2024 (LI); Trib. Santa Maria Capua Vetere, 26 luglio 2023 (LI); Trib. Pistoia, 9 febbraio 2017, n. 133.
[173] Trib. Rimini, 21 gennaio 2022 (LI); Trib. Milano, 10 maggio 2019, n. 4538; Trib. Nola, 4 Maggio 2018 (LI).
[174] This consideration is extremely common and shared essentially by all cases under discussion. *E.g.*: Trib. Pavia, 16 gennaio 2018; Trib. Pistoia, 9 febbraio 2017, n. 133.
[175] Cass., 15138/2015 specified that the plaintiff had virtually lost her reproductive capacity due to the protracted hormonal treatment; Trib. Genova, 20 giugno 2016; Trib. Genova, 23 maggio 2017.
[176] In all cases cited, the applicant was diagnosed with either explicitly diagnosed with gender dysphoria or supervised by a mental health professional.
[177] *E.g.*: Trib. Ferrara, 20 maggio 2024 (LI); Trib. Roma, 24 luglio 2023 (LI); Trib. Santa Maria Capua Vetere, Sez. I, 27 ottobre 2022; Trib. Vicenza, 7 agosto 2020, n. 1342.

As for *physical* transformations, the interpretation of this requirement varies from case to case, although surgery on genitals is no longer required. Courts seem to routinely assess the appearance of the applicant, altered through hormone therapy.[178] In some instances, courts have positively viewed further bodily changes, such as the appearance or removal of body hair,[179] breast augmentation or removal,[180] distribution of body fat, muscle composition,[181] as well as the gendered conformation of facial traits (for instance, through rhinoplasty).[182]

Finally, the constitutional doctrine obliges the applicant to change their *behaviour*. At times, courts may state without further explanation that the applicant behaves in accordance with their gender identity.[183] In some cases, courts considered in positive terms that the applicant displayed the 'stereotypical' behaviour of the sex/gender in which they sought legal recognition.[184] At other times, the personal attributes considered included the job of the applicant, evaluated on the basis of their association with masculinity or femininity.[185] Courts may judge the attitude of the applicant,[186] (including an assessment of whether the mannerisms were 'natural', as opposed to, presumably, artificial),[187] clothes,[188] make-up[189] and

[178] *E.g.*: Trib. Padova, 17 giugno 2024 (LI); Trib. Padova, Sez I, 23 maggio 2024 (LI); Trib. Ferrara, 20 maggio 2024 (LI); Trib. Torino, 27 marzo 2024 (LI); Trib. Pavia, 1 marzo 2024 (LI); Trib. Trieste, 13 febbraio 2024 (LI); Trib. Ascoli Piceno, 16 gennaio 2024 (LI); Trib. Pisa, 17 Ottobre 2023, Sez. Civile (LI); Trib. Novara, 9 settembre 2023; Trib. Messina, 3 gennaio 2023; Trib. Santa Maria Capua Vetere, 26 luglio 2023 (LI); Trib. Roma, 24 luglio 2023 (LI); Trib. Santa Maria Capua Vetere, Sez. I, 27 ottobre 2022 (LI); Trib. Civitavecchia, 8 febbraio 2022 (LI); Trib. Rimini, 21 gennaio 2022 (LI); Trib. Agrigento, 12 gennaio 2021 (LI); Trib. Genova, 15 dicembre 2020, n. 2112; Trib. Perugia, 21 settembre 2020, n. 994; Trib. Busto Arsizio, 11 marzo 2020 (LI); Trib. Milano, 5 dicembre 2019, n. 11278; Trib. Milano, 11 luglio 2019, n. 6914; Trib. Milano, 1 marzo 2019, n. 2081; Trib. Milano, 13 febbraio 2019, n. 1431; Trib. Lamezia Terme, 29 gennaio 2019 (LI); Trib. Novara, 27 novembre 2018, n. 1087; Trib. Frosinone, 19 luglio 2018 (LI); Trib. Nola, 4 maggio 2018 (LI); Trib. Pavia, 16 gennaio 2018; Trib. Trento, 29 settembre 2017; Trib. Roma, 4 agosto 2017, n. 15902; Trib. Bari, 22 maggio 2017, n. 2642; Trib. Pistoia, 9 febbraio 2017, n. 133; Trib. Genova, 20 giugno 2016.

[179] *E.g.*: Trib. Novara, 9 settembre 2023; Trib. Santa Maria Capua Vetere, 26 luglio 2023 (LI); Trib. Civitavecchia, 8 febbraio 2022 (LI); Trib. Genova, 23 maggio 2017 (LI); Trib. Pistoia, 9 febbraio 2017, n. 133; Trib. Genova, 20 giugno 2016.

[180] *E.g.*: Trib. Milano, 6 marzo 2019, n. 2295; Trib. Milano, 13 febbraio 2019, n. 1431; Trib. Frosinone, 19 luglio 2018 (LI); Trib. Genova, 20 giugno 2016, n. 2178.

[181] *E.g.*: Trib. Novara, 9 settembre 2023; Trib. Civitavecchia, 8 febbraio 2022 (LI).

[182] *E.g.*: Trib. Milano, 6 marzo 2019, n. 2295; Trib. Genova, 20 giugno 2016.

[183] *E.g.*: Trib. Torino, 27 marzo 2024 (LI); Trib. Cuneo, 23 febbraio 2024 (LI); Trib. Milano, 26 aprile 2023.

[184] *E.g.*: Trib. Santa Maria Capua Vetere, Sez. I, 27 ottobre 2022 (LI); Trib. Santa Maria Capua Vetere, 12 maggio 2017, n. 1617.

[185] *E.g.*: Trib. Bari, 27 settempre 2016, n. 4801; Trib. Perugia, 23 gennaio 2018, n. 116. Neither of these decisions specifies the job of the applicant, but only the court's evaluation thereof. The latter decision considers the applicant's job, but only to find a conflict: the applicant identifies as female despite their profession.

[186] *E.g.*: Trib. Benevento, 10 novembre 2022; Trib. Mantova, 21 aprile 2017; Trib. Genova, 19 gennaio 2017, n. 425.

[187] *E.g.*: Trib. Pisa, 17 ottobre 2023, Sez. Civile (LI); Trib. Santa Maria Capua Vetere, 26 luglio 2023.

[188] This is common. For a few examples: Trib. Padova, Sez I, 23 maggio 2024 (LI); Trib. Roma, 24 luglio 2023 (LI); Trib. Rimini, 21 gennaio 2022 (LI); Trib. Milano, 17 febbraio 2020, n. 1479; Trib. Genova, 19 gennaio 2017, n. 425.

[189] *E.g.*: Trib. Monza, 4 gennaio 2021; Trib. Milano, 1 marzo 2019, n. 2081.

voice,[190] way of moving and gesticulating,[191] or whether the trans person has already proven that they can live conformingly with their gender identity, for example, by enrolling at university under the name associated with the claimed sex (so-called *carriera alias*).[192] In some decisions, the sexual orientation of the applicant was considered.[193]

3.3. Penalties and rewards

Finally, applicants who fail to prove on hierarchical observation that they conform to the fussy and stereotyped expectations are subjected to a system of penalties and rewards. In his analysis of disciplinary power, Foucault defined rewards as all those forms of recognition that improve the social status of individuals ('stars, prizes, badges, privileges, etc.'). The systems of penalties, conversely, include an array of different forms of hardship, ranging from social humiliation to having to repeat the demeaning tasks that have been assigned (and failed).[194] Penalties and rewards may or may not be administered through law.[195]

Referring to the imposition of standards of femaleness on cis women, Bartky has argued that rewards for complying with gender norms may include social appreciation and personal satisfaction. Similarly, social exclusion and the loss of male patronage can be among the disciplinary penalties.[196] Feder has demonstrated how the 'schoolyard tribunal' exercises the 'microphysics of power' over gender non-conforming boys. Social rejection, peer judgement, repudiation, teasing, and name-calling are among the disciplinary penalties inflicted.[197] Focusing on the medical setting in the United States, Spade has identified the authorization to undergo the physical transformation desired by trans people as a reward, and exclusion from the process of medical transition as a sanction.[198] A similar effect is at play in the context of gender recognition. The reward lies in the successful outcome of the application. Conversely, the applicant who does not conform to the expected standards might, in principle, see their application denied—an affliction, though not necessarily in doctrinal terms.

[190] *E.g.*: Trib. Padova, 17 giugno 2024 (LI); Trib. Busto Arsizio, 11 marzo 2020; Trib. Genova, 19 gennaio 2017, n. 425.
[191] *E.g.*: Trib. Benevento, 10 novembre 2022 (LI); Trib. Pisa, 17 Ottobre 2023; Trib. Genova, 15 dicembre 2020, n. 2112.
[192] *E.g.*: Trib. Milano, 24 aprile 2023.
[193] *E.g.*: Trib. Milano, 5 dicembre 2019, n. 11278; Trib. Milano, 6 marzo 2019, n. 2295; Trib. Bari, 7 febbraio 2019, n. 585; Trib. Mantova, 21 aprile 2017.
[194] Foucault, *supra* note 154, at 15; Hunt & Wickham, *supra* note 157, at 21; Havis, *supra* note 155, at 115; Dreyfus & Rabinow, *supra* note 157, at 157–59.
[195] Ewald, *supra* note 161, at 138–39.
[196] Bartky, *supra* note 156.
[197] Feder, *supra* note 156, at 50.
[198] Spade, *supra* note 156, at 319.

4. Conclusion

Italian law on gender recognition enshrines an ascriptive form of identity. Legal sex is associated with an objective dimension to be ascertained. The elements on which such an identity relies are the 'sex characteristics' as spelled out by the Constitutional Court, namely the 'psychological, physical, and behavioural' elements that must change if recognition is to be granted. Experts—health professionals and judges—are called upon to determine whether the person qualifies for legal reclassification. While gender recognition in its medico-behavioural dimension does go some way towards protecting trans people, it also regiments them by spelling out which 'diverse' identities are acceptable and which are not.

Several factors underlie this model. First, legal sex is defined as the outcome of a balance between the rights of the applicant and other interests and rights in tension with it. The primary justification has traditionally been the preservation of the 'certainty of legal relations', which, in the context of legal sex, mostly refers to gender relations and to constitutional heteronormativity. Of course, sex categories serve other interests in Italy as well—as the Constitutional Court itself made clear in its 2024 decision concerning nonbinary recognition. Nevertheless, family law principles seem to be the real winners in this story. That said, additional cultural and doctrinal factors come into play. Trans identity has consistently been understood in pathological terms, and the centrality of the right to health, although useful for providing a solid foundation for gender recognition, has facilitated medical involvement. Overall, medico-behavioural requirements, with their aura of 'seriousness' and rigour, seem to make it possible to reconcile the existence of trans people with public authorities' desire to maintain a firm grip on sex reclassification.

The definition of a rights-bearer has compelled courts to determine whether individuals seeking recognition meet the criteria. This has led to forms of control that include the constituent elements of disciplinary power. Courts hierarchically observe the applicant, create norms, and dole out rewards and penalties (by granting or possibly denying recognition), thereby ensuring that individuals adhere to a binary sex/gender. The Italian case shows how law and medicine can combine to create a correspondence between the definitions of sexed individuals and legal sex. Evidently, rights have an ambivalent dimension here. Italian courts and Parliament have constructed a definition of the proper beneficiary of the right, and that definition is ultimately imposed on the applicants. Gender recognition empowers those individuals who manage to have their identity recognized, but it also allows a normalizing structure to take hold. Gender constitutionalism produces the very subjects on whom it rests.

5

The Socio-Behavioural Model

France*

1. Controlling identities beyond medicalization: The socio-behavioural model

With Law 2016-1547 'On the modernization of justice in the XXI century' (henceforth, Law J21),[1] the French Parliament entirely de-medicalized the procedure for gender recognition. The *Code Civil* now ensures the right to change the registered 'sex' for every person 'who proves, with a sufficient gathering of facts, that the sex designation in her civil status record does not coincide with that in which she presents herself and in which she is known'.[2] Among such facts, the law includes name change, the person's presentation in social settings, and the sex/gender in which the person is known, for example, by family, friends, and colleagues.[3] Medical evidence, while not proscribed, can no longer be required by courts—which are in charge of ruling on applications for gender recognition.[4] As the Court of Cassation denied recognition to nonbinary identities in 2017,[5] the possibility of changing one's legal sex is limited to the male/female binary. Given the emphasis on gender performance and social acknowledgment, I will refer to this right as 'socio-behavioural'.

Why did the French Parliament impose socio-behavioural standards for recognition? Furthermore, how does the socio-behavioural model operate? In this chapter, I explore how and why gender diversity can be controlled *even* in a de-medicalized legal setting. To address these questions, I first argue that the socio-behavioural model represents an ascriptive type of legal identity (as opposed to an

* This chapter draws on, at times reproduces, and expands on Stefano Osella, The Legal Regime of Gender Identity: A Comparative Enquiry 70–120 (7 May 2019) (Ph.D. Dissertation, European University Institute).

1 Loi n. 2016-1547 du 18 novembre 2016 de modernisation de la justice du XXIe siècle. Law J21 was not limited to gender recognition but was part of a general reform of civil justice in France. It also reformed the rules for the change of name. Everyone with a legitimate interest can obtain a name change through a de-judicialized procedure under the control of the registrar and the public attorney, who can oppose the request if legitimate interest seems to be lacking (Code Civil [C. Civ.][Civil Code], Arts. 60 and 61).

2 C. civ., Art. 61-5.

3 C. civ., Art. 61-5.

4 C. civ., Art. 61-6.

5 Cour de cassation [Cass.] [supreme court for judicial matters], 1e civ., 4 May 2017, n. 16-17.189.

Gender Diversity in Public Law. Stefano Osella, Oxford University Press. © Stefano Osella 2026.
DOI: 10.1093/9780198935070.003.0005

elective one).[6] Indeed, this form of gender recognition assumes that legal identities are based on 'certain … social standards, considered to be objective', which are assessed by an external authority.[7] As such, I contend that the socio-behavioural model does not represent a conceptual change vis-à-vis the medico-behavioural one. Without intending to diminish the importance of this development for trans people, who are no longer required to undergo medical interventions that may be invasive and coercive, it is still the public authorities who have the power to 'discover' and determine the legal sex of individuals.

Second, I show that the socio-behavioural model has been established to preserve control over citizens' civil status and to safeguard the *indisponibilité de l'état des personnes* (henceforth, 'the inalienability of civil status of the person' or, for brevity, 'inalienability').[8] This principle is of paramount importance in French law and, possibly, to the national ethos. Centrally, it is crucial to the preservation of the gender order in public law. I moreover argue that this standard of recognition—centred on social perception—has been influenced by the original doctrinal grounding in the right to privacy. Privacy-based gender recognition is mostly intended to prevent undesired 'outings' of trans people—for example, when a person's identification documents indicate a sex category that is not congruent with the appearance of the same person. This implies an understanding of the trans individual as someone who acquires the appearance associated with the other binary sex/gender. To be sure, gender recognition is now grounded in the right to identity, too. Nevertheless, 'appearances' have remained central to the law.

Third, I demonstrate how a specific beneficiary of gender recognition is produced through such socio-behavioural standards. The socio-behavioural model delineates what a man or a woman should be in law and excludes from recognition those who fall outside this definition. To be clear, the behavioural standards established by the French Parliament seemingly comply with the case law of the European Court of Human Rights (ECtHR), which bars compulsory sterilization.[9] Furthermore, the socio-behavioural model allows individuals to embody forms of diversity and to redefine maleness and femaleness. French law places no restrictions on classifying, for example, individuals with the anatomy associated with femaleness as men, or the other way round. Pregnant fathers and begetting

[6] Ruth Rubio-Marín and I have initially discussed the French model (especially its constitutional aspects) and referred to it as 'binary ascriptive' in Stefano Osella & Ruth Rubio-Marín, *Gender Recognition at the Crossroads: Four Models and the Compass of Comparative Law*, 21 INTERNATIONAL JOURNAL OF CONSTITUTIONAL LAW 574, 585–88 (2023). For this use of 'ascriptive' and 'elective', *see*: Jessica A. Clarke, *Identity and Form*, 103 CALIFORNIA LAW REVIEW 747 (2015).

[7] Clarke, *supra* note 6, at 751.

[8] This translation is taken from the jurisprudence of the ECtHR: A.P., Garçon, and Nicot v. France, Apps. No. 79885/12, 52471/13, and 52596/13 (6 Apr. 2017), https://hudoc.echr.coe.int/eng?i=001-172913.

[9] A.P., Garçon, and Nicot v. France, Apps. No. 79885/12, 52471/13, and 52596/13 (6 Apr. 2017), https://hudoc.echr.coe.int/eng?i=001-172913.

mothers have now become possible. Nevertheless, 'subjects' of recognition are still presupposed and produced to uphold the principle of the inalienability of civil status.

Socio-behavioural recognition seems to be underexplored in international scholarship. This produces a gap that needs filling, for practical purposes too. On the one hand, the imposition of medical requirements is widely contested by human rights lawyers. On the other hand, gender self-determination is encountering fierce resistance.[10] Accordingly, the 'socio-behavioural' solution might perhaps be perceived as an acceptable compromise between the medicalization of gender identity and a system of self-determination.[11] For these reasons, a thorough treatment of the concept is in order.

2. 'Sex' in the civil status and the gender order in public law

In France, the sex of every person must be registered in the civil registries at birth.[12] The law does not define 'sex'.[13] However, sex assignment is typically based on genital examination.[14] This practice is legally grounded in a 1903 decision by the Court of Cassation, where sex was defined for the purpose of marriage as that which was apparent from one's external genitalia.[15] Although not explicitly stipulated, the child must be named in accordance with their legal sex.[16] Finally, despite the absence of any statutory indication, registration is binary, as the Court of Cassation confirmed in 2017 and as the law regulating intersexuality clarifies.[17]

[10] *See* Chapter 2.

[11] For example, this is suggested in: Davina Cooper et al., King's College, Abolishing Legal Sex Status: The Challenge and Consequences of Gender-Related Law Reform. Future of Legal Gender Project Final Report 26 (2022), https://www.kcl.ac.uk/law/research/future-of-legal-gender-abolishing-legal-sex-status-full-report.pdf.

[12] C. civ., Art. 57(1).

[13] On the legal notion of sex: Philippe Reigné, *La Notion Juridique de Sexe*, *in* MON CORPS A-T-IL UN SEXE 302 (Eveline Peyre & Joëlle Wiels eds., 2015).

[14] Marie-Xavière Catto, *La Mention du Sexe à l'État Civil*, *in* LA LOI ET LE GENRE: ÉTUDES CRITIQUES DE DROIT FRANÇAIS 29, 32 (Marc Pichard, Stéphanie Hennette-Vauchez & Diane Roman eds., 2014). More complex procedures are required when a child presents genital ambiguities: Anne-Marie Rajon, *L'Épreuve Corporelle: l'Intersexualité à la Naissance*, *in* L'ÉTAT CIVIL DANS TOUS SES ÉTATS 71, 72–73 (Claire Neirinck ed., 2008).

[15] Cass., 6 Apr. 1903, in [1904] DALLOZ 395, as discussed in Marie-Xavière Catto & Stefano Osella, *The Sexed Subject*, *in* THE CAMBRIDGE COMPANION TO GENDER AND THE LAW 25, 36–37 (Stéphanie Hennette-Vauchez & Ruth Rubio-Marín eds., 2023). For a historical overview of how legal sex was litigated in court: Gabrielle Houbre, *Un «sexe indéterminé»? L'Identité Civile des Hermaphrodites entre Droit et Médicine au XIX siècle*, 48 REVUE D'HISTOIRE DU XIXE SIÈCLE 63 (2014).

[16] Frédrerique Le Dujet-Thomas, *Les Normes Relatives au Prénom: Une Perméabilité Aux Stéréotypes de Genre?*, *in* LA LOI ET LE GENRE. ETUDES CRITIQUES DE DROIT FRANÇAIS 86 (Stéphanie Hennette-Vauchez, Marc Pichard & Diane Roman eds., 2014).

[17] Cass., 1e civ., 4 May 2017, n. 16–17189. The possibility of a third sex was already ruled out by Cour d'appel [CA] [regional court of appeal], 18 Jan. 1974, RECUEIL DALLOZ 196 (1974).

The French civil registration dates back to the French Revolution, when a uniform, state-managed system to record all citizens was introduced.[18] The establishment of such a system was a fundamental step in the transition from the *ancien régime* subjecthood to Republican citizenship.[19] Symbolically, civil registration and the civil status of the person became 'the great lady'—'*la grande dame*'—of Republican France,[20] and registration at birth came to be regarded as a Republican baptism.[21] The Constitution reserves the regulation of civil registration to the domain of legislation (*reserve de loi*), confirming its importance.[22]

Civil registration has a public law function in France. It includes elements that are presumed to be permanent throughout one's life, thereby allowing for the unequivocal identification of individuals.[23] These facts might arguably be understood as a representation of a pre-legal reality.[24] By being so designed, civil registration can be seen as a stabilizer of the legal status of each person, that is, of the legal relations between the individual, fellow citizens, and the state. As Anne-Marie Leroyer argues, the effective exercise of public authority (*puissance publique*) has historically required the certainty of the legal positions of every person.[25] The importance of civil registration in public law is confirmed by the consideration that this institution has been central in the construction of the state itself, indispensable as it is for the exercise of some of its functions—for example, taxation, military service, and personal identification.[26]

Nevertheless, the notion that registration neutrally represents reality and is subtracted from legal and political choices has been criticized by French scholars. To start with, as Marc Pichard highlights, registration attributes a status and thus creates legal relations.[27] In other words, it does not solely record facts. Furthermore,

[18] For a historical perspective, *see*: Laurence Hérault, *«Le Sexe de l'Enfant Est Légitime». À Propos de la Mention de Sexe à l'État Civil et de sa Modification*, *in* État Civil et Transidentité. Anatomie d'une Relation Singulière 23 (Jérome Courduriès, Christine Durlens & Laurence Hérault eds., 2021); Gérard Noiriel, *The Identification of the Citizen: The Birth of the Republican Civil Status in France*, *in* Documenting Individual Identity: The Development of State Practices in the Modern World 28 (Jane Caplan & John Thorpey eds., 1999).

[19] Noiriel, *supra* note 18. Arguably, civil registration also enshrined the patriarchal order in which women were subject to considerable disadvantages vis-à-vis men, *see* Florence Bellivier, Droit des Personnes ¶ 47 and ¶ 66 (2015).

[20] Anne-Marie Leroyer, *La Notion d'État des Personnes*, *in* Ruptures, Mouvements, et Continuité de Droit. Autour de Michelle Gobert 247, 256 (2004).

[21] *See* Antoine Mandret-Degeilh, *Le Baptême Républicain: Usage Institutionnels et Usages Profanes des Symbol Republicain*, *in* La Republique et Ses Symboles. Un Territoir des Signes 265 (Évelyne Cohen & Gérard Monnier eds., 2013); Gérard Noiriel, *L'Identification des Citoyens. Naissance de l'État Civil Républicain*, 13 Genèses 3 (1993).

[22] Constitution [Const.], Art. 34.

[23] Bellivier, *supra* note 19, ¶ 47.

[24] Leroyer, *supra* note 20, at 263–64.

[25] *Id.* at 250–56.

[26] Éric Millard, *Le Rôle de l'État Civil dans la Construction de l'Etat*, in Mélanges en l'honneur du Doyen F.-P. Blanc (2011), https://hal.science/halshs-00617835.

[27] Marc Pichard, *La Mention du Sexe dans les Actes de l'État Civil*, *in* État Civil et Transidentité. Anatomie d'une Relation Singulière 55, 63 (Jérome Courduriès, Christine Dourlens & Laurence Hérault eds., 2021) (connecting sex assignment to the notion of status).

Marie-Xavière Catto observes that, as revealed by the selection of elements that determine the civil status of the person, registration fosters collective identities and social arrangements deemed to be preferable.[28] Similarly, Danièle Lochak states that sex categories do not simply photograph reality but rather contribute to creating it by attaching different legal consequences to being of one or the other sex.[29] The reality that sex registration contributes to creating, clearly, relates not only to the establishment and upholding, but also to the transformation in an egalitarian sense, of the gender order in public law.[30] That said, as Stéphanie Hennette-Vauchez and Marc Pichard argue, civil registration in France has also come to legitimate and protect individual identity, thus revealing a deep-seated tension between its regulatory and protective functions.[31]

To be sure, 'gender order' should not necessarily be read in this context as a synonym for 'patriarchy' but, more neutrally, as referring to all legal positions that assume the existence of sex legal categories. The gender order is indeed transforming in French law, for example, thanks to the advancements in women's equality and family law. The 2013 opening to same-sex marriage and adoptive filiation[32] and the right of single women and women in lesbian couples to be recognized as mothers of a child born via assisted reproductive technology[33] exemplify this evolution.[34]

Although in transformation, the gender order has not disappeared and remains grounded in the binary,[35] as clarified by the Court of Cassation in its 2017 decision on nonbinary recognition.[36] As I argued before, in this judgment, the French top court denied the application of an intersex, nonbinary person to be registered as 'neuter' or, alternatively, 'intersex'. This was the last word pronounced domestically on a controversy that had had varying results before lower courts.[37] The Court

[28] Marie-Xavière Catto, *Le Critère de l'Apparence Physique dans les Décisions de Changement de Sexe*, *in* La Bicatégorisation de Sexe entre Droit, Normes Sociales et Sciences Biomédicales 155, 158 (Marie-Xavière Catto & Julie Mazaleigue-Labaste eds., 2021).

[29] Danièle Lochak, *Le Droit/les Droits à l'Épreuve de la Non-Binarité. Reflexiones Conclusives*, *in* Le(s) Droit(s) à l'épreuve de la Non-Binarité 263, 265 (Olivia Bui-Xuan ed., 2023).

[30] Stéphanie Hennette-Vauchez & Marc Pichard, *Conclusion: La Fondamentalisation de l'État Civil, in Identité et État Civil, in* Identité et État Civil. Évolutions Contemporaines 281, 296–300 (Amélie Gogos-Gintrand & Stéphanie Moracchini-Zeidenberg eds., 2024).

[31] *Id.*

[32] Loi n. 2013-404 du 17 mai 2013 ouvrant le mariage aux couples de personnes de même sexe.

[33] Loi n. 2021-1017 du 2 août 2021 relative à la bioéthique, Art. 1.

[34] In this context, it may be debated whether the sex category of 'woman' is maintained and what function it serves in the pursuit of equality. On this point: Marie-Xavière Catto, *Garder la Catégorie Juridique de «Femme»?*, *in* Qu'Est-ce Qu'Une Femme? Catégories Homme/Femme: Débats Contemporains 131, 137–38 (Patricia Lemarchand & Muriel Salle eds., 2023).

[35] For a historical and sociological perspective on the connection between the preservation of the binary and the gender order: Michal Raz, *Bicatégorisation*, *in* Encyclopédie critique du genre 87 (Juliette Rennes ed., 2016); Elsa Dorlin, *Sexe, Genre et Intersexualité: La Crise comme Régime Théorique*,18 Raisons Politiques 117 (2005).

[36] Cass., 1e civ., 4 May 2017, n. 16-17.189.

[37] The Tribunal de Grande Instance [TGI] [court of first instance] observed that French law does not expressly forbid a third sex. It further considered that Article 8 of the European Convention on Human Rights protects the rights of trans people to have their identity recognized. The TGI also considered

of Cassation acknowledged the existence of a right to gender recognition under Article 8 of the European Convention on Human Rights (ECHR). Nevertheless, it defined the binary as a 'founding element' of social and legal organization. It stated that recognition of a 'neuter sex' would have far-reaching consequences for the system. The Court, moreover, added that the interference with the plaintiff's right to private life under Article 8 of the ECHR was not disproportionate since the applicant appeared masculine and lived 'consistently' in said legally registered sex. The Court of Cassation followed the advice of the Advocate General, who had argued that French law is based on the binary,[38] with the male-female dyad being not only a legal and customary reality,[39] but also a necessary element to achieve women's equality[40] and regulate filiation relations,[41] something that seems to be confirmed by the recent case law on trans parenthood.[42] To be sure, the necessity of the binary to the legal order has been subject to some contestation by scholars.[43] Nevertheless, multiple legal and constitutional provisions presuppose and explicitly refer to the male-female dyad.[44]

The findings of the Court of Cassation were legitimated at the supranational level in 2023, when the ECtHR ruled that the recognition of a nonbinary category falls within the margin of appreciation of the states.[45] On the one hand, the ECtHR confirmed that nonbinary people may have their right to identity affected if recognition were not granted.[46] On the other hand, the ECtHR reaffirmed the legitimacy of the public interest in preserving the binary as a criterion of legal and social

that the applicant was an intersex person and that intersex persons are a tiny minority, incapable of creating significant organizational problems for a binary legal system (TGI Tours, 20 Aug. 2015). The CA Orleans reversed this decision (22 Mar. 2016, n. 14, www.legifrance.gouv.fr). The CA considered that the applicant's appearance was masculine. It also observed that he was married to a woman with whom he had adopted a child. The CA concluded that they were not living as an 'intersex' or 'neuter' and, to rephrase informally, he could pass as a man. It also considered that recognizing a nonbinary legal status was a matter of great moral and legal complexity. Laurence Brunet & Marie-Xavière Catto, *«Homme et femme, la Cour Créa». Note Sous Cass. 1er Civ., 4 Mai 2017, n.16-17189, in* La Bicatégorisation de Sexe entre Droit, Normes Sociales et Sciences Biomédicales 75 (Marie-Xavière Catto & Julie Mazaleigue-Labaste eds., 2021) (providing a thorough comment on the decision). I previously discussed this case in Stefano Osella, *When Comparative Law Walks the Path of Anthropology: The Third Gender in Europe*, 23 German Law Journal 920, 929–32 (2022).

38 Opinion of the first Advocate General Ingall-Montagnier, 21 Mar. 2017 (on file with author).
39 *Id.* ¶ 1.
40 *Id.*
41 *Id.*
42 See Section 3.4 of the present chapter.
43 *E.g.*: Jean-Paul Vauthier & François Vialla, *Hermès ou Aphrodite: Puisqu'il Faut Choisir*, 24 Recueil Dalloz 1399, 1402 (2017).
44 *E.g.*: Art. 1, 3, and the Preamble to the 1946 Constitution. *See* Aude Mirkovic, *La Dualité des Énonciations Relatives au Sexe Dans les Actes de l'État Civil Constitue-t-Elle «un Élement Fondateur de l'Organisation Sociale et Juridique»?, in* Le(s) Droit(s) à l'épreuve de la Non-Binarité 71 (Olivia Bui-Xuan ed., 2023).
45 Y v. France, App. No. 76888/2017 (31 Jan. 2023), https://hudoc.echr.coe.int/eng?i=001-222780.
46 Y v. France, App. No. 76888/2017, ¶¶ 75–76 (31 Jan. 2023), https://hudoc.echr.coe.int/eng?i=001-222780.

organization by making explicit reference to 'family law, filiation, procreation, and equality between men and women'.[47] Combined with the lack of consensus regarding the recognition of nonbinary identity, the rejection of the applicant's claim was inevitable.

In this context, the principle of the inalienability (*indisponibilité*) of one's civil status—which has primarily been weighed against gender recognition in France—becomes crucial. Taken literally, inalienability would prevent all acts of wilful 'disposition' of one's own legal status.[48] Nevertheless, wilful changes to one's civil status may occur numerous times throughout a person's life (from single to married, from foreigner to citizen, etc.), and those changes are normally considered to be valid. Rather than total immutability, therefore, inalienability can be seen as a 'principle of controlled changeability', requiring procedural safeguards (such as the control of a judge)[49] and barring status changes that conflict with the *ordre public*,[50] which in this context refers to the structures of gender.[51]

3. Identity as appearance: The road to de-medicalization

3.1. Background: Medicalization of gender recognition and the preservation of the gender order

Gender recognition was introduced in France in 1992, following a judgment by the ECtHR.[52] Before that, for almost twenty years, the Court of Cassation had ruled that inalienability did not allow voluntary changes of legal sex.[53] In four decisions

[47] Y v. France, App. No. 76888/2017, ¶89 (31 Jan. 2023), https://hudoc.echr.coe.int/eng?i=001-222780.

[48] Claire Neirinck, *Les Characteres de l'État Civil, in* L'État Civil Dans Tous Ses États 41, 42–43 (Claire Neirinck ed., 2008); Céline Kuhn, *Droit et Transsexualisme: La Consécration d'Une Metamorphose, in* Bioéthique et Genre 201, 202 (Anne-Françoise Zattara-Gros ed., 2013).

[49] Bellivier, *supra* note 19, ¶ 48.

[50] Leroyer, *supra* note 20, at 265–68.

[51] For a discussion of the gender order and sex categories in French public law: Bui-Xuan, *supra* note 29; Pichard, Hennette-Vauchez & Roman, *supra* note 14; Philippe Reigné, *L'Intersexuation et la Mention de Sexe à l'État Civil,* (32) Recueil Dalloz 1915, 1917 (2016); Danielle Lochak, *Dualité de Sexe et Dualité de Genre dans les Normes Juridiques, in* Mélanges Andrée Lajoie 661 (Pierre Noreau & Louise Rolland eds., 2008). Heterosexual marriage was central to this gender order: Philippe Reigné, *Sexe, Genre, et État des Personnes,* (42) La Semaine Juridique—Edition Générale 1140, ¶¶ 6–10 (2011); Daniel Borrillo, *Le Sexe et le Droit: De la Logique Binaire des Genres et la Matrice Hétérosexuelle de la Loi,* (1) Jurisprudence. Revue Critique, Université de Savoie, Le Genre Une Question de Droit 263 (2011); Daniel Borrillo, *Pour Une Théorie du Droit des Personnes et de la Famille Émancipée du Genre, in* Droit des Familles, Genre, et Sexualité 16 (Nicole Gallus ed., 2012); Michèle-Laure Rassat, *Sexe, Médicine, et Droit, in* Melanges a Pierre Raynaud 667 (1985).

[52] B v. France, App. No. 13343/1987 (25 Mar. 1992), https://hudoc.echr.coe.int/eng?i=001-57770; Cass., ass. plén., 11 Dec. 1992, in (5) La Semaine Juridique 21991 (1993).

[53] The overview of the law before the 1992 decision of the Court of Cassation draws on Jean Pierre Branlard, Le Sexe et l'État des Personnes. Aspects Historique, Sociologique, et Juridique (1993); Jacqueline Rubellin-Devichi, *Défense et Illustration du Droit Français à l'Égard du Transsexualisme, in* Sur l'Identité Sexuelle: À Propos du Transsexualisme 131 (Marcel Czermak

in 1990, the Court stated that 'transsexual' people, even if they had lost their original sex characteristics through medical treatments, could not acquire those of the other sex/gender and were thus excluded from recognition.[54] When one looks through the veneer of this biology-centred narrative, public law considerations can, however, be discerned. For example, in 1985, Michèle-Laure Rassat had argued that transsexual identity posed questions for the organization of the state (e.g., military conscription; gender segregated facilities), social security law (e.g., age of retirement), and family (that is, heteronormative) arrangements.[55] As argued by Michelle Gobert in 1990, the *juge rapporteur* of the Court of Cassation expressed concern about 'transsexual' people marrying in their new legal sex and adopting children, thus clarifying the threat gender recognition posed to the heterosexual foundation of family law.[56]

The 1992 case of *B v. France* (henceforth, *B.*) was the breakthrough.[57] The ECtHR granted the application of a post-operative trans woman. She had claimed that, 'by failing to allow the indication of her sex to be corrected in the civil status [records] ... and on her official identification documents, the French authorities forced her to disclose intimate personal information to third parties [and this created] great difficulties' in her professional life.[58] The ECtHR ruled that this constant outing violated her right to private life.[59] This decision, *nota bene*, did not establish a right to gender recognition based on the right to identity. The ECtHR instead enunciated a right for 'transsexual' people to be protected from the adverse consequences of, so to speak, involuntary outings. Only with the 2002 cases *Christine Goodwin v. UK* and *I. v. UK* was a fundamental right to gender recognition as an integral part of identity declared.[60]

& Henry Frignet eds., 1996). *See*: Cass., 1e civ., 15 Dec. 1975, n. 73-12787; Cass., 1e civ., 30 Nov. 1983, n. 82-13808; Cass., 1e civ., 3 Mar. 1987, n. 84-15691; Cass., 1e civ., 31 Mar. 1987, n. 85-141876; Cass., 1e civ., 7 June 1988, n. 86-13698; Cass., 1e civ., 10 May 1989, n. 87-17111.

[54] Cass., 1e civ., 21 May 1990, n. 88-12163; Cass., 1e civ., 21 May 1990, n. 88-12250; Cass., 1e civ., 21 May 1990, n. 88-12829; Cass., 1e civ., 21 May 1990, n. 88-15858.

[55] *See* Rassat, *supra* note 51, at 667–71.

[56] Michelle Gobert, *Le Transsexualisme ou la Difficulté d'Exister*, (49) La Semaine Juridique Edition Générale—JPC, doctr 3475, ¶ 14 (1990). For a broader discussion of the consequences of gender recognition, especially for marriage, *see*: *Id.* at ¶ 15.

[57] B v. France, App. No. 13343/1987 (25 Mar. 1992), https://hudoc.echr.coe.int/eng?i=001-57770.

[58] B v. France, App. No. 13343/1987, ¶ 43 (25 Mar. 1992), https://hudoc.echr.coe.int/eng?i=001-57770.

[59] B v. France, App. No. 13343/1987, ¶ 63 (25 Mar. 1992), https://hudoc.echr.coe.int/eng?i=001-57770; Art. 8 ECHR.

[60] Christine Goodwin v. United Kingdom, App. No. 28597/1995 (11 July 2002), https://hudoc.echr.coe.int/fre?i=001-60596; I. v. United Kingdom, App. No. 25680/1994 (11 July 2002), https://hudoc.echr.coe.int/spa?i=001-60595. Refer to: Damien Gonzalez-Salzberg, Sexuality and Transsexuality Under the European Convention on Human Rights: A Queer Reading of Human Rights Law (2019) (discussing these decisions at length).

B. rapidly resonated in France. In 1992, the Court of Cassation granted gender recognition to people 'suffering from the transsexualism syndrome'.[61] The Court described that 'transsexual' people

> no longer possess all the characteristics of their original sex after having undergone medical and surgical treatments for therapeutic reasons, and [have] acquired a physical appearance resembling the other sex which corresponds to their social behaviour.[62]

The Court did not retract its insistence on the centrality of the inalienability of civil status, and its implications on the gender order. Yet it concluded that no conflict should arise as long as recognition was limited to the described beneficiaries. This right was implicitly limited to unmarried people, clearly to avoid same-sex marriages.[63]

The implementation of this doctrine centred on the appearance of the applicant and on the associated medical transition, and exhibited all the characteristics of disciplinary power as laid out in Chapter 4—hierarchical observation; evaluation through norms; penalties and rewards.[64] First, ordinary courts in charge of assessing the applications (*actions d'état*) were called to scrutinize the applicants. Medical expertise played a crucial role, with doctors summoned as expert witnesses and serving as gatekeepers of the medical and legal process. As anthropologist Laurence Hérault has argued, medicalization reinforced binary conceptions of gender.[65] Applicants were carefully examined for compliance with gender standards. An overall transformation of their bodies seemed to be required.[66]

[61] Cass., ass. plén., 11 Dec. 1992, n. 91-11900.

[62] *Id.*

[63] *See* Virginie Larribau-Terneyre, *Transsexualism et Couple*, (5) DROIT DE LA FAMILLE 11 (2013). This requirement was confirmed when some courts rejected applications lodged by transsexual applicants who intended to remain married in their birth-assigned legal sex. TGI Caen, 9 Jan. 2003, unpublished, reported by Laurence Mauger-Vielpeau, *Le Transsexualisme et le Code Civil*, (9) DROIT DE LA FAMILLE, ÉTUDE 18, ¶ 31 (2005); TGI Besançon, 19 Mar. 2009, n. 08/02219, Jurisdata 2009-024072; TGI Brest, 15 Dec. 2011, n. 11/00975, Jurisdata n 2011-027855.

[64] ALAN HUNT & GARY WICKHAM, FOUCAULT AND LAW: TOWARDS A SOCIOLOGY OF LAW AS GOVERNANCE 21 (1994); HUBERT L. DREYFUS & PAUL RABINOW, MICHEL FOUCAULT: BEYOND STRUCTURALISM AND HERMENEUTICS 153–60 (2d ed. 1983); Devonya D. Havis, *Discipline*, *in* THE CAMBRIDGE FOUCAULT LEXICON 110 (Leonard Lawlor & John Nale eds., 2014). *See* Chapter 1.

[65] Laurence Hérault, *Constituer des Hommes et des Femmes: La Procedure de Transsexualisation*, 42 TERRAIN 95 (2004).

[66] Cass., 1e civ., 18 Oct. 1994, n. 93-10.730; CA Paris, 1e ch., Section C, 30 Apr. 1993, Jurisdata 21472; CA Versailles, 1e ch., 1e Section, 14 Oct. 1993, Jurisdata 045036; CA Aix-en-Provence, 1e civ., section A, 7 Mar. 1995, Jurisdata 40180; CA Lyon, 2e ch., section A, 4 June 2009, Jurisdata 006810. A few courts denied recognition for failing to achieve full transformation: CA Poitiers, 3e civ., 15 Dec. 2004, Jurisdata 274567; CA Papeete, civ., 15 Mar. 2012, n. 147, Jurisdata 2012-023696; CA Limoges, civ., 20 Mar. 2012, Jurisdata 2012-005346. Gender recognition could however be granted without phalloplasty: CA Aix-en-Provence, 6e civ., section A, 9 Nov. 2001, Jurisdata 157510. In some cases, gender recognition was granted without treatments for health reasons (CA Rennes, 26 Oct. 1998, (35) RECUEIL DALLOZ 508 (1999)) or for the specific socio-legal vulnerability of the applicant (CA Poitiers, 4e civ., 20 Dec. 2006, Jurisdata 330472).

A psychiatric diagnosis and the therapeutic purpose of surgical and medical treatments were key to obtaining gender recognition.[67] Second, behavioural changes were also required, including mannerisms, clothing style, and general presentation. Applicants had to recount a lifelong history of pain and identification in the other sex/gender.[68] If the applicant did not comply with this list of requirements, recognition could be denied.

3.2. Towards the socio-behavioural model

Contestation of medical requirements and resistance from the Court of Cassation

As argued in the literature, a push in the evolution of the preconditions for gender recognition originated at the supranational level.[69] In 2009, the Council of Europe's Commissioner for Human Rights Thomas Hammarberg issued a report (the Hammarberg report) where he condemned the sterilization requirement,[70] and invited Member States to abolish all medical preconditions for gender recognition.[71] In 2009, following the recommendation of the Commissioner for Human Rights, the *Haute Autorité de la Santé* proposed making gender recognition conditional solely on undergoing hormonal therapy.[72] On 29 April 2010, the Parliamentary Assembly of the Council of Europe called on Member States to ensure identity recognition without 'the obligation to undergo sterilisation or other medical procedures, such as sex reassignment surgery and hormonal therapy'.[73] Domestic developments concerning the pathological status of trans identity took place at the same time.[74] Following the Hammarberg report, French MPs started

[67] Post-operative transsexual people were refused gender recognition in a few decisions because their treatment was not carried out within a therapeutic process under psychiatric care: CA Paris, 1e ch., section C, 14 June 1994, Jurisdata 024843; CA Agen, 1e ch., 13 Dec. 1994, Jurisdata 050821. Apparently, in one case, gender recognition was granted without the certainty of the diagnosis. CA Bordeaux, 25 Jan. 1993, CAHIERS JURISPRUDENCE AQUITAINE 210 (1993), reported by Rubellin-Devichi, *supra* note 53, at 138.

[68] CA Nancy, 3 ch., 9 Jan. 2012, n. 11/01043, Jurisdata 2012-006036; CA Aix-en-Provence, 6e civ., section A, 9 Nov. 2001, Jurisdata 2001-157510; CA Agen, 1 ch., 30 May 1996, Jurisdata 044069.

[69] Corinne Fortier & Laurence Brunet, *Changement d'État Civil des Personnes «Trans» en France: Du Transsexualisme à la Transidentité, in* DROIT DES FAMILLES, GENRE ET SEXUALITÉ 63, 105 (Nicole Gallus ed., 2012).

[70] Thomas Hammarberg, Commissioner for Human Rights, Council of Europe, Human Rights and Gender Identity, CommDH/IssuePaper(2009)9 (29 July 2009).

[71] *Id.* at 18.

[72] Haute Autorité de la Santé, Situation Actuelle et Perspectives d'Evolution de la Prise en Charge Medicale du Transsexualisme en France 40-41 (Nov. 2009).

[73] Parliamentary Assembly of the Council of Europe, Resolution 1728 (2010), Discrimination on the Basis of Sexual Orientation and Gender Identity, ¶ 16.11.2 (29 Apr. 2010).

[74] On 16 May 2009, the Ministry of Health announced that trans identity should no longer be considered a psychiatric illness in France. The Ministry clarified that 'transsexualism' would be moved from the list of 'severe anxiety disorders' to the 'off the list' section in the Code of Social Security. *See* François Vialla, *Iphis ou Atalante: la Transidentité Saisie par le Droit, in* LES ASSISES DU CORPS

to address questions to the government. They suggested that requiring gender confirmation surgery violated human dignity,[75] and that medical requirements were humiliating and expensive,[76] arbitrary and inconsistently applied.[77] With the *circulaire* of 14 May 2010, the Ministry of Justice responded by emphasizing that the 1992 standards of the Court of Cassation were aimed at the *irreversible* transition of the applicant.[78] The *circulaire* directed public prosecutors to endorse applications for gender recognition upon the establishment of irreversible transition through hormonal therapies.[79] Some openings could be found in the case law, which at times granted recognition without surgery.[80]

The Court of Cassation cemented the irreversibility-based doctrine with four decisions in 2012–2013. Three of these decisions regarded appeals lodged by post-operative 'transsexual' people.[81] Despite the medical documentation presented, the applicants were asked to undergo further medical examination. On refusal, their claims were denied. They appealed, arguing that their human rights to personality, equality, and physical integrity had been infringed upon.[82] In the fourth case, the applicant essentially contested both the diagnosis and the irreversibility requirements, arguing that they violated the same human rights.[83] All appeals were rejected, as the applicants did not offer evidence of the 'irreversible transformation of their appearance'.[84] The irreversible transformation of the appearance and the psychiatric diagnosis were then justified by the Court as a proportionate balancing of the applicant's right to private life with legal certainty and the inalienability of civil status.[85]

TRANSFORMÉ. REGARDS CROISÉS SUR LE GENRE 240 (Jacques Mateu, Mathieu Reynier & François Vialla 2010); Arnaud Alessandrin, *Du 'Transsexualisme' a la 'Dysphorie de Genre': Ce Que le DSM Fait des Variances de Genre*, 9 SOCIO-LOGOS ¶ 7 (2014), https://journals.openedition.org/socio-logos/2837. The announcement was followed by Décret n. 2010-125 du 8 février 2010 portant modification de l'annexe figurant à l'article D. 322-1 du code de la sécurité sociale relative aux critères médicaux utilisés pour la définition de l'affection de longue durée «affections psychiatriques de longue durée».

[75] This was the question posed by Senator Roger Madec (17 Sept. 2009, n. 10128, p. 2190), https://www.senat.fr/questions/base/2009/qSEQ090910128.html.

[76] Jean-Luc Pérat posed this question in the *Assemblee Nationale* (8 Dec. 2009, n. 65910, p. 11633) http://questions.assemblee-nationale.fr/q13/13-65910QE.htm. For the answer of the government, in the person of the Ministry of Justice: 2 Mar. 2010, p. 2452, https://www.senat.fr/questions/base/2009/qSEQ090910128.html.

[77] Oral question n. 0832S by Senator Maryvonne Blondin (25 Feb. 2010, p. 411) https://www.senat.fr/questions/base/2010/qSEQ10020832S.html.

[78] Circulaire de la DACS n° CIV/07/10 du 14 mai 2010 relative aux demandes de changement de sexe à l'état civil (NOR: JUSC1012994C).

[79] *Id.*

[80] *E.g.*: CA Nancy, 3e civ., 2 Sept. 2011, Jurisdata 031585. *See*: Sophie Paricard, *Transsexualisme. À Quand la Loi?*, (1) DROIT DE LA FAMILLE, ÉTUDE 2 ¶¶ 17–26 and specifically note 33 (2012).

[81] Cass., 1e civ., 7 June 2012, n. 10-26.947, 757; Cass., 1e civ., 7 June, 2012, n. 11-22.490, 758; Cass., 1e civ., 13 Feb. 2013, n. 11-14.515.

[82] C. civ. Art. 9 and Art. 16; Arts. 8 and 14 ECHR.

[83] Cass., 1e civ., 13 Feb. 2013, n. 12-11.949.

[84] Cass., 1e civ., 7 June 2012. n. 10-26.947, 757; Cass., 1e civ., 7 June 2012, n. 11-22.490.

[85] For a discussion: François Vialla, *La Transidentité: Une Jurisprudence en «Équilibre Instable»*, MÉDICINE ET DROIT 105 (2013); Sophie Paricard, *Transsexualisme: La Cour de Cassation*

Nevertheless, irreversibility was an unclear requirement. Leaving aside that, arguably, no aspects of individual appearance can be irreversible, this formulation was criticized for being vague and for making uniform application difficult.[86] Regardless, it soon came to be interpreted as sterilization.[87] With some exceptions,[88] courts generally demanded the—psychiatrically supervised—loss of fertility of the applicant, achieved with[89] or without surgery (e.g., through protracted hormonal treatment).[90]

Cracks in the irreversibility doctrine: Further human rights concerns

In 2013, the *Commission Nationale Consultative des Droits de l'Homme* (CNCDH) criticized the diagnostic precondition for being pathologizing and stigmatizing, as well as the irreversibility doctrine for being opaque and effectively a sterilization requirement.[91] However, the CNCDH rejected gender self-determination. Civil status and the system of registration were deemed too important, not only for identifying citizens, but also as a symbol.[92] The CNCDH recommended instead a de-medicalized (and yet not entirely self-determined) model of recognition.[93] In 2015, the Parliamentary Assembly of the Council of Europe invited the Member States to provide quick and transparent procedures for gender recognition and to abolish all compulsory medical and psychiatric treatments.[94] Albeit in an *obiter*

Sonnerait-Elle le Glas de la Libéralisation? Note sous Civ. 1re, 7 Juin 2012, n° 10-26.947 (1re espèce) et n° 11-22.490 (2e espèce), 5 Droit de la Santé 880 (2012).

[86] Philippe Reigné, *Le Changement de Sexe devant la Cour de Cassation. Le Juge, l'Expert et l'Irréversibilité,* (26) La Semaine Juridique Edition Générale 753 (2012); Paricard, *supra* note 80, ¶¶ 17–26 (criticizing the overall ambiguity of French law). On the ambiguity of the notion of irreversibility: Fortier & Brunet, *supra* note 69.

[87] Reigné, *supra* note 86, ¶ 3. For a more optimistic reading of 'irreversibility' as a potentially positive development capable of questioning the surgery requirement: François Vialla, *L'Irreversibilité en Question*, 25 Recueil Dalloz 1648 (2012), commenting on CA Versailles, 1 ch., 22 Mar. 2012, Jurisdata 2012-005712. As specified below in the text, the ECtHR considered that the requirement of irreversibility of one's appearance coincided with sterilization, in the 2016 decision in *A.P., Garçon, and Nicot v. France.*

[88] Courts could consider a transition irreversible without surgery on primary sex characteristics. Nevertheless, an overall transformation—inclusive of hormone therapy, psychiatric counselling, and treatments to change secondary sex characteristics and behavioural transformation—was still required: CA Versailles, 1 ch., 22 Mar. 2012; CA, 1e ch., 13 Dec. 2012, Jurisdata 2012-029416; CA Metz, 11 Oct. 2016, Jurisdata 2016/021430.

[89] CA Nîmes, ch. civ., 19 Feb. 2014, n. 13/03142 (*www.dalloz.fr*); TGI Bobigny, 3e ch., 3 section, 18 Mar. 2013, Jurisdata 2013-009176. For a commentary, *see*: Philippe Reigné, *Changement d'État Civil: l'Immobilisme des Juges du Fond*, 6 Droit de la Famille, comm. 82 (2013).

[90] CA Nancy, 3 ch. civ., 10 Apr. 2015, Jurisdata 2015-008034; CA Douai, 1e ch., 1 section, 24 Mar. 2014, n. 218/2014 (*www.dalloz.fr*).

[91] Commission Nationale Consultative des Droits de l'Homme [National Consultative Commission of Human Rights] (CNCDH), Avis sur l'identité de genre et sur le changement de la mention de sexe à l'état civil (NOR: CDHX1320077V), ¶¶ 17–23 (27 June 2013).

[92] *Id.* ¶ 28–29.

[93] *Id.* ¶¶ 25–31.

[94] Parliamentary Assembly of the Council of Europe, Resolution 2048 (2015), Discrimination against Transgender People in Europe, ¶ 6.2 (22 Apr. 2015).

dictum, the Court of Strasbourg arguably held in *Y.Y. v. Turkey*[95] that the sterilization requirement infringed on the right to physical integrity.[96]

In 2016, the French Ombudsperson—the *Défenseur des Droits*—declared that requiring the irreversible transformation of one's appearance was unclear, discriminatory, and burdensome.[97] Ultimately, he deemed it to be incompatible with *Y.Y. v. Turkey*. The right to gender recognition, he considered, could not be interpreted as requiring sterilization.[98] Compulsory psychiatric supervision was also criticized for being discriminatory and stigmatizing.[99] Notably, the *Défenseur* targeted the principle of the inalienability of civil status, criticizing it as a manifestation of a past social order.[100] The *Défenseur*, moreover, highlighted that a person's civil status was not solely determined by biology, citing as examples adoption and assisted reproductive technologies.[101] Hence, also considering the risks of stereotyping that behavioural evaluations entail, he suggested a procedure based on self-declaration.[102]

The Court of Strasbourg ultimately ruled that the irreversibility requirement infringed on Article 8 of the ECHR in its 2017 decision, *A.P., Garçon, and Nicot v. France*.[103] The case was decided *after* Law J21 of 2016 had been passed. The applicants had contested that the irreversible change in one's appearance involved sterilization and claimed that this infringed on the right to be free from torture and inhumane or degrading treatment,[104] and on the rights to identity and physical integrity.[105] Furthermore, the applicants had challenged the diagnosis requirement and the overreliance on medical expertise in the procedure. For its part, the French government had opposed that the medically achieved irreversibility was imperative to uphold the principle of the inalienability of civil status.[106]

The ECtHR acknowledged that irreversibility of one's appearance in practice required either surgical sterilization or hormonal therapies likely to cause loss of fertility.[107] The Court ruled that this infringed on Article 8 of the ECHR, as it subjected trans people to the 'impossible' choice between gender recognition and

[95] Y.Y. v. Turkey, App. No. 14793/08 (10 Mar. 2015), https://hudoc.echr.coe.int/eng?i=001-153134.

[96] Y.Y. v. Turkey, App. No. 14793/08, ¶ 119 (10 Mar. 2015), https://hudoc.echr.coe.int/eng?i=001-153134.

[97] Défenseur des Droits [Ombudsperson], Decision Cadre MLD-MSP-2016-164, 7–11 (24 June 2016).

[98] *Id.* at 11–16.

[99] *Id.* at 16–17.

[100] *Id.* at 16.

[101] *Id.* at 15.

[102] *Id.* at 20–21.

[103] A.P., Garçon, and Nicot v. France, Apps. No. 79885/12, 52471/13, and 52596/13 (6 Apr. 2017), https://hudoc.echr.coe.int/eng?i=001-172913.

[104] Art. 3 ECHR.

[105] Art. 8 ECHR.

[106] A.P., Garçon, and Nicot v. France, Apps. No. 79885/12, 52471/13, and 52596/13, ¶¶ 104–08 (6 Apr. 2017), https://hudoc.echr.coe.int/eng?i=001-172913.

[107] A.P., Garçon, and Nicot v. France, Apps. No. 79885/12, 52471/13, and 52596/13, ¶¶ 116–20 (6 Apr. 2017), https://hudoc.echr.coe.int/eng?i=001-172913.

the preservation of their physical integrity.[108] Nevertheless, it found that the diagnostic requirement did not have a direct impact on physical integrity and clarified that states retain a wide margin of appreciation in the matter.[109] The Court also held that the diagnosis of gender dysphoria ensures that no irreversible physical change is made without due consideration.[110] Ultimately, it concluded that the overreliance on expert assessment did not violate Article 8 of the ECHR.[111]

3.3. The socio-behavioural model

With Law J21 of 2016, Parliament filled the legislative vacuum that had lasted for decades.[112] The right to gender recognition is now granted to all people of age and emancipated children, even though at least one instance of recognition of an underage person *not* emancipated has been recorded.[113] Applicants have to provide various pieces of evidence ('gathering of facts') to prove that their civil status no longer corresponds to the lived sex/gender in which they are known. Medical certifications, though not prohibited, cannot be required.[114] Once a court ascertains that the applicant meets the preconditions, it orders the reclassification and name change (if necessary) on the birth certificate.[115] Gender recognition does

[108] A.P., Garçon, and Nicot v. France, Apps. No. 79885/12, 52471/13, and 52596/13, ¶132 (6 Apr. 2017), https://hudoc.echr.coe.int/eng?i=001-172913.

[109] A.P., Garçon, and Nicot v. France, Apps. No. 79885/12, 52471/13, and 52596/13, ¶¶ 139-40 (6 Apr. 2017), https://hudoc.echr.coe.int/eng?i=001-172913.

[110] A.P., Garçon, and Nicot v. France, Apps. No. 79885/12, 52471/13, and 52596/13, ¶ 141 (6 Apr. 2017), https://hudoc.echr.coe.int/eng?i=001-172913.

[111] A.P., Garçon, and Nicot v. France, Apps. No. 79885/12, 52471/13, and 52596/13, ¶¶ 149-54 (6 Apr. 2017), https://hudoc.echr.coe.int/eng?i=001-172913. For a discussion of the decision: Damian A. Gonzalez-Salzberg, *An Improved Protection for the (Mentally Ill) Trans Parent: A Queer Reading of AP, Garçon and Nicot v France*, 81 The Modern Law Review 526 (2018); Benjamin Moron-Puech, *L'Arrêt* A. P., Nicot et Garçon c. France *ou la Protection Insuffisante par le Juge Européen des Droits Fondamentaux des Personnes Transsexuées'*, La Revue des Droits de l'Homme (3 May 2017), http://journals.openedition.org/revdh/3049.

[112] Previously, some bills were proposed: Proposition de loi visant à la simplification de la procédure de changement de la mention de sexe dans l'état civil, enregistré à la Présidence de l'Assemblée Nationale (22 Dec. 2011).

[113] With decision 21/01282 of 25 January 2022, the CA Chambery granted recognition to a seventeen-year-old child who was represented by their parents. The Court of Appeal reasoned that the lack of references to non-emancipated children in the law does not entail that other subjects are excluded from it (Articles 371ff of the Civil Code). For a comment: Marie-Xavière Catto, *Le Sexe Assigné Contesté et Modifié avant la Majorité (Note sous CA Chambéry, 25 janvier 2022, inédit)*, La Revue des Droits de l'Homme (29 Mar. 2022), http://journals.openedition.org/revdh/14588. A different matter is the question of medical transition, which is not discussed in this chapter. It is worth mentioning that this topic has been a subject of political controversy. In 2024, the political group Les Republicans registered bill n. 435 to limit the medical transition of underage people ('visant à encadrer les pratiques médicales mises en œuvre dans la prise en charge des mineurs en questionnement de genre'). This bill attracted the criticism of the French Ombudsperson (Avis du Défenseur des Droits n°24-05 sur la Proposition de Loi n°435 (2023–2024) Visant à Encadrer les Pratiques Médicales Mises en œuvre dans la Prise en Charge des Mineurs en Questionnement de Genre, déposée au Sénat le 19 mars 2024).

[114] C. civ., Arts. 61-5 and 61-6.

[115] C. civ., Art. 61-7.

not affect the obligations towards other people or the parental relations established prior to the modification.[116] This model of gender recognition protects the *possession d'état* ('possession of status').[117] This is a well-established concept in French private law.[118] It can be understood as the legal protection of the *verité sociologique* ('sociological truth').[119] As Paricard argues, the main elements that constitute the possession of status are indeed protected in the 2016 law on gender recognition: *tractatus* (appearance), *fama* ('being known as' in one's social circles), and *nomen* (name, in this case, change of name).[120] In practice, being socially recognizable as belonging to one sex/gender or the other is the determining factor to obtain gender recognition.[121]

This socio-behavioural right is the outcome of an effort to balance identity rights with the principles—primarily inalienability—of the civil status. The reform of gender recognition began with an amendment proposed by a group of socialist MPs in the *Assemblée Nationale* when Law J21 was being drafted.[122] Human rights concerns prompted the initiative. In its first version, legislators wanted to grant a right based on a de-medicalized and de-judicialized procedure,[123] considered to be the application of the rights deriving from the ECHR.[124] The control of the application was, in this first proposal, demanded to the public prosecutor (*procureur*). Privacy and self-determination seemed central to the debates. Arguably, the trans person was understood as transforming themselves and acquiring the looks associated with the other binary sex/gender. References were made to the case law and

[116] C. civ., Art. 61-8.

[117] Project de loi portant application des mesures relatives à la justice du XXIème siècle, Report n. 839 by Yves Détraigne, 21 Sept. 2016, 106. For a discussion: Philippe Reigné, *Changement d'État Civil et Possession d'État du Sexe dans la Loi de Modernisation de la Justice du XXI Siècle. À Propos de la Loi n. 2016-1547 du 18 Novembre 2016*, (51) LA SEMAINE JURIDIQUE 1378 (2016).

[118] For example, it applies to some filiation relations, as detailed by Article 311-1 of the Civil Code. *See*: Sophie Paricard, *Modification de la Mention du Sexe à l'État Civil et Respect de l'Integrité Corporelle: Quels Enjeux?*, *in* IDENTITÉ ET ÉTAT CIVIL. ÉVOLUTIONS CONTEMPORAINES 175, 187 (Amélie Gogos-Gintrand & Stéphanie Moracchini-Zeidenberg eds., 2024).

[119] Sophie Paricard, *Du Sexe par Possession d'État à la Consécration de l'Identité du Genre?*, *in* PERSONNES ET FAMILLES DU XXIE SIÈCLE. ACTES DU COLLOQUE DE PAU DU 30 JUIN 2017 31, 34 (Jean-Jacques Lemouland & Daniel Vigneau eds., 2018).

[120] *Id.*

[121] Paricard, *supra* note 118, at 187, citing JEAN HAUSER & DANIÈLE HUET-WEILER, TRAITÉ DE DROIT CIVIL. LA FAMILLE 249 (2d ed. 1993); Catto, *supra* note 28, at 178–79.

[122] Amendment n. 282 (Rect) presented by Pascale Crozon, François Binet, Florence Delauney and others, introducing Article 18 quarter on the text n. 3726 (May 12, 2016). *See also* the discussion by: Pascale Crozon, Assemblée Nationale, XIV Legislature, Constitution of 4 Oct. 1958, Ordinary Session 2015–2016, *Compte Rendu Integral*, Second Session, of Thursday, 19 May 2016. The first mentioning of gender recognition in relation to Law 2016-1547 appears to be by Sergio Coronado and others, on 29 April 2016 (Amendment n. CL89, subsequently rejected). All the Parliamentary debates are available at the institutional websites of the Senate (https://www.senat.fr/dossier-legislatif/pjl14-661.html) and of the National Assembly (https://www.assemblee-nationale.fr/14/dossiers/justice_21e_siecle.asp). For a report of the debates, see Report n. 3726 Jean-Marie Clément & Jean-Yves Le Bouillonnec (Assemblée Nationale, XIV Legislature, Constitution of 4 Oct. 1958, 6 May 2016).

[123] Amendement n. 282 (Rect), *supra* note 122.

[124] *Id.*

soft law that had developed up to that point, including Resolutions 1728 (2010)[125] and 2048 (2015)[126] of the Parliamentary Assembly of the Council of Europe, as well as to the 2013 report by the CNCDH and to the jurisprudence of the ECtHR.

However, the government opposed this proposition, seeing it as compromising the inalienability of civil status. The Ministry of Justice emphasized the importance of legal security (*sécurité juridique*), thereby confirming the necessity of a judicial procedure.[127] Throughout the parliamentary debates, references to the inalienability of civil status were made, at times emphatically, for example, when civil registration was defined as an ancient French tradition.[128] Hérault furthermore reports that legislators feared social opposition to gender recognition similar to that against same-sex marriage.[129] Before the promulgation of the bill into a law, a group of MPs contested it before the Constitutional Council. Their main argument was that the new right to gender recognition attributed excessive importance to the 'will of the individual'. It thus allegedly compromised the principle of the inalienability of civil status,[130] which is of vital importance to the social order and to the position of the person in the family and the public sphere.[131] The new law, the MPs further argued, would diminish legal security and, thereby, the dignity of French citizens as protected in the Preamble of the 1946 Constitution.[132] The

[125] Resolution of the Parliamentary Assembly of the Council of Europe 1728 (2010) on Discrimination on the Basis of Sexual Orientation and Gender Identity.

[126] See Amendement n. 282, *supra* note 122, introducing Article 18 quarter on the text n. 3726 (12 May 2016). See also the *compte rendu integral* delivered by Pascale Crozon on 19 May 2016 (Assemblée Nationale, XIV Legislature, Constitution of 4 Oct. 1958, Ordinary Session 2015–2016).

[127] Marie-Xavière Catto, *Changer de Sexe à l'État Civil depuis la Loi du 18 Novembre 2016 de Modernisation de la Justice du XXIe Siècle: Un Bilan d'Application*, (9) CAHIERS DROIT, SCIENCES & TECHNOLOGIE 107 ¶ 39 (2019); François Vialla, *État Civil (Changement de Sexe): 'Démédicalisation' de la Procedure*, (27) RECUEIL DALLOZ 1561 (2016). See the answer of the Ministry of Justice Jean-Jacques Urvoas, in the *compte rendu integral* of 12 July 2016 (Assemblée Nationale, XIV Legislature, Constitution of 4 Oct. 1958, first session, 12 July 2016).

[128] For example, one legislator claimed a genealogy to the 1539 ordinances of Villers-Cotterêts. *See* the report n. 3904, delivered on 30 June 2016, by Jean-Marie Clément & Jean-Yves Le Bouillonnec (Assemblée Nationale, XIV Legislature, Constitution of 4 Oct. 1958).

[129] Laurence Hérault et al., Mission de Recherche Droit et Justice, État Civil de Demain et Transidentité. Rapport Final 154 (May 2018), https://hal.science/hal-02054506v1/file/15-24-Rapport-final_État-civil-de-demain-et-transidentité_mai-2018%281%29.pdf. A coalition of right-wing parties, traditionalist Catholics, and the clergy had indeed mobilized to oppose equal marriage. Although ultimately unsuccessful, these activists were vocal and posed a significant political challenge. *See* Michael Stambolis-Ruhstorfer & Josselin Tricou, *Resisting 'Gender Theory' in France: A Fulcrum for Religious Action in a Secular Society*, *in* ANTI-GENDER CAMPAIGNS IN EUROPE: MOBILIZING AGAINST EQUALITY (Roman Kuhar & David Paternotte eds., 2017); SARA GARBAGNOLI & MASSIMO PREARO, LA CROISADE «ANTI-GENRE». DU VATICAN AUX MANIFS POUR TOUS (2017).

[130] The MPs complained of two other constitutional breaches that are not directly related to the discussion at hand and will not be here examined (Conseil constitutionnel [CC] [Constitutional Court], decision n. 2016-739, 17 Nov. 2016, ¶ 65, https://www.conseil-constitutionnel.fr/decision/2016/2016739DC.htm). *See* Osella & Rubio-Marín, *supra* note 6, at 587.

[131] Referral to the Constitutional Council, 17 October 2016, presented by the minimum number of sixty members of the National Assembly, on the application of Article 61, paragraph 2, of the Constitution, dealt with in Decision no 2016-739 DC, https://www.conseil-constitutionnel.fr/les-decisions/decision-n-2016-739-dc-du-17-novembre-2016-saisine-par-60-deputes.

[132] *Id.*

Constitutional Council judged that the de-medicalization of the procedure did not violate human dignity and upheld the constitutionality of the newly legislated right.[133]

Ultimately, the law entered into force, and, despite the innovations it brought, it was not immune to criticisms. In 2016, when the bill was still being debated, the *Défenseur des Droits* had stressed the difficulty of establishing social requirements respectful of trans identity. Evaluation would depend on the sensitivity of the court, leaving excessive room for heterogeneous, and stereotyped, interpretations.[134] Scholars echoed such criticisms.[135] In response to the *Défenseur*, the Ministry of Justice issued an interpretative *circulaire* to guide the application of the law in May 2017.[136] It suggested that the legislature had intended to protect the lived gender identity of trans people.[137] The Ministry also underlined that the 'facts' listed in the law as a basis for recognition are not exhaustive, and that courts can rely on other facts, too.[138] The *circulaire* thus offered an interpretation of the law capable of opening it up to circumstances beyond the social sphere of the person, including self-identification.[139] The *circulaire* underlined that it is not for society to determine the sex/gender in which applicants live.[140] The Ministry specified that '[i]t is the willingness of the person to present themselves in society as belonging to the gender they intimately experience that can allow the sex claimed to be brought into line with that recorded in the civil registry.'[141]

That said, the *circulaire* did not suggest a declaratory procedure—which would go against the grain of the law. Even though 'willingness' was therein said to be key to recognition, the applicant was still supposed to prove it. However, borrowing the effective words of Catto, 'How to establish the willingness of the person? How to convince the judge that the person is convinced? . . . The rejection of a procedure based on self-declaration entails the presence of material elements [of proof].'[142] The law remains, therefore, ascriptive.

[133] CC, decision n. 2016-739, 17 Nov. 2016, ¶ 67. *See* Osella & Rubio-Marín, *supra* note 6, at 587.
[134] Défenseur des Droits, *supra* note 97, at 19–21.
[135] Paricard, *supra* note 119, at 46; Catto, *supra* note 127, ¶ 45.
[136] Circulaire de presentation des dispositions de l'Article 56 de la Loi n. 2016-1547 du 18 Novembre 2016 de modernisation de la justice du XXIe siècle concernant les procedures judiciaries de changement de prénom ed de modification de la mention du sexe à l'état civil (NOR: JUSC1709389C) (31 May 2017).
[137] *Id.* at 6.
[138] *Id.*
[139] *Id.*
[140] *Id.*
[141] *Id.*
[142] Catto, *supra* note 127, ¶ 8.

3.4. The socio-behavioural model in practice

The right envisioned by the French Parliament has an ambivalent dimension, similar to the medico-behavioural model in Italy. On the one hand, individuals seeking gender recognition can obtain it without medical preconditions. As a result, the socio-behavioural model destabilizes entrenched notions of maleness and femaleness, and people can embody legal sex differently. On the other hand, this diversity is only tolerated up to a point. This right has been crafted in such a way that it only protects the identity of those who conform to well-established gender norms. In fact, I argue that it has been '"ground[ed]" upon [a] given conception of humanity or attribute of the human rights bearer [and therefore] can always be unmasked ... as a particular and unavoidably exclusionary interpretation of the human'.[143] This reading seems to be confirmed in the application of the law. The socio-behavioural right arguably operates as a disciplinary mechanism, exhibiting the main characteristics of hierarchical observation, evaluation through norms, and a system of penalties and rewards.[144] Although there have been changes in the content of the gender norms applied—no medical requirements are needed—the structure that produces sexed subjects remains the same as before Law J21.

To begin with, courts and applicants maintain a *hierarchical relationship* to one another. It is the judge who has to be persuaded that the applicant deserves recognition and who has the ultimate say over it. This is unsurprising: As Hérault observes, the role of a judge in France involves scrutiny and evaluation, unlike that of registrars, who may limit themselves to simply receiving a declaration.[145] Admittedly, however, in comparison to the medico-behavioural model, the number of authorities that applicants must deal with is reduced, with doctors having lost their role as gatekeepers of legal recognition.[146]

Applicants are then minutely examined for conformity to gender norms.[147] In practice, gender recognition is overwhelmingly based on external assessment and validation.[148] Name change is considered to be a reliable indicator of one's new lived identity.[149] The appearance of the person also weighs in. Courts may, for example, consider one's clothing, recognition in the social circle,[150]

[143] Ben Golder, Foucault and the Politics of Rights 89 (2015).

[144] Hunt & Wickham, *supra* note 64; Dreyfus & Rabinow, *supra* note 64; Havis, *supra* note 64. *See* Chapter 4.

[145] Laurence Hérault, *«Le Sexe de l'Enfant Est Légitime» À Propos de la Mention de Sexe à l'État Civil et de sa Modification»*, *in* État Civil et Transidentité. Anatomie d'une Relation Singulière 23, 49 (Jérome Courduriès, Christine Durlens & Laurence Hérault eds., 2021).

[146] Reportedly, on one occasion a TGI required the applicant to produce medical certificates: Défenseur des Droit, Décision-Cadre n. 2020-136, 5 (18 July 2020).

[147] The implementation of Law J21 presented in the text builds on the analyses of: Catto, *supra* note 127; Hérault et al., *supra* note 129, at 42–46; Paricard, *supra* note 118.

[148] In one case, the TGI seemed to grant recognition based on the self-determination: TGI Saint Pierre, ch. civ., 2 June 2017.

[149] Catto, *supra* note 127, ¶ 26.

[150] TGI Paris, 14 Nov. 2017, n. 17/05786.

behaviour,[151] and physical resemblance to standards of the claimed sex/gender,[152] including the acquisition of secondary sexual characteristics—for instance, having a goatee.[153]

The Court of Cassation confirmed the centrality of social perception in the socio-behavioural right in the third sex case.[154] Denying the application for nonbinary recognition, the Court also ruled that the applicant, legally classified as a male, did not suffer disproportionate interference with their right to identity due to their masculine appearance. It should be mentioned that the Court might have misunderstood the plaintiff, who was not demanding recognition in order to avoid being 'outed' and to be able to 'pass' undisturbed. Rather, they wanted to be recognized as nonbinary because that was how they identified, and they wanted to have their identity acknowledged. Regardless, the Court's reasoning showed that gender recognition is still based on appearance.[155] Interestingly, the ECtHR, in its 2023 decision on the same case, somewhat chastised the Court of Cassation for this conclusion. It stated that the Court of Cassation had confused 'the concept of identity with the concept of appearance' and ignored the fact that the applicant—in the specific case—presented themselves as masculine because they were constrained by the lack of a nonbinary option in French law.[156]

In short, as Paricard explains, the socio-behavioural model requires a gender performance:

> Presenting as a woman involves displaying attitudes considered feminine (a more supple gait, sitting with crossed legs, measured gesticulation), wearing feminine clothes (such as dresses, skirts, and heels), keeping long hair, doing make-up, and removing body hair. It also means avoiding an appearance that could be confusing (having a beard, moustache or goatee). Presenting as a man similarly is a matter of cultural and social constructs [and might involve] wearing trousers, keeping short hair, sitting with legs apart, and avoiding visible elements of the other sex (braids ...).[157]

Medical transformations can still be considered, even though they are no longer required by law, as the courts themselves have made clear. However, while no longer necessary, medicalization seems to be helpful in proving one's case.[158] In fact, as anthropologist Jerome Courduriès suggests, judges may even be more positively

151 TGI Paris, 23 May 2018.
152 TGI Bobigny, 21 Nov. 2017.
153 TGI Evry, 1a ch., 9 Oct. 2017, n. 17/04792.
154 Cass., 1e civ., 4 May 2017, n. 16-17,189.
155 Catto, *supra* note 28, at 170.
156 Y v. France, App. No. 76888/17, ¶ 88 (31 Jan. 2023), https://hudoc.echr.coe.int/eng?i=001-223027.
157 Paricard, *supra* note 118, at 188.
158 Catto, *supra* note 127, ¶¶ 15–24.

predisposed towards applicants who have undergone medical treatments, as doing so allows for a clearer transition.[159]

With regard to the types of evidence accepted, Catto observes that courts may also consider 'documentary' materials.[160] Catto highlights that everything that records the sex/gender or the name under which the applicant lives can be considered, such as 'social media accounts, loyalty program membership cards . . . , utility bills, correspondence. . . ., telephone records, and public transportation passes [*Pass Navigo*]'.[161] The applicant's physical appearance at the hearing, in photographs, *etcetera*, may also be examined.[162] Courts may also evaluate testimonial evidence:[163] family, friends, acquaintances, and other people belonging to the social circle of the applicant may be called on to testify. Courts have consistently exhibited a willingness to consider evidence demonstrating that the applicant has been known as a person of the claimed sex/gender for a considerable time, sometimes several years.[164]

In fairness, Catto points out that French courts have in some cases avoided over-reliance on stereotypes. Also, the 'trapped in the wrong body narrative', with its echoes of profound malaise, no longer seems required by courts.[165] This might be seen as a positive development in terms of gender equality. Still, it bears relatively little influence on the mechanisms that preserve the stability of sex categories and the gender order in the law that builds on them. Regardless of *what* norms are examined, a detailed examination takes place nonetheless. In short, French law makes gender recognition the outcome of an *ensemble* of repeated acts. Echoing Butler's definition, these 'deeds' that constitute gender—these 'acts, gestures, and enactments'—are 'performative' because they become the inner core of identity that they are supposed to reflect.[166]

Finally, if the applicant fails the tests, they cannot be recognized in their gender identity. All benefits that are associated with gender recognition are denied to them. In this way, recognition and denial of recognition operate as a *reward* or a *penalty*, respectively, thereby constituting the 'third' leg of disciplinary power.

[159] Jerôme Courduriès, *Les Juges et les Trans. Vers une Approche Relationnelle du Genre dans les Tribunaux Français*, *in* ÉTAT CIVIL ET TRANSIDENTITÉ. ANATOMIE D'UNE RELATION SINGULIÈRE: GENRE, IDENTITÉ, FILIATION 131, 148–49 (Jérôme Courduriès, Christine Dourlens & Laurence Hérault eds., 2021).

[160] Catto, *supra* note 127, ¶ 31.

[161] Catto, *supra* note 127, ¶ 32. Hérault et al., *supra* note 129, at 43–47, discussing: TGI Nanterre, pole civ., 17 Oct. 2017, n. 16/09227; CA Montpellier, 3e ch. B, 15 Mar. 2017; TGI Paris, pole famille, 28 Nov. 2017, n. 17/07135; TGI Nanterre, 17 Oct. 2017, n. 17/06267; TGI Creteil, 1e ch., n. 16/09330.

[162] TGI Creteil, 1 ch., 7 Dec. 2017, n. 17/05750. On the relevance of the appearance at the hearing: Courduriès, *supra* note 159, at 155.

[163] Catto, *supra* note 127, ¶ 31.

[164] Hérault et al., *supra* note 129, at 42–46.

[165] Catto, *supra* note 127, ¶¶ 48–49.

[166] JUDITH BUTLER, GENDER TROUBLE: FEMINISM AND THE SUBVERSION OF IDENTITY 185 (2d ed. 1999).

3.5. Back to the body? The question of trans parenthood

With the abolishment of medical requirements, sterilization in particular, trans people can preserve their reproductive capacity after recognition. As a consequence, trans people have started demanding 'gender alignment'.[167] By gender alignment, I refer to the registration of the trans parent in the birth certificate of their children according to the parental denomination consistent with their legal registration: namely, trans men as fathers, and trans women as mothers.[168] Gender alignment is arguably integral to the right of identity of trans people. Further rights are, however, at stake, for example, privacy and family life, not to mention the rights of the family members, and especially of the children, of the trans person.[169] Although still a relatively new demand, its centrality is evinced by its inclusion in the Yogyakarta Principles + 10[170] and by the human rights litigation before the ECtHR. The latter has, however, established that the matter still falls within the margin of appreciation of the states.[171]

Hérault defined trans parenthood—fatherhood in particular—as culturally unthinkable in our societies.[172] Trans people have been traditionally understood as sterile. This may be a consequence of the still pervasive 'trapped-in-the-wrong-body' narrative that postulates that *all* trans people desire a physical change that entails the elimination of the original sex characteristics.[173] Trans people have, moreover, been considered ill-equipped to be parents because of the moral stigma attached to gender diversity.[174] Structural limits have traditionally compounded

[167] The term appears to be common currency in the field: Alice Margaria, *Trans Men Giving Birth and Reflections on Fatherhood: What to Expect?*, 34 International Journal of Law, Policy and the Family 225 (2020); Lara Karaian, *Pregnant Men: Repronormativity, Critical Trans Theory, and the Re(conceive)ing of Sex and Pregnancy in Law*, 22 Social and Legal Studies 211 (2013); Sheelagh McGuinness & Amel Alghrani, *Gender and Parenthood: The Case for Realignment*, 16 Medical Law Review 261 (2008).

[168] For a more extensive discussion of the limits on trans parenthood, *see*: Alice Margaria & Stefano Osella, *Trans Birthing Men: A New Legal Puzzle Between Cultural and Structural Limits*, *in* Biomedical Practices in the Middle East and Europe: The Impact of Religion and Culture (Marie-Claire Foblets & Federica Sona eds., forthcoming 2026). For a brief previous discussion of the case of trans parenthood in France and its impact on the preservation of the binary, *see* Osella, *supra* note 37.

[169] Daniela Alaattinoglu & Alice Margaria, *Trans Parents and the Gendered Law: Critical Reflections on the Swedish Regulation*, 21 International Journal of Constitutional Law 603 (2023).

[170] The Yogyakarta Principles Plus 10—Additional Principles and State Obligation on the Application of International Human Rights Law in Relation to Sexual Orientation, Gender Expression and Sex Characteristics to Complement the Yogyakarta Principles, Principle 24(i), which declares that: 'States shall ... [i]ssue birth certificates for children upon birth that reflect the self-defined gender identity of the parents.'

[171] O.H. and G.H. v. Germany, App. Nos. 53568/18 and 54741/18 (4 Apr. 2023), https://hudoc.echr.coe.int/eng?i=001-223924.

[172] Laurence Hérault, *Procréer à la Manière des Femmes, Engendrer en Tant Qu'Homme*, *in* La Parenté Transgenre 81 (Laurence Hérault ed., 2014).

[173] Peter Dunne, *Transgender Sterilisation Requirements in Europe*, 25 Medical Law Review 554 (2017).

[174] Sonia K. Katyal & Ilona M. Turner, *Transparenthood*, 117 Michigan Law Review 1593 (2019); Carlos A. Ball, The Right to Be Parents: LGBT Families and the Transformation of Parenthood 183 (2012).

the cultural ones, especially considering the heteronormative rules of family law that presuppose specific forms of reproduction to establish family links.[175] The much criticized[176] *mater semper certa* rule, which assigns motherhood to the person who bears the child, and the presumption of paternity for the man married to the mother, are cases in point.[177]

Although Article 61-8 of the Civil Code provides that gender recognition does not affect filiation relations established before the amendment of legal sex, no legislative rule explicitly governs relationships established thereafter. However, in 2020, the Court of Cassation denied the claim of a trans woman to be recorded as the 'mother' of the child whom she had begotten.[178] The plaintiff was legally female and married to a cis woman, who had given birth to the child. She claimed that the misalignment between her legal sex and parental designation infringed on her right to identity, as well as the rights of her child, in particular to registration, protected by the New York Convention on the Rights of the Child.[179] The Court of Cassation rejected the argument and clarified that French law, as in force at the time, did not allow the presence of two biological mothers nor of neutral designations such as 'biological parent'—which the Court of Appeal of Montpellier had identified as the proper designation of the plaintiff. While the plaintiff enjoyed a right to have her biological relation to the child acknowledged by law, she had to be registered as the 'father', considering the general rules on establishing motherhood in French law. The Court also established that the right of children to registration and to know their origins,[180] as well as privacy and family life, read together with equality,[181] required the plaintiff to be registered as the child's father. This decision ran counter to the opinion of the *Défenséur des Droits*.[182]

The Court of Appeal of Toulouse,[183] to which the Court of Cassation had assigned the file after deciding the main principles concerning the case, in fact granted the claim of the plaintiff. Considering the legal gap on the reproductive rights of trans people,[184] this court found that the right to private life of the parent,

[175] Marie Mesnil, *Quel Genre pour la Parenté Trans? Le Trois Lectures de l'Identité Sexuée*, *in* La Bicatégorisation de Sexe entre Droit, Normes Sociales et Sciences Biomédicales 201, 202–04 (Marie-Xavière Catto & Julie Mazaleigue-Labaste eds., 2021). As acknowledged in the text, these rules have however evolved after the 2021 *loi de bioethique* which opened options to lesbian parenthood.

[176] Marcela Iacub, L'Empire du Ventre. Pour une Autre Histoire de la Maternité (2004); Courtney M. Cahill, *The New Maternity*, 133 Harvard Law Review 2223 (2020); Jessica A. Clarke, *Pregnant People*, 119 Columbia Law Review 173 (2019).

[177] For a discussion of the law in England and Wales: Chapter 8.

[178] Cass., 1e civ., 16 Sept. 2020, n. 18-50.080. The case was previously decided by the TGI of Montpellier (22 July 2016, n. 15/05019), which had rejected the claim. The CA Montpellier (3 ch. A and B, 14 Nov. 2018, n. 16/06059) also rejected the claim, but ordered that the applicant be recorded in the civil registry neither as 'father' nor 'mother', but rather as 'biological parent'.

[179] Article 7.

[180] Cass., 1e civ., 16 Sept. 2020, n. 18-50.080.

[181] Articles 8 and 14 ECHR.

[182] Défenseur des Droits, Décision-cadre n. 2020-136, 28 June 2019.

[183] CA Toulouse, ch. 6, 9 Feb. 2022, n. 20/03128.

[184] This gap had not been filled by the *loi de bioethique* of 2021.

together with the best interests of the child, made the registration of the plaintiff as a *mother* imperative. The Court of Appeal of Toulouse also invoked the 2021 law on bioethics, which opened assisted reproductive technologies to lesbian couples, thus making it possible to register two mothers on the birth certificate.

As a result of this decision, the French legal framework appears somewhat uncertain. On the one hand, the decision of the Court of Appeal of Toulouse was favourable to the applicant. Nevertheless, this judgment does not seem uncontroversially grounded in the law, and its compliance with the principles established by the Court of Cassation could be debated.[185] Admittedly, the new law on bioethics, which was passed after the decision of the Court of Cassation, changed the rules on filiation that had limited the plaintiff's demand.[186] With this reform, the need to gatekeep gender alignment might have become less pressing. On the other hand, if one also considers that the Court of Strasbourg has not to date ruled in favour of trans parents, the right to be registered in line with one's gender identity rests on feeble grounds. Even more importantly, the *Conseil Constitutionnel*, called upon to decide on the constitutionality of some aspects of the law on paternity leave and its implications for the equality of same-sex couples and couples including a trans parent (*inter alia*), ruled that trans men are entitled to maternity leave when they give birth in 2025.[187] Although the full implications of this judgment cannot be explored here and more research is needed, it *prima facie* appears that the *Conseil Constitutionnel* has aligned itself with the Court of Cassation. It reinforced the tie between 'biology' (so to speak) and the rules on establishing filiation when it stated:

> According to a constant jurisprudence of the Court of Cassation, transgender people who have modified their sex in the civil status registry may only rely on the means of establishing filiation that reflect physiological reality [*réalité physiologique*] to obtain recognition of legal filiation with their child.[188]

Be that as it may, it is interesting to note that the (mis)recognition of trans parents arguably appears to bring the body back to the centre of the law, carving out an exception to the socio-behavioural model established in 2016.[189] The case of

[185] Sophie Paricard, *La Parenté Transgenre: Une Décision Inédite. Toulouse, 9 Févr. 2022, n. 20/03128*, DALLOZ ACTUALITÉ (1 Mar. 2022).
[186] Pierre Michel, *Filiation Biologique et Mère Transgenre: La Double Filiation Maternelle Biologique Consacrée par la Cour d'Appel de Toulouse Note sous CA Toulouse, ch. 6, 9 février 2022, n° RG 20/03128*, in LA REVUE DES DROITS DE L'HOMME (21 Mar. 2022), http:// journals.openedition.org/revdh/14560.
[187] CC, decision No. 2025-1155, 8 Aug. 2025, https://www.conseil-constitutionnel.fr/decision/2025/20251155QPC.htm. This case concerned 'Arts. L. 1225-35 of the Labour Code and L. 623-1 of the Social Security Code, in the version following Law No. 2020-1576 of 14 Dec. 2020 on funding social security for 2021'. For an analysis: Mila Petkova & Benjamin Moron-Puech, *Vers un Notariat au Service des Personnes Transgenres?*, REVUE JURIDIQUE PERSONNES & FAMILLE 307 (2026).
[188] CC, decision No. 2025-1155, 8 Aug. 2025, ¶ 20.
[189] Paricard, *supra* note 118, at 178–81.

trans parenthood seems to confirm the understanding of legal sex as the outcome of balancing opposing principles. Paisley Currah, focusing on the United States, has observed that the different criteria used by the various government agencies to define sex (and, to that effect, to determine recognition) demonstrate that legal sex serves different purposes in different settings.[190] In the same spirit, French legislators believed that the *verité sociologique* was enough to ensure the inalienability of civil status and the principles of the gender order in a changing legal system. However, when the stability of filiation rules is at stake, the narrow reading of French law, following the Court of Cassation's decision, suggests a retrenchment of narratives of the body and biology.

4. Conclusion

In this chapter, I hope to have demonstrated that the socio-behavioural model represents an ascriptive form of gender recognition. Legal sex is grounded in social and behavioural criteria that are clearly assessable by a third party. Sex is to be discovered, not declared. Medical transformations are not necessary, but identity recognition is granted to those who perform sex/gender in a socially intelligible fashion. These preconditions define an ideal rights-bearer, a subject of recognition who, unlike in the Italian case, is not repulsed by and in anguish over their own anatomy, but who still conventionally lives, presents, and is acknowledged as a person of the gender in which they seek recognition. Given the impossibility of obtaining nonbinary recognition, they must position themselves within the male-female binary.

I have shown that socio-behavioural preconditions are motivated by the need to safeguard the inalienability of civil status. Although connected to the gender order and, to some extent, heteronormativity, the French case shows that the ramifications of sex categories in the legal system go beyond merely preserving heteronormativity. As the Court of Cassation stated in 2017, binary categories are a 'founding' element of social and legal organization and are connected to a multitude of public interests, including equality. Second, control over gender recognition is also exerted for cultural reasons, as safeguarding the inalienability of civil status has been given considerable emphasis throughout the various changes in the law.

Third, we may suggest that the tremendous amount of attention that had been directed to medicalization could have been a factor influencing the development of a socio-behavioural model in France. At the same time, the insistence on socio-behavioural preconditions is consistent with the recurring doctrinal grounding

[190] Paisely Currah, Sex Is as Sex Does: Governing Transgender Identity (2022).

in privacy. Privacy was outspokenly the rationale behind gender recognition up until 2016, based on the *B v. France* case and subsequent case law by the Court of Cassation. That is not to say that privacy remains to date the only doctrinal foundation of gender recognition. In compliance with the law of the Council of Europe, so consequential for French legal developments, the protection of identity is now central, too. Yet it is hard not to discern a continuity between the various stages in the evolution of this right, as well as the persisting importance of individual appearances in the reasoning of French courts and legislature.

As to *how* the socio-behavioural model operates, a disciplinary apparatus underpins the right. The subject of recognition presupposed by the legislature and defined by the law is repeatedly affirmed by the courts. This right is paradoxical in that it not only grants an important demand to the person but also enables an entire structure of normalization. In this sense, the similarity between the medico-behavioural and the socio-behavioural forms is quite evident. In short, the socio-behavioural model demonstrates how an externally imposed normative gender identity and, more importantly, a normative gender expression, are still at the core of important legal, possibly constitutional, principles.

Ultimately, one wonders if this compromise can be satisfactory and durable, especially vis-à-vis the increased protection of trans rights. In a time of increased protection of gender self-determination, movements in France, as well as in many other jurisdictions, can be directed towards the abolishment of the requirements of the socio-behavioural model, as seems to be the case with bills promoting a self-declaratory procedure that were officially put before the Senate[191] and the National Assembly in 2024.[192] In June 2025, the Défenseur des Droits issued a new framework decision and urged the government to implement gender self-determination through a swift process based on the individual's declaration.[193] The outcome of such bills is still unknown, but surely they suggest the next step in the recognition of trans identity: de-judicialization and self-determination, to which the next chapter is dedicated.

[191] Proposition de loi visant à faciliter la reconnaissance du genre à l'état civil, n. 490, enregistré à la Présidence du Sénat le 2 avril 2024.

[192] Proposition de loi visant à faciliter la reconnaissance du genre à l'état civil, n° 656, déposée le mardi 3 décembre 2024.

[193] Défenseur des Droits, Décision-cadre n°2025-112.

6

The Self-Determination Model

Colombia

1. Self-determination to the fore

At times, gender recognition goes beyond de-medicalization, and gender self-determination is achieved by trans advocates. When this is the case, those eager to modify their legal sex can declare their intention to a public authority, without being required to meet any standards or otherwise prove their eligibility. Gender self-determination has been a central demand of trans advocacy for a few decades now, due to its inclusivity and the absence of the controls that we encountered in, for example, Italy and France.[1] This right is slowly gaining traction in international human rights soft law and at the supranational level.[2] For example, the Parliamentary Assembly of the Council of Europe and the Commissioner for Human Rights have repeatedly called for gender self-determination.[3] The European Parliament has endorsed it,[4] as have the Inter-American Court of Human Rights (IACtHR)[5] and the Inter-American Commission for Human Rights.[6] At the national level, gender self-determination could be found in at least twenty-four jurisdictions in 2023.[7] While still exceptional, it is hardly the one-of-a-kind rarity

[1] Phyllis Randolph Frye, *Preface to Appendix: The International Bill of Gender Rights*, *in* Transgender Rights (Paisely Currah, Richard Juang & Shannon Price Minter eds., 2006); Zowie Davis, Sex/Gender and Self-Determination (2021).

[2] Refer to: Chapter 2.

[3] Parliamentary Assembly of the Council of Europe, Resolution 2048 (2015) on Discrimination against Transgender People in Europe (22 Apr. 2015); Commissioner for Human Rights of the Council of Europe, Human Rights and Gender Identity and Expression (Mar. 2024).

[4] Resolution 2021/2243(INI), of the European Parliament on Intersectional Discrimination in the European Union: The Socio-Economic Situation of Women of African, Middle-Eastern, Latin-American and Asian Descent, ¶ 50 (6 July 2022); Resolution 2018/2878(RSP) of the European Parliament on the Rights of Intersex People, ¶ 9 (14 Feb. 2019).

[5] Identidad de Género, e Igualdad y No Discriminación a Parejas del Mismo Sexo, Advisory Opinion OC-24/17, Inter-American Court of Human Rights, (Ser. A) No. 24, ¶ 95 (24 Nov. 2017).

[6] Informe sobre Personas Trans y de Género Diverso y Sus Derechos Económicos, Sociales, Culturales y Ambientales, Inter-American Commission on Human Rights, OEA/Ser.L/V/II. Doc. 239 (7 Aug. 2020); Violencia contra Personas Lesbianas, Gay, Bisexuales, Trans e Intersex en América, Inter-American Commission on Human Rights, OAS/Ser.L/V/II.rev.2 Doc. 36 (12 Nov. 2015).

[7] For an overview of the laws on gender self-determination in 2023: Ido Katri, *The Perils of Gender Self-Determination: Global Shifts in Sex Reclassification Law and Policy*, 71 The American Journal of Comparative Law 707 (2023).

Gender Diversity in Public Law. Stefano Osella, Oxford University Press. © Stefano Osella 2026.
DOI: 10.1093/9780198935070.003.0006

that it might have been in 2012, when Argentina—the first country on the world stage to do so—legislated it.[8]

Colombia not only fits, but arguably is the crown jewel of this trend.[9] Over the course of a few years, the Colombian Constitutional Court has produced an abundant and theoretically sophisticated jurisprudence with queer and, to some extent, decolonial overtones. The result is a constitutional doctrine of self-determination that has been applied to multiple cases where the right of identity of trans people has come into conflict with other public interests or fundamental rights, for example, conscription into mandatory military service and age requirements for retirement benefits.[10] The Constitutional Court has granted a right to gender self-determination with 'fluid' characteristics, allowing for multiple subsequent changes. With some specific tweaks motivated by the best interests of the child, the Constitutional Court has granted a right to gender self-determination to underage persons too.

This chapter illustrates the development and the characteristics of this model of recognition. It contributes to the existing scholarship by offering a detailed analysis of landmark decisions that define the development and features of this recognition model. It pays particular attention to the constitutional dynamics at play and to its theoretical implications, both in terms of queer and decolonial theory.[11] The main argument put forward is that gender self-determination ensures that legal sex reflects, at least to some extent, the autonomously defined identity of the applicant, thereby being liberating for trans people. This capacity of self-representation reached its acme in 2022, when a third gender option was introduced—a development that will be explored in Chapter 7. Furthermore, self-determination has the potential to challenge Eurocentric epistemologies of gender and thus to contribute

[8] Law No. 26.743, 23 May 2012 (Arg.).

[9] Stefano Osella & Ruth Rubio-Marín, *Gender Recognition at the Crossroads: Four Models and the Compass of Comparative Law*, 21 International Journal of Constitutional Law 575, 595–97 (2023) (briefly identifying the Colombian case as a 'self-determination' model). Isabel C. Jaramillo-Sierra has connected the abundant constitutional output of the Colombian Court to the instrument of *tutela*. The *tutela* is a writ that allows every person to immediately obtain protection of human rights. It is disciplined by Article 86 of the Constitution and has become an increasingly important instrument among the constitutional actions in the Colombian legal system (Jan Boesten, Constitutional Origin and Norm Creation in Colombia: Discursive Institutionalism and the Empowerment of the Constitutional Court (2022); Las Acciones Constitucionales. Reflexiones sobre sus Avances y Retos (Maria Lucia Torres-Villareal & Paola Marcela Iregui-Parra eds., 2020). Jaramillo-Sierra reports that, to date, the number of all *tutelas*—not just concerning gender or trans rights—decided by the courts can be counted in the millions (Isabel C. Jaramillo-Sierra, *Women and LGBTQIA+ Rights in Colombia*, *in* Women, Gender, and Constitutionalism in Latin America 67, 70–71 (Francisca Pou Gimenez, Veronica Undurraga & Ruth Rubio-Marín eds., 2024)).

[10] The case law of the Court was implemented with Decreto [Presidential Decree] 1227, 4 junio 2015, which added Section 4 to Decreto 1069, 26 mayo 2015.

[11] For a general overview of gender self-determination in Colombia and for a more sustained socio-legal discussion of the subject, *see*: Isabel C. Jaramillo, *The Story of the Recognition of Sexual Identity as a Source of Harm in Colombian Constitutional Law*, *in* Trans Rights and Wrongs: A Comparative Study of Legal Reform Concerning Trans Persons 437 (Isabel C. Jaramillo & Laura Carlson eds., 2021); Jaramillo-Sierra, *supra* note 9.

to decolonizing gender in the law. This is evident in the Colombian case law, where the Constitutional Court has connected self-determination to a broader decolonial approach in gender constitutionalism.

The Colombian case shows that, even when limited to the binary, self-determination constitutes an important step towards the disestablishment of conventional and binary legal categories. When a right to self-define legal sex is enacted, the exclusion of nonbinary people from such a right becomes conceptually difficult. Furthermore, when public authorities no longer define and certify the characteristics that demonstrate belonging in a sex category—as happens with self-determination—they cease to define the subject of recognition. As the boundaries of the sexed subject become hazier, the law no longer lays the groundwork for the development of the gender disciplinary apparatus that we encountered in Italy and France. Hence, it is not much of an exaggeration to say that gender self-determination has earth-shattering potential when it comes to the constitutional gender order and gender in public law.

Although I do not offer a comprehensive explanation of all of the factors underlying the evolution of Colombian constitutional law regarding gender recognition, a few observations can serve as a starting point for future research. First, structural changes unfolded at the constitutional level, as LGBTQI+ rights were recognized by the Constitutional Court,[12] especially those of intersex people, as explained in Chapter 3. The result has been a weakening of constitutional heteronormativity and a heightened acceptance of bodies that defy the binary.[13] Second, trans identity has been culturally revalued by the Constitutional Court as fully dignified. Explaining the reasons behind this cultural transformation is beyond the scope of this chapter. It is nonetheless worth pointing out the critical role of trans activists in Colombia,[14] and especially their contributions to the case law of the Constitutional Court through the submission of *amici* briefs. Finally, from a doctrinal point of view, the Court has grounded gender recognition in the right to *vivir como quiera*—that is, living as one wishes—which, in turn, has been grounded in dignity, the right to which is enshrined in Article 1 of the Colombian Constitution. The Colombian Constitutional Court protects free will, even when it comes to individual sex classification.

Methodologically, the choice to include Colombia in this study is motivated by the richness of its case law—an abundance that, in fact, makes a discussion thereof in its entirety infeasible in a comparative monograph. Since a selection is necessary, I have included the decisions that scholars and the Court itself have identified

[12] Julieta Lemaitre Ripoll, *Love in the Time of Cholera: LGBT Rights in Colombia*, 6 SUR-International Journal on Human Rights 73 (2009); Jaramillo, *supra* note 11, at 441.

[13] Judith Butler, Gender Trouble: Feminism and the Subversion of Identity 33 (2d ed. 1999).

[14] Daniel A. Verástegui-Mejía & Geronimo P. Céspedes, *Memorias de Resistencia: El Movimiento Social Trans en Colombia*, 58 Revista de Estudios Colombianos 50 (2021).

as foundational. Finally, the analysis contemplates cases that recognize other forms of gender diversity—such as ancestral identities—to show the theoretical potential of self-determination.

As per usual, some caveats are in order. First, as Isabel C. Jaramillo suggests, we have little knowledge of the limits that trans people seeking recognition meet in practice.[15] Jaramillo argues that the scarce data available suggest that self-declaration 'does not seem to have been resisted by notaries in charge of the implementation'.[16] Second, trans people may run into obstacles to recognition in various forms of structural discrimination that might in practice prevent them from seeking a change of legal sex.[17] Third, violence against LGBTQI+ people, especially racialized ones, is widespread in Colombia,[18] as it is elsewhere. Such violence is a reminder that, despite the progress of constitutional law, grassroots work to foster dignity and inclusion remains needed. As Jaramillo-Sierra argues, stopping violence is at the core of trans demands. Nevertheless, self-determination 'has empowered middle-class and professional trans persons to become more vocal and support the larger process of societal transformation involved in their claims'.[19] But more fundamentally, we should not forget that gender self-determination has been a crucial demand of *travestí* activism, with its broader links to intersectional and anti-capitalist demands.

Finally, this chapter intervenes in a debate on gender self-determination that has been intense and contentious. It is worth emphasizing that, even though the Constitutional Court of Colombia has undeniably looked very favourably on the demands of gender-diverse people, echoes of the blowback from gender-critical feminists and anti-gender advocacy can be traced in a few dissenting opinions.[20] It is also useful to bear in mind that, in the Latin American context, hostility to the so-called gender ideology has triggered social mobilization[21] and, in Colombia,

[15] Jaramillo, *supra* note 11, at 447.

[16] *Id.* at 449.

[17] For example, trans men are not exempt from military service (Ley [L.] 1861/2017, Art. 12), although serving might represent a danger to their lives and well-being and other categories of men enjoy an exemption. The only alternative for them is to be declared unfit for service, possibly after invasive and humiliating examinations. If trans men do not comply with these requirements, they cannot receive the *tarjeta militar*—a document certifying the successful completion of military duties—which is required for many purposes in civilian life, including applying for jobs in the public and private sectors. Arguably, this treatment hinders various rights, including gender recognition, as the development of trans identity is limited by these circumstances. (Jhonnatan Espinosa Rodríguez et al., Hombres trans y libreta militar en Colombia (2021) https://www.dejusticia.org/publication/hombres-trans-y-libreta-militar-en-colombia/; Corte Constitucional [C.C.] [Constitutional Court], 22 mayo 2019, Sentencia C-220/19; C.C., 6 agosto 2019, Sentencia C-356/19). Note, all decisions can be found at https://www.corteconstitucional.gov.co/. Henceforth, all decisions already cited in full will be reported with the number and year only.

[18] Jaramillo, *supra* note 11, at 447; Colombia Diversa, La Realidad de la Discriminación (Dec. 2023) https://colombiadiversa.org/c-diversa/wp-content/uploads/2023/11/Resumen-ejecutivo-Informe-Colombia-Diversa.pdf.

[19] Jaramillo-Sierra, *supra* note 9, at 93.

[20] For an overview, refer to Chapter 2.

[21] Flávia Biroli & Mariana Caminotti, *The Conservative Backlash Against Gender in Latin America*, 16 Politics and Gender 1 (2020).

even played a part in the 2016 rejection of the peace accord between the government and the FARC anti-government fighters.[22]

My aim in this chapter is not to muster a defence of the results achieved by the Colombian Constitutional Court; rather, I would like to suggest that this Court represents a potentially inspiring example regarding the method with which cases of gender recognition have been decided. The Court has taken as a point of departure the existence of a right to gender recognition, which is an established, albeit relatively novel, human right.[23] Against this background, the Court has examined whether and to what extent gender self-determination might affect competing interests or rights, and has offered what it believes to be an adequate balance among them. This is not to say that the Constitutional Court has always correctly assessed all principles involved. But it is to say that the Court's approach appears to be inspired by pragmatic and empirical considerations, without dogmatic overtones.[24] The Court, in short, has foregrounded proportionality and strived to assess matters *in concreto*.

2. The earlier doctrine of gender recognition

2.1. Sex as a fact

In Colombian law, civil status clarifies the legal position of every person in the family and society.[25] In principle, the various registries that constitute the civil status record facts, sex included,[26] which determine the set of legal positions of each person.[27] Although nonbinary recognition was granted by the Colombian Constitutional Court in 2022,[28] at the time of writing, options at birth appear to be in most cases binary.[29] Changes to a person's civil status, sex included, are permitted by the general law on the civil status. An official act from a notary (*escritura*

[22] Ana Cristina González Velez & Laura Castro, *Colombia: Educación Sexual, Diversidad, y Paz: El Entramado de la 'Ideología de Género'*, *in* Develando la Retórica del Miedo de Los Fundamentalismos: La Campaña 'Con Mis Hijos No Te Metas' en Colombia, Ecuador, y Perú (Ana Cristina González Vélez et al. eds., 2018); José Fernando Serrano-Amaya, *La Tormenta Perfecta: Ideología de Género y Articulación de Públicos*, 27 Sexualidad, Salud, y Sociedad 150 (2017).

[23] Holning Lau, *Gender Recognition as a Human Right*, *in* The Cambridge Handbook of New Human Rights 193 (Andreas von Arnault, Kerstin von der Decker & Susi Mart eds., 2020).

[24] Unlike other courts, such as the UK Supreme Court and the other courts discussed in Chapter 8.

[25] L. 1260, 27 julio 1970, Art. 1.

[26] L. 1260/1970, Art. 52.

[27] Defensoria del Pueblo, Trans-Formando Derechos. Derechos de las Personas Transgénero in Colombia (2018), https://directoriosaludtrans.com/wp-content/uploads/2024/10/7.-Trans-formando-derechos-de-las-personas-transgenero-en-Colombia-2018-defensoria-del-pueblo.pdf.

[28] C.C., 4 febrero 2022, Sentencia T-033/22.

[29] Intersex children whose sex is hard to determine may, however, be recorded without 'ticking the box', so to speak. C.C., 16 julio 2013, Sentencia T-450A/13. For a discussion of intersexuality in Colombia, *see* Chapter 3.

publica) or a judicial decision is required. Before *Decreto* 1227 of 2015, which implemented the 2015 constitutional doctrine on gender self-determination, the necessary procedures to amend legal sex were judge-made only.

The Constitutional Court had ruled that gender recognition required a judicial procedure in 1994,[30] when it found that sex categories were intended to reflect an objective element on which family and social relations are built.[31] Sex could not be declared; it had to be verified, and the declaratory procedure before a notary was judged ill-fit to the purpose.[32] The Constitutional Court, to be clear, did not rule out gender recognition, but it deemed necessary a judicial procedure, possibly to assess requirements that, however, remained unspecified—most likely, they were intended to be medical.[33] In addition to being unclear, the 1994 judgment appears contradictory, too. The emphasis on the factual reality of sex was indeed the outcome of a value judgment. The Court did not rule that recording sex as a fact was an objective worth pursuing per se. It was not the reality of sex—however defined—that the Constitutional Court was after, but arguably the stability of legal categories that such a factual reality seemingly allowed. Lacking any grounding of gender recognition in fundamental rights, and given the pre-eminence of public interests based on the stability of sex categories, transition was allowed but subjected to judicial controls.

Circumstances of the time might explain this outcome. The 1991 Constitution had granted a multiplicity of rights, including gender equality, and seen a significant feminist mobilization during the constituent process.[34] However, the text of the Constitution has attracted scholarly criticism for its heteronormativity.[35] Admittedly, as Julieta Lemaitre Ripoll argued, the Constitutional Court, with many progressive decisions, 'extended the right to equality and human dignity to include protections against sexual orientation discrimination'.[36] However, at the time of the 1994 decision, these advances were yet to come.

[30] C.C., 8 noviembre 1994, Sentencia T-504/94. This discussion expands the analysis previously presented in Stefano Osella & Ruth Rubio-Marín, *The Right to Gender Recognition Before the Colombian Constitutional Court: A Queer and Travesti Theory Analysis*, 40 Bulletin of Latin American Research 650, 656 (2021).

[31] C.C., T-504/94, ¶ 2 (Fundamentos juridicos).

[32] C.C., T-504/94, ¶¶ 4 and 6 (Fundamentos juridicos).

[33] This is suggested by the Constitutional Court in the following case law: C.C., 13 febrero 2015, Sentencia T-063/15, ¶ 7.2.3 (Consideraciones y fundamentos).

[34] Julieta Lemaitre, *Feminist Legalism: Colombian Constitution-Making in the 1990s*, *in* Women as Constitution-Makers: Case Studies from the New Democratic Era (Helen Irving & Ruth Rubio-Marín eds., 2019).

[35] Lina Céspedes-Báez & Jorge Sarmiento-Forero, *¿Cómo Mira el Estado? Constitución de 1991 y Compromisos de Género del Estado Colombiano*, 13 Revista Estudios Socio-Jurídicos 389, 398 (2011).

[36] Lemaitre Ripoll, *supra* note 12, at 75.

2.2. Towards gender self-determination

The purported 'factuality' of sex was short-lived. As discussed in Chapter 2, the Constitutional Court banned involuntary gender reassignment of intersex children in decision T-477/95 and established that 'sex is an unmodifiable element of the identity of each person and only the person, with full knowledge and properly informed, can consent to sex reassignment'.[37] The person was defined as the 'master' (*dueña*) of themselves and their actions.[38] As of 1999, the Constitutional Court started to refer to the binary as a cultural construct and to intersexuality as a source of richness.[39] In the ensuing case law, the Court reiterated these notions over and over again.[40] In the following years, the Constitutional Court protected the rights of trans people, for example, shielding them from discrimination[41] and guaranteeing access to gender-affirming healthcare.[42] LGB individuals also increasingly had their rights safeguarded—including protection of same-sex unions and their right to live as a family in 2011.[43]

Against this background, the Constitutional Court laid the groundwork for a reconceptualization of legal sex in a case concerning public funding for gender confirmation treatments as well as gender recognition. Despite falling short of establishing a general right to gender self-determination, the Court reaffirmed that multiple constitutional principles—including dignity and free development of personality—entail granting recognition,[44] and stated that

> [t]he sexual identity of the person ... concerns what they consider in their inner self and what they want to manifest to others.... [I]t becomes vitally important to protect [trans people's] fundamental rights to the free development of personality, self-determination, and human dignity. ... [T]he State cannot impose any barrier on the individual deciding their life development, their way of being, or their sexual condition.[45]

[37] C.C., 23 octubre 1995, Sentencia T-477/95, ¶ 13.1. *See also*: Ruth Rubio-Marín & Stefano Osella, *Between Rights and Pragmatism: Intersexuality Before the Colombian Constitutional Court*, *in* The Legal Status of Intersex Persons (Jens Scherpe, Anatol Dutta & Tobias Helms eds., 2018).

[38] C.C., T-477/95, ¶ 15.1.

[39] C.C., 12 mayo 1999, Sentencia SU-337/99, ¶ 91 (Aclaración final).

[40] *See* Chapter 3.

[41] C.C., 4 mayo 2011, Sentencia T-314/11.

[42] C.C., 29 octubre 2012, Sentencia T-876/12.

[43] C.C., 26 julio 2011, Sentencia C-577/11. Same-sex marriage followed with: C.C., 28 abril 2016, Sentencia SU-216/16.

[44] C.C., 8 noviembre 2012, Sentencia T-918/12, ¶¶ 3.3. and 7.3 (Consideraciones y fundamentos). *See also*: Jaramillo, *supra* note 11, at 444; Osella & Rubio-Marín, *supra* note 30 (connecting this decision to the creation of a right to gender recognition in Colombia).

[45] C.C., T-918/12, ¶ 3.4 (Consideraciones y fundamentos).

Limits on such rights, the Court stressed, are legitimate only if necessary to protect the rights of others or to serve public interests.[46] Gender self-determination, the Court highlighted, does not harm third parties.[47]

3. The doctrine of self-determination

3.1. Sex determination and legal identity[48]

In 2015 came the breakthrough, with decision T-063/15.[49] This case originated from a *tutela* filed by a trans woman, requesting to use the more expedite, cheaper, and less cumbersome notarial procedure instead of the judicial one. The Court granted the *tutela* and established a doctrine of gender self-determination.[50]

First, the Court elaborated a doctrinal and theoretical basis of gender recognition.[51] It grounded such a right in dignity.[52] This principle ensures the autonomy of each person to live 'as they wish' (*vivir como quiera*), 'well', and 'without being humiliated' (*sin humillaciones*). The Court also invoked the right to free development of personality[53] and referred to the rights to legal personality and to be recognized before the law.[54] At the same time, the decision acknowledged opposing interests, such as stability of civil status and the certainty of legal and social positions.[55] From a theoretical perspective, the Court borrowed the definition of gender identity from the Yogyakarta Principles. It considered that sex is not determined by genitalia alone, but is rather a complex of factors, identity included. Likewise, it did not regard trans identity as pathological but as a valid life option.[56] For these reasons, the Court concluded that individual sex cannot be seen as merely 'objective',[57] and that cis and trans identities are equally respectable in the eyes of the law.[58]

At this point, the Court moved to the proportionality analysis. It reasoned that a judicial procedure requires time-consuming scrutiny and validation. This procedure is often based on medical evidence and stereotyped evaluations that 'force

[46] C.C., T-918/12, ¶ 3.2 (Consideraciones y fundamentos).
[47] C.C., T-918/12, ¶ 3.3 (Consideraciones y fundamentos).
[48] This section draws on and expands Osella & Rubio-Marín, *supra* note 30.
[49] The case also concerned the name change of a trans person. The Court confirmed that having a name that reflects one's gender identity is part of the more general right to identity and of the right to determine one's own life plan (T-063/15, ¶ 4.4.1. (Consideraciones y fundamentos)).
[50] For a doctrinal discussion of the decision: Julia Sandra Bernal Crespo, *Los Derechos Fundamentales de la Personas Transgénero*, 38 Revista Mexicana de Derecho Constitucióнal 229 (2018).
[51] C.C., T-063/15, ¶ 4 and ¶ 4.5 (Consideraciones y fundamentos).
[52] Art. 1 *Constitución Politica* [C.P.].
[53] C.C., T-063/15, ¶ 4; Art. 16 C.P.
[54] Art 14. C.P.
[55] C.C., T-063/15, ¶ 7.2.6 (Consideraciones y fundamentos). *See also*: Decreto ley 1260/1970, Art. 1.
[56] C.C., T-063/15, ¶ 5.2–5.3 (Consideraciones y fundamentos).
[57] C.C., T-063/15, ¶¶ 5.2–5.3 (Consideraciones y fundamentos).
[58] C.C., T-063/15, ¶ 7.2.4 (Consideraciones y fundamentos).

the person to position themselves at one extreme or the other on a heteronormativity scale'.[59] This statement echoes the connection between institutional heterosexuality and the binary theorized by Judith Butler, who identified in obligatory heterosexuality the need to preserve two stable, mutually exclusive sexes.[60] The Court considered that the less invasive (declaratory) notarial procedure could preserve legal and social certainty, if needed with further corroboration such as witnesses, a previous name change, or—repeating that trans identity is not a pathology—optional medical records.[61]

The decision was not unanimous. Justice Guerrero Perez objected that sex in a person's civil status should be grounded in biological facts, as self-ascription might undermine the function of civil status registration. The justice also objected that the Court's approach resembled 'more activism than science'.[62] Justice Guerrero Perez mobilized the narrative that animates anti-gender advocacy. And yet, this dissent displays the same contradiction as the 1994 decision, where 'science' was not pursued for its own sake, but as an instrument to cement control over sex categories. While Guerrero Perez's criticism of the Court's balancing exercise could be legitimate, it should have been supported with some kind of empirical evidence that was not offered.[63]

As Juliana Jaramillo argued, decision T-063/15 had radiating effects in the field of politics.[64] As the Court requested many interventions from civil society, the proceedings offered a platform for creating alliances among various organizations, especially between networks of trans activists and institutional and academic actors. These alliances would continue in the aftermath of the decision, when cooperation with the government was needed to implement the right established by the Court.

On 4 June 2015, the President of the Republic enacted decree 1227 of 2015, implementing the decision. The preamble of decree 1227 of 2015 states that gender recognition should not be understood as a change vis-à-vis a previous reality, but, rather, as a correction of a mistake made at birth when a legal sex not conforming

[59] C.C., T-063/15, ¶ 7.2.3 (Consideraciones y fundamentos).

[60] BUTLER, *supra* note 13.

[61] C.C., T-063/15, ¶ 7.2.7 (Consideraciones y fundamentos).

[62] C.C., T-063/15, Salvamento de Voto del Magistrado Guerrero Perez, ¶¶ 3–4.

[63] I have already expressed my reservations about the positions of gender critical 'radfems' in Ruth Rubio-Marín & Stefano Osella, *La Autodeterminación de Género: Gender Critical Radfems a la Prueba de la Proporcionalidad*, IBERICONNECT BLOG (1 Feb. 2021), https://www.ibericonnect.blog/2021/02/la-autodeterminacion-de-genero-gender-critical-radfems-a-la-prueba-de-la-proporcionalidad/.

[64] Juliana Jaramillo, *La Corte Constitucional de Colombia y el Reconocimiento Legal de la Identidad de Género: Redes de Movilización Legal e Impacto Judicial*, 60 REVISTA DERECHO DEL ESTADO 29, 47–55 (2024); José Fernando Serrano-Amaya, Manuel Alejandro Rodríguez Rondón & Natalia Daza-Niño, *Public Policies Toward LGBT People and Rights in Latin America*, *in* OXFORD RESEARCH ENCYCLOPEDIA OF POLITICS 15 (2020), https://oxfordre.com/politics/view/10.1093/acrefore/9780190228637.001.0001/acrefore-9780190228637-e-1261. On the notion of radiating effects: Marc Galanter, *The Radiating Effect of Courts*, *in* EMPIRICAL THEORIES ABOUT COURTS (Keith Boyum & Lynn Mather eds., 1983); LEILA KAWAR, CONTESTING IMMIGRATION POLICY IN COURT: LEGAL ACTIVISM AND ITS RADIATING EFFECTS IN THE UNITED STATES AND FRANCE (2015).

to the identity of the person was assigned. The decree provides binary options,[65] as the Constitutional Court had not discussed the question of nonbinary recognition. The decree further requires a sworn oath from the applicant for recognition.[66] This oath must include a reference to the 'sociocultural construction that the person has of their identity'.[67] Only one sex change within a ten-year period was allowed.[68]

The ten-year restriction and the limitation to the binary were removed by the Court in 2022. The case concerned a *tutela* lodged by a *travesti* person, who could not gain recognition on the basis of decree 1227 of 2015. At the risk of overgeneralization, *travesti* is a regional identity with strong political overtones[69] that usually refers to people assigned male at birth who present themselves 'as "females" according to manners, dress and make-up',[70] and yet reject standard binary labels.[71] Malú Machuca Rose wrote: '[*t*]*ravesti* is the refusal to be trans, the refusal to be woman, the refusal to be intelligible.'[72] Considering the restrictions that temporal limits might place on individuals with such characteristics, the Constitutional Court ruled that mandatory intervals are disproportionate, discriminatory, and can hinder one's self-actualization.[73]

3.2. Gender recognition beyond the amendment in civil registries

With several decisions concerning military duties, the Constitutional Court established not only that individuals have the right to self-declare their legal sex, but also that self-determination entails the right to be treated according to one's identity, *regardless* of formal legal classification.

With decision T-476/14, the Court ruled in favour of a trans woman who was denied the possibility of obtaining a government job because she could not present a *libreta militar*, the document that certifies the successful completion of military service.[74] The Constitutional Court granted the *tutela* and ordered the public authority to review its decision. The Court understood the recognition of gender identity to be derived from the right to dignity. It also considered developments

[65] The Court recognized a nonbinary option in 2022, as discussed in Chapter 7.
[66] Decreto 1227/2015, Art. 2.2.6.12.4.5.
[67] Decreto 1227/2015, Art. 2.2.6.12.4.5, par. 1.
[68] Decreto 1227/2015, Art. 2.2.6.12.4.6.
[69] Lohana Berkins, *Un Itinerario Politico del Travestitismo, in* SEXUALIDADES MIGRANTES: GÉNERO Y TRANSGÉNERO 127 (Dana Maffía ed., 2003).
[70] Giuseppe Campuzano, *Contemporary Travesti Encounters with Gender and Sexuality in Latin America*, 52 DEVELOPMENTS 75 (2009).
[71] DON KULICK, TRAVESTÍ: SEX, GENDER AND CULTURE AMONG BRAZILIAN TRANSGENDERED PROSTITUTES 225–38 (1998).
[72] Malù Machuca Rose, *Giuseppe Campuzano's Afterlife*, 6 TSQ: TRANSGENDER STUDIES QUARTERLY 239, 243 (2019).
[73] C.C., T-033/22, ¶¶ 61–65.
[74] C.C., 9 julio 2014, Sentencia T-476/14. *See also*: Jaramillo, *supra* note 11, at 444. The facts in the case point to the conclusion that the applicant had not changed her legal sex in the civil registries.

taking place at the supranational level, where the Inter-American Court of Human Rights had repeatedly referred to the right of identity and gender identity.[75] Ultimately, it established that 'if a person identifies as a transgender woman, and defines her identity in public and social life as a transgender woman, then subjecting her to a [legal] requirement of the gender in which she does not identify [such as completing military service] … is a failure to recognize her right to develop gender identity, that is, to self-determination.'[76]

This judgment served as a starting point for expanding self-determination, which the Court further developed in landmark decision T-099/15.[77] The case concerned a trans woman, legally male, who was fined for failing to comply with the mandatory military service for Colombian male citizens.[78] The plaintiff had manifested her identity to military authorities in vain.[79] The Court ruled that, since the plaintiff identified as a woman, she could not be legally treated as a male regardless of her legal sex. In reaching this conclusion, the Court relied on the same theoretical and doctrinal apparatus that grounded the earlier decision T-063/15;[80] moreover, it referred to the sex/gender binary as a 'cultural construct'.[81]

The Court acknowledged that the rules on mandatory military service are connected to public interests of constitutional status. For example, they relate to the preservation of the national territorial integrity and public order.[82] Nevertheless, military authorities, the Constitutional Court continued, unjustifiably degraded the plaintiff, who was treated as a man 'despite being a woman' (*a pesar de ser mujer*).[83] The possibility that individuals might abuse the system—for example, by declaring to be female to dodge the draft—was acknowledged.[84] However, the Constitutional Court also underlined the general obligation to presume good faith from citizens,[85] and encouraged public authorities to denounce all those 'unscrupulous people' who make false statements to avoid their military obligations.[86]

[75] Gelman v. Uruguay, Inter-American Court of Human Rights (ser. C) No. 221 (24 Feb. 2011); Contreras and Others v. El Salvador, Inter-American Court of Human Rights (ser. C) No. 232 (31 Aug. 2011); Atala Riffo and Daughters v. Chile, Inter-American Court of Human Rights (ser. C) No. 239 (24 Feb. 2012).

[76] C.C., T-476/14, ¶ III (Análisis del caso concreto).

[77] C.C., 10 marzo 2015, Sentencia T-099/15. This decision cannot be seen as a mere confirmation of the previous doctrine. For a different opinion: Jaramillo, *supra* note 11, at 444, fn. 18.

[78] L. 48, marzo 3, 1993, Art. 14. The decision specifies that the applicant is legally classified as a male in several passages, for example: T-099/15, ¶ 34 (Consideraciones). *See* also the *Aclaració de Voto* of Justice Jorge Ignacio Pretelt Chaljub.

[79] C.C., T-099/15, ¶¶ 1–5 (Antecedentes).

[80] C.C., T-099/15, ¶ 36 and ¶ 40 (Consideraciones).

[81] C.C., T-099/15, ¶ 39 (Consideraciones). Marco Antonio Ruiz Nieves criticized the Court for focusing its attention on trans men and women only, thus giving the idea of binary normativity: Marco Antonio Ruiz Nieves, *El Concepto Transgénero en las Sentencias de Tutela (Colombia)*, 13 Revista Verba Iuris 95, 107 (2018).

[82] C.C., T-099/15, ¶¶ 87–91 (Consideraciones).

[83] C.C., T-099/15, ¶ 98 (Consideraciones).

[84] This objection was also central to the dissenting opinion of Justice Jorge Ignacio Pretelt Chaljub.

[85] Art. 83 C.P.

[86] C.C., T-099/15, ¶ 99 (Consideraciones).

Finally, although there was no expedited mechanism to change legal sex at the time of the facts, the decision nonetheless clarified that military authorities could not require medical, judicial, or other evidence to exempt the applicant from military service.[87] This doctrine was essentially restated in the following jurisprudence.[88]

As expected, institutional actors raised concerns with this doctrine. In the subsequent and similar case C-584/15, the state attorney (*Procuradór General de la Nación*) conjured 'gender ideology'. They referred to such a notion as a 'pseudo-theory with scientific pretention that advances the belief that the distinction between men and women, despite the obvious genetic, anatomical and psychological differences, are not determined by biological sex ... [but] by time- and context-specific culture.'[89] The Court did not thoroughly engage with this objection, as it appeared more concerned with balancing principles than with rewriting ontological rules about gender. In his *aclaración de voto* to decision T-099/15, Justice Pretelt Chaljub highlighted the risk of cis men fraudulently posing as trans women to avoid conscription. In the dissent to the subsequent C-006/16, he connected the exclusion of *cis* women from mandatory military service to sex-based discrimination. He referred to the risk of sexual violence during conflict, which would ostensibly target cis women—implicitly—*only*. This claim, it should be mentioned, raises questions, especially in the Colombian context, where LGBTQI+ people, as well as women, have been targeted during the military conflict between the government and the FARC rebels.[90] Justice Pretelt Chaljub furthermore referred to sex-based discrimination in the job market, which could possibly further deteriorate the position of cis women should they be subjected to military duties.[91] That said, Justice Pretelt Chaljub did not oppose the exemption of trans women from military service, but insisted on limiting such an exemption to those who had previously changed their legal sex in the civil registry[92]—a procedure that, as we have seen, is ultimately based on self-determination.

87 C.C., T-099/15, ¶ 103 (Consideraciones).

88 C.C., 8 septiembre 2015, Sentencia C-584/15; C.C., 21 enero 2016, Sentencia C-006/16. These cases were slightly different. They concerned the constitutionality of the law that explicitly excluded women from military service, without explicitly explaining whether trans women were excluded too. The Constitutional Court ruled that the law was constitutional because the correct interpretation of the term 'woman' encompasses both trans and cis women.

89 C.C., C-584/15, ¶ V (Concepto del Procurador General de la Nación).

90 Claudia Marcela Alvarez Hurtado & Vanessa Cuenca Riva, *Trayectorias de Reconstrucción de Tejido Social de las Mujeres Trans Víctimas de Desplazamiento Forzado en el Marco del Conflicto Armado: Caso del Municipio Neiva (Huila), 2019*, *in* CÁTEDRA UNESCO: DERECHOS HUMANOS Y VIOLENCIA: GOBIERNO Y GOBERNANZA: REFLEXIONES PARA LA CONSTRUCCIÓN DE POLÍTICAS PÚBLICAS DESDE ABAJO EN TORNO AL DESPLAZAMIENTO FORZADO EN COLOMBIA (Marcela Gutierrez Quevedo & Ángela Marcela Olarte Delgado, 2020). References to the violence against LGBTQI+ people are also included in: Colombia Diversa, Fundación Grupo de Acción y Apoyo a Personas Trans and Diversas Incorrectas Informe sombra para el Comité de la CEDAW-Situación de Mujeres Lesbianas, Bisexuales y Trans en Colombia 2013–2018 (2019).

91 C.C., C-006/16, Salvamento de Voto del Magistrado Jorge Ignacio Pretelt Chaljub, ¶ 2.2.13.

92 C.C., C-006/16, Salvamento de Voto del Magistrado Jorge Ignacio Pretelt Chaljub, ¶¶ 2.4.12–2.4.13.

More recently, the Constitutional Court has focused on the notion of 'woman' and the various expressions used to mark the feminine gender—such as 'female worker' (*trabajadora*) and 'mother'—contained in the law concerning maternity leave.[93] The case concerned the constitutional validity of these expressions, which do not include pregnant trans men or nonbinary people, nor these categories of persons who had just delivered a child. The Court ruled that the law is constitutionally valid if such terms are interpreted as inclusive of gender-diverse people too. Technically, this judgment does not extend a legal status conforming to one's gender identity; rather, people legally classified as males are granted rights and benefits established for females. However, this decision shows how the Constitutional Court of Colombia detaches identity from formal legal status to ensure the equality of trans (and nonbinary) people, and endeavours to carve out a space for gender-diverse people in a system that has been constructed around traditional and binary sex categories.

3.3. The transformative power of gender self-determination

Gender self-determination can be transformative for trans people. The jurisprudence of the Constitutional Court modified the legal notion of sex, adopting a system of sex election,[94] which 'is akin to a contractual right to opt into or out of a particular identity'.[95] The Colombian Court ruled that the purpose of the law is to register, and not assess, identity as defined by the person,[96] and guarantee them the set of legal positions corresponding to the lived, rather than formalized, self. Unlike the medico-behavioural and the socio-behavioural models, self-determination is detached from specific recognition requirements. There are no standards to which individuals must conform to change their legal sex. The jurisprudence of the Constitutional Court guarantees each person's freedom to be categorized in the sex they choose, and allows them to live and manifest their gender identity in diverse and unconventional forms. At a more practical level, self-determination can be quicker and less expensive.[97]

[93] C.C., 24 agosto 2023, Sentencia C-324/23. The case concerned the constitutional validity of several passages of Art. 236 Código Sustantivo del Trabajo (Labour Code) (C.S.T.).

[94] Jessica A. Clarke, *Identity and Form*, 103 California Law Review 747, 763–69 (2015).

[95] *Id.* at 763.

[96] On this point: Osella & Rubio-Marín, *supra* note 9, at 595. *See also*: Ruth Rubio-Marín & Stefano Osella, *El Nuevo Derecho Constitucional a la Identidad de Género entre la Libertad de Elección, el Incremento de Categorías y la Subjetividad y Fluidez de sus Contenidos. Un Análisis desde el Derecho Comparado*, 40 Revista Española de Derecho Constitucional 45, 61–66 (2020).

[97] I have previously expanded the transformative power of self-determination in Osella & Rubio-Marín, *supra* note 30. *See also*: Marie-Xaviere Catto & Stefano Osella, *The Sexed Subject*, *in* The Cambridge Companion to Gender and the Law 25, 48–52 (Stephanie Hennette-Vauchez & Ruth Rubio-Marín eds., 2023).

Not only is sex self-determined under the Colombian constitutional doctrine, but, since 2022, there are no time limitations. In protecting gender-fluid identities, the Constitutional Court of Colombia altered one element of sex categorization (fixity) that has been considered crucial to ensuring stability and certainty in the system.[98] This focus on permanence responded, Paisley Currah and Lisa Jean Moore have suggested, to the belief 'that one "always will be" either male or female', laying bare a cultural understanding of gender that spills over into the law. At the same time, it also reflected the administrative concern with pursuing the 'imperative to render the citizenry, a collection of "identifiable, corporeal bodies," easily legible. … This bureaucratic fear of "not knowing" a citizen evokes a central problem of modern statehood.'[99] On the other hand, despite the possibility of expansive interpretations of the constitutional doctrine, the options for reclassification in Colombia were restricted to the male–female binary until 2022, thus to some extent limiting gender self-determination.[100]

The right to gender self-determination defined by the Colombian Constitutional Court is transformative from the perspective of gender constitutionalism, too. This is because it questions some of the fundamental assumptions upon which the separate sphere doctrine is built, which, in turn, lies at the core of the constitutional gender order.[101] Central to this doctrine are indeed 'patriarchal and heteronormative gender roles'.[102] These different roles have long been rooted in the bodies of the subjects that populate this system. For example, in his work detailing the history of the notion of 'sex', Thomas Laqueur connected the understanding of (physical) sex as a binary to the cultural and political circumstances of the eighteenth and nineteenth centuries, arguing that the 'creation of a bourgeois public sphere … raised with a vengeance the question of which sex(es) ought legitimately to occupy it. And everywhere biology entered the discourse'.[103] Likewise, Carole Pateman underlined the importance of making 'natural beings recognizable' for social contract theorists to 'smuggle social characteristics [which would be in the social contract] into the natural condition'.[104] Gender self-determination questions these assumptions because the 'patriarchal and heteronormative gender roles' and the ostensible 'natural condition' differences between the sexes supposedly reflected in the law

[98] Catto & Osella, *supra* note 97, at 50.

[99] Paisely Currah & Lisa Jean Moore, *'We Won't Know Who You Are': Contesting Sex Designations in New York City Birth Certificates*, 24 Hypatia 113, 127 (2009).

[100] Marlene Wayar, a prominent *travesti* activist, made precisely this point when criticizing self-determination in Argentina: Marlene Wayar, *¿Qué pasó con la T?*, Pagina 12 (11 May 2012), https://www.pagina12.com.ar/diario/suplementos/soy/1-2436-2012-05-11.html.

[101] Ruth Rubio-Marín, Global Gender Constitutionalism and Women's Citizenship: A Struggle for Transformative Inclusion 295–309 (2022).

[102] Ruth Rubio-Marín, Wen-Chen Chang, Kelley Loper & Mara Malagodi, *Gender Constitutionalism in Asia: A Comparative Framework*, *in* Gender, Sexuality and Constitutionalism in Asia 1, 1 (Wen-Chen Chang, Kelley Loper, Mara Malagodi & Ruth Rubio-Marín eds., 2023).

[103] Thomas Laqueur, Making Sex: Bodies and Gender from the Greeks to Freud 194 (1990).

[104] Carole Pateman, The Sexual Contract 41 (1988).

are entirely detached from legal identity. As the boundaries between legal sexes become porous, the legitimacy of using sex categories as an instrument to pursue legal (at times, constitutional) objectives is called into question.

The third transformation entailed by self-determination is theoretical. This right indeed undermines the structure of the gender order in the law. To be clear, scholars have questioned the disruptive potential of self-determination on the gender legal order. For example, Ido Katri argued that, far from displacing sex categories, gender self-determination could serve to merely revise the existing system, ensuring a degree of inclusion of trans people while legitimating the persistence of sex categories.[105] Aeyal Gross wrote that 'the binary hierarchical categories of gender and sexuality (i.e., men/women and heterosexual/homosexual) are themselves part of the problem, as this structure mandates that every person must have a gender or sexual orientation.'[106] Gender self-determination, in this context, 'represent[s] an attempt at offering freedom of, but not freedom from, sexual orientation and gender identity'.[107] This is why some theorists have argued for the importance of going beyond trans and disestablishing sex categories altogether.[108]

Admittedly, gender self-determination leaves sex categories in place. However, without a set of characteristics that individuals must possess to change their legal sex, the categories lose rigidity.[109] To borrow from Butler, the 'production and normalization of masculine and feminine' no longer take place.[110] Writing about self-determination in Argentina, Martín De Mauro Rucovski stated that

> the political and legal power of [self-determination] is indubitably located in exposing the malleability of categories like masculinity and femininity .... In this sense, the recognition in the LIG [*ley de identidad de genero,* that is, the law that introduced self-determination] is not tied to specific identities—not transgender, *travesti*, or transmasculine—but rather accounts for the undecidability of gendered ways of living.[111]

Gender self-determination, therefore, can be understood as profoundly questioning the gender structure in the law, especially when we understand gender as a system where meaning is created. Butler seemed to have understood gender as just such a system of signification when they wrote:

[105] Katri, *supra* note 7, at 742–44.

[106] Aeyal Gross, *Post/Colonial Queer Globalisation and International Human Rights: Images of LGBT Rights*, 4 Jindal Global Law Review 98, 127–28 (2013).

[107] *Id.*

[108] Heath Fogg Davis, Beyond Trans: Does Gender Matter? (2017). *See* Chapter 8.

[109] Refer also to: Osella & Rubio-Marín, *supra* note 30; Catto & Osella, *supra* note 97, at 48.

[110] Judith Butler, Undoing Gender 42 (2004).

[111] Martín De Mauro Rucovsky (Ian Martin trans.), *The Travesti Critique of the Gender Identity Law in Argentina*, 6 TSQ: Transgender Studies Quarterly 223, 232 (2019).

> [G]ender is the apparatus by which the production and normalization of masculine and feminine take place along with the interstitial forms of hormonal, chromosomal, psychic, and performative that gender assumes.[112]

The gender order in public and constitutional law, in other words, should not be limited to the mere presence of categories, but understood as the presence of such categories combined with a specific set of meanings that, as happens in the medico-behavioural and socio-behavioural system of recognition, is imposed on individuals.

4. Expanding self-determination and including ancestral identities

Multiple identities might be understood as gender-diverse without necessarily fitting the globalized category of trans, for example, certain Indigenous identities from South America. The Colombian Constitutional Court acknowledged such identities in 2021.[113] The case concerned a *tutela* successfully lodged by a legally recognized trans woman to whom a pension fund had refused to pay benefits at the retirement age established for women, treating trans women like men.[114] The Court confirmed its doctrine on gender self-determination and offered one more example of a balance between 'constitutionally imperative' public interests and trans demands.[115] The pension fund justified its denial with reference to the principle of legality—*Decreto* 1227 of 2015 did not change the law concerning pensions[116]—and to the sustainability of pension schemes, allegedly imperilled by trans women's earlier retirement.[117] The fund further pointed to risks of fraudulent behaviour, such as men posing as trans women to enjoy benefits before their due time.[118] The Court ruled in favour of the applicant. It referred to the constitutional duty of presuming good faith on the part of the citizen,[119] and stressed the necessity of envisioning less invasive means to achieve these legitimate objectives. For example, the Court suggested that the pension fund conduct a statistical study on the impact of earlier retirement of trans women, or compile details of cases demonstrating bad faith on the part of the person applying to retire. In brief, the decision drew a few lines in the sand: limits on gender recognition must

[112] BUTLER, *supra* note 110, at 42.

[113] C.C., 9 diciembre 2021, Sentencia SU-440/21, ¶¶ 53–59. For an initial analysis of this decision, *see* Stefano Osella, *Come Evolve il Diritto all'Identità di Genere? Fattori Strutturali, Culturali, e Dogmatici nella Giurisprudenza Costituzionale Italiana e Colombiana. Un'Analisi Comparata*, DIRITTI COMPARATI 1, 35–36 (2023), https://www.diritticomparati.it/bozza-automatica-170/.

[114] L. 100, 23 diciembre 1993, Art. 33.

[115] C.C., SU-440/21, ¶ 117.

[116] C.C., SU-440/21, ¶ 112.

[117] C.C., SU-440/21, ¶ 113.

[118] C.C., SU-440/21, ¶ 116.

[119] Art. 83 C.P.; C.C., SU-440/21, ¶ 120.

be proportionate and based on empirical data, and legitimate objectives, such as those at stake, cannot be pursued with carpet-bombing policies, so to speak, but with targeted measures.[120]

This said, the innovative potential of this decision lies in the acknowledgement of the existence of multiple gender identities, including 'cis', 'trans', and 'ancestral' identities,[121] which the Court made after citing the 2020 report of the Inter-American Commission on Human Rights.[122] In that report, the Inter-American Commission had recognized the discrimination suffered by individuals who live sex/gender and sexuality in ways that are typical 'of some indigenous people on the continent'.[123] For example, the Commission referred to the *muxhe* of Mexico—birth-assigned males who show patterns of behaviour associated with femaleness, and who yet reject being identified as women and might be understood as nonbinary. The Commission also mentioned the *wigunduguid*, a two-spirit identity of the Kuna people of Panama. These precolonial identities, the Commission pointed out, were targeted by colonial violence, and deserve recognition because of the several and intersecting forms of discrimination that they have suffered and continue to suffer.[124] The Constitutional Court of Colombia confirmed its stance on such 'vernacular' gender identities in 2022, when it recognized a *travesti* person and their gender fluidity. To do so, it removed the temporal restrictions on gender self-determination that were contained in *Decreto* 1227 of 2015.[125]

As these decisions suggest, gender self-determination and its capacity to include 'ancestral' identities can be understood as an attempt to decolonize the law concerning sex, mainly as such recognition could be used to challenge the Eurocentric classificatory systems of individuals and, clearly, of the 'conquered'.[126] Indeed, as Maria Lugones has argued, the imposition of a binary system of gender (which, I add, reflects in the law) has been part of the colonial project. The imposition of the European state form—and, in general, the dynamics of exploitation that characterized European colonization—required the establishment of a gender

[120] Justice Cristina Pardo Schlesinger filed a dissenting opinion (*salvamento de voto*). She criticized the majority opinion for uncritically accepting the so-called gender ideology that is grounded in existentialist and historical materialist Marxism and for being—recalling the dissent to decision T-063/15—more grounded in activism than science: C.C., 440/21, Salvamento de Voto della Magistrada Cristina Pardo Schlesinger, ¶ 6.

[121] C.C., SU-440/21, ¶ 56.

[122] Informe sobre Personas Trans y de Género Diverso y Sus Derechos Económicos, Sociales, Culturales y Ambientales, Inter-American Commission on Human Rights, OEA/Ser.L/V/II. Doc. 239 (7 Aug. 2020).

[123] *Id.* ¶ 92.

[124] *Id.* ¶¶ 94–96.

[125] The Court had previously granted the possibility of multiple name-changes (C.C., 28 julio 2017, Sentencia C-114/17, ¶ 38.8).

[126] For a general perspective on decoloniality: Anibál Quijano (Michael Ennis trans.), *Coloniality of Power, Eurocentrism and Latin America*, 1 NEPANTLA 533 (2000); ANIBÁL QUIJANO: FOUNDATIONAL ESSAYS ON THE COLONIALITY OF POWER (Walter Mignolo, Rita Segato & Catherine Walsh eds., David Frye trans., 2024).

system.[127] When applied to Indigenous cultures, the 'gender system [has a dark side that] was and is thoroughly violent'.[128] It entails the imposition of European understandings of maleness and femaleness, the exclusion of people who do not fit such standards from 'participation in rituals, decision making, and economics; [and] their reduction to animality, to forced sex with white colonizers, to such deep labor exploitation that often people died working'.[129] The imposition of European standards of gender was also understood as part of the 'civilizing mission [that] was present in the ideological conception of conquest and colonization' and that 'justified enormous cruelty'.[130] Scott Lauria Morgensen, starting from the consideration that 'settler epistemology' is part of colonization, argued that such an epistemology included 'the European establishment of Western heteropatriarchal and binary sex/gender systems in settler societies'.[131] Today's legacies of this colonization resonate in

> a cissexist biological essentialism that divides the world's population into supposedly distinct 'races'; presents sex as binary …; presents gender and race as hierarchical; and imposes compulsory heterosexuality and conformity to cissexist standards as the only natural, legal, moral, viable, and desirable sexual orientations and gender identities.[132]

Examples of the erasure of gender diversity abound. Examining a sampling of historical and ethnographic accounts, Michael Horswell explained the symbolic, religious, and social roles of those whom we would today call gender-diverse people in pre-Colombian Andean societies. Horswell also reported how missionaries took pride in 'punishing' these people, whom they viewed as devious.[133] The violence was so widespread that, at times, it reached the level of a 'gendercide'. Although not referring to Colombia, Deborah Miranda discussed the systematic elimination of the *Joyas*—whom we might understand as gender-diverse people—from southern California.[134] Brooklyn Leo offered an account of the violence committed by Spanish *conquistadores* on individuals who defied conventional understandings

[127] Maria Lugones, *Heterosexualism and the Colonial/Modern Gender System*, 22 Hypatia 186 (2007); Lugones builds on the insights of Oyéronké Oyewùmí, The Invention of Women: Making an African Sense of Western Gender Discourses (1997).

[128] Lugones, *supra* note 127, at 206.

[129] *Id.*

[130] Maria Lugones, *Toward a Decolonial Feminism*, 25 Hypatia 742, 744 (2010).

[131] Scott Lauria Morgensen, *Theorising Gender, Sexuality, and Settler Colonialism: An Introduction*, 2 Settler Colonial Studies 2, 13 (2012).

[132] Claudia Sofía Garriga-López & Juliana Martínez, *Transfeminist Latinx America*, 10 TSQ: Transgender Studies Quarterly 301, 302 (2023).

[133] Michael J. Horswell, *Toward an Andean Theory of Ritual Same-Sex Sexuality and Third Gender Subjectivity*, *in* Infamous Desire. Male Homosexuality in Colonial Latin America (Pete Sigal ed., 2003).

[134] Deborah A. Miranda, *Extermination of the* Joyas*: Gendercide in Spanish California*, 16 GLQ: A Journal of Lesbian and Gay Studies 253 (2010).

of sex/gender.[135] Referring to *travesti* people, Giuseppe Campuzano denounced the violence that was perpetrated against 'any gender identity or sexual orientation which contradicted or challenged heteronormativity'.[136]

All of this helps to clarify and amplify Lugones's argument that '[c]olonialism... imposed a new gender system that created very different arrangements for colonized males and females than for white bourgeois colonizers. Thus, it introduced many genders and gender itself as a colonial concept'.[137] Lugones argued that understanding the historical—and specifically colonial—origin of gender in the region (as the Constitutional Court does) is 'an attempt to move, dislodge, complicate what has faced me and others engaged in liberatory/decolonial projects as hard barriers that are both conceptual and political'.[138] These notions can be 'barriers to the conceptualization and enactment of liberatory possibilities as decolonial possibilities'.[139] As Morgensen wrote, '[a]nticolonial feminist and queer accounts show that ... that liberation will follow disturbing all that colonisation taught, so that distinctive ways of life might be recalled or imagined.'[140] Protection of ancestral identities, including *travesti*, therefore has a central role in recovering cultural notions and rendering justice to individuals whom colonizers attempted to erase. Gender self-determination—that is, granting recognition to individuals whose very existence decentres notions of gender from Eurocentric standards—seems to be part and parcel of a broader decolonial project.

Needless to say, gender self-determination alone is insufficient to decolonize gender and must be accompanied by broader anti-capitalist and intersectional forms of equality. For example, Andres García Becerra, writing about *travestis* in Colombia, emphasized the importance of socio-economic rights.[141] Finally, we ought not to forget other dynamics of epistemic colonization, as even gender recognition—as well-intentioned as it might be—still has the potential to export a form of identity—the trans identity as conceptualized in the global North—that, as David Valentine has demonstrated, has the potential to erase other gender epistemologies.[142] As Claudia-Sofia Garriga-Lopez and Juliana Martinez have argued:

> [t]he centrality of decoloniality for Latin American transfeminisms can also be seen in the reappropriation and resignification of certain terms.... The use of the

[135] Brooklyn Leo, *The Colonial/Modern [Cis]Gender System and Trans World Traveling*, 35 Hypatia 454, 464 (2020).
[136] Campuzano, *supra* note 70, at 80.
[137] Lugones, *supra* note 127, at 186.
[138] *Id.* at 187.
[139] *Id.*
[140] Morgensen, *supra* note 131, at 5.
[141] Andres García Becerra, *Tacones, Siliconas, Hormonas y Otras Críticas al Sistema Sexo-Género. Feminismos y Experiencias de Transexuales y Travestis*, 45 Revista Colombiana de Antropología 119 (2009).
[142] David Valentine, Imagining Transgender: The Ethnography of Category (2007).

term *travesti* signals a refusal of the term transgender, which is imported from the global North and often carries with it a binary notion of gender.[143]

5. A Limit to gender self-determination? The question of trans children

5.1. Gender self-determination and the need for supervision: A brief detour

This account would be incomplete without a discussion of the specific form taken by children's constitutional right to gender self-determination in Colombia. Indeed, the Constitutional Court defined the right to gender self-determination of children by balancing, on the one hand, autonomy and identity and, on the other hand, the principle of the best interests of the child and the need for supervision that the latter entails.[144] The specific standards set by the Constitutional Court for trans children demonstrate once again how the determination of legal sex represents the outcome of value judgments.

To understand why the Constitutional Court of Colombia has established a different mechanism of gender self-determination for children, some cursory references to psychological and bioethical literature might be helpful. Matters seem relatively straightforward when it comes to underage people who have attained a sufficient level of maturity—let us think of adolescents nearing majority. As stated by 118 healthcare professionals in the most recent edition of the Standards of Care for the Health of Transgender and Gender Diverse People, favouring social transition of trans adolescents, including aspects of gender recognition, can benefit mental health and well-being.[145] At the same time, these professionals suggested that it could be advantageous for trans adolescents to have recourse to professional help—not as an attempt to influence their identification, but to ensure that they are not left without support in what is a challenging decision.

More complicated is the case of younger, prepubescent children. The reason for this complication lies in the fact that some gender-diverse children develop a cis identity as they grow up (so-called desisters) and thus de-transition. A social detransition can be a distressing event in itself. Additionally, it may be feared that

[143] Garriga-López & Martínez, *supra* note 132, at 303.
[144] Art. 44 C.P.
[145] For a discussion of the standards of care of trans adolescents and children: Eli Coleman et al., *Standards of Care for the Health of Transgender and Gender Diverse People, Version 8*, 23 International Journal of Transgender Health sup1 S1, S-52 (2022). For a sociological perspective: Tey Meadow, Trans Kids: Being Gendered in the Twenty-First Century 176 (2018). For an introduction to the 'gender affirmative approach', *see* Diane Ehrensaft, The Gender Creative Child: Pathways for Nurturing and Supporting Children Who Live Outside Gender Boxes (2016).

social transition may encourage medical transition. If this is the case, further ethical concerns may arise. If medical transition is likely to be unjustified for individuals who eventually desist, then social transition (which might be seen as enabling medical transition) could also be problematic.[146] No professional consensus exists. As explained by Simona Giordano, on whose account these bioethical remarks draw, health professionals have developed different approaches to social (and medical) transition: 'gender-affirming' care, which 'allow[s] the child to express the affirmed gender';[147] 'live in your skin', which attempts to discourage trans identity and might be considered a form of 'reparative' therapy;[148] 'watch and wait', in principle supportive of trans identity, which allows a degree of social transition, for example, in the domestic sphere, but discourages full transition before puberty.[149]

To further complicate the scenario, Giordano has pointed out that data on de-transition may not be the best indicator of the chances of persistence of a *specific* child. She also underlined that the connection between social and medical transition, as well as the impact of de-transition, remains unclear. This uncertainty, Giordano contends, suggests that decisions on the social transition of children should be made not by weighing future and hypothetical benefits and risks, but rather on *present* ones. Numerous studies demonstrate that 'children thrive when they are allowed to live in the gender that is most authentic to themselves. Those who are unable to affirm their identity … are much more likely to suffer anxiety and depression, compromised school performance, suicidal ideation, and carry out suicide attempts than those who are in supporting environments.'[150]

Be that as it may, one aspect seems relatively uncontroversial. Social (and legal) transition must be approached with care when it comes to children, and psychological support appears necessary. As Diane Ehrensaft—a child psychologist and advocate of gender-affirming care—underlined, clinicians do not 'rubber-stamp' children's declarations, but engage in a listening process with the purpose of understanding whether the choice to transition comes from the child and whether parents are supportive.[151] This makes it clear why the self-determined procedure established for adults may not serve trans children best, and why special procedures to support them in an age-appropriate fashion might be necessary.

[146] Simona Giordano, Children and Gender: Ethical Issues in Clinical Management of Transgender and Gender Diverse Youth, from Early Years to Late Adolescence 90–92 (2023).

[147] *Id.* at 95.

[148] On this point, *see* Diane Ehrensaft, *Treatment Paradigms for Prepubertal Children*, *in* Pediatric Gender Identity 171, 182 (Michelle Forcier, Gerrit Van Schalkwyk & Jack L Turban eds., 2020).

[149] Giordano, *supra* note 146, at 95.

[150] Simona Giordano, *Importance of Being Persistent: Should Transgender Children Be Allowed to Transition Socially?*, 45 Journal of Medical Ethics 654, 659 (2019).

[151] Ehrensaft, *supra* note 148, at 181.

5.2. Gender self-determination and 'free, qualified, and informed' consent—or, the limits on gender self-determination

The first case decided by the Constitutional Court of Colombia concerned a—rather significant—bureaucratic detail. *Decreto* 1227 of 2015 listed the *cedula de ciudadania*—an identification document released to people when they reach the age of majority (eighteen)—among the documents to be attached to the application for gender recognition.[152] The applicant, an underage seventeen-year-old person, was unable to produce it. The *notaría* declined the application and instructed the applicant to lodge a judicial claim. A *tutela* was consequently filed.

The Court argued that, *prima facie*, self-determination should be enjoyed by adults and children alike, and yet children's autonomy can be limited, depending on the age of the child and the effects of their choices. To establish some guidelines to determine the question of legal transition of children, the Court first noted that support from the applicant's parents strengthened the application. Second, it invited authorities to consider professional evidence from 'therapists, social workers, and other professionals in relevant areas'. Third, the maturity of the child and their proximity to being of age was also found to be relevant. Fourth, the Court advised considering the consequences of the decision to transition,[153] which, although not trivial, is not irreversible either, as *Decreto* 1227 of 2015 allows de-transition after ten years.[154]

A few months later, the Constitutional Court confirmed that excluding children from a notarial procedure and self-determination, demanding a judicial procedure instead, pursues a 'constitutionally imperative' objective,[155] namely, ensuring the supervision necessary to safeguard the best interests of the child.[156] Nevertheless, the Constitutional Court observed that, despite being suitable for the purpose, the judicialization of the procedure is not necessary, as notaries can support trans children too, and children may be mature enough to decide on their identity.[157] The Court underlined that the decision of the child must be free from external interference or coercion, informed, and qualified—in this case, qualified as non-permanent, given the possibility of reverting back without much trouble after ten years.[158]

Administrative Instructions 12 of 27 April 2018 interpreted this case law narrowly, requiring a minimum age of seventeen, a joint declaration of child and parents, and professional certificates, that is, 'medical documents [*conceptos*] that

[152] C.C., 3 agosto 2017, Sentencia T-498/17.

[153] C.C., T-498/17, ¶¶ 5.5.1–5.5.4 (Consideraciones). Subsequently, the Court ruled that the consent of one of the parents is sufficient. C.C., 23 marzo 2022, Sentencia T-105/22.

[154] This limit was removed by the Constitutional Court with decision C.C., T-033/22.

[155] C.C., 15 noviembre 2017, Sentencia T-675/17, ¶ 22.1.

[156] C.C., T-675/17, ¶ 22.2.

[157] C.C., T-675/17, ¶¶ 22.3–23.

[158] C.C., T-675/17, ¶ 29.

prove the existence of a previous process tending to reaffirm the gender identity of the minor'.[159] While not clearly defined, the recognition of a child's gender identity seemed to require some kind of medical transition—a requirement that, while not explicitly banned for trans children, was at odds with the previous constitutional case law.

5.3. The expansion of self-determination

In 2019, the Constitutional Court extended gender recognition to younger children and stressed the illegitimacy of any medical preconditions.[160] The case concerned a ten-year-old child, represented by their mother, who had applied for gender recognition on their behalf.[161] The *notaría*, enforcing Administrative Instructions 12 of 2018, denied the request and invited the applicant to lodge a judicial claim.

The Court did not consider the young age of the applicant to be an impediment. It cited scientific literature attesting that trans identity can manifest as early as age five or six and consolidate between five and seven,[162] and recalled the case law on intersex children, in which the identity of the child was deemed sufficiently developed at age five. The Constitutional Court added that applicants' maturity should be assessed *in concreto*,[163] considering the specific development of the child.[164] While confirming the doctrine of free, informed, and qualified consent, the Court added that no medical evidence can be required for gender recognition—not even in the case of children.

Regardless of any possible criticism of this approach, the Administrative Instruction 1 of 12 January 2020 laid down the new criteria. The *Superintendencia de Notariado y Registro* required an assessment of maturity *in concreto*; proscribed the use of all medical evidence; and imposed an assessment of the 'free, informed, and qualified consent'. It is the duty of the notary, the *Superintendencia* established, to assess that such requirements are met.[165]

[159] Ministerio de la Justicia y Superintendencia de Notariado y Registro, Instrucción Administrativa 12, Cumplimiento Decisión Judicial T- 675 de 2017—Requisitos que permiten la modificación del componente sexo de los menores de edad transgénero en el Registro del Estado Civil, ¶iii (2 May 2018), https://servicios.supernotariado.gov.co/instrucciones_administrativas.html.

[160] C.C., 27 septiembre 2019, Sentencia T-447/19 (the prohibition of 'physical, medical, and psychological evidence' can be found throughout the decision and in very clear terms at ¶ 106).

[161] Even though the child was intersex, the Court repeatedly insisted that the case concerned exclusively gender identity and was to be regarded as a case of trans rights (C.C., T-447/19, ¶¶ 69–70).

[162] C.C., T-447/19, ¶¶ 67–68.

[163] C.C., T-447/19, ¶ 94.

[164] C.C., T-447/19, ¶¶ 92–95.

[165] Superintendencia de Notariado y Registro, Instrucción Administrativa 1, Cumplimiento Decisión Judicial T- 447/2019—Requisitos que permiten la modificación del nombre y la corrección del componente sexo en el Registro Civil de los menores de edad, Arts. 1–4 (13 Jan. 2020), https://servicios.supernotariado.gov.co/instrucciones_administrativas.html.

Finally, although strictly speaking different from recognition in civil registries, the case law concerning the right of trans students to be treated according to their identity in school interactions can also be informative in this context.[166] With multiple decisions, the Constitutional Court has protected the right of trans students to be free from discrimination in educational establishments—for example, by being allowed to wear the uniform associated with the sex/gender they feel more comfortable in. Thanks to these multiple decisions, students can obtain a degree of social recognition in school settings, regardless of any changes to their legal identity.

6. Conclusion

On 31 July 2024, a bill on gender recognition was introduced before the Colombian Parliament. The bill adopts self-determination as a standard and protects a self-defined legal sex in various areas of interaction with the state, including military service, education, and athletic competitions.[167] Every trans person is entitled to as many changes as they need. The bill also introduces four options of legal classification: male, female, nonbinary, and trans or *travesti*. No limits are imposed on the gender recognition of trans children, who are seemingly treated like adults—a provision, it should be pointed out, whose conformity to the constitutional jurisprudence could be challenged. The bill also guarantees protection from intersectional discrimination, participation in social and cultural life, and establishes measures to support unhoused trans people, among others. In the words of the proponents, the bill aims to 'establish a comprehensive framework to contribute to the full exercise of the rights of people with gender diverse identities, through the elimination of all forms of injustice, exclusion, discrimination and violence in the private and public sphere'.[168] The press has already hailed the bill as the 'most robust' legislative protection of gender diversity at the global level.[169] In late 2025, the *Registraduría Nacional del Estado Civil* introduced four options for the sex marker on the national ID with an administrative measure: male, female, nonbinary and 'trans'.[170]

[166] *See* C.C., 12 diciembre 2016, Sentencia T-701/16; C.C., 17 febrero 2017, Sentencia T-100/17; C.C., 26 febrero 2016, Sentencia T-063/18, as cited by the Constitutional Court in C.C., 23 junio 2019, Sentencia T-192/20, ¶ 14. *See also* C.C., 4 julio 2024, Sentencia T-261/24; C.C., 4 noviembre 2014, Sentencia T-804/14; and C.C., 14 octubre 2020, Sentencia T-443/20.

[167] Proyecto de ley [bill] de 31 julio 2024 n. 122/2024C, Art. 12.

[168] Proyecto de ley [bill] de 31 julio 2024 n. 122/2024C, Exposición de Motivos, https://www.camara.gov.co/ley-de-identidad-de-genero.

[169] Camila Osoria, *Lina Quevedo: 'El de Colombia es el Proyecto de Ley Trans Más Robusto a Nivel Mundial'*, El País América Colombia (13 July 2024), https://elpais.com/america-colombia/2024-07-31/lina-quevedo-el-de-colombia-es-el-proyecto-de-ley-trans-mas-robusto-a-nivel-mundial.html.

[170] Registraduría Nacional del Estado Civil, *Categorías 'No Binario' (NB) y 'Trans' (T) Fueron Incluidas en el Campo 'Sexo' de Registros Civiles y Todos los Documentos de Identidad* (28 Nov. 2025), https://www.registraduria.gov.co/Categorias-no-binario-NB-y-trans-T-fueron-incluidas-en-el-campo-sexo-de.html.

Regardless of whether and when it will become law, the bill reflects the constitutional jurisprudence and the self-determination model enshrined therein. This model offers the highest degree of recognition to trans men and women, ancestral identities, *travestis*, and, as of 2022, nonbinary and gender-fluid people. The Colombian Constitutional Court has indeed protected gender identity in nearly absolute terms, as all forms of 'assessments and validations' have been proscribed. Adding to its inclusiveness of gender-diverse people, the Colombian case also exposes the places where conventional binary labels, Eurocentrism, and colonization intersect and interact in the legal domain. When one examines Colombian jurisprudence acknowledging 'ancestral' identities, the association of the imposition of a legal binary with Eurocentrism immediately comes to mind. Gender self-determination, as developed by the Colombian Constitutional Court, teaches us that gender equality cannot be separated from an intersectional analysis.

Admittedly, this approach invites further discussion—and possibly criticism. Normative research into gender self-determination, comprising both conceptual and empirical aspects, would certainly be important. But be that as it may, it is undeniable that the jurisprudence of the Constitutional Court has transformed sex categories in public law, shifting legal identity from ascription to election. The differences vis-à-vis the other models discussed in this book are striking. In Italy and France, the person's declaration is subjected to approval by courts, and the possibility of achieving gender recognition is tied to a process whereby the 'proper' subject of recognition is very narrowly defined. Colombia, on the other hand, has shifted the power to determine legal identity from the state to the individual. As a result, the fundamentals that lead to the forms of disciplinary control over gender identity are, in principle, disestablished. It should be noted, however, that the role of the state and of public law does not simply disappear. Instead, it changes. The force of the law is redirected from imposing identities to acknowledging and fostering them. Sex registration is not simply a lazy exercise; it forces the state into the role of changing the understanding of legal sex and creating inclusion for gender-diverse people—with possible cultural spillovers that certainly warrant more investigation. This endeavour, arguably, is carried forward with nonbinary recognition—as is discussed in the next chapter.

7

'All Thirdness Is Not Alike': The Right to Nonbinary Recognition and Its Inner Tensions

1. Introduction

The existence of nonbinary people—individuals whose gender identity diverges from the male–female dichotomy—has long been discussed in history and anthropology.[1] Often confused with intersexuality, nonbinary is an identity, a 'deeply felt internal and individual experience of gender'.[2] As Serena Nanda has argued, nonbinary identities are widespread and often acknowledged and respected among human societies.[3] Although they are often associated with an exoticized Orient, nonbinary identities have long been present in Western societies, too.[4] Sex/gender thirdness takes on different forms depending on contextual factors and other identity markers that might influence nonbinary people's self-understanding and expression, including race, nationality, background, and religion.[5]

Nonbinary people and their claims are becoming more conspicuous by the day. Admittedly, nonbinary people remain largely invisible in the eyes of the law. Although the number of jurisdictions recognizing a nonbinary legal sex is increasing, most still do not.[6] Recognition at the constitutional level is even rarer. As we have seen, the preservation of binary categories seems to be crucial in defining the gender order in public law, which is built around the separate spheres doctrine.[7] Nevertheless, nonbinary recognition is now granted in several

[1] The title of this chapter reproduces verbatim an expression found in: Lawrence Cohen, *The Pleasures of Castration: The Postoperative Status of Hijras, Jankhas, and Academics*, *in* Sexual Nature, Sexual Culture 276, 277 (Paul R. Abramson & Steven D. Pinkerton eds., 1995).

[2] Yogyakarta Principles: Principles on the Application of International Human Rights Law in Relation to Sexual Orientation and Gender Identity (Mar. 2007).

[3] Serena Nanda, Neither Man nor Woman: The Hijras of India 128 (2d ed., 1999).

[4] One example is the *femminielli* from Naples: Marzia Mauriello, An Anthropology of Gender Variance and Trans Experience in Naples: Beauty in Transit (2021); Maria Carolina Vesce, Altri Transiti: Corpi, Pratiche, e Rappresentazioni di Femminielli e Transessuali (2017).

[5] Stefano Osella, *When Comparative Law Walks the Path of Anthropology: The Third Gender in Europe*, 23 German Law Journal 920, 926–29 (2022).

[6] Zhan Chiam et al., ILGA World, Trans Legal Mapping Report 2019: Recognition Before the Law (2020).

[7] Ruth Rubio-Marín, Global Gender Constitutionalism and Women's Citizenship: A Struggle for Transformative Inclusion (2022). *See* Chapter 1 (Introduction).

Gender Diversity in Public Law. Stefano Osella, Oxford University Press. © Stefano Osella 2026.
DOI: 10.1093/9780198935070.003.0007

jurisdictions, at times also as a constitutional right. Developments have taken place primarily at the national level. A right to legal thirdness is mostly absent at the international level or, if present, only in the form of soft law.[8] Notably, on 31 January 2023, the European Court of Human Rights (ECtHR) ruled that French authorities had not violated Article 8 of the European Convention on Human Rights (ECHR) when they refused to recognize a third legal sex.[9]

Legal thirdness manifests in various forms, which this chapter aims to explore. As per usual in this book, the focus will be on how gender identity recognition interacts with legal principles and values that build on legal sex—as a set of legal positions or a status—and how such principles and values might influence the formation of the right to nonbinary recognition. The chapter discusses the challenges posed by a third legal sex for the complex of legal positions and public interests that build on sex categories—or what I call the gender order in public law. Crucially, it shows how, depending on the characteristics of such a right, the introduction of nonbinary recognition may either reinforce or disestablish the system of legal categories, favouring or relinquishing control over individual identities. Furthermore, all of the models identified in this chapter will be assessed to understand the challenges and opportunities that they offer to nonbinary people.

In this chapter, I identify and discuss three main models of nonbinary recognition. The first one is *embodied recognition*, whereby a third option is granted to applicants who meet externally assessable preconditions, such as embodying physical and/or behavioural diversity.[10] Different physical characteristics might be the result of medical operations—as recognized in the Australian case law—or a congenital condition—as, arguably, is constitutionally recognized in Germany and was legally in force until the 2024 law on self-determination.[11] This form of recognition ostensibly safeguards legal certainty and minimizes deviations from the legal structures defined around the binary. Embodied recognition can therefore

[8] Giovanna Gilleri, Sex, Gender and International Human Rights Law: Contesting Binaries (2024); Sandra Duffy, *Contested Subjects of Human Rights: Trans- and Gender-Variant Subjects of International Human Rights Law*, 84 Modern Law Review 1041 (2021); Pieter Cannoot & Mattias Decoster, *The Abolition of Sex/Gender Registration in the Age of Gender Self-Determination: An International Human Rights Analysis*, 1 International Journal of Gender, Sexuality & Law 26, 29–34 (2020).

[9] Y v. France, App. No. 76888/17 (31 Jan. 2023), https://hudoc.echr.coe.int/eng?i=001-223027.

[10] Embodied recognition is an ascriptive identity. I decided to adopt the label 'embodied' because the crucial constitutional cases that describe its functioning refer to specific forms of embodiment. For the discussion of 'ascriptive' identity, refer to: Stefano Osella & Ruth Rubio-Marín, *Gender Recognition at the Crossroads: Four Models of Recognition and the Compass of Comparative Law*, 21 International Journal of Constitutional Law 574 (2023). The label 'ascriptive' is borrowed from: Jessica A. Clarke, *Identity and Form*, 103 California Law Review 747 (2015). I have previously used the terms employed in this Chapter ('embodied recognition' and 'self-determination') in Osella, *supra* note 5. For a brief discussion of nonbinary recognition, *see also*: Marie-Xaviere Catto & Stefano Osella, *The Sexed Subject, in* The Cambridge Companion to Gender and the Law 25, 52–55 (Stéphanie Hennette-Vauchez & Ruth Rubio-Marín eds., 2023).

[11] Gesetz über die Selbstbestimmung in Bezug auf den Geschlechtseintrag [SBGG], 19 June 2024. At the legislative level, this new law makes Germany an illustration of self-determination. However, the previous legal and jurisprudential developments in this jurisdiction offer an example of embodied nonbinary recognition.

function to maintain the stability of the complex of legal positions and public interests that build on sex assignment.[12]

The second model is *self-determination*. In this case, there are no preconditions for accessing nonbinary recognition. The Colombian Constitutional Court offers a prime example of nonbinary self-determination granted as a matter of constitutional right. This court's jurisprudence offers insights into how nonbinary recognition can interact with constitutional principles that presuppose the exclusive existence of males and females. Self-determination arguably comes at a cost in terms of legal certainty. Nevertheless, it favours inclusivity, not only of gender-diverse people, but of cultural diversity more generally. As the Colombian case shows, nonbinary self-determination has been used in a decolonial discourse to reaffirm identities that were oppressed by European colonization in Latin America. Crucially, nonbinary self-determination has the potential to transform the gender order in public law in a profound way.

Third comes *redistributive recognition*, a model that we encounter in the decisions of the Supreme Courts of Nepal, Pakistan, and India. We can understand redistributive recognition as an instrument for achieving substantive equality and remedying the rampant discrimination from which trans and nonbinary people suffer. These decisions foreground local identities that differ from the globalized understanding of transness. For clarity, these courts have adopted different standards for granting recognition, which can be defined as either embodied (Pakistan) or self-determined (India and Nepal). Nevertheless, their distinctive characteristics and similarities in reasoning lead me to devote a separate section to them. The decisions included in this model serve as a helpful reminder of the Eurocentrism of the binary gender order in public law, as well as of the multiple functions and transformative potential of nonbinary recognition.

The comparison of these forms of legal thirdness enables us to understand the challenges that nonbinary recognition presents in public and constitutional law. It also clarifies the different ways in which courts (and, to a lesser extent, legislatures) have responded to them. Legal comparison allows us to conclude that public authorities, such as courts or legislatures, may either use nonbinary recognition pragmatically to preserve the stability of the gender order in the law or to revolutionize it, depending on context-specific factors.

Before proceeding, a methodological note is in order. As mentioned, this chapter aims to provide a taxonomy of nonbinary recognition forms and to examine the interactions of this right within legal systems previously structured around the binary. For this reason, I have drawn on the jurisprudence of multiple

[12] This dynamic appears to reflect what Grietje Baars terms 'sexage' (Grietje Baars, *Queer Cases Unmake Gendered Law, Or, Fucking Law's Gendering Function*, 45 AUSTRALIAN FEMINIST LAW JOURNAL 15, 22 (2019)). For a discussion of intersex embodiment and its correlation with the 'third gender', *see* FAE GARLAND & MITCHELL TRAVIS, INTERSEX EMBODIMENT: LEGAL FRAMEWORKS BEYOND IDENTITY AND DISORDER 51–77 (2023).

jurisdictions. These jurisdictions were selected because their respective apex courts granted nonbinary recognition in different forms. These courts also extensively considered the issue of nonbinary recognition in relation to conflicting public interests and fundamental rights. While this chapter provides criteria to classify forms of nonbinary recognition, it does not aim to offer a comprehensive overview of all the different forms that this right may take within the identified categories.[13] Rather, the more modest goal of this research is to capture the various interactions between the right to nonbinary recognition and the public interests or fundamental rights that rely on legal sex.

2. Embodied recognition

2.1. Embodied recognition without rights: The *Norrie* case

Embodied recognition is linked to meeting certain specific preconditions, which can be behavioural, social, or physical. Among these preconditions, restricting gender recognition to individuals with particular bodily characteristics seems to be an ancient practice. In France, a third legal category was discussed in the immediate aftermath of the introduction of the 1810 *Code Napoleon*. Some jurists argued that 'hermaphroditic' children should *not* be registered as males or females. They suggested waiting to fully appreciate the development of the child. When such a development was no longer uncertain, a binary legal identity could be assigned.[14] Other scholars examined the possibility of annotating the registries to include, for example, the category 'undetermined sex'.[15] A distinct registration was recommended by some as a matter of scientific positivism: being 'hermaphrodites', these children could not accurately be registered as either males or females.[16]

As already discussed in Chapter 3, 'hermaphrodites' generated social anxiety. A third legal category was intended to prevent the social consequences of incorrect registration and to safeguard the morals of the time. French proposals for registering intersex children in a different sex category were 'aimed at better controlling unruly sexes, not to make space for alternative ones'.[17] Undetected (so to

[13] For such a taxonomy: Osella & Rubio-Marín, *supra* note 10.

[14] Gabrielle Houbre, *Un «sexe indéterminé»? L'Identité Civile des Hermaphrodites entre Drot et Médicine au XIX siècle*, 48 REVUE D'HISTOIRE DU XIXE SIÈCLE 63, 67 (2014).

[15] *Id.* at 67–73.

[16] Anne E. Linton, *Hermaphrodite Outlaws: Ambiguous Sex and the Civil Code in Nineteenth-Century France*, 138 REPRESENTATIONS 87, 92 (2017).

[17] Geertje Mak, *Doubtful Sex in Civil Law: Nineteenth and Early Twentieth Century Proposals for Ruling Hermaphroditism*, 12 CARDOZO JOURNAL OF LAW & GENDER 197, 198 (2005). *See also*: Houbre, *supra* note 14, at 69–74. *See* also GARLAND & TRAVIS, who effectively speak of '[i]ntersex as a placeholder for binary sex' (*supra* note 12, at 52–55).

speak) intersex people were seen as a threat to morals and marriage.[18] If wrongly assigned to one sex/gender, 'hermaphrodites' could enter segregated spaces, with all the moral panic that could ensue. The establishment of a third category was not driven by the concern for the welfare of gender-diverse people. On the contrary, the special regime might have entailed a limitation of their rights—for example, by inhibiting their capacity to inherit property, hold public office, and marry.[19] In some European countries, the discussion did not remain at the level of academic speculation. As Geertje Mak reports, the 1792 Prussian *Landrecht* envisioned special procedures for the assignment of a special sex status to intersex people, introducing *ad hoc* procedures to re-register them.[20]

Embodied recognition persists to this day. Today's version can however be considerably different from these historical examples. Fundamentally, when granted, it has been a positive response to a demand raised by stakeholders. Yet embodied recognition may still be used to protect a public interest in the legal certainty of public registries. The 2014 *Norrie* case decided by the High Court of Australia is a telling example of this stance.[21] In fact, as Grietje Baars notes, embodiment is in this case used to preserve the personal identification function of the legal system.[22] To be sure, the law on gender recognition in Australia, at the federal and local level, has evolved to a significant degree since 2014. At the time of writing (2025), changes are being made towards demedicalization, and, at times, self-determination. Interestingly, the 2024 decision of the Federal Court in *Tickle v. Giggle for Girls*, although not directly concerned with the recognition of a nonbinary identity, has confirmed that 'sex is not confined to being a biological concept referring to whether a person at birth had male or female physical traits, nor confined to being a binary concept'.[23] Nevertheless, the *Norrie* case remains authoritative and

[18] Linton, *supra* note 16, at 93.
[19] *Id.* at 92.
[20] Mak, *supra* note 17, at 201–02.
[21] NSW Registrar of Births, Deaths and Marriages v. Norrie [2014] HCA 11 (hereinafter, NSW Registrar of Births, Deaths and Marriages v. Norrie).
[22] The interpretation of the Australian case presented here is informed by Baars, *supra* note 12, at 27–30.
[23] Tickle v. Giggle for Girls Pty Ltd (No 2) [2024] FCA 960 ¶ 55. The Federal Court of Australia also underlined that 'sex, as it is deployed in the SDA… is changeable and not necessarily binary' ¶ 59. The Tickle v. Giggle for Girls case concerned a trans woman who had been barred from accessing a social media app designed for cis women only. The Federal Court ruled in her favour. The appeal of this decision is currently pending (https://www.fedcourt.gov.au/services/access-to-files-and-transcripts/online-files/giggle-for-girls-v-roxanne-tickle). More research is needed to understand whether this judgment grounds a right to binary and nonbinary self-determination in Australia as a matter of anti-discrimination law. For a broader discussion of trans law in the jurisdiction: Sarah Moulds, *Making the Invisible Visible Again: Pathways for Legal Recognition of Sex and Gender Diversity in Australian Law*, 7 Griffith Journal of Law & Human Dignity 246 (2019). As a federal system, the legal framework for gender recognition in Australia is fragmented and has been defined as 'a hotchpotch' (Rachel Wallbank, *The Legal Status of People Who Experience Difference in Sexual Formation and Gender Expression in Australia*, *in* The Legal Status of Transgender and Transsexual Persons 498 (Jens Scherpe ed., 2015)). At the federal level, the 2013 Australian Government Guidelines on the Recognition of Sex and Gender (as updated in November 2015) offer an additional category for registration (M; F; X) (¶ 19). This document also specifies that '[t]he preferred Australian Government approach is to collect and

a clear example of how controls over legal sex can be present also in nonbinary systems. The High Court granted a third sex (non-specific) status to a nonbinary applicant—Norrie—after they acquired a nonbinary bodily shape following medical and surgical treatments. The applicant was born with male sex characteristics and had undergone a 'sex affirmation procedure' to correct, in the words of the applicant, a 'sexual ambiguity'. Yet Norrie believed that such treatments had ultimately failed. Hence, they applied for a 'non-specific' sex registration in the Births, Deaths, and Marriages Register of New South Wales. As then legally required,[24] they attached to their application two (supportive) statutory declarations by medical practitioners.[25] After having been denied by the registrar and by two courts, the claim reached the ultimate appellate level.

The decision of the High Court was not rendered in a vacuum. The High Court had ruled on the rights of trans people before. Although a degree of openness to the protection of gender identity was evident, the perspective remained medico-behavioural.[26] The Australian Government had previously recommended the possibility of using an X marker when gender information is to be collected.[27] Earlier case law had also contemplated the possibility of a nonbinary categorization.[28] Consistent with such openings, the High Court first acknowledged that the possibility of an 'ambiguous' (neither-male-nor-female) legal sex had been contemplated both in the text of the civil registry law and in the Court's own precedents.[29] It then rejected the opposing view of the registrar, which had cautioned that a third legal category would generate confusion in the binary legal system.[30]

use gender information' (¶ 16). Gender is intended to be 'a person's personal and social identity. It refers to the way a person feels, presents and is recognised within the community. A person's gender may be reflected in outward social markers, including their name, outward appearance, mannerisms and dress' (¶ 13). An application to change gender information at the federal level can be supported, among various ways, by the submission of 'a state or territory birth certificate, which specifies their gender. A document from a state or territory Registrar of Births, Deaths and Marriages recognising a change of sex and/or gender will also be seen as sufficient evidence' (¶ 24(c)). At the state level, some states have moved towards gender self-determination: Victoria (Births, Deaths and Marriages Registration Amendment Act 2019, adding Part 4A to the Births, Deaths and Marriages Registration Act 1996) and New South Wales (Equality Legislation Amendment (LGBTQI+) Act 2024, adding Part 5A to the Births, Deaths and Marriages Registration Act 1995).

[24] Births, Deaths and Marriages Registration Act 1995 No. 62, Art. 32DB.

[25] Baars, *supra* note 12, at 27 (offering an overview of the facts).

[26] AB v. Western Australia (2011) 244 CLR 390 (hereinafter, AB v. Western Australia). Concerning marriage: The Attorney-General for the Commonwealth v. 'Kevin and Jennifer' and Human Rights and Equal Opportunity Commission, 30 FAMILY LAW REPORTS 1 (2003).

[27] Australian Government Guidelines on the Recognition of Sex and Gender (July 2013), and cited in Baars, *supra* note 12, at 29.

[28] AB v. Western Australia, 402 ¶ 23. Theodore Bennett reports that Court of Appeal of New South Wales had excluded such a possibility in a previous decision in R. v. Harris. Bennett refers to the reason given by Mathews J in the decision and, specifically, to the difficulties that a third sex might create for the legal system. Theodore Bennett, *'No Man's Land': Nonbinary Sex Identification in Australian Law and Policy*, 37 UNSW LAW JOURNAL 847, 850–51 (2014).

[29] NSW Registrar of Births, Deaths and Marriages v. Norrie, ¶¶ 33, 36–40. *See* also Births, Deaths and Marriages Registration Act 1995 No. 62 Art. 32(b).

[30] NSW Registrar of Births, Deaths and Marriages v. Norrie, ¶¶ 28–29 and ¶¶ 43–44.

On the one hand, the High Court seemed to suggest that the sex of the individual was ultimately of lesser importance in the specific legal system. Indeed, it stated that: '[f]or the most part, the sex of the individuals concerned is irrelevant to legal relations. … The chief, perhaps the only, case where the sex of the parties to the relationship is legally significant is [heterosexual] marriage.'[31] On the other hand, however, the High Court ruled that the applicant should not be required to be registered as male or female, as either designation would be 'inaccurate'.[32]

The *Norrie* decision did not go uncriticized, even though it opened up a possibility for individuals with characteristics similar to the applicant's. From the standpoint of nonbinary people, it has been argued that introducing a third category with the specific characteristics defined by the High Court might flatten the many different intra-category differences. Furthermore, a nonbinary option strictly tied to physical 'ambiguity' seemed ultimately to reinforce the male and female binary categories as the healthy and 'uncontaminated' ones.[33] Though in a different context, the High Court's words echo the earlier debates on nonbinary registration. This is not to suggest that the High Court intended that the nonbinary category serves merely as an instrument to control gender-diverse people. After all, it was Norrie who presented the claim. However, as Baars underlines, central to this case is the 'correctness of the register' and of 'the bureaucratic system of registration, and by extension gender regulation and reproduction—even if that necessitated a third gender category'.[34]

2.2. The right to an embodied nonbinary recognition[35]

Embodied recognition, with its stabilizing potential, has also been defined as a fundamental right. This is arguably the case in German constitutional law.[36] In 2017, the Federal Constitutional Court (FCC) granted a nonbinary option to individuals whose '[sex/]gender development' (*Geschlechtsentwicklung*) deviates from male and female and who permanently identify as nonbinary.[37] Some

[31] NSW Registrar of Births, Deaths and Marriages v. Norrie, ¶ 42. At the time of the decision, marriage was limited to heterosexual couples (S. 5(1) of the Marriage Act 1961). The Marriage Amendment (Definition and Religious Freedoms) Act 2017 introduced same-sex marriage in Australia.

[32] NSW Registrar of Births, Deaths and Marriages v. Norrie, ¶ 46.

[33] Dylan Davis, *The Normativity of Recognition: Non-Binary Gender Markers in Australian Law and Policy*, *in* Advances in Gender Research 227, 236 (Vasilikye Demos & Marcia Texler Segal eds., 2017).

[34] Baars, *supra* note 12, at 29.

[35] This section is much indebted, partly reproduces, and expands the research presented in Osella, *supra* note 5, at 935–39.

[36] For a thorough discussion of sex registration law in Germany: Susanna Rossbach, Das personenstandsrechtliche Geschlecht. Zu Vergangenheit, Gegenwart und Zukunft des Geschlechtseintrags in den Personenstandsregistern (2025).

[37] Bundesverfassungsgericht [Federal Constitutional Court][BVerfG], 10 Oct. 2017, 1 BvR 2019/16, ¶ 35. The English translation of the decision is taken from the official website of the Federal Constitutional Court (https://www.bundesverfassungsgericht.de/SharedDocs/Entscheidungen/EN/

scholars have suggested that this decision should be read expansively as protecting self-determination.[38] Yet, the German Parliament in 2018 and the Federal Court of Justice (FCJ) in 2020 applied this decision more narrowly and limited recognition to intersex people only.[39] Although the specific characteristics of the plaintiff (an intersex nonbinary person) were consequential for the outcome of the FCC's 2017 judgment, the resulting definition of a more restrictive embodied recognition standard was also driven by the public interest in controlling sex categories. In June 2024, the German legislature granted gender self-determination, inclusive of a nonbinary option, to all people, endosex and intersex alike.[40] The new law has thus replaced the first legislative implementation of the FCC's 2017 ruling. Although, at the level of legislation, Germany is now a model of self-determination, the constitutional framework appears more open to debate. In any case, the study of the German approach remains essential to discerning how a right to nonbinary recognition can be crafted in such a way that it still preserves the stability of the gender order in public law.

The FCC's 2017 decision concerned a 2013 amendment to the Personal Status Law (*Personenstandgesetz*).[41] As discussed in Chapter 3, the 2013 law had introduced the possibility of a blank—sexless—registration for intersex children, whose parents were allowed 'not to tick the box'.[42] Angelika von Wahl shows how the 2013 law was preceded by several years of intersex activism which, although primarily focused on involuntary medical interventions, also demanded flexible forms of

2017/10/rs20171010_1bvr201916en.html). However, in this specific passage, I have added 'sex' to 'gender'. The original German uses the term '*Geschlechtsentwicklung*'. '*Geschlechts*' might mean both 'sex' and 'gender'. The interpretation of this expression—whether it means 'sex' intended as 'biological characteristics' or 'gender', thus possibly inclusive of 'gender identity'—has been debated, as detailed in the text. To preserve the ambiguity of the original German, I used therefore 'sex/gender'.

[38] Anna Katharina Mangold & Susanna Roßbach, *Das Grundrecht auf geschlechtliche Selbstbestimmung*, 78 JuristenZeitung 756, 759 (2023); Dana-Sophia Valentiner, *Geschlechtsidentität und Verfassungsrecht*, *in* Geschlecterfragen in Recht. Interdisziplinäre Überlegungen 129, 143–44 (Magdalena Januszkiewicz et al. eds., 2022); Chris Ambrosi, *Die Dritte Option: Für Wen?*, VerfBlog (29 Nov. 2017), https://verfassungsblog.de/die-dritte-option-fuer-wen/.

[39] Bundesgerichtshof [BGH] [Federal Court of Justice], 22 Apr. 2020, XII 383/19, ¶¶ 14, 18–22, and 32, http://juris.bundesgerichtshof.de/cgi-bin/rechtsprechung/document.py?Gericht=bgh&Art=en&nr=106062&pos=0&anz=1. Intersex people could obtain recognition under the 2018 law that was passed after the 2017 decision of the FCC: Gesetz zur Änderung der in das Geburtenregister einzutragenden Angaben, 22 Dec. 2018, which incorporated § 45b of the Personnenstandsgesetz [PStG].

[40] Gesetz über die Selbstbestimmung in Bezug auf den Geschlechtseintrag [SBGG], 21 Jun. 2024.

[41] Gesetz zur Änderung personenstandsrechtlicher Vorschriften, 7 May 2013, incorporating paragraph § 22(3) of the Personnenstandsgesetz.

[42] PStG, § 22(3). Following scholarly interpretation and a decision of the FCJ in 2016, intersex adults were eventually allowed to choose the 'sex-less' option too. Jens T. Theilen, *Intersexualität, Personenstandsrecht und Grundrechte*, 67 Das Standesamt 1, 4 (2014); Susanne Lilian Gössl, *Die Eintragung im Geburtenregister als 'Inter' oder 'Divers'*, 68 Das Standesamt, 171, 172 (2015). BGH, 22 June 2016, XII ZB 52/15, marg. 23, https://www-juris-de.bls.idm.oclc.org/perma?d=KORE301182016.

registration.[43] Following the concluding observations of the CEDAW Committee in 2009,[44] the German Government invited the Ethics Council to study the rights of intersex people and advise on the best way to safeguard them.[45] In 2012, the German Ethics Council stated that 'the compulsory categorization of intersexed people as belonging to either the female or male sex constitutes a grave interference with those persons' right to self-determination and right of personality'.[46]

The 2013 law was far from perfect. As Susanna Roßbach documents, scholars pointed out that the set of legal positions of a sexless person was all but clear.[47] Roßbach also argues that the law was ambiguous regarding whether the sexless status was mandatory or, instead, optional. The text was prescriptive. Yet, the legislative intent was protective. The protective spirit of the law was therefore hardly compatible with a mandatory registration—a matter that was subsequently resolved in favour of optionality via administrative interpretation.[48] The law was also unclear in relation to the possibility of adults being classified as sexless. This issue was clarified by a 2016 decision in which the FCJ determined that intersex adults were allowed to choose the 'sexless' option based on the general rules on amending the birth registry.[49] To be sure, all this was not ideal from the perspective of intersex and nonbinary people. Furthermore, the uncertainty generated by the 2013 law was, as Anna Katharina Mangold suggests, strategic.[50] It limited nonbinary recognition to a minimum and avoided a thorough adaptation of the legal system to be fully inclusive of a nonbinary identity. Ultimately, it helped preserve the binary structure of the law. Nevertheless, the 2013 law was also an unprecedented challenge to the legal binary system. Crucially, it paved the way to the subsequent developments.

The sexless status was at the core of the 2017 decision of the FCC. The absence of a positive nonbinary sex option was targeted by the *Dritte Option* campaign—a group of activists that mobilized for nonbinary recognition. This advocacy group pushed forward the demand for recognition of a person, Vanja, who was both

[43] Angelika von Wahl, *From Object to Subject: Intersex Activism and the Rise and Fall of the Gender Binary in Germany*, 28 Social Politics 755 (2021); Angelika von Wahl, *From Private Wrongs to Public Rights: The Politics of Intersex Activism in the Merkel Era*, 31 German Politics 59 (2022).

[44] Committee on the Elimination of Discrimination Against Women, Concluding Observations on the Combined Sixth Periodic Report of Germany, U.N. Doc. CEDAW/C/DEU/CO/6 nr. 62 (12 Feb. 2009).

[45] Von Wahl, *From Private Wrongs to Public Rights*, *supra* note 43, at 67.

[46] Ethikrat [German Ethics Council], Intersexuality 129–30 (23 Feb. 2012).

[47] Rossbach, *supra* note 36, at 61–70.

[48] *Id.*

[49] BGH, 22 June 2016, XII ZB 52/15, marg. 23, https://www-juris-de.bls.idm.oclc.org/perma?d=KORE301182016. The case referred to: §§ 48.I, 47.II, no. 1 PStG in conjunction with § 22.III PStG. *See also*: Theilen, *supra* note 42; Gössl, *supra* note 42.

[50] Anna Katharina Mangold, *Nicht Mann. Nicht Frau. Nicht Nichts: Ein Verfassungsblog-Symposium*, VerfBlog (12 Nov. 2017), https://verfassungsblog.de/nicht-mann-nicht-frau-nicht-nichts-ein-verfassungsblog-symposium/.

nonbinary and *intersex*.[51] The lack of a positive nonbinary option resulted in a mismatch between the legal and the lived identity of the plaintiff, who could not avail themselves of the 2013 law because of their positive nonbinary (and not genderless) identity. This mismatch, the plaintiff argued, impinged on their constitutional right to free development of personality, self-image, and the possibility to 'move about in public and to be seen by others as a nonbinary person'.[52] After unsuccessful attempts to rectify the personal status at the administrative level and, subsequently, lower courts,[53] the case was decided in favour of the plaintiff by the FCC. The Court granted a right to nonbinary recognition to people who permanently identify as nonbinary and have a variation of sex/gender development.

The decision laid down a two-fold doctrinal foundation of the right to nonbinary recognition. First, the FCC ruled that the impossibility of using a positive nonbinary option encroached on the right to identity as an emanation of the right to free development of personality.[54] The law required sex registration without allowing a third positive sex entry. The option offered by the 2013 law (leaving the sex marker blank) was deemed not to be a valid alternative by the FCC. Indeed, it did not grant a positive recognition of the plaintiff's identity, thus forcing them to tolerate a non-representative registration.[55] Gender equality was the second ground. Recalling the case law of the Court of Justice of the European Union, the FCC considered that gender equality protected gender identity too.[56]

The FCC examined in detail the constitutionally grounded justifications for the interference with the right to nonbinary recognition. First, the Court dismissed the argument that the reference to men and women in the equality clause[57] could be interpreted as a restriction or a denial of nonbinary identities.[58] Second, the Court rejected the argument that nonbinary recognition might affect the rights of third parties. The third option, the FCC established, is not forced on anyone—not even on people with a variation of sex/gender development, who remain free to retain a binary identity. Third, the FCC acknowledged the financial and bureaucratic costs that the addition of a third option would entail. Nevertheless, it considered them acceptable in light of the constitutional right at stake. To be sure, the Court established that the general right to personality does not give a right to register *any* gender identity. Yet the legislature, the Court added, is free to dispense

[51] The person was asking to be reclassified as 'inter/other' (in German, *inter/divers*) or, alternatively, simply 'other' (*divers*). BVerfG, 10 Oct. 2017, 1 BvR 2019/16, ¶ 1.

[52] BVerfG, 10 Oct. 2017, 1 BvR 2019/16, ¶ 48.

[53] The application had been previously rejected by the FCJ (BGH, 22 June 2016, XII ZB 52/15); by the Higher Regional Court in Celle (Oberlandesgericht [Higher Regional Court] [Olg], 21 Jan. 2015, 17 W 28/14); and by the District Court in Hannover (Amtsgericht [AG] [District Court], 13 Oct. 2014, 85 III 105/14).

[54] This right is grounded in: Grundgesetz [GG] [Basic Law], Art. 2(1), Art. 1(1).

[55] BVerfG, 10 Oct. 2017, 1 BvR 2019/16, ¶ 41–55.

[56] BVerfG, 10 Oct. 2017, 1 BvR 2019/16, ¶¶ 56–64.

[57] GG, Art. 3(2).

[58] BVerfG, 10 Oct. 2017, 1 BvR 2019/16, ¶ 50–55.

of sex categories in the law altogether. Fourth, the FCC acknowledged that the state has an interest in preserving the binary categorization as a matter of regulatory interests. There are legal provisions that build on the binary. However, the FCC considered that any potential legal uncertainty caused by the addition of a third sex category had in fact already been triggered by the 2013 law. In fact, the FCC underlined that a third positive option might even increase certainty relative to a permanently unticked box, which could have been left blank erroneously.[59] The Court also found that the addition of a nonbinary category did not as such change the 'permanent nature' (*Dauerhaftigkeit*) of civil status, which does not depend on the number of sex categories recognized.[60]

The FCC's decision remains rather ambiguous, and the precise contours of the recognition that it grants have been the subject of debate. On the one hand, the expression 'variations of sex/gender development' might be interpreted in a restrictive fashion, as limited to intersex people in conformity with medical parlance.[61] The same FCC seems to link this expression to the notion of 'disorders of sex development' (DSD), or, in other words, intersexuality.[62] This narrow reading, Jens Theilen argues, appears more faithful to the text of the decision.[63] On the other hand, the judgment was contextualized as the Court's answer to the questions posed by the plaintiff. The FCC never explicitly excluded from recognition endosex people. Some passages of the judgment, moreover, seem to attach considerable weight to the self-identification of the applicant,[64] in light of which the exclusion of nonbinary endosex people might seem unreasonable.[65] Roßbach

[59] BVerfG, 10 Oct. 2017, 1 BvR 2019/16, ¶¶ 51–54.

[60] BVerfG, 10 Oct. 2017, 1 BvR 2019/16, ¶ 55.

[61] For example, the Federal Association of Medical Doctors speaks of 'Varianten des Geschlechtsentwicklung' to refer to intersexuality: Stellungnahme des Bundesartzkammer zum Regierungsentwurf eines Gesetzes zum Schutz von Kindern mit Varianten des Geschlechtsentwicklung (BT-Drs. 19/24686) (8 Jan. 2021), https://www.bundesaerztekammer.de/politik/stellungnahmen-gesetzgebung; Stellungnahme der Bundesärztekammer „Versorgung von Kindern, Jugendlichen und Erwachsenen mit Varianten/Störungen der Geschlechtsentwicklung (Disorders of Sex Development, DSD)" (30 Jan. 2015), https://www.bundesaerztekammer.de/fileadmin/user_upload/_old-files/downloads/pdf-Ordner/Stellungnahmen/BAeK-Stn_DSD.pdf.

[62] BVerfG, 10 Oct. 2017, 1 BvR 2019/16, ¶ 9.

[63] Jens Theilen, *Developments in German Civil Status Law on the Recognition of Intersex and Non-Binary Persons: Subversion Subverted*, *in* Protecting Trans Rights in the Age of Gender Self-Determination 95, 102 (Eva Brems, Pieter Cannoot & Toon Moonen eds., 2020); Jens Theilen, *Beyond the Gender Binary: Rethinking the Right to Legal Gender Recognition*, 3 European Human Rights Law Review 249, 255 (2018). Refer also to Peter Dunne & Jule Mulder, *Beyond the Binary: Towards a Third Sex Category in Germany?*, 19 German Law Journal 627, 641–42 (2018).

[64] *E.g.*: At ¶ 58, the FCC states that Article 3(3) of the Basic Law not only protects men and women from gender-based discrimination, but also individuals who 'do not identify with either sex/gender'. For a discussion: Chris Ambrosi, *Die Dritte Option: Für Wen?*, VerfBlog (29 Nov. 2017), https://verfassungsblog.de/die-dritte-option-fuer-wen/. At ¶ 59, the FCC refers to the vulnerability of people whose gender identity is 'neither woman nor man' in a society where the binary is so central: Mangold & Roßbach, *supra* note 38, at 757–60. *See also*: Anna Katharina Mangold, Maya Markwald & Cara Röhner, Rechtsgutachten zum Verständnis von 'Varianten der Geschlechtsentwicklung' in § 45b Personenstandsgesetz 11–12 (2 Dec. 2019), https://eufbox.uni-flensburg.de/index.php/s/WwkHJkHaEaHpkQk#pdfviewer.

[65] Ambrosi, *supra* note 64.

points to the emphasis placed by the FCC on the need to protect 'the gender identity of persons who cannot be assigned to either the male or female sex/gender'.[66] Anna Katharina Mangold, Maya Markwald, and Cara Röhner have also suggested that the expression 'variations of sex/gender development' could encompass all nonbinary people, regardless of their physical characteristics.[67] This interpretation could be reinforced if the decision is read against the jurisprudence that the FCC has developed over time on the right to gender recognition.[68] Finally, it is much more certain that the FCC insisted on the required permanence of gender identity. Although gender-fluid people were not explicitly excluded from constitutional franchise, and an expansive reading might be sustainable, interpreting the FCC's decision as protecting fluid identities would not be without challenges. In conclusion, despite the possibility of expansive interpretations, this 2017 judgment does not appear to grant self-determination—at least, not in unequivocal terms. It is an ambiguous decision at best, especially when compared with other decisions at the comparative level that grant self-determination, and a narrow reading along the lines of embodied recognition appears plausible.

Be that as it may, the lack of clarity gave the legislature some margin of manoeuvre. Under the 2018 law that enacted the FCC's decision,[69] applicants wishing to amend their legal status were required to provide medical certification of their intersex condition to the administrative authorities.[70] If medical certification was not available, or if the intersex condition could no longer be proved or could only be proved with an invasive evaluation, applicants could swear an oath about their original 'variation of sex development'.[71]

The parliamentary debates that led to the 2018 law are illuminating on the values underlying embodied recognition in a predominantly binary legal system. Limiting the third option to people with a physical variation was connected to legal principles, arguably of constitutional standing, such as the certainty of civil status. Outside the more narrowly legal domain, one MP seemingly linked the protection of physical intersexuality only to the resistance against gender ideology.[72] Some opposition was also mustered based on a rhetoric of naturalness and adherence to

[66] ROSSBACH, *supra* note 36, at 71, referring to ¶ 40 of the decision.

[67] Mangold, Markwald & Röhner, *supra* note 64, at 6–15.

[68] On this point: Dunne & Mulder, *supra* note 63, at 642. Beginning in 1978, the FCC has developed an extensive body of case law on the right to gender recognition, repeatedly affirming the importance of protecting what nowadays is referred to as gender identity. Valentiner offers a detailed summary of the case law: *supra* note 38, at 130–41.

[69] Gesetz zur Änderung der in das Geburtenregister einzutragenden Angaben, 22 Dec. 2018.

[70] The faithfulness of the law to the ruling has been questioned: Helen Lindenberg, *Das Dritte Geschlecht. Eine Bewertung des Gesetzesentwurfs zur Einführung des Geschlechtseintrages, divers' sowie möglicher Folgeregelungen*, NZFAM—NEUE ZEITSCHRIFT FÜR FAMILIENRECHT 1062, 1063 (2018).

[71] PstG, § 45(b), as modified by Gesetz zur Änderung der in das Geburtenregister einzutragenden Angaben, 22 Dec. 2018.

[72] Deutscher Bundestag [Federal Parliament], 13 Dec. 2018, 8330 C, https://dip.bundestag.de/vorgang/gesetz-zur-änderung-der-in-das-geburtenregister-einzutragenden-angaben/239069. See in particular the position of Marc Henrichmann (at 8330). On 'gender ideology': Beatrix von Storch (at 8332).

a presumed 'factual reality' to avoid the possibility that individuals might change their civil status without serious reasons.[73]

Admittedly, the notion of 'variations of sex development' contained in the 2018 law was not interpreted uniformly by courts. Limited instances of more liberal readings, in which these 'variations' have been recognized in the subjective self-identification of the applicant, have been recorded.[74] As a response, the government issued administrative guidelines to specify that 'transsexual' people were not covered by the 2018 law. Furthermore, it wielded the option of criminal prosecution—for perjury or forgery of a medical certificate[75]—in cases of endosex people trying to obtain recognition in the third option.[76]

The FCJ restricted the application of the 2018 law in April 2020. The plaintiff was a nonbinary (genderless) endosex person—or, to cite the FCJ, a person with a 'merely perceived intersexuality'—who had been denied nonbinary recognition.[77] The FCJ rejected their appeal and established that the right granted with the 2018 law was exclusively 'connected to the impossibility of assigning a female or male sex/gender on the basis of physical characteristics'.[78] To buttress its point, the FCJ recalled the Chicago Consensus on the Disorders of Sex Development and the 2015 statement of the Council of German Medical Doctors on Variations of Sex Development[79]—whose terminology was echoed by the Federal Constitutional Court and the law.[80] Interpreting this provision more inclusively, the FCJ ruled, would infringe on the separation of powers, going beyond the intention of Parliament, and would upset the civil status law that was, at the time, 'as a whole tied to biological sex'.[81]

[73] Ha Mi Le & Benedict Ertelt, *Zwischen Unbehagen und Ignoranz. Die Anhörung im Gesetzgebungsverfahren zur 'Dritten Option'*, VERFBLOG (29 Jan. 2018), https://verfassungsblog.de/zwischen-unbehagen-und-ignoranz-die-anhoerung-im-gesetzgebungsverfahren-zur-dritten-option/.

[74] Oberlandesgericht [OLG] Düsseldorf, 11 June 2019, I-25 Wx 76/17, FAMRZ 2019, 1663; Amtgericht [AG] Münster, 16 Dec. 2019, 22 III 36/19, FAMRZ 2020, 626. On the other hand, giving a more restrictive interpretation of the law: OLG Nürnberg, 3 Sept. 2019, 11 W 1880/19, FAMRZ 2019, 1948.

[75] Strafgesetzbuch [Criminal code] [StGB], § 156 and § 278.

[76] Rundschreiben zum Gesetz zur Änderung der in das Geburtenregister einzutragenden Angaben, StAZ 2019, S. 151 (RdSchr. d. BMI v. 10.4.2019 - V II 1 - 20103/27#17).

[77] After the registrar's office and the local court (*Amtgericht* Wuppertal) initially declined the application to change the official sex marker, the higher regional court in Düsseldorf (OLG Düsseldorf) ruled on 11 June 2019 (I-25 Wx 76/17, FAMRZ 2019, 1663) that the sex entry was to be amended. The supervisory authority for registry offices appealed this decision again. The case thus came to the FCJ. The expression (merely) 'perceived intersexuality' (*(lediglich) empfundene Intersexualität*) can be found throughout the decision to refer to the applicant, for example, in the introductory summary at point (b).

[78] BGH, 22 Apr. 2020, XII 383/19, ¶ 32.

[79] Stellungnahme der Bundesärztekammer 'Versorgung von Kindern, Jugendlichen und Erwachsenen mit Varianten/Störungen der Geschlechtsentwicklung (Disorders of Sex Development, DSD)' (30 Jan. 2015), https://www.bundesaerztekammer.de/fileadmin/user_upload/_old-files/downloads/pdf-Ordner/Stellungnahmen/BAeK-Stn_DSD.pdf.

[80] BGH, 22 Apr. 2020, XII 383/19, ¶¶ 14, 18–22.

[81] BGH, 22 Apr. 2020, XII 383/19, ¶ 25 and ¶ 27.

To be sure, the FCJ did grant recognition of the applicant's nonbinary identity. Yet it relied on the 1980 Transsexual People Act—which, as of November 2024, is no longer in force.[82] This law secured recognition for binary 'transsexual' people who had identified in the other binary sex/gender for at least three years, will likely identify as such permanently, and had obtained supporting opinions from two 'experts'. Leaving aside the practical disadvantages for nonbinary people of a longer and more invasive judicial procedure,[83] the FCJ considered that the procedures established by the 1980 Transsexual People Act conferred permanence and certainty to the legal status, upon which depend 'rights, duties, and family positions'.[84] The establishment of a different procedure for nonbinary people and intersex people who also identify as nonbinary, the FCJ continued, did not infringe on gender equality. Nonbinary people and intersex nonbinary people were considered dissimilar and thus could be treated differently, only the latter being a deviation from a person's 'biological sex'.[85] The FCJ, in other words, was transparent in connecting embodiment, legal control, and the interests underlying civil status registration.

The decision of the FCJ led to some different views among commentators. Some argued that the FCJ had operated correctly, differentiating the legal treatment of two situations that are factually distinct—the nonbinary recognition of endosex and intersex people, respectively.[86] Others pointed out that the decision of the FCJ was not in line with the ruling of the FCC,[87] or, at least, with a liberal interpretation thereof. Regardless, what seemed uncontroversial was the attempt of the court to preserve control over the nonbinary option in an attempt to preserve stability in a still largely binary legal system.

The FCJ's decision had been appealed to the FCC. However, the application appears to have been withdrawn following the enactment of the gender self-determination law in 2024.[88] The appeal had targeted the necessity of sex registration at birth, as well as the restrictive interpretation of the 2018 law.[89] The main claim of the appeal appeared to centre on the need to revise the interpretation of 'variations of sex/gender development' to include cases of nonbinary people with standard physical characteristics and to endorse an interpretation of the law that

[82] BGH, 22 Apr. 2020, XII 383/19. For a comment: Jens Theilen, *Der biologische Essentialismus hinter 'lediglich empfundener Intersexualität'*, VERFBLOG (22 May 2020), https://verfassungsblog.de/der-biologische-essentialismus-hinter-lediglich-empfundener-intersexualitaet/.

[83] On this point: Anna Katharina Mangold, Friedrike Boll & Katrin Niedenthal, Verfassungsbeschwerde ¶ B.I.4.cc (15 June 2020) (on file with author).

[84] BGH, 22 Apr. 2020, XII 383/19, ¶¶ 43–44. *See also*: BVerfG, 11. Jan. 2011, 1 BvR 3295/07, ¶ 66.

[85] BGH, 22 Apr. 2020, XII 383/19, ¶¶ 45–49.

[86] Anatol Dutta & Matteo Fornasier, *Anmerkung zu BGH, Beschluss vom 22.4.2020—XII ZB 383/19*, FAMRZ ZEITSCHRIFT FÜR DAS GESAMTE FAMILIENRECHT 1009, 1015–17 (2020); Judith Froese, *Anmerkung zu BGH, Beschluss vom 22.4.2020—XII ZB 383/19*, 75 JURISTENZEITUNG 856, 859 (2020).

[87] Valentiner, *supra* note 38, at 146–47.

[88] Mangold, Boll & Niedenthal, *supra* note 83. For the withdrawal announcement, *see* FRIEDRICH-Ebert-Stiftung für Freiheitsrechte e.V. (GFF), Mein Geschlecht bestimme ich!, https://freiheitsrechte.org/themen/soziale-teilhabe/selbstbestimmter-geschlechtseintrag.

[89] PStG, § 21(1).

complies with the (expansive reading of the) 2017 decision of the FCC. The application pinpointed the lack of valid justifications to deny a self-determined identification. Notably, the claim insisted on the importance of having specific and well-documented explanations of how the legal assignment of sex at birth, and the limitations on recognition throughout life, serve the regulatory interests of the state.[90] A decision granting self-determination might arguably have been transformative of the German constitutional approach to gender diversity and dispelled all possible doubts about the 2017 decision.

Be that as it may, the 2024 self-determination law now grants individuals the right to obtain recognition (male, female, 'other') with a simple declaration, or to refrain from declaring altogether. This right is granted to adults and children alike.[91] The possibility of such a law had been discussed at least since 2017, when the German Parliament for the first time called out for a broader reform of the Transsexual People Law, but saw a turning point with the 'Traffic Light' coalition resulting from the 2021 elections.[92] Procedurally, the applicant is required to register the intention to change their legal sex with the registry office.[93] After a three-month waiting period, they will have to reiterate their intention and specify that they understand the consequences of their actions, at which point recognition will become effective.[94] The declaration can be reneged by the applicant after one year, thus adding some legislative protection to gender fluidity.[95]

The law reveals the possible tensions between gender recognition and competing interests and rights, as well as the centrality of the legal assignment of a binary sex to the pursuit of constitutionally grounded interests. So, for example, limits to recognition are instated in cases of gender quotas,[96] as well as to access to changing rooms and segregated facilities and athletic competitions.[97] Limits to gender recognition are also put in place when it comes to the defence needs of the state.[98]

To wrap it up, the FCC crafted a right characterized by a degree of uncertainty. To be sure, 'embodied recognition' grants a right to a long-invisible segment of the

[90] Mangold and Roßbach have highlighted that references to such regulatory needs are far too generalized, thus questioning whether the binary is necessary: Mangold & Roßbach, *supra* note 38, at 759.

[91] While not deviating from the self-determination model, the law establishes special procedures for children and when a conflict arises between parents and children concerning gender recognition (SBGG, § 3).

[92] As explained by Rossbach, *supra* note 36, at 186–90. The 'Traffic Light' coalition included The Green Party, the Liberal Democratic Party, and the Social Democratic Party.

[93] SBGG, § 4.

[94] SBGG, § 2.

[95] SBGG, § 5(1).

[96] The legal sex to be considered for the computation of quotas is the one at the moment of the appointment to the body in question (SBGG, § 7).

[97] The determination of the sex of the person for this purpose is left to the specific regulatory entities or private bodies (SBGG, §§ 6(2) and 6(3)).

[98] The legal assignment to the male sex remains unaltered in case of defence needs (SBGG, § 9).

population and challenges, at least to some extent, the binary legal system.[99] On the other hand, legislators, courts, and—to a lesser extent—the government relied on the ambivalence of the constitutional decision and on the intersex embodiment to *limit* nonbinary identity to a small, and manageable, subset of gender-diverse people and thus safeguard the gender order in public law. This came with exclusionary effects for nonbinary people whose embodiment differed from the norm.

3. Self-determined recognition

3.1. A self-determined, nonbinary, and fluid identity

To date, some constitutional courts have granted a third option based on self-determination. In these cases, courts have unequivocally avoided, if not rejected, establishing any standards that applicants must meet to be reclassified as nonbinary. Furthermore, all assumptions about identity permanence have been abandoned in the case law of these courts, thus protecting gender-fluid people who may repeatedly change legal sex over time. A self-determined and fluid nonbinary option represents a clean break from the traditional form of sex categorization entrenched in public law. Not only does this system make recognition possible for subjects that were unthinkable in the conventional classification and forsake any pretence of permanence that was and still is a central staple of sex categorization, but it also requires a complete rethinking of the rights and duties based on binary categories—in other words, of the gender order in public law. Perhaps most importantly, this system no longer aims to define its subjects, but, at least to a large extent, endeavours to protect them, thus changing the relationship between gender-diverse people and the law from erasure to recognition.

Although the Belgian Constitutional Court was the first to read a self-determined and fluid nonbinary identification into the Constitution in 2019,[100] it is the Colombian Constitutional Court that has more thoroughly expanded and fully operationalized this doctrine. The turning point was decision T-033/22. The Constitutional Court of Colombia ruled that Presidential Decree 1227 of 2015, which limited recognition to the binary and capped on the number of changes one could make to their civil status to two legal transitions maximum, with a mandatory minimum ten-year interval between them,[101] violated the rights of gender-fluid

[99] Anna Katharina Mangold, *Symposium on the 'Third Option': 'Not Man, Not Woman, Not Nothing'*, IACL-AIDC BLOG (16 Jan. 2018), https://blog-iacl-aidc.org/the-third-gender/2018/5/28/i2tnkkxpwywkbpinwn5wva1fmlb449; Berit Völtzmann, *The Same Freedom for Everyone*, IACL-AIDC BLOG (23 Jan. 2018), https://blog-iacl-aidc.org/the-third-gender/2018/5/28/symposium-on-the-third-option-not-man-not-woman-not-nothing-the-same-freedom-for-everyone.

[100] Constitutional Court, 19 June 2019, 99/2019. I presented an anthropological analysis of the decision in Osella, *supra* note 5.

[101] Decreto [Presidential Decree]1227 de 2015.

and nonbinary people. As discussed in Chapter 6, the 2015 Presidential Decree was the result of a constitutional decision of the same year in which the Court had protected gender self-determination[102] based on dignity,[103] the free development of personality,[104] and legal personality.[105] Although in the 2015 decision the Court was clear in rejecting any preconditions on gender recognition, it remained silent on nonbinary identities and the possibility of having multiple transitions recognized. Nevertheless, the Presidential Decree implemented this ruling narrowly, imposing restrictions where the Court had been vague.[106]

The T-033/22 decision removed such limits.[107] The case concerned a person identifying as a *travesti* with female characteristics. After a change of name, they obtained legal recognition in the female sex in 2015—a choice that did not reflect their identity but that at least to some extent shielded them from the constant ridicule, marginalization, and humiliation they had to endure. In 2019, the plaintiff requested the *Registraduría Nacional del Estado Civil* to erase the sex designation from their ID or, alternatively, to replace the 'F' with an 'X' or 'indeterminate'. The *Registraduría* denied the application. The *cédula de ciudadanía*—an identification document provided to people of age—is based directly on the civil registry, which, at the time, only included binary options. The plaintiff claimed that the misrecognition of their identity had severe consequences for their rights, including their right to health.[108] For example, they experienced difficulties in accessing medical treatments, as they needed medication for their prostate, but individuals registered as female could not obtain the treatment. In 2021, well before the minimum ten-year interval had elapsed, they once again applied for recognition in a different sex, but the *Notaría* denied it.

The Constitutional Court granted the claim for nonbinary recognition.[109] First, the Court stated that the right to free development of personality,[110] in combination with dignity, guarantees to each person the right to define themselves and the elements that constitute their being, including gender identity, autonomously and without interference. The right to define themselves, the Court added, has a further dimension in terms of legal personality.[111] Protecting gender identity cannot

[102] Corte Constitucional [C.C.][Constitutional Court], 13 febrero 2015, Sentencia T-063/15. All decisions are available on the website of the Constitutional Court: https://www.corteconstitucional.gov.co. Hereinafter, all decisions are cited in shortened form, by reference to their number only.
[103] Constitución Politica de Colombia [C.P.], Art. 1.
[104] Art. 16 C.P.
[105] Art. 14 C.P.
[106] Refer to: Stefano Osella & Ruth Rubio-Marín, *The Right to Gender Recognition Before the Colombian Constitutional Court: A Queer and Travesti Theory Analysis*, 40 Bulletin of Latin American Research 650 (2021).
[107] *See* Chapter 6 and Stefano Osella, *La Storia di Due Corti, Fattori Strutturali, Culturali, e Dogmatici nella Giurisprudenza Costituzionale Italiana e Colombiana. Un'Analisi Comparata*, Diritti Comparati 1, 35–37 (2023), https://www.diritticomparati.it/bozza-automatica-170/.
[108] Art. 49 C.P.
[109] *See* Chapter 6.
[110] Art. 16 C.P.
[111] C.C., 4 febrero 2022, Sentencia T-033/22, ¶¶ 28–29.

be separated from the possibility of manifesting this essential trait of one's identity in full and obtaining recognition and respect at the legal level. Ensuring the correspondence between gender identity and individual legal categorization (including how it is displayed on the ID), the Court found, is indispensable to ensuring social involvement, self-recognition, and participation in the state and society.[112] The lack of a third option was found to misrecognize nonbinary people and their experience and to be an obstacle to the free exercise of their rights and a source of discrimination. The Court articulated the significance of this decision,[113] acknowledging the distress that the applicant had had to endure. Furthermore, doubling down on its earlier refutation of Eurocentric sex epistemologies, the Court referred to the 'hijra, meti, lala, skesana, motsoalle, mithli, kuchu, kawein, queer, muxé, fa'afafine, fakaleiti, hamjensgara and two-spirits'.[114]

The Court also discussed the terminology for categorizing nonbinary people. After considering a few options, the Court picked 'nonbinary' (*no binario*), which it considered to be the most respectful term, as it grants nonbinary people a positive identification. This term was preferred over 'undetermined' or 'neuter', which both suggested an absence of identity, and 'X', which the Court deemed inadequate to give visibility to nonbinary people. The Court also noted that manifold forms of thirdness can be found, and that an open category where the person decides on their denomination might therefore be more inclusive. Nevertheless, the Constitutional Court argued that the proliferation of denominations might affect the equality of nonbinary people, especially in relation to affirmative action and public policies that could otherwise work in their favour. With this excursus into terminology, the Constitutional Court demonstrated its intense engagement with the politics of identity and its willingness to transform the law and the constitutional system to be more inclusive.[115]

This approach was reaffirmed in the subsequent case law. In 2024, the Constitutional Court decided another case on the nonbinary designation on the electronic version of the *cédula de ciudadanía*.[116] In ruling in favour of the applicant, who had been denied this designation, the Court reasoned that the electronic *cédula de ciudadanía* is necessary for personal identification purposes and is the basis for the exercise of civil and political rights.[117] It also grants every person the right to express their gender identity and facilitates interactions between individuals, society, and the state.[118] In being denied this right, the plaintiff had suffered

[112] C.C., T-033/22, ¶¶ 30–32.
[113] C.C., T-033/22, ¶¶ 61–62.
[114] C.C., T-033/22, ¶ 45. For a discussion of the decolonial potential of gender self-determination, *see* Chapter 6.
[115] C.C., T-033/22, ¶¶ 70–86.
[116] C.C., 16 diciembre 2024, Sentencia T-527/24.
[117] C.C., T-527/24, ¶ 65.
[118] C.C., T-527/24, ¶ 66.

from structural discrimination, as their rights to equality, free development of personality, and legal personality had been encroached upon.

3.2. Transforming the binary gender order in public law

Following the T-033/22 ruling, the Colombian Constitutional Court decided several cases on the legal status of nonbinary people. These judgments clarify that nonbinary recognition is not only a matter of designations in civil registries and identification documents, but also entails several legal positions that need to be rethought once the legal system opens up to gender diversity. To be sure, all forms of nonbinary recognition, to some extent, lead to the transformation of legal systems structured around the binary. Nevertheless, the self-determination model enacted by the Constitutional Court of Colombia is bound to accelerate the pace of transformation as individual transitions are no longer restricted. Given the rapid tempo with which the Colombian Court releases judgments, the examples reported here are unlikely to be comprehensive. Nevertheless, they illustrate the complexities and transformations that nonbinary self-determination entails.

In 2023, the Constitutional Court ruled that the provisions concerning maternity leave for pregnant women and working mothers should also apply to nonbinary people.[119] It reasoned that trans and nonbinary people, being a historically discriminated group, are entitled to special constitutional protection. At the same time, the Court established that the rationales behind maternity leave—protecting the health of pregnant women and new mothers and guaranteeing adequate care to newborn children—should be interpreted in accordance with the constitutional principle of equality. In 2025, the Court expansively interpreted the provisions that confer rights on and protect from discrimination breastfeeding 'women', 'mothers', and 'female workers' (*trabajadoras*) to include nonbinary people.[120] The Court argued that the aim of these provisions is to eliminate discrimination against lactating people, and noted the possibility that some nonbinary people can also lactate and breastfeed.

The possible tensions with women's rights did not go unnoticed. However, the Court explained that the expansion of rights to nonbinary people

> is in no way intended to misrecognize the progress achieved by groups who have historically been discriminated against. Quite the contrary, [this recognition] has the purpose of continuing to expand the scope of fundamental rights, which necessarily requires a permanent revision of the reality and of the experiences that

[119] C.C., 24 agosto 2023, Sentencia C-324/23. The decision also referred to trans men.
[120] C.C., 27 febrero 2025, Sentencia C-071/25. The decision also referred to trans men.

demand the activation of constitutional guarantees for people who do not enjoy visibility and protection in the legal system.[121]

In case C-408/23, the Constitutional Court examined the legal void on the statutory retirement age of nonbinary people. Although the Constitutional Court declined jurisdiction and deferred to the legislature, it made a point of commenting on the importance of creating a system that does not exclude nonbinary people.[122] Finally, in decision T-401/25 regarding the release of the *libreta militar* with a nonbinary marker,[123] the Colombian Constitutional Court ordered the national army to update its internal procedures to recognize nonbinary individuals.[124] The Court openly criticized the resistance opposed by some institutions—such as the army—to recognizing nonbinary identity and defined it as a form of discrimination.[125] In very clear terms, it stated that nonbinary recognition is a constitutional obligation.[126] Crucially for the argument presented here, the Court arguably established a doctrine that requires the state and its institutions to change the structures based on a past understanding of binary identity to include nonbinary people.

Further progress appears to be in store in Colombia. As mentioned in Chapter 6, the 2024 bill on gender recognition introduces a number of sex categories that individuals can choose from, based on their own self-determination. In addition to male and female, individuals will be able to identify as nonbinary and *travesti*, bringing the total number of positive sex options to four.[127] Legislators have emphasized—and, arguably, even celebrated—gender plurality in several parts of the bill, critically referencing the 'cultural' origins of the binary,[128] thus continuing the trail that the Constitutional Court has been blazing since 1995. In November 2025, the *Registraduría Nacional del Estado Civil* announced that the options 'no binario' and 'trans' were added to the *cédula de ciudadanía* through a regulatory measure.[129]

[121] C.C., C-071/25, ¶ 107.

[122] C.C., 11 octubre 2023, Sentencia C-408/23.

[123] As explained in Chapter 6, the 'libreta militar' is the document that certifies the successful completion of military service. It appears to be widely required in civilian life, too, and it carries importance in multiple daily activities.

[124] C.C., 29 septiembre 2025, Sentencia T-401/25.

[125] C.C., T-401/25, ¶ 53.

[126] C.C., T-401/25, ¶¶ 58–59.

[127] Proyecto de ley [bill] 122 de 2024 'Por el cual se expide la Ley Integral de Identidad de Género', Art. 14, https://www.camara.gov.co/ley-de-identidad-de-genero-883/. For an introduction to the bill, *see* Chapter 6.

[128] Proyecto de ley [bill] 122 de 2024, Art. 3, definition of 'Persona Trans/Transgenero' and 'Persona no binaria'.

[129] Registraduría Nacional del Estado Civil, Categorías 'No Binario' (NB) y 'Trans' (T) Fueron Incluidas en el Campo 'Sexo' de Registros Civiles y Todos los Documentos de Identidad (28 Nov. 2025), https://www.registraduria.gov.co/Categorias-no-binario-NB-y-trans-T-fueron-incluidas-en-el-campo-sexo-de.html.

In sum, by not setting specific criteria for achieving a change of legal status, the Court has paved the way for nonbinary self-determination to contribute to disestablishing mechanisms of gender signification in law. It has, therefore, granted the most inclusive form of gender recognition. The recognition of a *travesti* person also highlights the importance of acknowledging gender diversity from a decolonial perspective—something that emerged in relation to self-determination as well, but that becomes even more evident with the recognition of legal thirdness. The Colombian case demonstrates that this diversity extends beyond gender and intersects with culture and race. Self-determination opens up avenues for forms of intersectional recognition: it empowers individuals who find themselves at the intersection of multiple axes of discrimination to gain recognition and protects a multiplicity of constitutional rights. Nevertheless, self-determination comes at a cost in terms of legal certainty, as the state renounces control over the transition between categories that are multiplied.

4. Redistributive recognition

Three jurisdictions in South Asia have been at the vanguard of the constitutional rights of nonbinary people. In 2007, the Supreme Court of Nepal recognized a third sex category and ordered all discriminatory measures against LGBTQI+ people to be repealed.[130] In 2009, the Supreme Court of Pakistan ordered identity recognition for trans and nonbinary people,[131] as well as several measures to protect their rights to inheritance, education, healthcare, and personal safety against violence, including at the hands of the police.[132] In 2014, the Supreme Court of India declared a general right to binary and nonbinary gender identity recognition, and issued a set of directives to ensure that trans and nonbinary people enjoy substantive equality.[133] These judgments were characterized by some ambiguity, and it was not immediately evident what standard of recognition they established. Ultimately, the Supreme Courts of Nepal and India clarified that their

[130] Sunil Babu Pant and Others v. Government of Nepal and Others (2008)1 Writ No. 917 2064 BS (2007 AD) 2NJALJ (2008) 261 (21 Dec. 2007) (hereinafter, Sunil Babu Pant v. HGM Nepal). This section is based on the English translation of the judgment, which is available at: https://www.icj.org/wp-content/uploads/2012/07/Sunil-Babu-Pant-and-Others-v.-Nepal-Government-and-Others-Supreme-Court-of-Nepal.pdf.

[131] The Supreme Court of Pakistan used different names in different orders, including 'eunuchs', 'unix', 'she-male', and 'transgender': Jeffrey A. Redding, *From 'She-Males' to 'Unix'*, *in* Regimes of Legality 258 (Daniela Berti & Devika Bordia eds., 2015).

[132] There have been several orders by the Supreme Court of Pakistan. The most relevant to the current discussion is Khaki v. Rawalpindi, Supreme Court of Pakistan (12 Dec. 2009). For a detailed account: Jeffrey A. Redding (trans. Daphne Romy-Masliah), *Les Droits Des Personnes Transgenres Au Pakistan (2009–2019)*, 80 Droit et Cultures (2020), https://journals.openedition.org/droitcultures/6516?lang=en.

[133] National Legal Service Authority v. Union of India (2014) 5 SCC 438 (India).

previous jurisprudence had introduced a self-determination standard. Moreover, gender self-determination was arguably enshrined in the text of the Constitution of Nepal.[134] In Pakistan, the case law was interpreted liberally by the legislature, which introduced self-determination.

These developments are remarkable. First, these courts granted nonbinary recognition much earlier than other constitutional or supreme courts. Second, the laws of these jurisdictions explicitly connect identity recognition and redistribution of resources. Recognition is understood *not only* as an element of personal autonomy validation but *also* as an instrument to remedy material disadvantages. Recognition is not primarily grounded in autonomy-derived rights but rather in equality. Admittedly, an element of redistribution is present in all forms of gender identity recognition, and equality is not an uncommon doctrinal ground. Nevertheless, the emphasis given to it in these decisions sets them apart as a distinct model in the comparative landscape. Third, the legal developments in these jurisdictions are characterized by references to local identities that defy globalized understandings of the binary, as well as of transness and gender diversity.

4.1. Nepal: From a flattening third sex to self-determination

The Supreme Court of Nepal was the first to grant a right to 'redistributive recognition' in *Sunil Babu Pant v. Government of Nepal*.[135] This 2007 case was promoted as a public interest litigation by a group of NGOs,[136] notably the LGBTQI+-rights-focused Blue Diamond Society (BDS).[137] Among other things, the plaintiffs asked for gender recognition (in the form of citizenship certificates) and anti-discrimination legislation for gender minorities.[138] They argued that the lack of adequate IDs caused material disadvantages to gender-diverse people, for example, by denying them crucial documents such as passports and residency registrations.[139]

The Supreme Court stated that the 2007 Interim Constitution mandated the Nepali state to ensure 'distributive justice', that is, to uplift 'the deprived and socially backward classes and communities ... to utilize the opportunity and enable them enjoy [*sic*] the rights equally as other people do'.[140] Furthermore, it

[134] Nepali Constitution of 2015, Art. 12.

[135] Sunil Babu Pant v. HGM Nepal.

[136] As specified in Sunil Babu Pant v. HGM Nepal: The Blue Diamond Society, Mitini Nepal (https://mitininepal.org.np), Cruise AIDS Nepal, and Parichaya Nepal.

[137] For an account of the work of the Blue Diamond Society: Kyle Knight, *Outliers: Sunil Babu Pant, the Blue Diamond Society, and Queer Organizing in Nepal*, 19 STUDIES IN NEPALI HISTORY AND SOCIETY 113 (2014).

[138] The analysis offered here will, however, focus on the recognition of gender identity.

[139] For a comment: Maria Federica Moscati & Hari Phuyal, *'The Third Gender Case' Decision of the Supreme Court of Nepal on the Rights of Lesbian, Gay, Bisexual, Transsexual and Intersex People*, 4 JOURNAL OF COMPARATIVE LAW 291 (2009).

[140] Sunil Babu Pant v. HGM Nepal, 266. *See* Art. 34, Interim Constitution of Nepal (2007).

explicitly rejected the notion that a different gender identity was a perversion. On the contrary, the Supreme Court reasoned that the exclusive existence of 'men and women', and the reduction of 'third sex' people to 'sexual perverts', were 'old notions' without value in light of the rights protecting the individual, such as equality and non-discrimination,[141] and of the principle of social justice, all enshrined in the Interim Constitution.[142] The Supreme Court established a duty of the state to recognize the third sex.[143] Furthermore, it ordered the state to 'make necessary arrangement for the people of third gender besides male or female'.[144] The Court did not establish any preconditions to achieve gender recognition. In fact, it ordered authorities to make provisions to protect trans people according to their 'self-feelings'[145]—an expression that, as Holning Lau and Mara Malagodi argue, seems to endorse gender self-determination.[146]

Scholars hailed this decision as great progress[147] even though its implementation was tardy and piecemeal.[148] Reportedly, there were instances of medical requirements being imposed by administrative authorities despite the judgment of the Court.[149] Nevertheless, *Pant* arguably had a transformative effect on the understanding of Nepali citizenship, leading the state to acknowledge that nonbinary people are part of the Nepali nation.[150] Subsequent developments strengthened the constitutional protection of nonbinary people in Nepal. In 2013, Lau and Malagodi report, the Supreme Court issued an order to the government to provide nonbinary people with passports matching their identity.[151]

[141] Sunil Babu Pant v. HGM Nepal, 276. *See* Art. 33, Interim Constitution of Nepal (2007).
[142] Sunil Babu Pant v. HGM Nepal, 276. *See* Art. 34, Interim Constitution of Nepal (2007).
[143] Sunil Babu Pant v. HGM Nepal, 278.
[144] Sunil Babu Pant v. HGM Nepal, 282. Art. 13, Art. 12, Arts. 2, 16, 17, International Covenant on Civil and Political Rights, 16 Dec. 1966, 999 U.N.T.S. 171 and Art. 10 International Covenant on Economic, Social and Cultural Rights, 16 Dec. 1966, 993 U.N.T.S. 3.
[145] Sunil Babu Pant v. HGM Nepal, 280–81.
[146] Holning Lau & Mara Malagodi, *Legal Gender Recognition in Nepal and Comparative Context*, 45 University of Pennsylvania Journal of International Law 269, 275 (2024).
[147] Michael Bochenek & Kyle Knight, *Establishing a Third Gender Category in Nepal: Process and Prognosis*, 26 Emory International Law Review 33 (2012).
[148] *Id.* A third gender column ('other') was added to the census only in 2011, and the first citizens' cards in the third gender were issued only in 2013. *See* Bret Boyce & Daniel Coyle, Institute of Development Studies, Development, Discourse, and Law: Transgender and Same-Sex Sexualities in Nepal, Evidence Report No. 13 (2013) https://opendocs.ids.ac.uk/opendocs/handle/20.500.12413/2839.
[149] Human Rights Watch, 'We Have to Beg So Many People': Human Rights Violations in Nepal's Legal Gender Recognition Practices 21–36 (2024), https://www.hrw.org/report/2024/02/15/we-have-beg-so-many-people/human-rights-violations-nepals-legal-gender. For a general overview of gender constitutionalism in Nepal: Mara Malagodi, *Gender Sexuality, and Constitutionalism in Nepal*, *in* Gender, Sexuality and Constitutionalism in Asia 281, 296 (Wen-Chen Chang, Kelley Loper, Mara Malagodi & Ruth Rubio-Marín eds., 2023).
[150] Boyce & Coyle, *supra* note 148.
[151] Dilu Buduja v. the Government of Nepal, the Office of the Prime Minister and Council of Ministers, et al., WO-0027/2011. The decision is not available in English. I relied on a summary that can be found in the Compendium of Landmark Judgments of the Supreme Court of Nepal on Gender Justice and Equality (2020) https://njanepal.org.np/pages/Compilation-Of-Decisions-Judgments/. A translation is also available in Human Rights Watch, *supra* note 149, at 94. *See*: Lau & Malagodi, *supra* note 146, at 277.

In 2015, a new Constitution entered into force. This document includes several articles that protect gender and sexual minorities.[152] In particular, Article 12 of the 2015 Constitution establishes that those who acquire Nepali citizenship by descent are entitled to have it in accordance 'with gender identity'. As Lau and Malagodi point out, this provision seems to ground a right to gender self-determination in the text of the Constitution[153]—something that is more the exception than the rule in the comparative landscape.[154] The Supreme Court protected self-determination once again in a 2017 decision concerning the implementation of the 2007 *Pant v. Nepal* judgment, emphasizing that gender self-determination is essential to fostering the self-respect of nonbinary people and allowing them to live with a sense of community and enjoy other rights.[155]

Despite its undeniable impact, the 2007 decision of the Supreme Court in *Pant* did not explicitly grant gender recognition *within the binary*, thus leaving trans people who identify as binary at a disadvantage. Admittedly, as underlined by Lau and Malagodi, the emphasis that the Supreme Court repeatedly placed on self-determination could hardly be compatible with a recognition limited to the binary.[156] Yet, as Sofia Aboim argues, *Pant* had flattened all gender diversity in the third sex, *de facto* disregarding the reality of trans people who live in a binary gender.[157] It is not surprising, then, that a case was eventually brought before the Supreme Court by a trans woman seeking legal recognition in a binary sex.[158] Lau and Malagodi report that the Supreme Court granted the claim in November 2023.[159]

4.2. Pakistan: Sexual thirdness as a 'disorder in the body'

As of 2009, the Supreme Court of Pakistan has issued multiple orders to recognize trans and nonbinary identities.[160] Despite the rights of LGB people remaining

[152] *See* Art. 18 and Art. 42. Refer to: Lau & Malagodi, *supra* note 146, at 291.

[153] Lau & Malagodi, *supra* note 146, at 276–77.

[154] *See* Chapter 2.

[155] Sunil Babu Pant v. Office of the Prime Minister and Council of Ministers et al., (2073/10/10), Decision n. 987, available in Human Rights Watch, *supra* note 149, at 76.

[156] Lau & Malagodi, *supra* note 146, at 276 and 296–97.

[157] Sofia Aboim, *Gender in a Box? The Paradoxes of Recognition Beyond the Gender Binary*, 8 Politics & Governance 231 (2020).

[158] Rukshana Kapali v. Government of Nepal, Petition to Supreme Court No. 077-WO-0973 (30 Nov. 2021).

[159] The final decision had been anticipated by an interim measure in January 2023, in which the Supreme Court ordered the university where Ms Kapali was enrolled to release the documentation that she needed according to her name and gender identity (Kapali v. Nepal, Order 079-WO-0681, available in Human Rights Watch, *supra* note 149, at 91). The Supreme Court of Nepal also restated the importance of gender identity in Adheep Pokhrel and Tobias Volz v. Ministry of Home Affairs, Department of Immigration, Khalikasthan et al., Certiorari, Mandamus, 079-WO-0198 (summary reported Human Rights Watch, *supra* note 149, at 51).

[160] This section substantially draws on: Muhammad Azfar Nisar, Governing Thirdness: State, Society, and Non-Binary Identities in Pakistan (2022). In this context, 'trans and nonbinary' is a

heavily restricted in the country,[161] the Supreme Court has explicitly aimed at remedying the widespread discrimination against trans and nonbinary people while at the same time tying sexual thirdness to bodily characteristics.[162]

These decisions were intended to remedy the ongoing subordination of gender-diverse people that originated under British colonial rule. Although forms of discrimination might predate colonization, trans and nonbinary people were generally granted a degree of social recognition and respect in precolonial times.[163] For example, Shahnaz Khan reports that people whom we might nowadays refer to as nonbinary used to act as advisors to local rulers, engaged in institutionalized and ritual forms of begging, and performed dances for celebrations of newborn children.[164] In return, they could be assigned land deeds and hereditary stipends that could be passed along in their communities, organized around the relationship between a *guru* and their disciples.[165]

British colonizers cracked down on gender diversity. 'Obscene' songs and dances were banned. Section 377 of the Penal Code criminalized all forms of sex other than penile-vaginal intercourse. The Criminal Tribes Act 1871, as amended in 1897, mandated registration and surveillance of all individuals who admitted to being or, after a medical examination, were found to be 'impotent'—that is, for the specific context of this book, gender-diverse.[166] The repression of gender-diverse identities was motivated by moral panic, as Jessica Hinchy suggests. Recurringly depicted as 'kidnappers, castrators and pimps of young Indian boys', trans and nonbinary people were perceived as 'filth' and 'polluting'.[167] In addition, they were perceived as a hindrance to the colonial governance of India. As colonial rule presupposed a clear separation between the public and private spheres, different and

reductive blanket term under which are grouped different identities that challenge binary notions of gender, but which is incapable of projecting the great intra-group diversity. Yet the terms trans, transgender, and nonbinary have been used in the literature: Shahnaz Khan, *What Is in a Name? Khwaja Sara, Hijra and Eunuchs in Pakistan*, 23 Indian Journal of Gender Studies 218, 219 (2016). I acknowledge that speaking of 'trans' and 'nonbinary' in this context might be very problematic, both theoretically and practically: Aniruddha Dutta & Raina Roy, *Decolonizing Transgender in India: Some Reflections*, 1 Transgender Studies Quarterly 320 (2014); Aniruddha Dutta, *Legible Identities and Legitimate Citizens*, 15 International Feminist Journal of Politics 494 (2013).

[161] Section 377 of the Pakistani Penal Code still criminalizes same-sex relations. For a brief overview, refer to the ILGA Database country report on Pakistan (https://database.ilga.org/pakistan-lgbti).

[162] For a general overview of the case law concerning gender diversity in Pakistan: Redding, *supra* note 132.

[163] For an account: Vanja Hamzić, Sexual and Gender Diversity in the Muslim World: History, Law and Vernacular Knowledge (2016).

[164] This was the case of one such identity: the *Khawaja Sara*. Although today they can be understood as nonbinary people in feminine attire, traditionally they also dressed as male and were generally assigned a higher social role than other forms of nonbinary identities: Shahnaz Khan, *Khwaja Sara, Hijra, and the Struggle for Rights in Pakistan*, 51 Modern Asian Studies 1283 (2017).

[165] *Id.* at 1285–89.

[166] Jessica Hinchy, Governing Gender and Sexuality in Colonial India. The Hijra, c. 1850–1900 (2019).

[167] *Id.* at 35–50, in particular at 46.

more public forms of sexuality were seen as threatening and as a peril for public health.[168] Furthermore, trans and nonbinary people challenged the binary understanding of the body that, according to some historians, took hold during the nineteenth century and relates to the establishment of the separate sphere doctrine.[169] In short, trans and nonbinary people were a part of the population that was illegible to the colonizing power and, therefore, not amenable to the state's 'wider-reaching schemes of enumeration, registration, and categorisation'.[170] Colonial authorities changed inheritance laws; stipends and land deeds could no longer be passed on from gurus to their disciples.[171] The discrimination continued after independence, with the government of Pakistan criminalizing all forms of non-heterosexual sex.[172] All of this was detrimental to the equality of trans and nonbinary people, who, because of the discrimination directed at them, often have to live off begging and sex work.[173]

It was against this background that the *Khaki* case took shape. In 2009, a lawyer, Dr Muhammad Khaki,[174] went before the Pakistani Supreme Court to protect the dignity of 'eunuchs'—that is, 'people of middle sex'. On 20 November 2009, the Supreme Court found that 'unix' (in the context of the decision, trans and nonbinary people) were unjustly discriminated against because 'of a disorder in their bodies'.[175] The Supreme Court ordered the National Database Registration Authority—the competent government agency—to record the 'exact status' of 'unix' in the census, after carrying out medical tests 'based on hormones'.[176] The Supreme Court also ruled that 'unix' are entitled to have their names registered in the electoral lists. It banned the violation of inheritance rights of trans and nonbinary people and mandated that special jobs be set aside for them, as the government had done for disabled people. The Court, finally, instructed police to stop violence against 'unix', and also to make sure that individuals *without* 'a disorder in their bodies' do not commit crimes and tarnish the reputation of (real) 'unix'.[177] These orders were largely replicated in the order of 23 December 2009, which also

[168] *Id.* at 50.
[169] *Id.* at 56. *See also*: THOMAS LAQUEUR, MAKING SEX: BODY AND GENDER FROM THE GREEKS TO FREUD (1990).
[170] *Id.*
[171] Khan, *supra* note 164, at 1287.
[172] Refer to: Section 377 of the Pakistani Penal Code and to The Offence of Zina (Enforcement of Hudood) Ordinance 1979.
[173] Khan, *supra* note 164.
[174] Khaki was a jurist and chair of the Insaaf Welfare Trust, a human rights NGO. This account is taken from: NISAR, *supra* note 160, at 1; HAMZIĆ, *supra* note 163, at 148; Redding, *supra* note 131, at 263.
[175] Khaki v. S.S.P. (Operation), Rawalpindi, Constitutional Petition No. 43 of 2009, ¶ 2 (4 Nov. 2009), https://www.law.cornell.edu/gender-justice/resource/khaki_v._rawalpindi.
[176] Khaki v. S.S.P. (Operation), Rawalpindi, Constitutional Petition No. 43 of 2009 (4 Nov. 2009).
[177] Khaki v. S.S.P. (Operation), Rawalpindi, Constitutional Petition No. 43 of 2009, ¶ 5 (4 Nov. 2009).

underlined the right of 'unix' to access educational institutions and healthcare.[178] In a similar fashion, the Supreme Court remarked that actions should be taken to prevent the status of 'unix' from being exercised by other persons.[179] Other orders followed in the coming years,[180] reportedly without mentioning the need for hormonal testing.[181] The Supreme Court, in brief, granted trans and nonbinary people a redistributive general right to recognition, which was strongly connected to sexual thirdness understood as a 'disorder in the body'. As Sadaf Aziz, Angbeen Atif Mizra, and Cristóbal Alvear-Garijo explain, equality and dignity, and the guarantee of full inclusion and citizenship to nonbinary people, were at the crux of these cases.[182]

These judgments represented a significant change of attitude towards gender minorities.[183] However, the Supreme Court has delineated a form of recognition related to the presence of certain physical characteristics, and equated being 'unix' to a disorder. As Muhammad Azfar Nisar argues, the case law of the Supreme Court creates a form of biology-centred and medicalized recognition, which facilitates the control and governance of sexual thirdness.[184] Relatedly, Jeffrey Redding argues that the Court felt the need to differentiate between real and 'fake' 'unix' to prevent the latter from benefitting from the recognition due to the former.[185] Furthermore, Nisar suggests, this focus on physical diversity is very similar to the emphasis that British colonizers had placed on the 'physical diversity' of 'eunuchs'—a physical diversity that, it should be recalled, had the function of making the entire category more legible.[186] This embodied approach to recognition appeared to be controversial among stakeholders. Khan reports that nonbinary people, when asked by local authorities to produce medical evidence to demonstrate their identities, reacted with protests and demanded gender self-determination.[187] This might in part explain why registration in the third sex did not really take off.[188] In short, it can be argued that there were different motivations for the controls, including the ostensible need to manage the legal positions of individuals and control welfare entitlements—thus suggesting a connection with the constitutional principle of equality.

[178] Khaki v. S.S.P. (Operation), Rawalpindi, Constitutional Petition No. 43 of 2009 (23 Dec. 2009). *See*: Arts. 22 and 25 Constitution of Pakistan.

[179] Khaki v. S.S.P. (Operation), Rawalpindi, Constitutional Petition No. 43 of 2009, ¶ 7 (23 Dec. 2009).

[180] These orders are reported by Redding, *supra* note 132.

[181] Khan, *supra* note 164, at 1295.

[182] Sadaf Aziz, Angbeen Atif Mizra & Cristóbal Alvear-Garijo, *Constitutionalism and Gender in Pakistan: A Counterpatriarchal Struggle*, *in* GENDER, SEXUALITY AND CONSTITUTIONALISM IN ASIA 311, 330–31 (Wen-Chen Chang, Kelley Loper, Mara Malagodi & Ruth Rubio-Marín eds., 2023).

[183] As reported by Khan, *supra* note 164, at 1293–95.

[184] NISAR, *supra* note 160, at 90–93.

[185] Redding, *supra* note 132, ¶¶ 14–15; Redding, *supra* note 131, at 269.

[186] NISAR, *supra* note 160, at 90–91.

[187] Khan, *supra* note 164, at 1295.

[188] Muhammad Azfar Nisar, *(Un)Becoming a Man: Legal Consciousness of the Third Gender Category in Pakistan*, 32 GENDER & SOCIETY 59, 70–76 (2018).

After the initial administrative implementation grounded in a biology-centred discourse,[189] the legislature passed the Transgender Persons (Protection of Rights) Act 2018. Incorporating several definitions contained in the Yogyakarta Principles, notably the notion of gender identity,[190] the 2018 Act grants gender self-determination to trans and nonbinary people.[191] The 2018 Act offers ample guarantees of non-discrimination in multiple areas, from inheritance to employment.[192] It enshrines the redistributive spirit that animated the decision of the Supreme Court and abandons the Court's attitude towards 'fake unix'. Civil society and scholars welcomed it positively.[193] Some decisions protecting trans people's self-determination have also been recorded.[194]

However, the fate of the 2018 Act is now in doubt. The Federal Shariat Court of Pakistan ruled that self-determination violates the precepts of Islam.[195] It also rejected the protection of gender identity and underlined that 'Islamic teachings are based on biological identity (sex) rather than self or social construction (gender)'.[196] As Zubair Assani argues, the Federal Shariat Court also manifested a preoccupation that the protection of gender identity might infringe on the rights of women. It has, however, underlined that intersex people are entitled to protection under Islamic law. Although the effects of the decision can be suspended while an appeal to the Shariat Appellate Bench of the Supreme Court is pending—which activists have committed to file[197]—the decision creates uncertainty regarding the rights of trans people.

[189] NISAR, *supra* note 160, at 94.

[190] Transgender Persons (Protection of Rights) Act 2018, S. 2 F. Refer to: International Commission of Jurists, Pakistan: Transgender Persons (Protection of Rights) Act, 2018: A Briefing Paper (Mar. 2020).

[191] Transgender Persons (Protection of Rights) Act 2018, S. 3.

[192] Transgender Persons (Protection of Rights) Act 2018, SS. 7–15.

[193] International Commission of Jurists, *supra* note 190. For a comment on the law: Jeffrey Redding, *The Pakistan Transgender Persons (Protection of Rights) Act of 2018 and Its Impact on the Law of Gender in Pakistan*, 20 AUSTRALIAN JOURNAL OF ASIAN LAW 103 (2019).

[194] Faiz Ullah v. P.P.S.C. and Ors (Writ Petition No. 3176 of 2021), https://translaw.clpr.org.in/case-law/faiz-ullah-vs-p-p-s-c-and-ors/, in which the Lahore High Court ruled that a person could self-identify for the purposes of employment law (in the context of a job reserved for female applicants).

[195] Shariat Petition No. 5/1 of 2020, https://database.ilga.org/api/downloader/download/1/PK%20-%20JUD%20-%20Federal%20Shariat%20Court%20S.P.%20No.%205%20of%202020%20(2023)%20-%20OR-OFF(en).pdf.

[196] Zubair Abbasi, *Balancing Gender Rights: Pakistan's Federal Shariat Court's Verdict on Self-Perceived Gender Identity*, OXFORD HUMAN RIGHTS HUB BLOG (31 May 2023), https://ohrh.law.ox.ac.uk/balancing-gender-rights-pakistans-federal-shariat-courts-verdict-on-self-perceived-gender-identity/.

[197] *Id.*

4.3. India: The tensions between control and self-determination[198]

The road to NALSA

In 2014, the Supreme Court of India decided *National Legal Service Authority v. Union of India* (*NALSA*),[199] a case that Rahul Rao saw as promising 'momentous redistributive gains for trans communities'.[200] In *NALSA*, the Supreme Court declared a constitutional right to gender recognition and issued several directives to improve the socio-economic conditions of Indian trans and nonbinary people. The Indian Supreme Court also granted recognition to remedy the social hostility, police harassment, discrimination, and exclusion from basic welfare services that trans and nonbinary people have to endure.[201] While acknowledging multiple identities, the *NALSA* decision foregrounds the *hijras*—birth-assigned males who identify as nonbinary or female. 'Hijra' should be understood not only as a gender identity, but also as a social and cultural one, as *hijras* create communities organized around kinship structures and characterized by distinct ritual and religious practices.[202] Albeit a turning point for gender-diverse people, this case is characterized by a degree of ambiguity, as it could be read as both granting self-determination and limiting recognition to individuals with specific medico-behavioural characteristics,[203] a matter that the Supreme Court subsequently solved in favour of self-determination. Furthermore, *NALSA* arguably defines a form of gender diversity that may lend itself to specific political and legal purposes.

The judgment in *NALSA* was not unanticipated. Indian courts had, to some extent, granted recognition of queer kinship for decades. This is true for the *guru–chela* (teacher–disciple) relationship that is a central feature of *hijra* communities.[204] State authorities have also enacted policies and laws to ensure the rights of gender-diverse people. For example, the state of Tamil Nadu passed legislation to

[198] This section partly draws and substantially expands on the research presented in Osella & Rubio-Marín, *supra* note 10, at 589. *See also*: Ruth Rubio-Marín & Stefano Osella, *El Nuevo Derecho Constitucional a la Identidad de Género entre la Libertad de Elección, el Incremento de Categorías y la Subjetividad y Fluidez de sus Contenidos. Un Análisis desde el Derecho Comparado*, 40 Revista Española de Derecho Constitucional 45, 57 (2020).

[199] National Legal Service Authority v. Union of India (2014) 5 SCC 438 (hereinafter, National Legal Service Authority v. Union of India).

[200] Rahul Rao, Out of Time: The Queer Politics of Postcoloniality 174 (2020).

[201] National Legal Service Authority v. Union of India, ¶¶ 5–6.

[202] For an ethnographic account: Nanda, *supra* note 3. In India, multiple nonbinary identities are present, differing according to characteristics such as religion, kinship structure, and geographical provenance: Gayatri Reddy, With Respect to Sex: Negotiating Hijra Identity in South India (2005).

[203] Aniruddha Dutta, *Contradictory Tendencies: The Supreme Court's NALSA Judgment on Transgender Recognition and Rights*, 5 Journal of Indian Law & Society 225 (2014).

[204] Mayur Suresh, *Possession Is 9/10th of the Body*, *in* Law like Love: Queer Perspectives on Law (Alok Gupta & Arvind Narrain eds., 2011).

provide nonbinary people with IDs and ensure them access to welfare services.[205] At the federal level, in 2011, the National Census permitted people to tick the 'other' box for the first time.[206] The Ministry of Social Justice and Empowerment created an Expert Committee to elaborate on possible forms of legal recognition in 2013.[207] This committee recommended that trans individuals be recognized in their legal sex of choice after a screening by a panel of experts.[208]

Courts likewise offered a degree of protection to the rights of LGBTQI+ people. The High Court of Delhi decriminalized same-sex intimacy in the 2009 *Naz Foundation* case. The Court established the unconstitutionality of the criminalization of same-sex intimacy contained in Section 377 of the Indian Penal Code (IPC), which had been in force since colonial times.[209] Public authorities, especially police, reportedly used Section 377 IPC against trans and nonbinary people, too. Moreover, as Siddharth Narrain argues, the narrative of the *Naz Foundation* judgment foregrounds decisional privacy, which can also be used to protect gender identity.[210] However, the Supreme Court overturned *Naz Foundation* in the 2013 *Suresh Kumar Koushal & Another v. Naz Foundation* decision.[211]

The NALSA judgment: A landmark achievement, with a few shortcomings

The 2014 *NALSA* case can be seen as a continuation of this process of expanding the rights of LGBTQI+ people, and specifically of trans and nonbinary persons.[212] The National Legal Service Authority, a public body tasked with the legal representation

[205] Committees were created to screen trans persons on the basis of a mixed set of externally assessable criteria, such as whether the person has undergone castration, is affiliated with the transgender community, and wears women's attire part- or full-time. Venkatesan Chakrapani, United Nations Development Program, Report 22, The Case of Tamil Nadu Transgender Welfare Board: Insights for Developing Practical Models for Social Protection Programmes for Transgender People in India (2012), https://www.undp.org/india/publications/case-tamil-nadu-transgender-welfare-board-insights-developing-practical-models-social-protection-programmes-transgender-people.

[206] Karan Gulati & Tushar Anand, *Inheritance Rights of Transgender Persons in India*, 7 Indian Law Review 1 (2023).

[207] Report of the Expert Committee on the Issues relating to Transgender Persons, submitted to the Ministry of Social Justice and Empowerment (27 Jan. 2014), https://prsindia.org/files/bills_acts/bills_parliament/2016/Expert_Committee_Report_(2014)_1.pdf.

[208] *Id.* at 31–34 (Chapter Four: Transgender Identity).

[209] Naz Foundation v. Government of NCT of Delhi, 160 (2009) DLT 277 (hereinafter, Naz Foundation v. Government of NCT of Delhi).

[210] Siddharth Narrain, *Crystallising Queerpolitics: The Naz Foundation Case and Its Implication for India's Transgender Communities*, 2 NUJS Law Review 455 (2009).

[211] Suresh Kumar Koushal & Another v. Naz Foundation & Others (2014) 1 SCC 1. The unconstitutionality of same-sex intimacy was eventually established by the Supreme Court in Navtej Singh Johar and Others v. Union of India (2018) INSC 790. *See* Rehan Abeyratne, Courts and LGBTQI+ Rights in an Age of Judicial Retrenchment 108–13 (2025) (offering a thorough, insightful analysis and reconstruction of the cases discussed in this section).

[212] Dipika Jain argues that *NALSA* should be compared with *Koushal*: Dipika Jain, *Shifting Subjects of State Legibility: Gender Minorities and the Law in India*, 32 Berkeley Journal of Gender, Law & Justice 39, 52 (2017). *See also*: Abeyratne, *supra* note 211, at 115 and 144–47 (providing an insightful discussion of the case and situating it within the broader context of constitutional transformations in India).

of marginalized sections of society, initiated the litigation.[213] The Supreme Court adopted a sympathetic tone and underlined the urgency of a constitutional intervention to support the multiple trans and nonbinary Indian identities, and most notably the *hijras*. On the one hand, the Supreme Court acknowledged the public interests associated with preserving the binary. Sex categories in India, the Court reasoned, are 'based on a person's sex assigned by birth ... [which] permits gender system [*sic*], including the law relating to marriage, adoption, inheritance, succession and taxation and welfare legislations'.[214] According to the Court, fundamental rights clashed with competing interests based on the 'biological' binary that the Indian system 'on the whole' recognized.[215] The Indian legal system was, and indeed is, largely gendered, with the binary informing central aspects of the relations between individuals and the state, as scholars have highlighted.[216]

On the other hand, the Supreme Court maintained that misrecognition causes deprivation and violence.[217] As such, it affects gender equality, enshrined in Article 14 of the Constitution. This article, the Supreme Court clarified, is not only intended to protect males and females, but also 'hijras/transgender' people.[218] Second, the expression of one's 'self-identified gender'—such as in 'dress, words, action or behavior'—was defined as integral to one's personality, and protected by the general freedom of expression.[219] Third, the due process clause[220]—'the heart and soul of the Indian Constitution'—ensures dignity, personal autonomy, privacy, and free development of one's personality, all rights that concur to ensure the recognition of gender identity.[221]

The decision ends with a list of directives that ensure gender diversity recognition. For example, the Supreme Court ordered that 'hijras, eunuchs, apart from binary gender, [must] be treated as "third gender" for the purpose of safeguarding their rights'.[222] Similarly, '[t]ransgender persons' right to decide their self-identified gender is also upheld.'[223] Furthermore, the Court instructed the government to treat trans and nonbinary people as it treats socially and educationally backward classes, meaning that the government should provide multiple measures to enhance their substantive equality, including reserved places in educational

[213] Legal Service Authority Act 1997, SS. 12–13.
[214] National Legal Service Authority v. Union of India, ¶ 49.
[215] National Legal Service Authority v. Union of India, ¶ 49 and ¶ 75.
[216] Gulati & Anand, *supra* note 206. *See*: Akshat Agarwal, *Supriyo and the Politics of Indian Family Law*, Indian Law Review (2025) (advance view), https://www.tandfonline.com/doi/full/10.1080/24730580.2025.2488234.
[217] National Legal Service Authority v. Union of India, ¶¶ 54–55.
[218] National Legal Service Authority v. Union of India, ¶ 54.
[219] National Legal Service Authority v. Union of India, ¶¶ 62–66.
[220] Art. 21 Constitution of India.
[221] National Legal Service Authority v. Union of India, ¶¶ 67–69.
[222] National Legal Service Authority v. Union of India, ¶ 129(1).
[223] National Legal Service Authority v. Union of India, ¶ 129(2).

establishments and public employment.[224] Finally, the Supreme Court also ordered the federal and the various state-level governments to provide better healthcare and run programmes aimed at promoting the visibility and respect of trans and nonbinary people.[225] Unquestionably, *NALSA* was a great victory for gender-diverse persons.

The decision is, however, ambiguous when it comes to the definition of beneficiaries of the rights that it provides. Jayna Khotari argues that the decision ought to be interpreted as granting self-determination.[226] The Supreme Court indeed emphasized 'self-determination' and the importance of a 'self-identified' gender in several passages of *NALSA*.[227] In the list of directives, furthermore, the Supreme Court ordered the federal and state governments to protect the right of 'transgender persons' to 'decide their self-identified gender … such as male, female or as third gender'.[228] Justice Radhakrishnan, who wrote one of the two opinions of which the judgment is made, emphasized that any evidence of medical treatments—such as hormones or gender confirmation surgery—cannot be required for recognition.[229] In the final directives, the full bench more limitedly ordered that 'any insistence for SRS [sexual reassignment surgery—but, *nota bene*, no mention is here made of hormone treatments or psychiatric supervision] is immoral and illegal'.[230] Justice Sikri's opinion, moreover, seems sympathetic to minorities and stated that the protection of human rights is required by the rule of law, even when such minorities are 'insignificant in numbers'.[231]

Nevertheless, in other passages, the Court seemed more inclined towards imposing some form of behavioural and medical preconditions. Justice Radhakrishnan appeared to recommend a 'psychological test' as a preferable alternative to a 'biological test'.[232] Aniruddha Dutta suggests that such a test might be linked to the finding of gender dysphoria in the trans applicant.[233] Justice Sikri's opinion asserts that 'a person has a constitutional right to get the recognition as male or female *after* SRS' (emphasis added).[234] When vernacular identities are discussed—for example, in the case of *hijras*—the ruling is also confusing.

[224] National Legal Service Authority v. Union of India, ¶ 129(3).
[225] National Legal Service Authority v. Union of India, ¶ 129(4–9).
[226] Jayna Khotari, *Trans Equality in India: Affirmation of the Right to Self-Determination of Gender*, 13 NUJS LAW REVIEW 1 (2020).
[227] National Legal Service Authority v. Union of India, ¶ 20, ¶ 74 and ¶ 99.
[228] National Legal Service Authority v. Union of India, ¶ 129(2).
[229] National Legal Service Authority v. Union of India, ¶ 20.
[230] National Legal Service Authority v. Union of India, ¶ 129(5).
[231] National Legal Service Authority v. Union of India, ¶ 123. Rehan Abeyratne interprets this statement as a direct response to the earlier 2013 *Koushal* judgment, which had restored the criminalization of same-sex intimacy under Section 377 of the Indian Penal Code, in part by reasoning that the law impacted only a 'minuscule fraction' of India's population (Suresh Kumar Koushal & Another v. Naz Foundation & Others, ¶ 43). *See* ABEYRATNE, *supra* note 211, at 115.
[232] National Legal Service Authority v. Union of India, ¶ 34.
[233] Dutta, *supra* note 203, at 232.
[234] National Legal Service Authority v. Union of India, ¶ 106 (emphasis added).

Throughout the case, they are portrayed as 'third gender',[235] even though their identity might be binary as well. For example, *hijras* may identify as women.[236] In the final directives, people in the broader 'transgender' category are granted a right to binary and nonbinary recognition. However, the Supreme Court ordered that *hijras* should be treated 'as third gender'. The Supreme Court decision also failed to give visibility to people who are assigned female at birth, such as trans men.[237] Finally, the Supreme Court, which ordered that all trans and nonbinary people be treated as members of socially and Educationally Backward Classes, seemed to ignore 'the variant caste identities of transgender individuals'[238] and the fact that 'members of the transgender community may belong to a wide range of castes'.[239]

As Gee Imaan Semmalar argues, we can read *NALSA* as an attempt to establish 'administrative legibility in order to provide state support'—which, it can be added, has constitutional implications—and a 'proper place' for trans people.[240] Interestingly, Dutta reports that gatekeeping of trans identities increased after the *NALSA* judgment.[241] Semmalar likewise notes that 'the question of who an "authentic" trans person is, who can claim and receive benefits from the State, has further intensified intra-community conflicts and definitional anxieties'.[242]

Furthermore, *NALSA* seems to define a nonbinary subject that fits the narratives of the government. Rahul Rao argued that the *NALSA* judgment delineated a notion of sexual diversity that is traditional and thus deemed to be politically palatable in a context of 'trans nationalism'.[243] The narrative of the decision indeed characterizes gender diversity as deeply rooted in Indian traditions. The opinion of Justice Radhakrishnan discusses at length the presence of gender diversity—mainly, *hijras*—in sacred Hindu texts, thus contrasting the Indian tolerance and celebration of diversity with the repressive attitude of the British. Nevertheless, as Semmalar observes:

[235] National Legal Service Authority v. Union of India, ¶¶ 70–75 and ¶ 108 (where, however, Justice Sikri concedes that *hijras* may identify 'either as women or "not men"').

[236] Gee Iman Semmalar, *Gender Outlawed: The Supreme Court Judgment on Third Gender and Its Implications*, Roundtable India (18 Apr. 2014), https://www.roundtableindia.co.in/because-we-have-a-voice-too-the-supreme-court-judgment-on-third-gender-and-its-implications/.

[237] Dipika Jain & Debanuj Dasgupta, *Law, Gender Identity, and the Uses of Human Rights: The Paradox of Recognition in South Asia*, 20 Journal of Human Rights 110, 113 (2021).

[238] *Id.*

[239] Jain, *supra* note 212, at 62.

[240] Gee Imaan Semmalar, *You Can't Fix Us: Trans Citizenship and the Classificatory Anxieties of the State*, *in* Desire and Its Discontents: Queer Politics in Contemporary India 192, 198 (Dipika Jain & Oishik Sircar eds., 2024) (referring specifically to National Legal Service Authority v. Union of India, ¶ 115).

[241] Ani Dutta, *Gatekeeping Transgender*, Raiot (4 Oct. 2016), https://www.academia.edu/30423956/Gatekeeping_Transgender.

[242] Semmalar, *supra* note 240, at 212–13.

[243] Rao, *supra* note 200, at 187.

> This [golden Hindu period narrative] completely ignores the Muslim cultural context within which several hijra gharanas have flourished beyond the restrictions of Hinduism, creating a syncretic culture that respects Islam within the transgender community.[244]

Vaibhav Saria argues that, with this narrative, the *NALSA* decision identifies an 'intelligible' form of gender diversity that is at the same time possibly heterosexual, but also politically and religiously significant, with direct links to the 'ascending Indian nationalism'.[245] Jennifer Ung Loh also suggests that the definition of gender-diverse identities in the *NALSA* judgment should be read against mounting Indian nationalism, as describing a form of gender variance that is essentially Indian (or Hindu) and hence acceptable, while at the same time excluding other forms of diversity that are imports and hence unacceptable.[246] Indeed, Rao observes, in 2014 homosexuality was understood as 'modern' and un-Indian in the Supreme Court's decision in *Koushal*.[247]

To sum up, Rehan Abeyratne points out that the 'use of history [in *NALSA*] plays into the nationalist narrative of the [Rashtriya Swayamsevak Sangh] and the [Bharatiya Janata Party]'.[248] As Dipika Jain argues, *NALSA* implements 'the state-sanctioned regulatory sexual regime which boxes gender fluidity'.[249] In conclusion, as Dipika Jain and Debanuj Dasgupta contend, the right to nonbinary recognition designed in the case law (and, *nota bene*, in the following legislation too) should be read in a neoliberal context that offers recognition to

> those who have historically been outside the folds of formal citizenship, if they perform 'certain prescribed codes of respectable citizenship'. The terms of recognition for queer subjects, in legal reform efforts, are based on 'the hegemonic constructs of the Hindu nation.'[250]

Post-NALSA: Legislative restrictions and judicial expansions

The judicial implementation of *NALSA* appears to have been uneven. Courts at the state level have treated the question of gender recognition differently. In some cases,

[244] Semmalar, *supra* note 236.

[245] Vaibhav Saria, *Begging for Change: Hijras, Law and Nationalism*, 53 CONTRIBUTIONS TO INDIAN SOCIOLOGY 133, 134, and 151 (2019).

[246] Jennifer Ung Loh, *Transgender Identity, Sexual Versus Gender 'Rights' and the Tools of the Indian State*, 119 FEMINIST REVIEW 39 (2018).

[247] RAO, *supra* note 200, at 189. It should be noted that, in 2023, the Supreme Court changed this narrative with its decision in Supriyo a.k.a Supriya Chakraborty & Abhay Dang v. Union of India thr. Its Secretary, Ministry of Law and Justice & other connected cases (2023) INSC 920, ¶¶ 81–106 (hereinafter, Supriyo v. Union of India), where it clarified that queerness is not 'un-Indian'.

[248] ABEYRATNE, *supra* note 211, at 146.

[249] Jain, *supra* note 212, at 70.

[250] Jain & Dasgupta, *supra* note 237, at 116, citing Oishink Sircar & Dipika Jain, *New Intimacies/Old Desires: Law, Culture and Queer Politics in Neoliberal Times*, 4 JINDAL GLOBAL LAW REVIEW 1, 12–13 (2012).

they have denied recognition to trans men and understood the *NALSA* ruling as encompassing only trans women and *hijras*.[251] Even when state courts have demonstrated remarkable openness, for example, stating that trans women are women, a clear application of a self-determination standard has been more doubtful.[252] At other times, they have granted self-determination.[253] The administrative implementation has also been criticized for being bureaucratic and complicated.[254]

The legislative implementation has been convoluted, too. Four bills have been presented to the Indian Parliament since 2014, none of which was approved. Eventually, the Transgender Persons (Protection of Rights) Act 2019 was passed.[255] Consistent with the 'redistributive' approach that characterizes the *NALSA* decision, several provisions granting equal access to education, healthcare, and employment have been added to the Act.[256] Nevertheless, this statute designs a mechanism whereby a district magistrate is given the authority to grant gender recognition 'if a person undergoes surgery to change gender'. Documentary evidence must be supplied by the applicant, including medical affidavits to demonstrate the completion of such surgery.[257] In sum, although this Act granted important rights and granted a degree of recognition to gender-diverse people, it can be argued that it 'placed new obstacles in the path toward legal recognition and social acceptance for India's gender diverse communities'.[258] Unsurprisingly, the constitutionality of the 2019 Act has been challenged, and, to the best of my knowledge, this claim is currently pending before the Supreme Court.[259]

[251] Jain, *supra* note 212, at 67. *See* Jackuline Mary v. The Superintendent of Police, Karur & Ors, W.P. No. 587.

[252] Viswanathan Krishna Murthy v. State of Andhra Pradesh, Criminal Petition Nos. 6783, 7064 & 6830 of 2022 (16 June 2025) (A.P. H.C.). For this reading of the case: Rishika Aggarwal, *Defining 'Woman' in Law? Contextualising the Indian High Court Judgment That Affirms Trans Women Are Women*, Oxford Human Rights Hub Blog (16 June 2025), https://ohrh.law.ox.ac.uk/defining-woman-in-law-contextualising-the-indian-high-court-judgment-that-affirms-trans-women-are-women/.

[253] For an overview, refer to the website 'Law and Sexuality', edited by Surabhi Shukla (https://lawandsexuality.com). For example, in Kantaro Kondagari @ Kajol v. State of Odisha and Ors WP (C) 4779 of 2022, the High Court of Orissa at Cuttack read the *NALSA* decision as enshrining gender self-determination, and thus protected the right of a trans woman who was applying for a survivor's pension after her father's passing. Apparently in a similar way, self-determination was protected by the High Court of Uttarakhand. Other courts, however, did not apply a self-determination test. In Smt. Surbhy Trivedi v. Gaurav Trivedi (Misc. petition no. 4820 of 2018), the High Court of Madhya Pradesh established that the gender identity of one of the spouses had to be medically tested in a case of marriage annulment (para 8).

[254] Dipika Jain & Gauri Pillai, *Bureaucratization of Transgender Rights: Perspectives from the Ground*, 14 Socio-Legal Review 98 (2018).

[255] Transgender Persons (Protection of Rights) Act 2019. *See* Aastha Khanna & Divesh Sawhney, *Legislative Review of the Transgender Persons (Protection of Rights) Act, 2019*, 24 Human Rights Brief 155, 160 (2021). *See also*: Transgender Persons (Protection of Rights) Rules 2020.

[256] Transgender Persons (Protection of Rights) Act 2019, SS. 13–15.

[257] Transgender Persons (Protection of Rights) Act 2019, S. 7.

[258] Abeyratne, *supra* note 211, at 149.

[259] Grace Banu Ganeshan & Ors. v. Union of India & Anr., W.P. (Civil) No. 406/2020, https://clpr.org.in/litigation/grace-banu-ganesan-ors-v-union-of-india-anr/.

Openings to gender diversity can however be observed in the case law. A few new judgments of the Supreme Court seem to have confirmed the reading of *NALSA* in terms of self-determination. The Supreme Court recognized the existence of a right to privacy in the 2017 decision in *Puttaswamy v. Union of India*.[260] As Shreya Atrey and Gautam Bhatia argue, the feminist-informed reasoning of *Puttaswamy* lends itself to the advancement of women and gender minorities, as the right to privacy defined by the Court encompasses protection of bodily integrity and of the liberty of taking 'intimate decisions'.[261] Abeyratne highlights that *Puttaswamy*

> was a landmark judgment. It firmly entrenched a constitutional right to privacy and did so in broad doctrinal terms that spoke both to the values underlying the Constitution and to the minority and disadvantaged communities who may call upon its protection in tangible ways.[262]

In 2018, in the wake of *Puttaswamy*, the Supreme Court decided *Navtej Singh Johar and Others v. Union of India*.[263] It reversed its own 2013 *Koushal* precedent that had upheld the criminalization of same-sex intimacy,[264] which had also affected trans and nonbinary individuals. In this judgment, there are repeated references to *NALSA* and to the protection of 'self-identified' gender identity granted therein.[265] Furthermore, the Supreme Court underlined that '[a]t the core of the concept of identity lies self-determination'.[266] Khotari suggests that *Navtej* and *NALSA* should be read together. As such, they establish 'that the right to self-determination, which is based solely on the person's own choice, has explicitly rejected the medical model of recognition of gender identity'.[267]

The Supreme Court seems to have taken a more definitive stance on the question of self-determination in the *Supriyo Chakraborty v. Union of India* decision of 27 October 2023. The case, which intervenes in the extremely complex Indian family law, rejected marriage equality and can be seen as a departure from the previously expansive case law concerning the rights of LGBTQI+ people in this jurisdiction.[268] Several passages of *Supriyo* refer to trans and other gender-diverse

[260] Justice K. S. Puttaswamy (Retd.) and Anr. v. Union Of India And Ors (2017) 10 SCC 1; AIR 2017 SC 4161.

[261] Gautam Bhatia & Shreya Atrey, *In Search of Principle: 70 Years of Gender Jurisprudence in India*, *in* Gender, Sexuality and Constitutionalism in Asia 259, 274 (Wen-Chen Chang, Kelley Loper, Mara Malagodi & Ruth Rubio-Marín eds., 2023).

[262] Abeyratne, *supra* note 211, at 130.

[263] Navtej Singh Johar and Others v. Union of India. *See* Abeyratne, *supra* note 211, at 130–35 (commenting on and systematizing the decision).

[264] Suresh Kumar Koushal & Another v. Naz Foundation & Others.

[265] For example: Navtej Singh Johar and Others v. Union of India, Opinion of Indu Malhotra, ¶ 16.1 and ¶ 17.2.

[266] Navtej Singh Johar and Others v. Union of India, ¶ 9.

[267] Khotari, *supra* note 226, at 6.

[268] For a discussion: Agarwal, *supra* note 216; Kushagr Bakshi, *Marriage, Courts, and Substantive Equality: A Transformative Interpretation*, 123 Michigan Law Review 519 (2024); Abeyratne, *supra* note 211, at 154–60 (commenting on and systematizing the decision in relation to same-sex marriage).

individuals. The Supreme Court retrospectively established that *NALSA* 'recognized the right of transgender persons to be identified by the gender identity of their choice, as well as their right to full protection under the Constitution, on equal terms with any other citizen of the country'.[269] It acknowledged the criticisms that were directed at *NALSA*, especially in relation to flattening 'the gender identities of hijras as belonging to the third gender alone'. Hence, *NALSA*, the Supreme Court insisted, 'must be read as recognizing the right of all transgender persons (including hijras and those who are socio-culturally known by other names) to be recognized by a gender of their choice'.[270]

All that glitters is not gold, though. The Court stated that 'if a transgender person is in a heterosexual relationship and wishes to marry their partner ... such a marriage would be recognized.'[271] This is not a particularly innovative statement. The High Court of Madras had already recognized a trans woman as a woman for the purposes of the Hindu Marriage Act 1955 in the 2019 decision in *Arunkumar v. Inspector General*.[272] The Court also added that 'intersex persons who identify as a man or a woman and seek to enter into a heterosexual marriage would also have a right to marry.'[273] While there is no explicit exclusion of nonbinary people from marriage, the silence on the matter leaves the marriage rights of nonbinary individuals in a limbo of uncertainty. This conclusion is in keeping with the previous lack of rules—and potential discrimination—that Akshat Agarwal argues has been enduring since the 2014 *NALSA* decision, and that is determined by the binary-normativity of the system of family law in India.[274]

On 17 October 2025, the Supreme Court of India delivered its judgment in *Kaushik v. Union of India*.[275] This decision concerns mostly the discrimination that trans and nonbinary people are exposed to in their daily interactions, and the shortfalls in the application of the Transgender Persons (Protection of Rights) Act 2019. A few interesting aspects of this case should be noted. First, the Supreme Court confirmed its self-determination doctrine, at least in principle.[276] Second, this decision is characterized again by a marked redistributive spirit. The Supreme Court stressed the constitutional importance of overcoming the 'practical hurdles' that 'transgender' people encounter when they need to change their sex markers. It also condemned the daily discrimination that 'transgender' people must face. Finally, the Court issued a detailed list of directives, 'suggesting', *inter alia*, the creation of adequate establishments to accommodate gender diversity.[277] In short, it

[269] Supriyo v. Union of India, ¶ 259.
[270] Supriyo v. Union of India, ¶ 259.
[271] Supriyo v. Union of India, ¶ 277.
[272] Arunkumar v. Inspector General (2019) AIR Madras 265.
[273] Supriyo v. Union of India, ¶ 277.
[274] Akshat Agarwal, *LGBT+ Rights Claims for Marriage Equality and the Possibilities of Transforming Indian Family Law*, 21 International Journal of Constitutional Law 1116, 1124 (2023).
[275] Jane Kaushik v. Union of India, (2025) INSC 1248 (hereinafter, Jane Kaushik v. Union of India).
[276] Jane Kaushik v. Union of India, ¶¶ 18, 78, and 178.
[277] Jane Kaushik v. Union of India, ¶¶ 198–99.

invited the government to create adequate structures to accommodate nonbinary people. At the same time, some questions arise at first blush. Namely, 'transgender' people appear to be defined as nonbinary only, thus possibly opening again the same doubts that were present in *NALSA* and possibly questioning the possibility to obtain recognition for trans binary people who fall outside established narratives. Although further research is necessary, a nationalist narrative might arguably be identified.[278]

To wrap up, the Indian case is characterized by deep tensions. The developments in this jurisdiction, though leading to self-determination, also show how the right to nonbinary recognition can be defined under-inclusively and in a manner that aligns with broader political and legal agendas. At the same time, the Indian cases demonstrate the transformative potential of constitutional law, as the Supreme Court foregrounded crucial constitutional principles to grant recognition to gender-diverse people and to guarantee a higher degree of socio-economic equality.

5. Conclusion

This chapter has identified and criticized three models of nonbinary recognition. In the first model—embodied recognition—nonbinary legal identity depends on possessing specific identifiable markers, such as bodily characteristics. For example, physical diversity can be the result of medical procedures, such as in the Australian *Norrie* case, or congenital, such as in the legal and jurisprudential framework that has developed in Germany until 2024. The Australian High Court made it explicit that embodied recognition can serve as an instrument to ensure legal stability—to the point that, in the reasoning of *Norrie*, the rights of the applicant fade into the background. The German Constitutional Court and, centrally, the FCJ and the German legislature in 2018, while foregrounding individual rights, have also drafted nonbinary recognition in a way that favours controls over individual applications and does not threaten the stability of the gender system.

An entirely different approach identified in this chapter—self-determined nonbinary recognition—is exemplified by decisions taken in Colombia. These decisions were the outcome of contestations to limits that had previously been imposed on nonbinary legal identity in a jurisdiction where gender self-determination had already been granted. In this context, self-determination has been 'enlarged' to include nonbinary people. This form of recognition prioritizes the rights of nonbinary people over the public interest and other rights that presuppose binary identities. In fact, the Colombian court was fully cognizant that self-determination

[278] There also appears to be some emphasis on national dimension of 'third gender' people (Jane Kaushik v. Union of India, ¶¶ 2–3).

comes at a cost in terms of legal stability and certainty. Nevertheless, it decided that the public interest in preserving the binary and controlling changes of personal status were outweighed by the rights of the person. Despite the instability it can potentially generate, gender recognition on the basis of self-determination guarantees inclusion. Amplifying the effects of gender self-determination with the inclusion of one (or possibly more) nonbinary options, this model of nonbinary recognition questions and transforms the basic structures of gender constitutionalism and its reliance on binary categories.

In general, recognition of gender identity can have positive effects on socio-economic equality of trans and nonbinary people. This socio-economic dimension is foregrounded in the redistributive model that we find in the case law of the Nepali, Pakistani, and Indian Supreme Courts. In these cases, socio-economic equality is not merely a welcome by-product of recognition, but rather its driving force. Courts steered their reasoning to remedy the deprivation that trans and nonbinary people endure. These decisions and the legal reasoning behind them create a bond between gender recognition and a *multitude* of rights—from equal access to employment and resources to the right to freedom from harassment and police violence.

But not all approaches to redistributive recognition are the same. The 2007 Nepalese Supreme Court decision ensured recognition based on self-determination to nonbinary people only; only recently has the binary option also been explicitly ensured. In the narrative of the Pakistani Supreme Court, redistributive recognition was arguably anchored to physical diversity—a connection which attracted significant criticism but that also allowed for controlling sexual thirdness and making it legible for legal and constitutional purposes. Finally, in India, nonbinary recognition was based on a largely ambiguous decision that has only recently been clarified, thus steering India more resolutely towards a right to gender self-determination. In all these jurisdictions—in Pakistan and India especially—we see a right that at once recognizes and yet defines gender diversity to allow the pursuit of legal, constitutional, and political purposes. As is the case in Germany and Australia, control over gender identities is multiplied beyond the binary, not disestablished.

Some courts have defined nonbinary recognition as a response to a history of colonial domination. Recognition includes and makes visible categories of people who had been oppressed by colonial authorities. This was manifest in Colombia, Pakistan, and India. To some extent, this was already noticeable when the Colombian Constitutional Court granted binary self-determination, as discussed in Chapter 6. However, the introduction of a nonbinary option makes the remedial potential of gender recognition particularly evident, because European colonizers heavily targeted people who did not fit into the male–female categories. The recognition of sexual thirdness is a first step to remedying the wrongs of the past. But more fundamentally for the purposes of this book, it brings into the limelight the racialized and Eurocentric dimension of binary identities, and thus of the subjects of constitutional and public law in many jurisdictions.

Finally, in each of these cases, we see the interplay among the demands of nonbinary people, the importance of preserving the binary in the legal system, and the existence of legal and constitutional principles that, in different ways, ground the recognition of gender diversity. In every instance, we learn that gender diversity lies at the core of public law.

8
Abolishing or Entrenching Categories? The Challenges Ahead

1. A fork in the road: Two challenges ahead

The discussion has up to this point centred on the recognition of gender diversity and the questions that the claims of intersex, trans, and nonbinary people pose for public law. Although challenging and even transformative for the system of sex categories, these claims were not primarily aimed at eliminating sex registration altogether. Rather, they were directed at carving out a space for gender-diverse people within a changing system of sex categories: sex categories, in principle, remain in place, but are modified to accommodate the demands of gender-diverse people. Nevertheless, activists and scholars have more recently contested the legal assignment of sex per se. They have, in other words, argued for expunging sex from the status of the person.

A handful of courts have considered this demand and reached different conclusions. This chapter offers an initial examination of the approaches to the question of a 'sex-less' civil status as discussed by the few constitutional courts that have examined the idea, classifying the results reached by these courts and suggesting some preliminary explanations for such conclusions. Three constitutional models for addressing the issue of a sex-less legal status are identified. The first is *constitutional necessity*: some constitutional courts have either implicitly or explicitly rejected the proposition of removing sex from the legal status of the person, judging that sex must remain a component of the individual civil status. Examples of this can be seen in Italy, France, and Colombia. The second approach is *constitutional neutrality*, as provided by the German, Austrian, and Belgian constitutional courts. All of them have ruled that sex registration is neither constitutionally forbidden nor mandated but rather remains at the discretion of the legislature. Third, we can hypothesize a *constitutional prohibition* of sex categories. If that were the case, sex categorization would be deemed unconstitutional. To the best of my knowledge, no court has thus far ruled in this sense. As per usual in this book, I do not aim to identify the variables that lead to one or the other model. Although it can be safely suggested that gender self-determination and nonbinary recognition make the constitutional permissibility of a sex-less status more likely, it cannot be said that they will necessarily lead to such an outcome, as the Colombian case shows. Be that as it may, from a theoretical perspective, I suggest that when gender

Gender Diversity in Public Law. Stefano Osella, Oxford University Press. © Stefano Osella 2026.
DOI: 10.1093/9780198935070.003.0008

self-determination is granted and multiple sex categories are available, the structure of the sex binary is questioned so profoundly that we might as well as ask whether it has already been altogether disestablished. This section of the chapter concludes with a few thoughts to guide future normative research.

The possibility of a sex-less legal status might seem far-fetched in this day and age, when a backlash against gender rights can be witnessed in many jurisdictions. Indeed, at the other end of the spectrum of possibilities, we may notice another complex issue in the relations between gender diversity and public law. Efforts to deny gender diversity can be observed across jurisdictions. They may include a re-affirmation of birth-assigned sex and the (re-)entrenchment of a biology-evoking narrative as an instrument to justify it. This chapter will therefore ask the question of the stoppages and backlashes against the global achievements of gender-diverse people. To this purpose, I will examine the law in the United Kingdom, and make passing references to other jurisdictions as well, such as Bolivia, Bulgaria, and Hungary.

I do not argue that either the elimination or the re-entrenchment of sex categories are the only possible or meaningful developments that lie ahead. Nevertheless, a few factors suggest focusing on these opposing tendencies. First, they have already been addressed in the comparative case law concerning constitutional and human rights and have been debated among scholars. Second, at a deeper level, both developments, in different ways, seem to challenge the very system of sex categories in public law. This system, as we have seen throughout this book, is shaped by a balancing of multiple principles in tension. Both erasing sex categories and denying gender diversity, each in its own way, would completely transform the results that have thus far been achieved.

2. The disestablishment of sex categories

2.1. Eliminating or preserving categories?

As I suggested before, the question of expunging sex categories from a person's civil status is central to public law.[1] Recently, it has been very much debated in the literature. Some scholars and activists have demanded an end to sex registration and envisioned a society (and law) 'beyond gender'.[2] Sex categories, some suggest,

[1] For an initial examination of these themes: Stefano Osella, *'De-Gendering' the Civil Status? A Public Law Problem*, 18 International Journal of Constitutional Law 471 (2020); Marie-Xavière Catto & Stefano Osella, *The Sexed Subject*, *in* The Cambridge Companion to Gender and the Law 25, 56 (Stéphanie Hennette-Vauchez & Ruth Rubio-Marín eds., 2023).

[2] *E.g.*: Principle 31, Yogyakarta Principles plus 10: Additional Principles and State Obligations on the Application of International Human Rights Law in Relation to Sexual Orientation, Gender Identity, Gender Expression and Sex Characteristics to Complement the Yogyakarta Principles (2017).

would no longer be used as an organizing principle of the legal system. Among other things, legal sex would not be relied on for: '(1) the allocation of legal and political rights, social and economic rewards, and respect; (2) the division of labor, including household labor and caring work as well as paid labor; (3) social expectations about appropriate forms of expression and behavior.'[3] The main argument that these activists and theorists put forward is that sex categories are detrimental in and of themselves, regardless of the recognition of gender diversity. Aeyal Gross argued that sex categories are inherently patriarchal, heteronormative, and hierarchical.[4] Ido Katri criticized gender self-determination because, paradoxically, it reinforces the mechanism of gender.[5] Heath Fogg Davis suggested that 'as long as sex-classification policies remain in place, they will always trigger [sex-identity] discrimination', which gender recognition will not solve. Indeed:

> Not everyone can or wants to assimilate into prevailing gender norms. Moreover, some people's statements about their sex identities will be rejected no matter what they do or say.[6]

Davina Cooper and Robyn Emerton argued that the legal assignment of sex disadvantages intersex, trans, and nonbinary people in and of itself. Sex registration, they suggested, is ill-suited to protect women. Sex categories were indeed devised as an instrument to facilitate the operation of the patriarchal gender legal order. Recognition, they also considered, is not a satisfactory solution. The permanence of a legal sex makes of 'gender ... a human characteristic' and obscures its cultural origins. Ultimately, Cooper and Emerton suggested that recognition entrusts 'state authorities [with] the power to determine which gender categories count and what they count for'.[7] Instead, Cooper and Emerton advanced the option of 'decertification'—namely, the state's withdrawal 'from registering, assigning, or guaranteeing a person's sex and gender'[8]—which would allow each person to live outside the gender order.[9]

Foregoing legal sex might appear easier said than done, but the fundamental strategy proposed by these scholars is centred on attaining the legitimate goals of sex categories through less intrusive and/or more effective means. A few examples

[3] Rogers Brubaker, Trans: Gender and Race in an Age of Unsettled Identities 119 (2016).

[4] Aeyal Gross, *Post/Colonial Queer Globalisation and International Human Rights: Images of LGBT Rights*, 4 Jindal Global Law Review 98, 127–28 (2013).

[5] Ido Katri, *The Perils of Gender Self-Determination: Global Shifts in Sex Reclassification Law and Policy*, 71 The American Journal of Comparative Law 707, 710 (2023). I respectfully disagree with this conclusion. Refer to Chapter 6 on Colombia.

[6] Heath Fogg Davis, Beyond Trans: Does Gender Matter 18 (2017).

[7] Davina Cooper & Robyn Emerton, *Pulling the Thread of Decertification: What Challenges Are Raised by the Proposal to Reform Legal Gender Status?*, 10 feminists@law 1, 5–6 (2020), https://journals.kent.ac.uk/index.php/feministsatlaw/article/view/938.

[8] *Id.* at 1.

[9] *Id.* at 7–8.

may clarify this point. Fogg Davis has argued that sex categories may yield less fruit than one may wish for.[10] Gender-segregated restrooms or facilities, for example, do not appear to ensure safety or privacy, and indeed advocates have devised other strategies to ensure that every user is safe and comfortable.[11] Referring to access to women-only spaces, such as shelters for violence survivors, washrooms, or changing rooms, Cooper and co-authors advise evaluating the threat posed by each user *in concreto*. This assessment would centre on examining personal elements such as biographical details, past history of violence, etc. instead of focusing on the sex assigned at birth or recorded in public registries. Cooper and co-authors have also suggested that sufficient public funding is a determining factor to ensure appropriately structured, well-maintained establishments where the privacy, safety, and comfort of every user is guaranteed.[12] The possibility of 'erasing' the legal category of women might clearly be of concern here. After all, women have long suffered and still suffer the effects of patriarchy and gender discrimination.[13] Nevertheless, it is worth mentioning that some feminist authors have problematized the preservation of the very category of 'woman' in the law. Marie-Xavière Catto has suggested the category of 'woman' is mentioned in French law mostly in relation to re-inscribing legal subordination or is at times superfluous (e.g., in relation to certain aspects of welfare law where men and women are treated equally), if not under-inclusive (e.g., pregnant trans men).[14]

Comprehensive reforms of the rules of athletic competitions—for example, considering the body composition and the strength of each athlete—may be used to preserve fairness in sports.[15] Employing precise language—combined with state-of-the-art informatic technologies—might be relied on to deliver health-related or welfare policies successfully. Instead of talking of maternity leaves for women, leaves for pregnant or birthing people might be designed—after all, not

[10] FOGG DAVIS, *supra* note 6.

[11] The abolishment of sex-segregated restrooms seemed to be a feminist demand before the debates on gender diversity became more polarizing. For example, Mary Anne Case makes an argument for the abolishment of 'urinary segregation' from a feminist perspective: Mary Anne Case, *Why Not Abolish Laws of Urinary Segregation?*, *in* TOILET: PUBLIC RESTROOMS AND THE POLITICS OF SHARING (Harvey Molotch & Laura Noren eds., 2010). In the same book, *see also*: Harvey Molotch, *On Not Making History: What NYU Did with the Toilet and What It Means for the World* 255, 264. It is here useful to recall that the—admittedly, limited—data available appear to suggest that sex-desegregated restrooms (and the inclusion of trans women in female toilets) do not make them less safe: Jody L. Herman, Andrew R. Flores & Elana Redfield, Williams Institute, Safety and Privacy in Public Restrooms and Other Gendered Facilities (Feb. 2025).

[12] Davina Cooper et al., King's College London, Abolishing Legal Sex Status: The Challenge and Consequences of Gender-Related Law Reform. Future of Legal Gender Project Final Report 21 (2022), https://www.kcl.ac.uk/law/research/future-of-legal-gender-abolishing-legal-sex-status-full-report.pdf; Cooper & Emerton, *supra* note 7.

[13] *See* GILA STOPLER, WOMEN'S RIGHTS IN LIBERAL STATES: PATRIARCHY, LIBERALISM, RELIGION AND THE CHIMERA OF RIGHTS (2025).

[14] Marie-Xavière Catto, *Garder la Catégorie Juridique de «Femme»?*, *in* QU'EST-CE QU'UNE FEMME? CATÉGORIES HOMME/FEMME: DÉBATS CONTEMPORAINS 131 (Patricia Lemarchand & Muriel Salle eds., 2023).

[15] FOGG DAVIS, *supra* note 6, at 111–40.

all people who become pregnant are women in the eyes of the law. Instead of reminding women or men to be screened for 'women-' or 'men-' only illnesses (let us think of uterine or prostate cancer), people with, say, a uterus or a prostate gland could receive the necessary information. After all, we are constantly reminded of the wonders of contemporary technologies and artificial intelligence. Thinking of a more personalized approach to healthcare (or other welfare areas) could perhaps be a convenient use of these powerful tools.

Sex registration, it has also been suggested, should not be understood in an all-or-nothing fashion. Sex categories, in other words, do not need to be either ubiquitous or entirely removed from the legal system. Intermediate solutions have been proposed. Cooper and co-authors, for example, suggest by way of compromise that legal sex might be preserved and some sensitive information retained, to be used solely for constitutionally imperative reasons. They refer to this approach as 'soft decertification'.[16] Catto advises downsizing the category of sex, which could be used solely when specific rights requiring categorization are at stake according to an ad hoc evaluation by administrative authorities.[17]

Other scholars disagree. Not only is the gender constitutional order rooted in binary categories, but, as said, important objectives are related to the binary. Laurie Shrage, for instance, has argued that equality-related purposes ultimately may justify the preservation of sex categories. Shrage has suggested that '[i]n most cases, the state only needs to track a person's lived sex, which can be verified by each individual',[18] but also noted that, with 'historic discrimination and victimization against women … we may need to consider not only a person's lived sex but past experiences of oppression', and thus retain categorizations based on sex assigned at birth.[19] Philippe Guez, while commenting positively on the French socio-behavioural model, has acknowledged that with the advancements of gender equality and with the legalization of same-sex marriage, the significance of sex in the legal status is diminished. However, Guez has also noted that essential aspects of (French) law still necessitate the legal assignment of sex.[20]

As we shall shortly see, the entrenchment of sex categories—ostensibly representing what is perceived to be a biological truth—is seemingly central to the legal demands of different movements, including gender-critical feminists and the opposers of the (so-called) gender ideology.[21] Although these groups have not, to the best of my knowledge, engaged in the debates over the preservation of sex categorization per se, their aversion to gender diversity recognition and insistence on

[16] Cooper et al., *supra* note 12, at 26.

[17] Catto, *supra* note 14.

[18] Laurie Shrage, *Does the Government Need to Know Your Sex?*, 20 The Journal of Political Philosophy 225, 246 (2012).

[19] *Id.* at 233.

[20] Philippe Guez, *Faut-il Supprimer la Mention du Sexe de la Personne à l'État civil?*, 8 Revue des Droits de l'Homme (online) (2015), http://journals.openedition.org/revdh/1660.

[21] *See* Chapter 2.

recording birth-assigned sex ('biological sex') is unlikely to be compatible with the notion of a sex-less legal status.

2.2. The contributions of courts

Constitutional necessity

Some courts or legislatures have implicitly required the presence of sex categories when they have imposed preconditions on gender recognition. In such cases, it appears that sex categories are deemed necessary to achieve constitutional aims. If the preservation of legal certainty and the stability of sex categories entails the imposition of specific requirements and an external assessment, then the presence of (stable and binary) sex categories is arguably legally required. This is even clearer in cases where courts have explicitly denied nonbinary recognition. The French Court of Cassation stated in 2017 that binary categories are 'foundational' to the French legal system.[22] The Italian Constitutional Court ruled that the binary shapes legal areas of constitutional importance.[23] The proposition of a sex-less status, under such circumstances, appears logically unfeasible.

That said, we should not conclude that sex categories are preserved only when gender diversity is either denied or limited. The Constitutional Court of Colombia has denied a claim for a sex-less legal status with judgment T-033/22,[24] even though it granted nonbinary self-determination and protected gender fluidity with the same decision and several precedents.[25] Judgment T-033/22 was the response to a *tutela* filed by a *travesti* person, both nonbinary and gender fluid, who did not manage to obtain gender recognition. The plaintiff argued, *inter alia*, that including sex in the person's civil status and displaying it on identification documents was a source of discrimination and a violation of privacy. The plaintiff also objected that, thanks to new technologies of identification (such as biometrics), a sex indicator is unnecessary for governance purposes.

The Court recognized that sex registration serves 'imperative' aims (*finalidades imperiosas*) such as personal identification and worthwhile public policies.[26] For example, it considered that including sex in the civil status is logically connected to

[22] As noted in Chapter 5, this statement has attracted a fair deal of scholarly criticism.

[23] Corte Costituzionale [Constitutional Court][Corte Cost.], 23 luglio 2024, n. 143.

[24] The plaintiffs asked for the elimination of sex from public display in identification documents only, while accepting that sex could be recorded in public registries and remain classified information (Corte Constitucional [Constitutional Court][C.C.], 4 febrero 2022, Sentencia T-033/22, ¶ 66). Nevertheless, the Court discussed 'the inclusion of this component [i.e. sex] in the civil registry and in the citizenship card [that is, the ID]' (C.C., T-033/22, ¶ 68). *See also*: Stefano Osella, *Come Evolve il Diritto all'Identità di Genere? Fattori Strutturali, Culturali e Dogmatici nella Giurisprudenza Costituzionale Italiana e Colombiana. Un'Analisi Comparata*, Diritti Comparati 1, 37–39 (2023), https://www.diritticomparati.it/bozza-automatica-170/.

[25] Refer to Chapters 6 and 7 for a discussion of the Colombian case law.

[26] C.C., T-033/22, ¶ 68.3.

the promotion of gender equality—not only of women, but also of gender-diverse people.[27] The Court did not discuss whether sex registration is necessary, but leapt to the last prong of the proportionality test (proportionality *strictu sensu*). To determine if the benefits of sex registration outweigh the disadvantages, the Court reasoned that sex, in Colombian law, reflects gender identity, and that since birth-assigned sex is not reported in the identification documents of trans people, the discrimination grounded in the mismatch between identity and sex markers is prevented. The Court thereby reaffirmed the constitutional imperative of sex registration and the rights necessitating it.[28]

Constitutional neutrality

The second approach is constitutional neutrality, which can be found in the judgments of the German Federal Constitutional Court (FCC), the Austrian Constitutional Court, and the Belgian Constitutional Court. These courts have veered towards constitutional neutrality in determining whether the lack of nonbinary recognition conforms to constitutional principles, stating that nonbinary people have a constitutional right to gender recognition that the legislature must protect either by introducing a nonbinary option or by eliminating registration altogether. The German FCC stated that '[t]he Basic Law does not require that civil registration be exclusively binary in terms of sex. *It neither requires that sex be governed by the law on the personal status*, nor is it opposed to the civil status recognition of a third gender identity beyond male and female.'[29] The gender equality clause in the Basic Law, the FCC further stated, does not require sex registration: 'The aim of this provision is mainly to eliminate discrimination against women based on sex but its aim *is not to codify [a sex/gender classification] in the law*.'[30] The FCC specified that, in addition to creating a third option, 'the legislature can dispense with the entry of sex/gender in civil registry matters altogether'.[31] Although this statement may well be an *obiter dictum*, as Rubio-Marín suggested,[32] the FCC stated it three times in the decision, leaving no doubt about the legitimacy of eliminating sex from the elements included in the civil status of the person. The Belgian Constitutional Court stated that 'the fact that the Constitution ... attributes special importance to the equality between men and women does not entail

[27] C.C., T-033/22, ¶ 68.4 (referring to 'the groups who are most vulnerable because of their gender').
[28] C.C., T-033/22, ¶ 69.
[29] Bundesverfassungsgericht [Federal Constitutional Court] [BVerfG], 10 Oct. 2017, 1 BvR 2019/16, ¶ 50, https://www.bundesverfassungsgericht.de/SharedDocs/Entscheidungen/EN/2017/10/rs20171010_1bvr201916en.html (emphasis added). The quotes in the text are taken from the official translation available on the website of the Federal Constitutional Court.
[30] BVerfG, 10 Oct. 2017, 1 BvR 2019/16, ¶ 50 (official translation) (emphasis added). The original German appears to speak of classifications ('geschlechtliche Zuordnung im Personenstandsrecht'). However, the official translation provided speaks of 'gender identity'.
[31] BVerfG, 10 Oct. 2017, 1 BvR 2019/16, ¶ 52 (translation mine).
[32] RUTH RUBIO-MARÍN, GLOBAL GENDER CONSTITUTIONALISM AND WOMEN'S CITIZENSHIP: A STRUGGLE FOR TRANSFORMATIVE INCLUSION 304–05 (2022).

that the categories "man" or "woman" can be considered as a basic principle of the Belgian constitutional order'.[33] In addressing the lack of nonbinary recognition, the Court concluded that '[t]here are ... several possibilities for remedying this unconstitutionality, including [the addition of a nonbinary category but] also *the possibility of removing the registration of sex or gender identity as an element of a person's status* [*état civil*]'.[34] The Austrian Constitutional Court has been less expansive, yet no less clear, on the point, stating that 'the legislature is in principle free to structure the civil status registry, as no constitutional provision requires the entry of a reference to sex/gender'.[35]

If legislatures opt to erase sex as part of the legal status, alternatives will need to be devised to safeguard the legitimate—and indeed, imperative—objectives underlying sex categories. This clearly refers to discrimination against women but also, as the Constitutional Court of Colombia suggested, the rights of trans and nonbinary people, who may also depend on accurate categorization for the effective exercise of their rights. Examples abound. For one, the nonbinary person who started the *Dritte Option* campaign in Germany desired to have their identity acknowledged and supported. And all cases that I have included in the redistributive recognition model insist on the importance of categorizing individuals as nonbinary or trans in order to provide them adequate protection.[36]

2.3. Concluding thoughts and perspectives of research

Future research should first discuss the constitutional *feasibility* of a sex-less legal status. To start with, the concrete circumstances that might possibly allow the relinquishment of sex categories should be identified to avoid that the analysis is merely speculative. In other words, discussing the idea of a sex-less status when the concrete legal circumstances are not present would run the risk of remaining an intellectual exercise. This means that, before engaging with doctrinal discussions, it would be important to isolate the variables that determine the concrete feasibility of a sex-less status. Comparative constitutional studies might in this sense indeed confirm themselves as a formidable tool of investigation. A preliminary observation might suggest that, when the recognition of gender diversity is restricted by medico-behavioural or socio-behavioural standards, or when nonbinary recognition is denied, a sex-less status is hardly thinkable.

[33] Cour Constitutionnelle [Constitutional Court], 19 June 2019, 99/2019, ¶ B.6.6. For a broader discussion of the right to gender recognition granted in the decision: Ruth Rubio-Marín & Stefano Osella, *El Nuevo Derecho Constitucional a la Identidad de Género entre la Libertad de Elección, el Incremento de Categorías y la Subjetividad y Fluidez de sus Contenidos. Un Análisis desde el Derecho Comparado*, 40 Revista Española de Derecho Constitucional 45, 66–69 (2020).

[34] Constitutional Court, 99/2019, ¶ B.7.3 (emphasis added).

[35] Verfassungsgerichtshof [VfGH] [Constitutional Court], 19 June 2018, G-77/2018, ¶ 6.2.

[36] Refer to Chapter 7.

Once the preconditions that are required to entertain the notion of a sex-less status are clarified, a doctrinal assessment of the various principles in tension would also be needed. While the outcome of this balancing exercise remains open, the comparative analysis offered in this book can serve as a starting point for understanding that we should avoid thinking of sex categories as somewhat 'ontologically' necessary. The sex status is a legal instrument. If alternative, less invasive and equally effective means of achieving the same legitimate objectives can be designed, general principles of constitutionalism lead to the conclusion that such alternative means must be preferred.[37] At the same time, the constitutional analysis might contemplate *alternative forms of registration*, mostly as a point of compromise among conflicting interests—for example, in the form of soft decertification as suggested by Cooper and co-authors or as limited recognition as proposed by Catto.

Second, the constitutional discussion of sex categories should start out from the transformation of sex registration in law. If the removal of sex is aimed at disestablishing the legal gender order, we must ask ourselves where such an order can be found. Does the legal gender order inhere in the sex label attached to each of us, or in the mechanism that attributes meaning to the label? We should not confuse sex designation with the meaning-making scaffolding that upholds it. Judith Butler noted that 'gender is the apparatus by which the production and normalization of masculine and feminine takes place'.[38] Jack Halberstam referred to gender as a 'grammar of power' and argued that subordination does not lie in the *content* of norms but in imposing them.[39] Sex designation is just the tip of the iceberg of the legal structure of sex. The gender order is maintained through many different norms, including those that are enforced when individuals seek to change their legal status. This is why self-determination, especially when inclusive of a nonbinary option, is a paradigmatic break in the definition of legal sex. Self-determination amounts to a rejection of hierarchical supervision and of the enforcement of gender norms that regulate transitions. Individuals may still be assigned a sex at birth based on physical examinations, thus making the sexual binary the default option. Even so, we must ask, echoing Chris Hutton, what remains of sex categories when additional options are introduced and when each person can determine what maleness and femaleness (or 'third-genderness') mean for them and obtain legal recognition.[40]

It should also be noted that, while self-determination may suffice to disestablish the mechanisms of definition and enforcement of gender norms, the elimination of

[37] Dean Spade, Normal Life: Administrative Violence, Critical Trans Politics, and the Limits of Law (2d ed. 2015).

[38] Judith Butler, Undoing Gender 42 (2004).

[39] Jack Halberstam, Trans*: A Quick and Quirky Account of Gender Variability (2018).

[40] Chris Hutton, *Legal Sex, Self-Classification and Gender Self- Determination*, 11 Law & Humanities 64, 78–79 (2017).

sex registration in no way guarantees that these mechanisms will be disestablished. Cooper and co-authors, for instance, made a case for abandoning sex registration, yet they also suggested that, in some sensitive legal areas such as gender equality, the sex status of the person should be preserved and determined by examining the person's 'lived gender'.[41] This conclusion might or might not be desirable or adequate. Regardless, adopting this standard would introduce a process of identity determination. After all, we saw that the socio-behavioural model in France defines and enforces subjects of recognition in a very specific and detailed fashion.[42] More explicitly, Cooper and Renz suggested that decertifying sex is unlikely to eliminate mechanisms of gender verification in the law. In pluralistic legal orders, institutions might impose standards and verify identities, for instance, in the case of single-sex private schools.[43]

Third, normative research should consider the transformations that the recognition of gender diversity—which might reasonably be a precondition for a sexless status—will bring about in the functioning and principles of civil registration. Stéphanie Hennette-Vauchez and Marc Pichard argue that sex registration can, in this day and age, be seen as a way of protecting 'identity' and not as an act of top-down identification.[44] The Constitutional Court of Colombia articulated a similar position when it insisted that the state must record and protect individual identity. In other words, *if* the choice of removing sex categories from the law is made to support gender-diverse people, then we should also ask what kind of registration we have in mind: one supporting every individual in their diversity, or one that operates through norms that would most likely not adequately represent human complexity and would impose standards that fit some predetermined legal objectives.

3. 'Biological sex' comes back: 'Gender-critical' feminism and anti-gender advocacy

On Monday, 20 January 2025, a few hours after solemnly taking the oath, the 47th President of the United States signed an executive order with the title 'Defending Women from Gender Ideology Extremism and Restoring Biological Truth to the Federal Government'.[45] The Executive Order establishes that 'it is the policy of the United States to recognize two sexes, male and female'. Gender identity is defined

[41] Cooper et al., *supra* note 12, at 39.
[42] *See* Chapter 5.
[43] Davina Cooper & Flora Renz, *If the State Decertified Gender, What Might Happen to Its Meaning and Value?*, 43 Journal of Law & Society 483 (2016).
[44] Stéphanie Hennette-Vauchez & Marc Pichard, *La Fondamentalisation de l'État Civil*, *in* Identité et État Civil: Évolutions Contemporaines 281 (Amélie Gogos-Gintrand & Stéphanie Moracchini-Zeidenberg eds., 2024).
[45] Exec. Order No. 14168 90 FR 8615 (2025).

as an 'ever-shifting [and self-assessed] concept' that replaces 'the biological category of sex'. This replacement, the Executive Order continues, is operated by 'gender ideology'. The notion of a 'biological sex' and the declared need to rely on it for legal purposes can be found again in the following executive orders concerning the military,[46] restricting gender-affirming medical care for children,[47] cutting resources to schools that support trans students,[48] and banning trans women from participating in athletic competitions as women.[49] Although the United States is not discussed in this book, the solemnity of the occasion points to the significance of this trend.[50]

Developments that, to varying degrees, are favourable to gender-diverse people have been at the core of this book. Nevertheless, a legal (re-)entrenchment of a binary, simplified, and biology-evoking[51] understanding of sex is noticeable in the comparative landscape. The forms of and reasons for this reaction are questions that I leave for future research. Now, I limit myself to pinpointing a few manifestations of this 'biological turn'. Furthermore, while I admit that discourses on 'biology' and 'biological truth' seem to hold sway in some jurisdictions, I also suggest that the 'biological sex' reaction confirms one fundamental argument of this book, namely, that identifying the criteria to determine sex (re)assignment is the outcome of a legal balancing exercise. Even a cursory overview shows that the decision to preserve birth-assigned sex is often justified by invoking legal objectives. Despite the 'biologistic' discourse, all these developments simply confirm that legal sex—far from solely reflecting a neutral biological fact—is the outcome of a balancing exercise of legal principles and values. As Judith Butler would say, it is, in other words, *gender*.

Constitutional lawyers should pay attention to the comeback of biological narratives on sex. First, this is because we see the mobilization of constitutional law to curb the rights of minorities, mostly through what Ruth Rubio-Marín has referred to as an 'erosive' constitutional jurisprudence. Restrictions on the recognition of gender diversity have been camouflaged by a fundamental rights discourse as measures to protect children or (cis) women whom the claims of gender diverse people would, presumably, imperil.[52] Constitutional amendments have also

[46] Prioritizing Military Excellence and Readiness, issued on 27 Jan. 2025 (Exec. Order No. 14183 90 FR 8757).

[47] Protecting Children from Chemical and Surgical Mutilation, issued on 28 Jan. 2025 (Exec. Order No. 14187 90 FR 8771).

[48] Ending Radical Indoctrination in K-12 Schooling, issued on 29 Jan. 2025 (Exec. Order No. 14190 90 FR 8853).

[49] Keeping Men Out of Women's Sports, 5 Feb. 2025 (Exec. Order No. 14201 90 FR 9279).

[50] For a discussion of these orders, *see* Ryan Thoreson, *Transgender Rights at a Crossroads in the United States*, VERFBLOG (13 Feb. 2025), https://verfassungsblog.de/transgender-rights-at-a-crossroads-in-the-united-states/.

[51] As explained in Chapter 2, the biological reality of sex is far from being simple and obvious.

[52] Ruth Rubio-Marín, *Anti-Gender Constitutionalism*, 21 EUROPEAN CONSTITUTIONAL LAW REVIEW 37 (2025). The application of the term 'camouflage' to this strategy is borrowed from Farrah Ahmed,

imposed restrictions on the recognition of gender diversity.[53] Second, this backlash has a deeper constitutional dimension as it re-entrenches binary and heteronormative understandings of gender that have arguably been at the core of gender constitutionalism since its inception.[54] Third, some of these developments appear to be connected to the ongoing assault on the rule of law and to the constitutional degradation that is taking place across jurisdictions.[55] As recently argued by Mara Malagodi and Elettra Stradella[56] and by Silvia Suteu,[57] the crisis of the rule of law in Europe is gendered: the degradation of constitutional values experienced in this region is *essentially* connected to a traditionalist understanding of sex and the family.

This section does not aim to provide a fully representative account of the re-entrenchment of biologistic narratives of sex in the law. Instead, taking my cue from Judith Butler's 2024 book, which identifies gender-critical feminism and the opposition to the so-called gender ideology as two primary sites of reaction to the rights of gender-diverse people, in this section I will discuss pertinent examples of these instances where the public law dimension comes to the fore.

3.1. Entrenching sex in the United Kingdom: Gender-critical arguments reach the Supreme Court

The legal background: The Gender Recognition Act 2004 and the 'endless' references to biology[58]

The developments in the United Kingdom exemplify the entrenchment of biology-inspired narratives of sex and the success of gender-critical claims. As mentioned

Constitutional Parasitism, Camouflage, and Pretense: Shaping Citizenship Through Subterfuge, 21 International Journal of Constitutional Law 285 (2023). For an introduction to the characteristics of this strategy: Gráinne de Búrca & Katherine G. Young, *The (Mis)appropriation of Human Rights by the New Global Right: An Introduction to the Symposium*, 21 International Journal of Constitutional Law 205 (2023).

[53] Rubio-Marín, *supra* note 52.

[54] *See* Chapter 1.

[55] Mara Malagodi, Stefano Osella & Elettra Stradella, *Gender, Populism, and Constitutional Degradation: Introduction to the Special Section*, 21 European Constitutional Law Review 1 (2025) (introducing the connection between constitutional degradation and 'anti-gender' rhetoric). *See also*: Stopler, *supra* note 13; Agniezska Graff & Elzbieta Korolczuk, Anti-Gender Politics in the Populist Moment (2022); Right Wing Populism and Gender: European Perspectives and Beyond 23 (Gabriele Dietze & Julia Roth eds., 2020).

[56] Mara Malagodi & Elettra Stradella, *Conceptualising the Link Between Constitutional Degradation and Gender Populism*, 21 European Constitutional Law Review 8 (2025).

[57] Silvia Suteu, *The Rule of Law Crisis Was Always Gendered: The Anti-Gender Playbook in Europe*, 21 European Constitutional Law Review 58 (2025).

[58] The use of 'endless' here refers to: Alex Sharpe, *Endless Sex: The Gender Recognition Act 2004 and the Persistence of a Legal Category*, 15 Feminist Legal Studies 57 (2007).

earlier, gender-critical feminists have seen the protection of trans identity rights as part of a reaffirmation of a system that imperils cis women (a term that they reject) and contributes to their discrimination. Although the safety, comfort, and equality of women are laudable and constitutionally imperative aims, the argument that such objectives might be compromised by gender recognition has been resisted by LGBTQI+ and feminist advocates.[59]

A medico-behavioural right to gender recognition has been introduced in the United Kingdom with the Gender Recognition Act 2004 (GRA 2004). The Act followed the condemnation of the United Kingdom by the ECtHR in *Christine Goodwin* and *I*,[60] several decisions of the European Court of Justice,[61] and a long jurisprudential, scholarly, and institutional debate.[62] The GRA 2004 allows trans people to change their legal sex after they have lived for two years in their 'acquired gender', have been diagnosed with gender dysphoria, and are committed to living in the 'acquired gender' until death.[63] The Act demands the applicant's oath along with medical evidence, such as reports submitted by medical practitioners.[64] The GRA 2004 does not require trans people to undergo hormonal treatment or surgery, even though Parliament had assumed that such treatments would take place.[65] In fact, the courts themselves raised doubts as to the practical possibility of obtaining a Gender Recognition Certificate—that is, the certificate that changes one's legal sex—without undergoing any medical treatments.[66] Applications are decided by a

[59] *See* Chapter 2.

[60] Christine Goodwin v. United Kingdom, App. No. 28597/1995 (11 July 2002), https://hudoc.echr.coe.int/eng?i=001-60596, and I. v. United Kingdom, App. No. 25680/1994 (11 July 2002), https://hudoc.echr.coe.int/spa?i=001-60595. *See* Damien Gonzalez-Salzberg, Sexuality and Transsexuality Under the European Convention on Human Rights: A Queer Reading of Human Rights Law (2019) (discussing these cases in depth).

[61] Case C-13/94, P. v. S. and Cornwall County Council, 1996 E.C.R. I-02143; Case C117/01 KB v. National Health Service Pension Agency, 2004 E.C.R. I-00541. *See also*: Case C-432/04, Sarah Margaret Richards v. Secretary of State for Work and Pension, 2006 E.C.R. I-3602 (filed before but decided after the introduction of the Gender Recognition Act 2004).

[62] I have discussed the evolution of English law prior to these developments in: The Legal Regime of Gender Identity: A Comparative Enquiry (7 May 2019) (Ph.D. Dissertation, European University Institute)(on file with author). Refer also to: Stephen Gilmore, *The Legal Status of Transsexual and Transgender Persons in England and Wales, in* The Legal Status of Transsexual and Transgender Persons 183 (Jens M. Scherpe ed., 2015). The legal debate largely focused on the denial of gender recognition based on the *Corbett* doctrine (which essentially entrenched birth-assigned sex in the law): Corbett v. Corbett (Otherwise Ashley) [1971] P. 83. Among the rich jurisprudential debates, it is also worth mentioning the 2003 *Bellinger* case with which, following the *Goodwin* and *I* decisions of the European Court of Human Rights, the (then) House of Lords issued a declaration of incompatibility under Section (S.) 4 of the Human Rights Act 1998 (Bellinger v. Bellinger [2003] UKHL 21).

[63] Gender Recognition Act 2004 (GRA 2004), S. 2.

[64] GRA 2004, S. 3.

[65] Sharpe cites a passage from the Hansards of the House of Commons in which Minister David Lammy explained that 'ultimately, [transsexuals] have surgical treatment if it is viable'. *See*: Sharpe, *supra* note 58, at 72.

[66] Carpenter v. Secretary of State for Justice [2015] EWHC 464 (Admin), [2015] 1 WLR 4111, ¶ 20.

Gender Recognition Panel that includes medical and legal professionals.[67] When a Gender Recognition Panel issues a Gender Recognition Certificate, the person 'becomes for all purposes [of] the acquired gender'.[68] Nevertheless, the Act details several exceptions and limitations to the rule, for example, concerning marriages, (in time) civil unions, equality law, sports, and succession to peerages. Such exceptions respond to the need to preserve the birth-assigned sex as a criterion for determining the legal status of trans people in some sensitive areas.

The GRA 2004 was at the time of its passing saluted as a pioneering piece of legislation.[69] Nonetheless, scholars have not spared it criticisms,[70] which have only intensified over time.[71] Indeed, even though the GRA 2004 should be understood as 'designed to facilitate gender recognition' and aimed at creating a 'statutory regime [that] is permissive rather than restrictive',[72] the intrusiveness of the procedure, the lack of transparency, and the difficulty of understanding the reasoning of the Gender Recognition Panels, as well as the necessity of securing a diagnosis of gender dysphoria have been targeted by scholars and activists.[73] Ascertaining if the applicant has in fact lived in the 'acquired gender' for two years prior to the application for recognition could be a particularly invasive part of the process. Details required to pass this 'lived gender' test could include the names that the applicant uses and possible deed poll changes, the pronouns by which the applicant is known, but also more intimate details such as the applicant's sexual drive.[74] A process of reform of the GRA 2004 started in 2015 with the work of the Women's

[67] GRA 2004, Schedule (Sch) 1.

[68] GRA 2004, S. 9.

[69] Alex Sharpe, *Gender Recognition in the UK: A Great Leap Forward*, 18 Social & Legal Studies 241 (2009); Sharon Cowan, *Looking Back (To)Wards the Body: Medicalization and GRA*, 18 Social & Legal Studies 247 (2009).

[70] *E.g.*: Sharpe, *supra* note 58, at 57; Alex Sharpe, *Transgender Marriage and the Legal Obligation to Disclose Gender History*, 75 The Modern Law Review 33 (2012).

[71] Peter Dunne, *Ten Years of Gender Recognition in the United Kingdom: Still a 'Model for Reform'*, Public Law 530 (2015).

[72] Jay v. Secretary of State for Justice [2018] EWHC2620 (Fam), [2019] Fam 87, ¶ 93.

[73] For an overview of the criticisms of the GRA 2004, *see* Dunne, *supra* note 71; for a discussion of how the GRA 2004 operates in practice, some of the main criticisms levelled against the law, and how it 'governs' sex in the United Kingdom: Flora Renz, Gender Recognition and the Law: Troubling Transgender People's Engagement with Legal Regulation (2024).

[74] These requirements were examined in AB v. Gender Recognition Panel [2024] EWHC1456 (Fam), [2025] 1 WLR (hereinafter, AB v. Gender Recognition Panel). In this decision, the High Court heard the appeal against a decision of a Gender Recognition Panel that had denied a Gender Recognition Certificate to a trans woman. Among the reasons given, the panel included concerns about the applicant's decision to interrupt testosterone blockers to preserve her 'male' sexual function. The Gender Recognition Panel averred that this decision conflicted with the applicant's stated aim to be recognized as a woman. Real women, the Gender Recognition Panel seems to suggest, do not need testosterone to be sexually active. McFarlane J differed from the Gender Recognition Panel in relation to the current significance of the decision of preserving the 'male' sexual function. The applicant, he argued, had resumed hormone intaking to block the production of testosterone. Nevertheless, McFarlane J acknowledged that the decision to preserve the 'male' sexual function indeed had 'a degree of ambivalence' (¶ 67). For an analytical discussion of the process of gender recognition, *see* Renz, *supra* note 73, at 21–56.

and Equality Committee of the House of Commons, but it was not successful. This attempted reform deserves deeper examination than that contained in the brief references that are possible here; for our purposes, suffice it to say that the process lasted approximately seven years and was eventually dropped by the government in the face of social opposition.[75]

The gradual entrenchment of the biologistic argument in the case law

The entrenchment of birth-assigned sex is noticeable in the case law, too. A few examples are arguably representative of this trend. First, English courts have denied trans parents the right to be recorded on the birth certificate of their children with a denomination that corresponds to their gender identity. Instead, they require the recording of the parental denomination usually associated with one's contribution to procreation, which is in line with one's birth-assigned sex. The case of Freddy McConnell, which Alice Margaria and I have discussed before, is crucial in this regard.[76] McConnell is a trans man with a Gender Recognition Certificate. He carried and delivered his child and asked to be recorded as the father on the child's birth certificate. This would have reflected his identity as a man and respected the social perception of the relationship between Freddy and his child. This request was denied, even though the impact of this denial on his right to privacy and family was uncontroversial and even though the Gender Recognition Act 2004 establishes that, after recognition, one belongs to the 'acquired gender' for 'all purposes'.[77]

Courts—especially the High Court—explained that McConnell's request could not be reconciled with the *mater semper certa* rule. This rule, central to family law and, presumably, to legal certainty, establishes that the person who delivers the child is the mother. Interestingly, MacFarlane J, the presiding judge who authored the judgment, stated that a person can be a 'mother' even though they are not female. By detaching motherhood from femaleness, this decision surely opened the door to queer interpretations of the law (does it get any queerer than a male

[75] Women and Equalities Committee, House of Commons, Transgender Equality: First Report of Session 2015–16, HC 390 (2015–16); on the importance of this Report, *see* Renz, *supra* note 73, at 1–4; on the reform and its social opposition, *see* Ruth Pearce, Sonja Erikainen & Ben Vincent, *TERF Wars: An Introduction*, 68 The Sociological Review 677 (2020).

[76] R (McConnell) v. Registrar General for England and Wales [2020] EWCA Civ 559; R(TT) v. Registrar General for England and Wales [2019] EWHC 2384 (Fam). I have previously analysed this case in Alice Margaria & Stefano Osella, *Recognizing Birthing Trans Fathers: A Legal Puzzle at the Intersection of Cultural and Structural Limits*, *in* Biomedical Practices in the Middle East and Europe: The Impact of Religion and Culture (Federica Sona, Marie-Claire Foblets, Shai Lavi & Hagai Boas eds., 2026, forthcoming) (discussing the cultural and structural limits to the recognition of trans parenthood and using the McConnell judgment as a case study). The brief description presented here draw on this previous research. *See also*: Alan Brown, *Trans Parenthood and the Meaning of 'Mother', 'Father' and 'Parent'*— R (McConnell and YY) v Registrar General for England and Wales *[2020] EWCA Civ 559*, 29 Medical Law Review 157 (2021); Amy Frieder, *Trans Parenthood in an Era of Assisted Reproductive Technology: Approaches to Defining Motherhood*, 34 Harvard Human Rights Journal 155 (2021); Alice Margaria, *Trans Men Giving Birth and Reflections on Fatherhood: What to Expect?*, 34 International Journal of Law, Policy, and the Family 225 (2020).

[77] GRA 2004, S. 9.

mother?), but ultimately failed to reflect the identity of the applicant. Besides, as McConnell repeatedly argued, despite the reasoning of the Court, motherhood remains associated with femaleness in the common social understanding—hence, his sense of misrecognition. English courts, in short, refused to treat McConnell as a male, and continued to treat him according to his birth-assigned sex. In this case, similar to the case on trans motherhood decided by the French Court of Cassation,[78] the birth-assigned legal sex was deemed preferable for preserving the stability of the legal system. Again, the question was not to determine the 'truth' concerning the parental relationship between McConnell and his child. After all, MacFarlane J insisted that mothers can be men—a conclusion that might well be objected to by those who deploy narratives of 'biological truth'. Rather, the decision was the outcome of a normative evaluation of concrete legal needs—in this case, the preservation of the principles of family law. Even though the McConnell case did not deploy a strong biology-evoking narrative, it can be argued that the fundamentals of this essentialist approach are central to the reasoning: birth-assigned sex and the act of procreation are interpreted as the 'right way' to determine the legal relationship between a child and their parents.

Second, in the *Elan-Cane* case, the Supreme Court of the United Kingdom (UKSC) denied the request of a nonbinary person to have their sex in their passport indicated with an X instead of the binary M/F.[79] The applicant, it should be noted, was not asking the Court to recognize a third sex as a legal status. Their request concerned only the addition of a nonbinary designation in a travel document. The UKSC acknowledged that the lack of a nonbinary designation interfered with the right to identity protected by Article 8 of the European Convention on Human Rights. Nevertheless, it also established that the sex designation in the passport reflects the legal sex of the person. In the United Kingdom, no third option is available. The UKSC also argued that the preservation of a binary sex designation relates to security purposes and to the overall coherence of the legal system, where binary categories are ubiquitous. The introduction of a nonbinary option—even if limited to the addition of a sex marker in a travel document without explicit changes to the overall structures of the legal system—would be complex and beyond the jurisdiction of the court.

The UKSC did not explicitly deny the request of the applicant with reference to biology. Nevertheless, it adopted the 'sex/biology' and 'gender/culture' divide, without paying much heed the criticisms that have been addressed to this

[78] Refer to Chapter 5.

[79] R (on the application of Elan-Cane) (Appellant) v. Secretary of State for the Home Department (Respondent) [2021] UKSC 56. Previously, both the Court of Appeal ([2020] EWCA Civ 363) and the High Court ([2018] EWHC 1530 (Admin), [2018] 1 WLR 5119) had dismissed the claim lodged by the applicant. Peter Dunne, *Traveling Beyond the Binary: No Right to Unspecified Passports Under the European Convention on Human Rights*, 79 THE CAMBRIDGE LAW JOURNAL 240 (2020).

distinction by gender theorists and scientists alike. Furthermore, the UKSC stated that '"sex" [is] associated with the idea of biological differences which are generally binary and immutable'.[80] The conclusions reached in *Elan-Cane* have been reaffirmed in the subsequent decision in *R (Castellucci) v. Gender Recognition Panel*.[81] In this decision, the High Court rejected the appeal lodged by a nonbinary applicant, who had been legally recognized as such in the United States, against a decision of a Gender Recognition Panel to deny them nonbinary recognition in the United Kingdom too.[82] These conclusions have been confirmed by the Court of Appeal, which deferred the introduction of a nonbinary identity to the legislature.[83]

Finally, the affirmation of a 'biological sex' discourse and its deployment to pursue a number of public interests reached its most evident point in the UKSC's 2025 decision in *For Women Scotland Ltd (Appellant) v. the Scottish Ministers (Respondent)*.[84] As specified by Sandra Duffy, this decision is to be read in the context of the ongoing 'moral panic' around trans people in the United Kingdom.[85] The UKSC had to determine whether the term 'sex' in the Equality Act 2010 had to be interpreted as 'biological sex' or whether it was inclusive of 'certified sex'. The crux of the case was whether the protection from sex discrimination that the Equality Act 2010 provides extended to trans people with a gender recognition certificate as members of the acquired sex. As the UKSC put it:

> The central question on this appeal is whether the [Equality Act] 2010 treats a trans woman with a [Gender Recognition Certificate] as a woman for all purposes within the scope of its provisions, or when that Act speaks of a 'woman' and 'sex' it is referring to a biological woman and biological sex.[86]

This question was consequential in the decision to grant trans people (trans women in particular) protection from sex discrimination, which, in turn, would entail granting them access to accommodations, services, and all measures designated

[80] R (on the application of Elan-Cane) (Appellant) v. Secretary of State for the Home Department (Respondent) [2021] UKSC 56, ¶ 3.

[81] R (Castellucci) v. Gender Recognition Panel [2024] EWHC54 (Admin), [2024] 2 WLR 1201.

[82] R (Castellucci) v. Gender Recognition Panel, ¶ 130.

[83] The King (on the application of Ryan Castellucci) v. Gender Recognition Panel and Minister for Women and Equalities [2025] EWCA Civ 167.

[84] For Women Scotland Ltd (Appellant) v. the Scottish Ministers (Respondent) [2025] UKSC 16 (hereinafter, For Women Scotland Ltd (Appellant) v. the Scottish Ministers (Respondent)). For a comment, *see* Flora Renz, *Law's Search for Biological Truth: For Women Scotland and the UK Supreme Court*, Radical Philosophy 3 (2025). The legal background of the case is quite complex and relates to the passing of the Gender Recognition Reform (Scotland) Bill 2022, which was subsequently vetoed by the UK Government. It is summarized in the introduction to the Judgment.

[85] Sandra Duffy, *Moral Panics and Legal Projects: Echoes of Section 28 in United Kingdom Transgender Discourse and Law Reform*, 1 Gender & Justice 78 (2025).

[86] For Women Scotland Ltd (Appellant) v. the Scottish Ministers (Respondent), ¶ 8.

for and granted to cis women (a term that the UKSC avoids).[87] This case was the outcome of litigation brought forward by the association *For Women Scotland*, 'a grassroots women's group founded in June 2018 amid growing unease about how women's rights would be affected by the Scottish Government's plans to reform the Gender Recognition Act to allow for self-declaration of sex', which aims to promote 'women's rights' (intended as women assigned as such at birth) and children's rights. Those in the group 'believe that there are only two sexes, that a person's sex is not a choice, nor can it be changed. Women are entitled to privacy, dignity, safety and fairness. Our legal rights should be protected and strengthened.'[88]

Before discussing the reasoning of the UKSC, a word on the Court's terminology is in order. Indeed, the lexicon adopted by the UKSC is indicative of its normative stance—so indicative, in fact, that the outcome of the decision was a foregone conclusion after the first few paragraphs. To start with, throughout the judgment, the UKSC refers to women (or men) and trans women (or trans men). As mentioned, no references to 'cis' women (or men) are made. Indeed, the use of the terms 'cis' or 'cisgender' gives equal dignity to trans and cis people. As B. Aultman argues, '[t]he terms *man* and *woman*, left unmarked, tend to normalize cisness—reinforcing the unstated "naturalness" of being cisgender.'[89] By omitting the 'cis' qualifier, the UKSC appears to establish a hierarchy of authenticity, arguably considering cis women and men (without qualifiers) as 'real' and 'natural', and reducing trans people to a simulacrum.

Second, the UKSC places considerable emphasis on 'biological sex' and does not use 'sex assigned at birth'. The former term is however politically loaded. According to Jessica Clarke, 'biological sex' gives a 'veneer of objectivity and scientism' to a normative notion and vision of the world and, mostly, to the denial of trans rights.[90] 'Biological' sex also gives a sense of simplicity and common sense to a question that is, in fact, extremely complicated. Indeed, throughout the decision, the UKSC appears to treat as obvious and self-evident the risks and inconveniences that would allegedly follow gender recognition, without, however, explaining them in detail. The UKSC could have easily used the term 'sex assigned

[87] For context, the Equality Act 2010 consolidates and amends UK equality law and prohibits discrimination based on several protected characteristics, including 'sex' and 'gender reassignment'. The Equality Act 2010 also consents a few exceptions to its prohibitions. Such exceptions are, broadly speaking, connected to the need to foster the equality of the protected individuals—for example, limits can be placed on the provision of services or on the access to segregated spaces. For a thorough discussion of the Equality Act 2010: Blackstone's Guide to the Equality Act 2010 (4th ed., Anthony Robinson, David Ruebain & Susie Uppal eds., 2021). For a more succinct account concerning the specific issues at stake, refer to: For Women Scotland Ltd (Appellant) v. the Scottish Ministers (Respondent), ¶¶ 112–50.

[88] 'About' (*For Women Scotland*), https://forwomen.scot/about/.

[89] B. Aultman, *Cisgender*, 1 Transgender Studies Quarterly 61 (2014). For another discussion of the terminology adopted by the UKSC, *see* Alan Brown, For Women Scotland *[2025] UKSC 16, [2025] 2 WLR 879: 'Paper Certificates', Gender Recognition Certificates and Other Legal Documents*, 14 *feminists@law* 1 (2025), https://journals.kent.ac.uk/index.php/feministsatlaw/article/view/1423/2464.

[90] Jessica A. Clarke, *Sex Assigned at Birth*, 122 Columbia Law Review 1822, 1859 (2022).

at birth'—to which, in fact, it referred[91]—and yet seemingly decided otherwise, aligning itself with gender-critical positions. This 'biological sex', it should also be noted, is almost certainly intended as binary. The narrative of the decision suggests so, as no explicit references to intersexuality are present—certainly a peculiar aspect of a decision that places references to biology at its heart. Furthermore, the UKSC had defined biological sex as binary in *Elan-Cane*, something from which it never distanced itself.

The UKSC concluded that 'sex' in the Equality Act 2010 ought to be interpreted as 'biological sex'. The Court saw 'no good reason why the legislature should have intended that sex-based rights and protections' afforded by the Equality Act 2010 should be inclusive of trans people and not limited to 'the distinct group of (biological) women and girls (or men and boys) with their shared biology leading to shared disadvantage and discrimination'.[92] To reach this conclusion, the UKSC first considered that the word 'sex' has a plain and unambiguous meaning. It then identified several provisions in the Act where 'sex' can exclusively be read as 'biological sex'. For example, the UKSC referred to all those provisions where sex discrimination is motivated by pregnancy or breastfeeding. The word 'sex' throughout the Act, the UKSC concluded, ought to be interpreted consistently to preserve clarity of meaning.

While this might be a standard approach to statutory interpretation, further normative evaluations come across in the judgment. Interpreting 'sex' as inclusive of 'certified sex', the UKSC held, would, for practical reasons, lead to self-identification as a main criterion in determining entitlements to group-based protections and rights. This would mean treating trans women (or men) as cis women (or men) in the context of positive actions or access to single-sex spaces, thus putting 'pressure' on 'women-only groups, organisations, and charities ... to include trans women'.[93] The UKSC further added that interpreting 'sex' as inclusive of 'certified sex' would have a 'chilling effect on lesbians who are no longer using lesbian-only spaces because of the presence of trans women (ie biological men who live in the female gender)'.[94] Same-sex orientation of lesbian women (but arguably also gay men), the UKSC considered, is the attraction towards a person of the opposite *biological* sex.[95]

Regarding separate or single-sex services, interpreting 'sex' in its 'biological meaning' would allow a 'service-provider [to] separate male and female users

[91] For Women Scotland Ltd (Appellant) v. the Scottish Ministers (Respondent), ¶ 6.
[92] For Women Scotland Ltd (Appellant) v. the Scottish Ministers (Respondent), ¶ 172. A discussion of whether the disadvantages experienced by women and girls is determined by biology falls entirely beyond the purposes of this chapter. Nevertheless, this understanding has received its fair share of criticism: *See* Chapter 2.
[93] For Women Scotland Ltd (Appellant) v. the Scottish Ministers (Respondent), ¶ 203.
[94] For Women Scotland Ltd (Appellant) v. the Scottish Ministers (Respondent), ¶ 207.
[95] For Women Scotland Ltd (Appellant) v. the Scottish Ministers (Respondent), ¶ 206. On this point, *see* Renz, *supra* note 84, at 6–7 (2025).

as obvious and distinct groups'.[96] Should the interpretation differ, trans women would be included in women-only spaces, and this would supposedly create 'practical difficulties'. Among them is the risk, the UKSC suggested, that trans women presenting as 'biological men' (but also men presenting as biological men) might have access to women-only spaces.[97] Similar considerations are made in relation to participation in sport, communal accommodations, equality duty in the public sector, and the armed forces. In short, the UKSC arguably considered that a departure from 'sex' in a 'biological' sense would ultimately extend the sex-based equality guarantees of cis men/women (but mostly, women) to trans men/women (but mostly, women), making the statute more confusing and favouring practical effects that are, in the opinion of a Supreme Court that has espoused gender-critical positions, undesirable.

It is not the purpose of this chapter to normatively criticize this judgment or approach,[98] regarding which I am largely unpersuaded. Surely, the conclusions reached by the UKSC could benefit from more sustained moral and empirical arguments. The reasoning, in fact, seems *prima facie* to get lost in a narrative where all normative conclusions are treated as self-evident. Be that as it may, what really seems self-evident is that the emphasis on 'biological sex' has little to do with the restoration of some 'biological truth', but rather conveys a balancing of principles that are (controversially) understood to be in tension—namely, the right of trans people against the rights of (cis) women. The UKSC is essentially attributing a certain meaning to birth-assigned sex that is read to be a guarantee of some legal and constitutional principles (such as equality).[99]

3.2. Gender recognition and the reaction to the (so-called) gender ideology: Hints for further research

Other examples of the reaction against the recognition of gender diversity can be found in Europe and Latin America. What characterizes these judgments is the explicit connection that they draw between the rejection of gender diversity

[96] For Women Scotland Ltd (Appellant) v. the Scottish Ministers (Respondent), ¶ 213.

[97] For Women Scotland Ltd (Appellant) v. the Scottish Ministers (Respondent), ¶ 213.

[98] For an engagement with the substantive arguments that the judgment (almost uncritically) endorses, refer to Chapter 2, and the questions that can be raised about the empirical foundations of gender-critical feminism.

[99] The implementation of the judgment in *For Women Scotland* falls outside the scope of this chapter. It is worth mentioning however that it appears to be ongoing. The Equality and Human Rights Commission is reviewing the Services, Public Functions and Associations Statutory Code of Practice. See Guidance: Services, Public Functions and Associations. Code of Practice, https://www.equalityhumanrights.com/equality/equality-act-2010/codes-practice/services-public-functions-and-associations-code-0. Refer also to: Research Briefing. Supreme Court judgment on the meaning of 'sex' in the Equality Act 2010: For Women Scotland (16 Dec. 2025), https://commonslibrary.parliament.uk/research-briefings/cbp-10259/.

recognition, heteronormativity, and traditionalist attitudes to family life. This connection is hardly a surprise. As has been mentioned several times already, identifying and acknowledging the link between institutional heterosexuality and the insistence on a stable and oppositional sex/gender binary, as theorized by Judith Butler, is a central feature of queer theory.[100] Politically, the background of such examples can be found in the opposition to the so-called gender ideology, which was introduced in Chapter 2.

The claims made by the coalition of social and legal actors that advocate against the so-called gender ideology (hereinafter, anti-gender advocacy) are making their way into constitutional law in multiple jurisdictions. Anti-gender advocates now benefit from a vast arsenal of doctrinal ammunition to keep waging lawfare against gender-related rights.[101] Anti-gender advocacy, it should be clarified, is not limited to the opposition of gender recognition rights. Nevertheless, trans identities have been a 'nightmare' for anti-gender advocates since the inception of the movement.[102] Of necessity, the following account is impressionistic, but it offers hints for further research.

As a caveat before proceeding, I should underline once again that 'gender-critical' arguments and 'anti-gender' advocacy do not entirely coincide. Anti-gender arguments, at least on their face, can be distinguished from gender-critical ones as they are outspokenly traditionalist, while gender-critical advocates locate themselves within the feminist movement. Nevertheless, both positions, even if grounded in different backgrounds, come to formulate legal demands concerning the recognition of gender diversity that are, by and large, similar. A combined presentation of their engagement with the law appears, therefore, appropriate, especially as their similarities have not gone unnoticed in the literature.[103] Furthermore, it should be noted that conservative or religion-based opposition to the rights of trans people does not appear to be necessarily articulated through the conceptual apparatus provided by the opposers of gender ideology, but might be found in other contexts and religious traditions, too.[104]

One example of anti-gender jurisprudence specifically targeting trans people can be found in Bulgaria. In 2018, the Bulgarian Constitutional Court established the incompatibility of the Council of Europe Convention on Preventing and Combating Violence against Women and Domestic Violence—also known as the

[100] Judith Butler, Gender Trouble: Feminism and the Subversion of Identity 30–31 (2d ed.1999).

[101] Rubio-Marín, *supra* note 52.

[102] Mary Anne Case, *After Gender the Destruction of Man: The Vatican's Nightmare Vision of the 'Gender Agenda' for Law*, 31 Pace Law Review 804 (2011).

[103] For a similar approach: Judith Butler, Who's Afraid of Gender (2024).

[104] As mentioned in Chapter 7, the Federal Shariat Court of Pakistan found the Transgender Persons Act 2018 incompatible with the principles of Islam on 19 May 2023.

Istanbul Convention—with the Bulgarian Constitution.[105] This decision must be contextualized in the political debate in Bulgaria and Central and Eastern Europe. As argued by Ivo Gruev, on whose account the description and the analysis here presented draw, the opposition in Bulgaria capitalized on the perceived threats to the traditional family and to the 'immutable, binary concept of biological sex with a notion of gender based on individual self-identification ... [and] on the potential legalization of same-sex marriage and the recognition of a "third gender"'.[106] The Constitutional Court argued that the definition of 'gender' contained in the Istanbul Convention would replace the 'biological definition of sex', and that the protection of gender-diversity rights would clash with the Bulgarian Constitution, which builds 'on the understanding of the binary existence of the human species'.[107] In other words, the Bulgarian Constitutional Court opposed a legal instrument that challenged the traditional gender order in public and constitutional law.

The Constitutional Court confirmed its position in 2021.[108] Unlike the 2018 case, this later judgment focused directly on the right to gender recognition, concluding that recognizing trans identity conflicts with the Constitution. It also clarified that circumscribing the definition of legal sex to that assigned at birth is functional to the heterosexuality of marriage, which is enshrined in the Constitution in Article 46. A 'biological' understanding of sex, the Court continued, is also connected to the protection of women and motherhood.[109] Finally, the judgment considered that denying diverse gender identities better serves the preservation of values associated with Eastern Orthodox Christianity, which, the Constitution states, 'shall be considered the traditional religion in the Republic of Bulgaria'.[110] In 2023, the Bulgarian Court of Cassation rendered a decision that largely aligns with the findings of the Constitutional Court.[111] The Court considered that gender recognition

[105] Council of Europe Convention on Preventing and Combating Violence against Women and Domestic Violence, 11 May 2011, C.E.T.S. No. 210; Decision No. 13/2018 (Constitutional Case No. 3/2018) (Bulg.). For a thorough discussion of this decision: Ivo Gruev, *Constitutionalizing Gender: Deterrence Instead of Equality*, INTERNATIONAL JOURNAL OF CONSTITUTIONAL LAW (forthcoming, on file with author). I thank Ivo Gruev for allowing me to cite this forthcoming piece. *See* also Radosveta Vassileva, *Bulgaria's Constitutional Troubles with the Istanbul Convention*, VERFBLOG (2 Aug. 2018), https://verfassungsblog.de/bulgarias-constitutional-troubles-with-the-istanbul-convention/. For the English translation of selected excerpts from this decision: (2022) 68 OSTEUROPA RECHT 189–93.

[106] Gruev, *supra* note 105. For a contextualization of anti-gender movements in Central and Eastern Europe: Suteu, *supra* note 57, at 58, and references therein, especially at footnote 5.

[107] Gruev, *supra* note 105.

[108] Interpretive Decision No. 15/2021 (Constitutional Case No. 6/2021) (Bulg.). The analysis presented here draws on: Teodora Petrova, *Value Judgments: The Dangers of the 'Traditionalist' Rhetoric of the Bulgarian Constitutional Court*, VERFBLOG (5 Nov. 2021), https://verfassungsblog.de/value-judgments/.

[109] Art. 47(2) Bulgarian Constitution. The translation is taken from constituteproject.org.

[110] Art. 13(4), Bulgarian Constitution.

[111] Interpretive Decision No. 2/2000 (Supreme Court of Cassation) (Bulg.). *See* Teodora Petrova, *Barring Legal Gender Reassignment in Bulgaria: Rights of Transgender People and Traditional Social Values*, VERFBLOG (2 Mar. 2023), https://verfassungsblog.de/barring-legal-gender-reassignment-in-bulgaria/.

is a menace to heterosexual marriage and parenthood. The Bulgarian case is particularly interesting because, while closing the door to gender diversity, it also restricted the rights of women. After all, the 'spectre' of gender diversity was used to argue the unconstitutionality of the ratification of the Istanbul Convention.

A biologistic understanding of sex can also be entrenched by way of constitutional amendments. The Hungarian Parliament adopted the Ninth Amendment to the 2011 Constitution on 15 December 2020. The newly added article (L)(1) of the Constitution 'protect[s] the institution of marriage as the union of one man and one woman' and 'the family as the basis of survival of the nation'.[112] Article XVI(1), which was also introduced with the Ninth Amendment, states that 'Hungary shall protect the right of children to a self-identity corresponding to their sex at birth and shall ensure an upbringing for them that is in accordance with the values based on the constitutional identity and Christian culture of our country'.[113] With Act XXX of 28 May 2020, the Hungarian Parliament had defined the legal notion of 'sex' as that assigned at birth 'determined on the basis of the primary sex [characteristics] or chromosomes'.[114] These reforms have been defined as an institutional commitment to homophobia, institutional heteronormativity, and transphobia,[115] and, needless to say, to the binary that these values presuppose. In 2023, the Constitutional Court of Hungary confirmed that the legal notion of sex is to be understood as a factual declaration of a biological reality and not as a representation of rights.[116] The case concerned the application of a trans person for gender recognition, which the presiding judge could not grant because it contradicted the law. As explained by Eszter Polgári and Tamas Dombos, on whose analysis I substantially draw, the Hungarian Constitutional Court insisted that 'sex at birth is a factual datum based on medical expert opinion'. Recording sex, so defined, 'cannot contradict human dignity'. But the Court did not explain how denying gender recognition is dignity compliant. At the same time, the Court cited numerous public interests, grounded in constitutional provisions, that would arguably require a binary and biologically based understanding of sex. In the words of Polgári and

[112] The translation is taken from: FRA—Fundamental Rights Agency of the European Union, The Fundamental Law of Hungary, https://fra.europa.eu/en/law-reference/fundamental-law-hungary-7. I am grateful to Alessia Riccioli for assisting me in locating the sources briefly presented in the text. *See* Alessia Riccioli, *Right-wing Populism and Gender Backlash: Reproductive Rights and the Constitutional Status of Women and LGBTQI + People* (manuscript, on file with author).

[113] The translation is taken from: European Commission for Democracy through Law, Hungary: Ninth Amendment to the Fundamental Law and Explanatory Memorandum, Opinion No. 1035/2021 (3 June 2021), https://www.venice.coe.int/webforms/documents/default.aspx?pdffile=CDL-REF(2021)045-e.

[114] The translation is taken from: Eszter Polgári & Tamas Dombos, *A New Chapter in the Hungarian Government's Crusade Against LGBTQI People*, VERFBLOG (18 Nov. 2020), https://verfassungsblog.de/a-new-chapter-in-the-hungarian-governments-crusade-against-lgbtqi-people/.

[115] *Id.*

[116] Alkotmánybíróság [AB] [Constitutional Court], 3058/2023. I rely on: Eszter Polgári & Tamas Dombos, *Ignorance and Evil: The Hungarian Constitutional Court on Legal Gender Recognition for Trans People*, VERFBLOG (21 Feb. 2023), https://verfassungsblog.de/ignorance-and-evil/.

Dombos, 'medical, penological, sport or labor law considerations also make [the exclusive registration of sex at birth] necessary and proportionate, although the proportionality is merely stated rather than demonstrated'.[117]

The backlash against the rights of gender-diverse people is not limited to Europe, as a 2017 judgment of the Plurinational Constitutional Tribunal of Bolivia demonstrates.[118] The case was promoted by a group of Bolivian MPs who were opposing several rights granted by the 2016 Law on Gender Identity (*Ley de Identidad de Género*).[119] The MPs raised the 'usual' objections to gender recognition. Invoking an array of constitutional provisions, they referred to the possible threats to women—in relation to employment quotas, separate facilities, etc.[120] Furthermore, they lamented a threat to traditional institutions, such as heterosexual marriage.[121] They also highlighted that the rights of trans people are a manifestation of 'gender ideology', and a denial of biological reality.[122]

On the one hand, the Constitutional Tribunal declared that the right to gender recognition is inherent to human dignity. It rebutted the position of the plaintiffs who had contended that the right to gender recognition introduced an abstract understanding of the person. Instead, the Constitutional Tribunal emphasized that, by focusing exclusively on birth-assigned sex, those who oppose the (so-called) gender ideology neglect the variability of human existence. Instead of understanding gender diversity as artificial, the court arguably considered the critiques of gender ideology and the ideologization of the binary as such.[123] On the other hand, the Tribunal ruled that allowing trans people to exercise the totality of rights that come with their newly acquired legal identity could be a threat to the heterosexuality of marriage[124] and to other interests and rights, including gender equality.[125] In short, despite rejecting the objections of anti-gender advocates and affirming a right to change legal sex designations, the court stopped short of recognizing a right to fully change one's legal status. Trans people will still be, in the eyes of the law, of their birth-assigned sex.

117 *Id.*

118 Sentencia Constitucional Plurinacional 0076/2017 (Tribunal Constitucional Plurinacional, Plena 2017) (Bol.) (hereinafter, Sentencia 00076/2017). Scholarship on this decision has been virtually absent. However, *see*: RUBIO-MARÍN, *supra* note 32, at 307. As clarified in Chapter 5 (on gender self-determination in Colombia), the debate on 'gender ideology' has been quite present in Latin America, too. For context: Gabriela Arguela-Ramirez, *The Twenty-First-Century Crusade Against Democracy, in Latin America: 'Gender Ideology' at the Frontline, in* GLOBAL PERSPECTIVES ON ANTI-FEMINISM: FAR-RIGHT AND RELIGIOUS ATTACKS ON EQUALITY AND DIVERSITY 27 (Judith Goetz & Stefanie Mayer eds., 2023).

119 They claimed that Articles 1, 3.2, 4.II, 7, 8, 9, 10, 11.II, 12.I, as well as the First Final Provision of the Ley de Identidad de Género (Ley 807 de 21 mayo 2016) infringed Articles 8.II, 9.2, 14.I, II, III, and IV, 58, 59, 60, 63, 64, 66, and 116 of the Bolivian Constitution.

120 Sentencia 00076/2017, ¶ I.1.1.a.

121 Sentencia 00076/2017, ¶ I.1.1.a.

122 Sentencia 00076/2017, ¶ I.1.1.d.

123 Sentencia 00076/2017, ¶ III.4.1–III.4.2.

124 Sentencia 00076/2017, ¶ III.4.6.i.

125 Sentencia 00076/2017, ¶ III.4.6.iii.

In conclusion, the denial of gender diversity and the entrenchment of narratives of 'biological' sex deserve thorough exploration. Future research will need to answer several questions. For example, what are the forms of this constitutional re-entrenchment of biologistic narratives? Why are the rights of such a numerically small minority catalysing such fierce opposition? Is the traditional understanding of 'sex' seeing a comeback into constitutional law, thus supplanting 'gender', as anti-gender advocates wish for, or are these developments mere 'blips' on the radar screen?

Despite the rejection of 'gender' and the celebration of 'sex', all cases mentioned in this chapter show that the choice to limit legal sex to that assigned at birth is the outcome of value judgments. In this sense, we see in the entrenchment of biology-evoking discourses in public law a legal mechanism that is not different from gender recognition—though, of course, its social effects can diverge. In both cases, sex is a proxy for achieving some purposes deemed valuable and is the outcome of a balancing exercise. Denying protection to gender identity is functional to some specific understandings of fundamental rights, the heteronormativity of marriage and filiation, as well as to other public interests—for example, the preservation of national traditions.

4. Conclusion

This chapter has examined two potential developments in the treatment of sex categories within public law. Both can be seen as reactions to the advancements in the rights of gender-diverse people. First, the chapter analysed how public law has responded to calls for eliminating sex as a legal status, which some advocates claim is the only strategy that can not only protect the rights of gender-diverse individuals, but also the rights of women and other people who, whatever the reason, are oppressed in a patriarchal gender system. Not only are sex categories harmful to those who fall outside the standard boxes, the argument goes, but they are also ultimately suboptimal—in legal terms, either not logically connected or unnecessary—for pursuing the otherwise worthwhile objectives that are invoked to legitimize categorization.

Courts have approached this question differently. While no court to date has concluded that the legal registration of sex is unconstitutional and must be removed, some have determined that sex categories must be preserved. This seems to be the case for binary and ascriptive systems of gender recognition—such as in France and Italy. Nevertheless, the preservation of sex categories has also been deemed necessary when a multiplicity of self-determined and fluid options are made available—as is the case in Colombia. Other courts have opted for constitutional neutrality—such as in Germany, Austria, and Belgium—ultimately deferring the decision about sex categories to parliamentary discretion. A bourgeoning scholarship is developing on the practical feasibility of erasing sex from a person's civil status. Future research will have to produce a more sustained constitutional analysis to answer the question of whether sex categories are necessary for public interests and rights grounded at the constitutional level. Furthermore, it will also be important to consider that the recognition of gender diversity has transformed the relationship between the individual and public authorities recording identities, from a top-down imposition to one of recognition and protection. This might possibly alter the normative conclusions concerning the creation of a sex-less status.

While the recognition of gender identity might lead to questioning sex categories altogether, the other reaction that is worth addressing is the backlash and the re-entrenchment of birth-assigned sex, scaffolded by a discourse in which references to biology take precedence. This trend can be observed in multiple jurisdictions, in Europe and beyond. It can be connected either to the gender-critical women's rights movement or to the moral conservative opposition to the so-called gender ideology. From a legal perspective, the 'comeback' of birth-assigned sex is to be understood as the attempt to secure some legal (and arguably constitutional) objectives, ranging from a much-contested approach to sex equality to the preservation of the traditional family and social values. Such objectives would, a few courts have held, be jeopardized should the protection of gender diversity come to pass. The normative considerations on which these decisions have been grounded have been the object of much criticism. My aim in this chapter is more modest; I have limited myself to highlighting the conceptual misunderstanding in which such notions have been trapped. Despite the grand narrative around biological 'truth', the only legal fact that can be ascertained is that the entrenchment of 'biological sex' is a legal strategy for achieving certain goals. Legal sex is the outcome of a normative mechanism of signification that largely, if not exclusively, rests on heteronormative assumptions and essentialist understandings of sex/gender. In other words, the determination of legal sex is not a mere reflection of a pre-discursive reality, but a wilful normative choice (whether well-intended or less so is a different question). In this sense, legal sex confirms itself to be nothing other than gender in another guise.

9
Conclusion

1. The arguments of the book

The study of the (mis)recognition of gender diversity presented in this book allows me to argue a few conclusive theses. First, sex characteristics and gender identity matter for the legal relationship between individuals and between the state and the individual—or for public law.[1] The connection between public law on the one hand and gender identity and sex characteristics on the other has long remained implicit. Gender identity and sex characteristics are seldom mentioned in constitutional instruments. Even when they are, it is normally to protect the rights of gender-diverse people, or, more rarely, to deny them. One is hardly accustomed to thinking of sex characteristics or gender identity as something with broader significance for public law.[2]

Nonetheless, gender diversity—or its erasure—is critical to public law, including several aspects of constitutional status. This centrality is proclaimed by courts, parliaments, and governments when gender-diverse people lodge claims for protection and recognition of their diversity. As a response to these claims, public authorities have invoked opposing legal and constitutional interests, and struck by and large a proportionality balancing. To cite Mattias Kumm, courts have engaged in a practice of 'Socratic contestation': they have had to explain their decisions and argue how a 'public action can be demonstratively justified by reasons that are appropriate in a liberal democracy'.[3] In doing so, they have revealed the conflict between gender diversity and the fundamentals of the gender order in the law.

Scholars working on gender constitutionalism have demonstrated that constitutional and public law build on the existence of 'men' and 'women', particularly when responding to the 'woman question'.[4] This book clarifies that public and

[1] Katherine G. Young, *Introduction: A Public Law of Gender*, *in* The Public Law of Gender: From the Local to the Global 1, 9 (Kim Rubenstein & Katherine Young eds., 2016).

[2] This would require a broader discussion concerning the place of gender studies in public law. Writing about care, Jaclyn Neo argues that we should expand our constitutional imaginary and bring gender studies into the centre of the discipline: Jaclyn Neo, *Constitutionalizing Care: How Can We Expand Our Constitutional Imaginary After Covid-19?*, 20 International Journal of Constitutional Law 1307 (2022).

[3] Mattias Kumm, *The Idea of Socratic Contestation and the Right to Justification: The Point of Rights-Based Proportionality Review*, 4 Law & Ethics of Human Rights 141, 142 (2010).

[4] Vicki C. Jackson, *Conclusion: Gender Equality and the Idea of a Constitution: Entrenchment, Jurisdiction, Interpretation*, *in* Constituting Equality: Gender Equality and Comparative Constitutional Law 349 (Susan H. Williams ed., 2009). For an overview, *see*: Introduction.

Gender Diversity in Public Law. Stefano Osella, Oxford University Press. © Stefano Osella 2026.
DOI: 10.1093/9780198935070.003.0009

constitutional law also rely on a cis-normative, binary, and, in fact, Eurocentric understanding of the individual.[5] Clearly, things are never static or monolithic. Various legal approaches to gender diversity can be identified. In some systems—it seems where cis-normative, heteronormative, and Eurocentric conceptions of sex/gender have been questioned—the protection of the individual and their diversity has been deemed a central responsibility of the state.

Second, the law on gender diversity reveals that the gender order is not entirely concerned with representing subjects that exist prior to the law. Political and legal theorists have already demonstrated that sex categories are an instrument of governance—not an act of positivistic depiction of some pre-political world.[6] This book contributes to clarifying that courts, parliaments, and governments in the discussed jurisdictions define the characteristics of male, female, and nonbinary people by balancing the claims of these persons against opposing public interests or fundamental rights and how this, in turn, shapes the sexed subjects of the system. It is worth emphasizing that the standardizing efforts are not limited to the binary but extend to some definitions of the third legal sex. To use a metaphor, this book clarifies that public law is not only a tailor, cutting cloth to dress the human body, but is also a plastic surgeon, intervening upon that body to ensure a good fit. I should also be clear that alternative models are gradually gaining traction in the comparative landscape. Such models present opportunities for transforming the notion of the sexed subject, shifting from a top-down definition to a bottom-up recognition.[7] In such cases, the effort to define the subject of legal sex is largely forsaken. But even then, we still observe the central role of public authorities, no longer in defining the sexed individual, but in protecting them.

For example, in Italy, one is not recognized as a man/woman because having transformed one's body, assumed appropriate mannerisms, and obtained a medical diagnosis reflects some deep truth about manhood or womanhood; one is because these criteria were deemed a reasonable compromise between the rights of gender-diverse people and various public interests. The same applies in the other jurisdictions discussed in the volume, including where 'biological' sex has been emphasized in the law. Nowhere is this clearer than in the United Kingdom. Despite all references to biology, English courts do not seem interested in representing (so to speak) nature per se but in mobilizing a biology-evoking discourse to achieve certain legal purposes. This reveals an aspect that many might find

[5] My debt to decolonial studies should be acknowledged. *See* Chapters 6 and 7 in particular, and authors cited therein.

[6] In particular: Paisley Currah, Sex Is as Sex Does: Governing Transgender Identity (2022); Dean Spade, Normal Life: Administrative Violence, Critical Trans Politics, and the Limits of Law (2d ed. 2015). For a broader overview of the debate, please refer to Section 3 of the Introduction.

[7] On the transformation of the sexed subject: Marie-Xavière Catto & Stefano Osella, *The Sexed Subject*, *in* The Cambridge Companion to Gender and the Law 25, 43–58 (Stéphanie Hennette-Vauchez & Ruth Rubio-Marín eds., 2023).

unpalatable: legal sex is always the result of an exercise in attributing meaning to some individual characteristics. In other words, legal sex has been 'gender all along'.[8]

Finally, this definition is legally enforced (also) through rights. Rights have an ambivalent function in this context.[9] From the individual perspective, they offer a coveted form of recognition. Structurally, they provide the gateway to challenge the existence of cis and binary identities in the law. And again, socratically, they force public authorities to provide reasons for action. When presented with the claims of gender diverse people, public authorities are indeed compelled to articulate the interests that conflict with recognition. They hence make explicit how the system relies on physical sex characteristics and gender identity. At the same time, courts and legislatures have defined the beneficiaries of such rights. Hence, they have created the conditions for 'enforcing' said characteristics on gender-diverse people. This ambivalent dimension of rights, though usually associated with medicalization, goes well beyond that and includes other forms of control, including the behavioural aspects. More than that, this pragmatic dimension may not simply be a 'convenient' side effect of rights, but might be deliberately sought after by courts and legal authorities (the Italian case is paradigmatic in this regard). All this becomes manifest if we raise our gaze from one to many jurisdictions. When we examine different models, we gain a vantage point of view to grasp the complexity of the interactions between gender diversity and public law.

In this book, I have endeavoured to be analytical and theoretical. I have not offered a 'solution' to the question of the recognition of gender diversity. This is because gender diversity matters differently across jurisdictions, depending on the specifics of each legal system. Any normative solution cannot be abstracted from the concrete social and legal circumstances where it operates. Furthermore, a more abstract understanding of these questions in public law is needed at this stage—even for normative purposes. This does not mean that this book is not written from a normative standpoint. As clarified in the Introduction, I align myself with the demands of gender-diverse people. To conclude, the lack of a normative argument does not mean the analysis here conducted lacks normative potential, either. Hopefully, this book might be the starting point for further research and for refining the understanding of our constitutional systems to make them more welcoming for gender-diverse people.

[8] Judith Butler uses this expression to discuss whether 'sex' (not legal sex) 'has been gender all along' (JUDITH BUTLER, GENDER TROUBLE: FEMINISM AND THE SUBVERSION OF IDENTITY 11 (2d ed. 1999).

[9] On this notion: BEN GOLDER, FOUCAULT AND THE POLITICS OF RIGHTS 88–113 (2015); Wendy Brown, *Suffering Rights as Paradoxes*, 7 CONSTELLATIONS 208 (2000); WENDY BROWN, STATES OF INJURY: POWER AND FREEDOM IN LATE MODERNITY (1995); Stefano Osella & Ruth Rubio-Marín, *Gender Recognition at the Crossroads: Four Models and the Compass of Comparative Law*, 21 INTERNATIONAL JOURNAL OF CONSTITUTIONAL LAW 574, 581–82 (2023); Stefano Osella, *Reinforcing the Binary and Disciplining the Subject: The Constitutional Right to Gender Recognition in the Italian Case Law*, 20 INTERNATIONAL JOURNAL OF CONSTITUTIONAL LAW 454 (2022).

2. Sex anatomy matters

The connection between the cis- and binary-normative legal order and the physical binary is clear in the law concerning intersex people. When children are born, they are assigned a binary legal sex. Their legal existence becomes, in many jurisdictions, inseparable from a sex—as a legal status—that is tied to their anatomy. The birth of an intersex child generates doubts as to their *sortability* into legal categories and therefore to their place in the legal system.[10]

Italian authorities have made manifest their perception of intersex people as a cause of legal instability. Mistaken assignments and future applications for gender recognition are feared. Adding to the cultural stigma that accompanies intersexuality, operations on intersex bodies might be encouraged to achieve legal stability. A rights discourse is mobilized because such treatments are ostensibly justified with reference to a controversial understanding of the child's best interests. In France, despite some recent developments, a combination of law and medicine has been used to ensure the legal assignment of a binary sex at birth. It can safely be said that, in these jurisdictions, public authorities put in place all necessary measures to encourage the creation of the bodies that they need.

Intersexuality may also be legally defended, at least to some extent. In Germany, intersex people have achieved the protection of their physical diversity through a process to which the Federal Constitutional Court and its recognition of nonbinary identity have been central. In Colombia, the protection of intersex physical integrity has preceded and contributed to nonbinary recognition. It has led to the creation of a legal order that is more complex and welcoming of differences. In both jurisdictions, the connection between a constitutional system that is open to gender diversity and the acceptance of intersex bodies comes to the fore. The Belgian case shows however that we should not assume that introducing a nonbinary option is necessarily conducive to protecting intersex physical integrity. Multiple reasons—far beyond the law—cause the erasure of intersex physical diversity. Nevertheless, the connection between the preservation of the binary legal order and the perceived 'problems' caused by intersex bodies emerges clearly from all the jurisdictions discussed.

3. Gender identity matters

Gender recognition entails a change in a person's legal status, that is, in their set of legal positions. This change is said to create legal uncertainty, as courts and legislatures have repeatedly asserted. Complete denial of the recognition of gender

[10] Julie A. Greenberg, Intersexuality and the Law: Why Sex Matters (2012).

diversity has been rejected by the courts and legislatures in the jurisdictions examined. In an age when gender identity is (increasingly) protected as a human right,[11] courts are called on to strike a balance among principles in tension. The result has often been a list of requirements for recognition, ensuring that only individuals exhibiting specific characteristics can be granted such a right. The imposition of requirements allows, at once, a degree of protection of identity and control over sex categories. This dynamic first reveals that men, women, and nonbinary people *with specific characteristics* are presupposed in law. Second, it clarifies the legal notion of sex: man, woman, and nonbinary identities are not intended to mirror images of an objective pre-legal reality. They are the outcome of a value judgment. Third, an entire legal mechanism may be put in place to define, police, and enforce these definitions.

In the *medico-behavioural* model, trans people can have their legal sex amended in conformity with their gender identity when they are medically supervised, possibly transform their bodies, and acquire a specific (that is, socially intelligible) behaviour. Italian law is a case in point. Men and women are described as subjects possessing specific 'psychological, physical, and behavioural' characteristics. Italian courts have held that requirements for gender recognition are necessary for numerous reasons, notably, to uphold the heterosexuality of marriage and the family. Italian law confirms the strict co-causation between institutional heterosexuality and the binary—a central tenet of queer theory. That said, cracks in the armour are discernible. Conflicting values are always at play in pluralistic societies and liberal orders. Nevertheless, there is no denying that trans and nonbinary people are perceived as 'trouble' for the system, and medico-behavioural preconditions are explicitly defined to contain such trouble.

Human rights lawyers have targeted mandatory medical treatments for gender recognition for being intrusive and coercive. Certain medical treatments in particular—think of sterilization—have received the lion's share of scholarly attention. The socio-behavioural model emerges as a step forward in the protection of the rights of trans people, who are no longer coerced into undergoing medical treatments to obtain gender recognition. This model was enacted in France, where the law requires trans people seeking to amend their legal sex to 'perform' sex/gender norms in a socially recognizable way. Despite opening to the demands of trans people, the socio-behavioural model is not immune to criticism, as it offers an opportunity for reifying gender stereotypes. Furthermore, socio-behavioural requirements exclude from recognition those who live gender identity in a non-standardized way.

[11] Holning Lau, *Gender Recognition as a Human Right*, *in* The Cambridge Handbook of New Human Rights 193 (Andreas von Arnauld, Kerstin von der Decken & Mart Susi eds., 2020); Michael O'Flaherty, *Sexual Orientation and Gender Identity*, *in* International Human Rights Law 305 (4th ed., Daniel Moeckli, Sangeeta Shah & Sandesh Sivakumaran eds., 2022).

Legally, the socio-behavioural model does not differ in its rationale and functioning from the medico-behavioural one. Very much like the medico-behavioural model, it is defined as an outcome of a balancing of principles. On the one hand, we find the identity rights of the person. On the other hand is the legal principle of the inalienability of civil status, with its public order implications. This is to say, the functioning of public registries is tied to a stable understanding of gender identity, with individuals avoiding (or limiting) changes throughout their existence by being required to uphold a specific gender performance. This brings further clarity to the debate: even though medico-behavioural requirements have been traditionally criticized as a governance instrument,[12] the analysis of the socio-behavioural model confirms from a legal standpoint that we should not focus on the content of the gender norm enforced on individuals, but rather on the *imposition* of a norm itself.[13]

In both the medico-behavioural and socio-behavioural models, we see that the definition of a rights-bearer triggers mechanisms that enforce gender norms on the person. As argued, this enforcement develops through a Foucauldian disciplinary apparatus. Clearly, trans people are not forced to undergo this mechanism; they can avoid it by deciding not to seek recognition. Strategic behaviour is always possible. Nevertheless, when individuals need recognition (something we learned 'lies at the heart of social justice'[14]), they have to pass through this process.

The *self-determination* model breaks with this mechanism. In Colombian law, each person can self-determine their legal identity without satisfying any requirements. Admittedly, individuals are limited in the options granted. But each person's self-declared identity is acknowledged and registered, and the law steers clear of imposing preconditions which individuals must satisfy. Legal sex, in other words, is left undefined. Despite the limitations encountered,[15] the absence of a definition of a rights-bearer allows individuals to embody different forms of maleness and femaleness (and, after 2022, nonbinary-ness) without being policed. Severed from definitions of identity, individuals who live sex/gender in different, provocative, or subversive ways can be legally recognized. This promotes 'gender

[12] The use of medical expertise to control gender diversity and sexuality has been long debated by many authors. Refer, for example, to MICHEL FOUCAULT, THE HISTORY OF SEXUALITY. VOLUME 1: AN INTRODUCTION (Robert Hurley trans., 1990); DAGMAR HERZOG, SEXUALITY IN EUROPE: A TWENTIETH-CENTURY HISTORY (2012). For a closer perspective on trans experiences: Dean Spade, *Mutilating Gender*, *in* THE TRANSGENDER STUDIES READER 315 (Susan Stryker & Stephen Whittle eds., 2006).

[13] For a theoretical perspective: JUDITH BUTLER, UNDOING GENDER 42 (2004); JACK HALBERSTAM, TRANS*: A QUICK AND QUIRKY ACCOUNT OF GENDER VARIABILITY 16 (2018).

[14] SALLY HINES, GENDER DIVERSITY, RECOGNITION AND CITIZENSHIP: TOWARDS A POLITICS OF DIFFERENCE 10 (2013).

[15] As we have seen in Chapter 6, gender recognition of children follows a slightly different logic, prompted by the need to balance the right to gender recognition with the principle of the best interests of the child.

trouble'. Although legal sex is not eliminated, self-determination empowers people 'to repeat it wrong', as Janet Halley would put it.[16]

The implications are of great interest because, considering the specifics of the Colombian context, identities that fall outside the Eurocentric understanding of sex/gender are allowed to emerge. The Colombian Constitutional Court has indeed noted that gender recognition can be one way to acknowledge identities that were misrecognized—and outright persecuted—under European colonization. The analysis of gender self-determination in Colombia thus reveals the Eurocentric assumptions of the system of categories entrenched in the law, and, by implication, its intersections with a plurality of identity markers, such as culture or ethnicity.

This transformation does not come without difficulties. Vocal opposition has been mustered against gender self-determination, which, some argue, conflicts with the equality of cis women, as well as with the best interests of the child. Gender self-determination (as well as gender recognition in general) might contradict traditionalist understandings of proper social ordering, as opponents of the so-called gender ideology have not failed to point out. Challenges also involve public law considerations regarding other public interests, such as the administration of welfare systems, national security, or equality rights, among others. Nevertheless, the Colombian Constitutional Court ultimately decided to protect individual diversity, compelled by the principle of dignity, which is foundational to the Colombian constitutional order.[17] When self-determination is granted, it should be noted that public law does not disappear. Rather, it acquires an important role in supporting the person and granting them the legal tools to preserve and inhabit their unique identities.

These models—which should *not* be read as a necessary or evolutionary trajectory—reveal three ways in which controls over identity can be exercised or relinquished. They show that control can take different forms and essentially depends on the introduction of definitions of sex—regardless of how sex is defined. They also show that the main challenges emerge when such definitions are relinquished. And they demonstrate that the relationship between the sexed individual, the state, and their consociates can evolve and transform towards greater inclusion, but that this puts the gender order in public and constitutional law under stress.

[16] The reference is to Butler's notion of 'gender trouble'. *See also*: Janet Halley, Split Decisions: How and Why to Take a Break from Feminism 138 (2007).

[17] Manuel José Cepeda Espinosa & David Lantau, Colombian Constitutional Law. Leading Cases 7 (2017).

4. Controlling identities beyond the binary matters

Nonbinary identity is a puzzle for legal and constitutional systems built on the binary. After all, liberal constitutionalism has the separate sphere tradition at its heart, and this tradition allows room for men and women only.[18] And yet the different ways in which nonbinary identities are recognized point to a more complex panorama. They suggest that the addition of a third category might not fatally challenge the system of legal sex on which the gender order predicates. Instead, the gender order could expand beyond the original categories.

First, we encountered *embodied recognition* in Australia and, at least up until 2024, in Germany, whereby recognition is granted to people with physical characteristics that differ from the standard definitions of maleness and femaleness.[19] Embodied recognition allows for stricter control over nonbinary identities and demonstrates that the addition of a third sex to the law does not entail the disestablishment of the gatekeeping mechanisms that we see at play in systems that are exclusively binary. *Nonbinary self-determination*, as encountered in Colombia, affords individuals the autonomy to define their own identity and relinquishes control over their sex status. While a legal sex is still present, the entire structure that attributes meaning to these categories is disestablished.

Finally, *redistributive recognition* can be encountered in India, Pakistan, and Nepal, although including these systems in a different category presents some taxonomical difficulties. If we were to focus exclusively on the standard of recognition, they would fall within either the 'embodied' or the 'self-determination' model. And yet, at the cost of some logical inconsistency, I believe that these systems deserve special attention because of the emphasis that they place on the redistributive aspects of recognition and because they acknowledge identities that European colonizers have attempted to wipe out. Redistributive recognition invites us to think that gender recognition has concrete, socio-economic consequences. It also allows us to entertain the idea that the project of building the binary through the law was an act of cultural imperialism, with very concrete practical repercussions that also intersect with class, ethnicity and socio-economic status. A focus on this model also helps us understand the Eurocentric and racialized dimensions that are part of the gender constitutional order when it is predicated on the binary.[20]

[18] Ruth Rubio-Marín, Global Gender Constitutionalism and Women's Citizenship: A Struggle for Transformative Inclusion (2022); Carole Pateman, The Sexual Contract (1988); Thomas Laqueur, Making Sex. Body and Gender from the Greeks to Freud 193–207 (1992).

[19] As clarified in Chapter 7, the German Parliament has legislatively introduced gender self-determination, including beyond the binary. Nevertheless, its development up to 2024 strictly limited nonbinary recognition to a specific subset of nonbinary people. From a constitutional standpoint, it is at least debatable whether German law reflects a model of 'embodied recognition' or one of 'self-determination'.

[20] On the racialized dimension of the gender order in constitutional law: Rubio-Marín, *supra* note 18, at 79.

5. Ongoing challenges

Two ongoing challenges might further influence the definition of the gender order in public and constitutional law. The first one concerns the assignment of legal sex and the possibility of a sex-less civil status. To the best of my knowledge, no court has to date found the inclusion of sex categories in a person's civil status to be constitutionally illegitimate. Some courts have instead determined that sex categories are necessary. Others have ruled constitutional neutrality and left it up to parliamentary discretion to decide whether sex categories in law should be maintained. Taken together, all these cases demonstrate the impact that the demand for recognition of gender diversity can have. After all, when sex is no longer assigned but freely chosen, and when the once-binary categories are multiplied, but where no definitions are given and no structure is envisioned to enact them, we are bound to ask ourselves what is left of the original system based on the assumption of cis and binary identities.[21]

Enacting a sex-less legal status would not be smooth sailing. Overcoming gender discrimination in society, in a system where individuals have no legal sex, presents practical and theoretical issues. The matter is crucial to public and constitutional law, especially because several of the rights and interests at stake have a constitutional dimension. At the same time, in an age of tremendous technological developments and transformations, we must ask ourselves whether legal sex is bound to remain the same. At the end of the day, sex categories are the legal aspect of a technology of governance that was developed hundreds of years ago. In a time when our very existence appears to be disaggregated in an endless heap of readable data, we are compelled to ponder whether sex categorization remains necessary at all.

The challenges ahead can be seen as a fork in the road. The demands of gender-diverse people have been met with backlash in some jurisdictions, where a re-affirmation of a biological narrative of sex is underway. In the United Kingdom, we have seen an increasing affirmation of birth-assigned binary sexes, ostensibly to preserve the consistency of the legal order and guarantee a particular understanding of women's rights. This reaffirmation has been accompanied by an emphasis on biological sex that gives a debatable sense (some might say a veneer[22]) of scientific grounding to these decisions. In Bolivia, Bulgaria, and Hungary, for their part, a similar entrenchment of biology-driven narratives has taken place in the context of the anti-gender advocacy rooted in traditionalist understandings of society. What is interesting, however, is that in all jurisdictions, the presumably 'objective', 'scientific' definition of legal sex has been revealed to be yet another act of balancing among interests in tensions—namely, the rights of trans and nonbinary

[21] Christopher Hutton, *Legal Sex, Self-Classification and Gender Self-Determination*, 11 Law and Humanities 64, 78–79 (2017).
[22] Jessica A. Clarke, *Sex Assigned at Birth*, 122 Columbia Law Review 1821 (2022).

people on the one hand and other public law, even constitutional, principles on the other. When the drumbeats quiet down, we see that even those pushing for the comeback of biology and opposing 'gender' in fact do not care much about biological sex itself, but rather about its political and legal uses.

6. Many questions and one wish

Much remains to be written. I am aware of many interesting cases, jurisdictions, and debates that I have been unable to include in this volume. Areas of the law where sex classification is central have also been left out—I think, for example, of sports law and the Caster Semenya case, on which the Grand Chamber of the European Court of Human Rights decided in July 2025.[23] I think of the still understudied international human rights law, which deserves further dedication and discussion. The list could continue indefinitely.

What seems certain, however, is that legal developments worldwide, the heated social and scholarly exchanges, as well as the political and legal reactions against the rights of gender-diverse people, all indicate that the questions examined in this book are unlikely to subside or be resolved any time soon. What is the future of sex categories, and with it of the legal gender order? Is it going to be disestablished? Is it going to be re-entrenched? What are the main factors that determine the success or failure of gender recognition? How will the many interests in tension be reconciled in a changing legal world, and how *should* they be reconciled? Legal comparison contains the answers to such questions. However, each answer must start out from the understanding of why sex characteristics and gender identity matter in public law, how they are relied upon, and how they are constructed within the legal system. In an age of polarizing debates, the starting point should be analytical clarity. I hope that, with this book, I have provided some of it.

[23] Semenya v. Switzerland, App. No. 10934/21 (10 July 2025), https://hudoc.echr.coe.int/eng?i=001-244348. *See*: Sylvia Tamale, Colonization and Afro-Feminism (2020) 92 (discussing the controversy surrounding Caster Semenya).

Index

For the benefit of digital users, indexed terms that span two pages (e.g., 52–53) may, on occasion, appear on only one of those pages.